TROY

and its Remains

Heinrich SCHLIEMANN

View of Hissarlik from the North.
after the excavations.

TROY and its Remains

A Narrative of
Researches and Discoveries
Made on the Site of Ilium,
and in the Trojan Plain

Edited by Philip Smith

ARNO PRESS • NEW YORK, 1976

First published 1875
Reprint Edition 1968 by Benjamin Blom, Inc.

Reprint Edition 1976 by Arno Press Inc.

LC# 68-21228
ISBN 0-405-09855-3

Manufactured in the United States of America

NOBLE OFFSET PRINTERS, INC.
NEW YORK 3, N. Y.

PREFACE BY THE EDITOR.

Dr. Schliemann's original narrative of his wonderful discoveries on the spot marked as the site of Homer's Ilium
by an unbroken tradition, from the earliest historic age of
Greece, has a permanent value and interest which can
scarcely be affected by the final verdict of criticism on the
result of his discoveries. If he has indeed found the fire-
scathed ruins of the city whose fate inspired the immortal
first-fruits of Greek poetry, and brought to light many
thousands of objects illustrating the race, language, and
religion of her inhabitants, their wealth and civilization,
their instruments and appliances for peaceful life and war;
and if, in digging out these remains, he has supplied the
missing link, long testified by tradition as well as poetry,
between the famous Greeks of history and their kindred in
the East; no words can describe the interest which must
ever belong to the first birth of such a contribution to the
history of the world. Or should we, on the other hand,
in the face of all that has been revealed on the very
spot of which the Greeks themselves believed that Homer
sang, lean to the scepticism of the scholar who still says :—
" I know as yet of one Ilion only, that is, the Ilion as sung
by Homer, which is not likely to be found in the trenches
of Hissarlik, but rather among the Muses who dwell on
Olympus ;" even so a new interest of historic and anti-
quarian curiosity would be excited by " the splendid ruins,"
as the same high authority rightly calls those " which

Dr. Schliemann has brought to light at Hissarlik." For what, in that case, were the *four cities*, whose successive layers of ruins, still marked by the fires that have passed over them in turn, are piled to the height of fifty feet above the old summit of the hill? If not even one of them is TROY, what is the story, so like that of Troy, which belongs to them?

> " Trojæ renascens alite lugubri
> Fortuna tristi clade iterabitur."

What is the light that is struggling to break forth from the varied mass of evidence, and the half-deciphered inscriptions, that are still exercising the ingenuity of the most able enquirers? Whatever may be the true and final answer to these questions—and we have had to put on record a signal proof that the most sanguine investigators will be content with no answer short of the truth*— the vivid narrative written by the discoverer on the spot can never lose that charm which Renan has so happily described as " la charme des origines."

The Editor may be permitted to add, what the Author might not say, that the work derives another charm from the spirit that prompted the labours which it records. It is the work of an enthusiast in a cause which, in our " practical" age, needs all the zeal of its remaining devotees, the cause of learning for its own sake. But, in this case, enthusiasm has gone hand in hand with the practical spirit in its best form. Dr. Schliemann judged rightly in prefixing to his first work the simple unaffected record of that discipline in adversity and self-reliance, amidst which he at once educated himself and obtained the means of gratifying his ardent desire to throw new light on the

---

* See the Appendix, pages 369, 370.

highest problems of antiquity, *at his own expense*. His readers ought to know that, besides other large contributions to the cause of learning, the cost of his excavations at Hissarlik alone has amounted to 10,000*l.* ; and this is in no sense the speculative investment of an explorer, for he has expressed the firm resolution to *give away* his collection, and not to *sell* it.

Under this sense of the high and lasting value of Dr. Schliemann's work, the present translation has been undertaken, with the object of laying the narrative before English readers in a form considerably improved upon the original. For this object the Editor can safely say, on behalf of the Publisher and himself, that no pains and cost have been spared; and Dr. Schliemann has contributed new materials of great value.

The original work* was published, at the beginning of this year, as an octavo volume, accompanied by a large quarto "Atlas" of 217 photographic plates, containing a Map, Plans, and Views of the Plain of Troy, the Hill of Hissarlik, and the excavations, with representations of upwards of 4000 objects selected from the 100,000 and more brought to light by Dr. Schliemann, which were elaborately described in the letter-press pages of the Atlas. The photographs were taken for the most part from drawings; and Dr. Schliemann is the first to acknowledge that their

---

* "*Trojanische Alterthümer. Bericht über die Ausgrabungen in Troja*, von DR. HEINRICH SCHLIEMANN. Leipzig, in Commission bei F. A. Brockhaus, 1874." It may be convenient to state here, lest the reader should be disappointed at finding no details of the excavations at Hissarlik in the first year (1870), that the work of that year was merely preliminary to the systematic researches of 1871-3. An account of that first year's work, and of the arguments which convinced Dr. Schliemann that he must search for Troy at Hissarlik and no where else, will be found in his earlier work, "*Ithaque, le Péloponnèse, et Troie.*"

execution left much to be desired. Many of his original
plans and drawings have been placed at our disposal ; and
an especial acknowledgment is due both to Dr. Schliemann
and Monsieur Émile Burnouf, the Director of the French
School at Athens, for the use of the admirable drawings of
the terra-cotta *whorls* and *balls* made by M. Burnouf and
his accomplished daughter. A selection of about 200
of these objects, which are among the most interesting of
Dr. Schliemann's discoveries, occupies the 32 lithographic
plates at the end of this volume. With the exception of the
first three Plates (XXI.–XXIII.), which are copied from
the Atlas, in order to give a general view of the *sections*
of the whorls and the chief *types* of the patterns upon them,
all the rest are engraved from M. Burnouf's drawings. They
are given in the *natural size*, and each whorl is accompanied by its section. The *depth* at which each object was
found among the layers of *débris* is a matter of such
moment (as will be seen from Dr. Schliemann's work) that
the Editor felt bound to undertake the great labour of
identifying each with the representation of the same object
in the Atlas, where the depth is marked, to which, unfortunately, the drawings gave no reference. The few
whorls that remain unmarked with their depth have either
escaped this repeated search, or are not represented in the
Atlas. The elaborate descriptions of the material, style
of workmanship, and supposed meanings of the patterns,
which M. Burnouf has inscribed on most of his drawings,
are given in the " List of Illustrations." The explanations
of the patterns are, of course, offered only as conjectures,
possessing the value which they derive from M. Burnouf's
profound knowledge of Aryan antiquities. Some of the
explanations of the patterns are Dr. Schliemann's ; and the
Editor has added a few descriptions, based on a careful
attempt to analyze and arrange the patterns according to

distinct types. Most of these types are exhibited on
Plates XXII. and XXIII.

The selection of the 300 illustrations inserted in the
body of the work has been a matter of no ordinary labour.
One chief point, in which the present work claims to be an
improvement on the original, is the exhibition of the most
interesting objects in Dr. Schliemann's collection in their
proper relation to the descriptions in his text. The work
of selection from 4000 objects, great as was the care it
required, was the smallest part of the difficulty. It is no
disparagement to Dr. Schliemann to recognize the fact that,
amidst his occupations at the work through the long days
of spring and summer, and with little competent help save
from Madame Schliemann's enthusiasm in the cause, the
objects thrown on his hands from day to day could only be
arranged and depicted very imperfectly. The difficulty was
greatly enhanced by a circumstance which should be noticed
in following the order of Dr. Schliemann's work. It dif-
fered greatly from that of his forerunners in the modern
enterprise of penetrating into the mounds that cover the
primeval cities of the world. When, for example, we follow
Layard into the mound of Nimrud, and see how the rooms
of the Assyrian palaces suddenly burst upon him, with
their walls lined with sculptured and inscribed slabs, we
seem almost to be reading of Aladdin's descent into the
treasure-house of jewels. But Schliemann's work consisted
in a series of transverse cuttings, which laid open sections
of the various strata, from the present surface of the hill to
the virgin soil. The work of one day would often yield
objects from almost all the strata; and each successive
trench repeated the old order, more or less, from the remains of Greek Ilium to those of the first settlers on the
hill. The marvel is that Dr. Schliemann should have been
able to preserve any order at all, rather than that he was

obliged to abandon the attempt in the later Plates of his
Atlas (see p. 225); and special thanks are due for his care
in continuing to note the depths of all the objects found.
This has often given the clue to our search, amidst the mixed
objects of a similar nature on the photographic Plates, for
those which he describes in his text, where the figures
referred to by Plate and Number form the exception rather
than the rule. We believe that the cases in which we have
failed to find objects really worth representing, or in which an
object named in the text may have been wrongly identified
in the Plates, are so few as in no way to affect the value
of the work. How much, on the other hand, its value
is increased by the style in which our illustrations have
been engraved, will be best seen by a comparison with the
photographic Plates. It should be added that the present
work contains all the illustrations that are now generally
accessible, as the Atlas is out of print, and the negatives
are understood to be past further use.

Twelve of the views (Plates II., III., IV., V., VI., VII. A
and B, IX., X., XI. A and B, and XII., besides the Great
Altar, No. 188) were engraved by Mr. Whymper; all the
other views and cuts by Mr. James D. Cooper; and the
lithographed map, plans, and plates of whorls and balls by
Messrs. Cooper and Hodson. In the description appended
to each engraving all that is valuable in the letter-press to
the Atlas has been incorporated, and the depth at which
the object was found is added. Some further descriptions
of the Plates are given in the "List of Illustrations."

The text of Dr. Schliemann's work has been translated
by Miss L. Dora Schmitz, and revised throughout by the
Editor. The object kept in view has been a faithful
rendering of the Memoirs, in all the freshness due to their
composition on the spot during the progress of the work.
That mode of composition, it is true, involved not a few of

those mistakes and contradictions on matters of opinion, due to the novelty and the rapid progress of the discoveries, which Dr. Schliemann has confessed and explained at the opening of his work (see p. 12). To have attempted a systematic correction and harmonizing of such discrepancies would have deprived the work of all its freshness, and of much of its value as a series of landmarks in the history of Dr. Schliemann's researches, from his first firm conviction that Troy was to be sought in the Hill of Hissarlik, to his discovery of the "Scæan Gate" and the "Treasure of Priam." The Author's final conclusions are summed up by himself in the "Introduction;" and the Editor has thought it enough to add to those statements, which seemed likely to mislead the reader for a time, references to the places where the correction may be found. On one point he has ventured a little further. All the earlier chapters are affected by the opinion, that the lowest remains on the native rock were those of the Homeric Troy, which Dr. Schliemann afterwards recognized in the stratum next above. To avoid perpetual reference to this change of opinion, the Editor has sometimes omitted or toned down the words "Troy" and "Trojan" as applied to the *lowest stratum*, and, both in the "Contents" and running titles, and in the descriptions of the Illustrations, he has throughout applied those terms to the discoveries in the *second stratum*, in accordance with Dr. Schliemann's ultimate conclusion.

In a very few cases the Editor has ventured to correct what seemed to him positive errors.* He has not deemed it any part of his duty to discuss the Author's opinions or to review his conclusions. He has, however, taken such

---

* Several misprints and wrong references in the original have been corrected. For the correction respecting the *débris* at Jerusalem (note to p. 218), the Editor is indebted to his friend Mr. George Grove.

opportunities as suggested themselves, to set Dr. Schliemann's statements in a clearer light by a few illustrative annotations. Among the rest, the chief passages cited from Homer are quoted in full, with Lord Derby's translation, and others have been added (out of many more which have been noted), as suggesting remarkable coincidences with the objects found by Dr. Schliemann.

From the manner in which the work was composed, and the great importance attached by Dr. Schliemann to some leading points of his argument, it was inevitable that there should be some repetitions, both in the Memoirs themselves, and between them and the Introduction. These the Editor has rather endeavoured to abridge than completely to remove. To have expunged them from the Memoirs would have deprived these of much of the interest resulting from the discussions which arose out of the discoveries in their first freshness; to have omitted them from the Introduction would have marred the completeness of the Author's summary of his results. The few repetitions left standing are a fair measure of the importance which the Author assigns to the points thus insisted on. A very few passages have been omitted for reasons that would be evident on a reference to the original; but none of these omissions affect a single point in Dr. Schliemann's discoveries.

The *measures*, which Dr. Schliemann gives with the minutest care throughout his work, have been preserved and converted from the French metric standard into English measures. This has been done with great care, though in such constant conversion some errors must of course have crept in; and *approximate* numbers have often been given to avoid the awkwardness of fractions, where *minute* accuracy seemed needless. In many cases both the French and English measures are given, not only because Dr. Schliemann gives both (as he often does), but for another sufficient reason. A chief key to the signifi-cance of the discoveries is found in the *depths* of the successive *strata* of remains, which are exhibited in the form of a diagram on page 10. The numbers which express these in *Meters* * are so constantly used by Dr. Schliemann, and are so much simpler than the English equivalents, that they have been kept as a sort of " memory key " to the strata of remains. For the like reason, and for simplicity-sake, the depths appended to the Illustrations are given in meters only. The *Table of French and English Measures* on page 56 will enable the reader to check our conversions and to make his own. The Editor has added an Appendix, explaining briefly the present state of the deeply interesting question concerning the *Inscrip-tions* which have been traced on some of the objects found by Dr. Schliemann.

With these explanations the Editor might be content to leave the work to the judgment of scholars and of the great body of educated persons, who have happily been brought up in the knowledge and love of Homer's glorious poetry, " the tale of Troy divine," and of

" Immortal Greece, dear land of glorious lays."

Long may it be before such training is denied to the imagination of the young, whether on the low utilitarian ground, or on the more specious and dangerous plea of making it the select possession of the few who can acquire it " thoroughly " :

Νήπιοι, οὐκ ἴσασιν ὅσῳ πλέον ἥμισυ παντός.

To attempt a discussion of the results of Dr. Schlie-

---

* The Anglicized form of the word is used as a matter of common sense and convenience. Dr. Schliemann does the same in German.

mann's discoveries would be alike beyond the province
of an Editor, and premature in the present state of the
investigation.   The criticisms called forth both in England
and on the Continent, during the one year that has
elapsed since the publication of the work, are an earnest
of the more than ten years' duration of that new War of
Troy for which it has given the signal.   The English
reader may obtain some idea of the points that have been
brought under discussion by turning over the file of the
" *Academy* " for the year, not to speak of many reviews of
Schliemann's work in other periodicals and papers.   Without plunging into these varied discussions, it may be well
to indicate briefly certain points that have been established,
some lines of research that have been opened, and some
false issues that need to be avoided.

First of all, the integrity of Dr. Schliemann in the
whole matter—of which his self-sacrificing spirit might
surely have been a sufficient pledge—and the genuineness
of his discoveries, are beyond all suspicion.   We have,
indeed, never seen them called in question, except in what
appears to be an effusion of spite from a Greek, who seems
to envy a German his discoveries on the Greek ground
which Greeks have neglected for fifteen centuries.*   In
addition to the consent of scholars, the genuineness and
high antiquity of the objects in Dr. Schliemann's collection
have been specially attested by so competent a judge as
Mr. Charles Newton, of the British Museum, who went
to Athens for the express purpose of examining them.†

---

* See the Letter of Mr. S. Comnos in the *Athenæum* of August 8th,
and the Answer of Dr. Schliemann in the *Academy* of November 7th,
1874.

† See Mr. Newton's Report, and the discussion thereupon, in the
Academy of February 14th, 1874, and in the 'Transactions of the Society
of Antiquaries.'

A letter by Mr. Frank Calvert, who is so honourably mentioned in the work, deserves special notice for the implied testimony which it bears to Dr. Schliemann's good faith, while strongly criticising some of his statements.*

Among the false issues raised in the discussion, one most to be avoided is the making the value of Dr. Schliemann's discoveries dependent on the question of the site of Troy as determined by the *data* furnished by the Iliad. The position is common to Schliemann and his adverse critics, that Homer never saw the city of whose fate he sang;—because, says Schliemann, it had long been buried beneath its own ashes and the cities, or the ruins of the cities, built above it;—because, say the objectors, Homer created a Troy of his own imagination. The former existence and site of Troy were known to Homer—says Schliemann—by the unbroken tradition belonging to the spot where the Greek colonists founded the city which they called by the same name as, and believed to be the true successor of, the Homeric ILIUM. Of this, it is replied, we know nothing, and we have no other guide to *Homer's Troy* save the data of the Iliad. Be it so; and if those data really point to Hissarlik—as was the universal opinion of antiquity, till a sceptical grammarian invented another site, which all scholars now reject—as was also the opinion of modern scholars, till the new site of Bunarbashi was invented by Lechevalier to suit the Iliad, and accepted by many critics, but rejected by others, including the high authority of Grote — then the conclusion is irresistible, that Schliemann has found the Troy of which Homer had heard through the lasting report of poetic fame: Ἡμεῖς δὲ

---

* The *Athenæum*, November 7th, 1874. Some of Mr. Calvert's corrections seem of importance, but we have not felt it right to use them in the absence of the reply which Dr. Schliemann will doubtless make, as he has done to his other critics.

κλέος οἶον ἀκούομεν.* But the corresponding *negative* does *not* follow; for, if Homer's Troy was but a city built in the ethereal region of his fancy, his placing it at Bunarbashi, or on any other spot, could not affect the lost site of the true Troy, *if such a city ever existed*, and therefore can be no objection to the argument, that the discovery of an ancient city on the traditional site of the heroic Troy confirms the truth of the tradition on both points—the *real existence* of the city, as well as its existence on this site. The paradox—that Troy never existed and that Bunarbashi was its site—was so far confirmed by Schliemann that he dug at Bunarbashi, and found clear evidence that the idea of a great city having ever stood there is a mere imagination. The few remains of walls, that were found there, confirm instead of weakening the negative conclusion; for they are as utterly inadequate to be the remains of the "great, sacred, wealthy Ilium," as they are suitable to the little town of Gergis, with which they are now identified by an inscription. In short, that the real city of Troy could not have stood at Bunarbashi, is one of the most certain results of Schliemann's researches.

The same sure test of downright digging has finally disposed of all the other suggested sites, leaving by the "method of exhaustion" the inevitable conclusion, that the only great city (or succession of cities), that we know to have existed in the Troad before the historic Grecian colony of Ilium, rose and perished—as the Greeks of Ilium always said it did—on the ground beneath their feet, upon

---

* *Iliad*, II. 486. See the full quotation at p. 346. Professor Max Müller quotes the same passage in favour of the non-reality of Homer's Troy; but surely the κλέος ἀκούομεν implies a positive tradition, and the οὐδέ τι ἴδμεν confesses ignorance of details only. Are Homer's Hellespont, and his Plain of Troy, watered by the Scamander and Simoïs, also "to be sought rather among the Muses who dwell on Olympus than" about "the Hill of Hissarlik"?

the Hill of Hissarlik. And that Homer, or—if you please —the so-called Homeric bards, familiar with the Troad, and avowedly following tradition, should have imagined a different site, would be, at the least, very surprising. This is not the place for an analysis of the Homeric local evidence; but, coming fresh from a renewed perusal of the *Iliad* with a view to this very question, the Editor feels bound to express the conviction that its indications, while in themselves consistent with the site of Hissarlik, can be interpreted in no other way, now that we know what that site contains.*

Standing, as it does, at the very point of junction between the East and West, and in the region where we find the connecting link between the primitive Greeks of Asia and Europe,† the Hill of Hissarlik answers at once to the primitive type of a Greek city, and to the present condition of the primeval capitals of the East. Like so many of the first, in Greece, Asia Minor, and Italy, the old city was a hill-fort, an Acropolis built near but not close upon the sea, in a situation suited at once for defence against the neighbouring barbarians, and for the prosecution of that commerce, whether by its own maritime enterprise, or by intercourse with foreign voyagers, of which the copper, ivory, and other objects from the ruins furnish decisive

---

* The excellent dissertation by Dr. Eckenbrecher, to which Schliemann refers at page 46, has just been republished in a revised edition, "*Die Lage des Homerischen Troja*, von Dr. GUSTAV VON ECKENBRECHER." With 2 Maps and a View of Hissarlik, 1875. The Author has purposely kept his argument in favour of the site at Hissarlik, from Homer and the later classical writers, distinct from what he distinctly accepts as its confirmation by Schliemann's discoveries.

† See the remarks on this point in the *Appendix*, p. 364. Lest the views here indicated should seem to be at variance with the frequent use of the term "pre-Hellenic" throughout this work, it may be well to explain, once for all, that "pre-Hellenic" is to be taken as signifying nothing else than "before the occupation of the site by the people of the historical Greek Ilium."

proofs.* This type is as conspicuously wanting at Bunarbashi, as it is well marked by the site of Hissarlik.

Like the other great oriental capitals of the Old World,
the present condition of Troy is that of a mound, such
as those in the plain of the Tigris and Euphrates, offering
for ages the invitation to research, which has only been
accepted and rewarded in our own day. The resemblance
is so striking, as to raise a strong presumption that, as
the mounds of Nimrud and Kouyunjik, of Khorsabad and
Hillah, have been found to contain the palaces of the
Assyrian and Babylonian kings, so we may accept the ruins
found in the mound of Hissarlik as those of the capital of
that primeval empire in Asia Minor, which is indicated by
the Homeric tradition, and proved to have been a reality
by the Egyptian monuments.†

This parallel seems to throw some light on a question,
concerning which Dr. Schliemann is forced to a result
which disappointed himself, and does not appear satis-
factory to us—that of the magnitude of Troy. As the
mounds opened by Layard and his fellow labourers contained only the "royal quarters," which towered above the
rude buildings of cities the magnitude of which is attested
by abundant proofs, so it is reasonable to believe that the
ruins at Hissarlik are those of the royal quarter, the only

---

* The *Phrygians* (of which race the Trojans were a branch) are
among the nations mentioned as having held in succession the supre-
macy at sea (θαλασσοκρατία).

† The evidence of the Egyptian monuments to the power of Troy,
and the bearing of that evidence on the date of the remains at Hissarlik,
are among the subjects which we must refrain from discussing, as both
too large and as yet too imperfectly investigated. It must suffice at
present to refer to the letters by M. FRANÇOIS LENORMANT in the
Academy for March 21st and March 28th, 1874, and to the two articles
in the *Contemporary Review* for June and July, 1874, which it is understood that Mr. GLADSTONE is about to republish under the title of
'*Homer and Egypt;* a Contribution towards determining the Place
of Homer in Chronology.'

really *permanent* part of the city, built on the hill capping the lower plateau which lifted the huts of the common people above the marshes and inundations of the Scamander and the Simoïs. In both cases the fragile dwellings of the multitude have perished; and the pottery and other remains, which were left on the surface of the plateau of Ilium, would naturally be cleared away by the succeeding settlers. Instead, therefore, of supposing with Schliemann, that Homer's poetical exaggeration invented the "Pergamus," we would rather say that he exalted the mean dwellings that clustered about the Pergamus into the "well-built city" with her "wide streets."

We cannot sympathize with the sentimental objection that, in proportion as the conviction grows that the Troy of Homer has been found, his poetry is brought down from the heights of pure imagination. Epic Poetry, the very essence of which is narrative, has always achieved its noblest triumphs in celebrating events which were at least believed to be real, not in the invention of incidents and deeds purely imaginary. The most resolute deniers of any historic basis for the story of Troy will admit that neither the scene nor the chief actors were invented by Homer, or, if you please, the Homeric poets, who assuredly believed the truth of the traditions to which the *Iliad* gave an immortal form. Any discovery which verifies that belief strengthens the foundation without impairing the superstructure, and adds the interest of truthfulness to those poetic beauties which remain the pure creation of Homer.

Leaving the Homeric bearings of the question to the discussion of which no speedy end can be anticipated, all are agreed that Dr. Schliemann's discoveries have added immensely to that growing mass of evidence which is tending to solve one of the most interesting problems in the history of the world, the connection between the East and

West, especially with regard to the spread of Aryan civilization.* Two points are becoming clearer every day, the early existence of members of the Greek race on the shores of Asia, and the essential truth of those traditions about the Oriental influence on Greek civilization, which, within our own remembrance, have passed through the stages of uncritical acceptance, hypercritical rejection, and discriminating belief founded on sure evidence.

It would seem as if Troy, familiar to our childhood as the point of contact in poetry between the East and West, were reappearing in the science of archæology as a link between the eastern and western branches of the antiquities of the great Aryan family, extending its influence to our own island in another sense than the legend of Brute the Trojan. How great an increase of light may soon be expected from the deciphering of the Inscriptions found at Hissarlik may be inferred, in part, from the brief account, in the Appendix, of the progress thus far made. In fine, few dissentients will be found from the judgment of a not too favourable critic, that " Dr. Schliemann, in spite of his over-great enthusiasm, ... *has done the world an incalculable service.*" †

The decipherment of the inscriptions will probably go far to determine the curious question of the use of the terra-cotta *whorls,* found in such numbers in all the four pre-Hellenic strata of remains at Hissarlik. That they had

---

* Those desirous of pursuing this study from its fountain-head may consult, besides the works quoted by Dr. Schliemann, SPIEGEL's ' Iranian Antiquities' (*Eranische Alterthumskunde,* Vols. I. and II., Leipzig, 1871, 1873).

† Professor Van Benschoten's ' Remarks on Dr. Schliemann's Discoveries,' in the ' Proceedings of the Sixth Annual Session of the American Philological Association, held at Hartford, July 1874.' We have been pleased to find this testimony, while correcting this sheet for press, in the *Academy* for January 9th, 1875.

some practical purpose may be inferred both from this very abundance, and from the occurrence of similar objects among the remains of various early races. Besides the examples given by Dr. Schliemann, they have been found in various parts of our own island, and especially in Scotland, but always (we believe) without decorations. On the other hand, the Aryan emblems and the inscriptions * marked upon them would seem to show that they were applied to, if not originally designed for, some higher use. It seems quite natural for a simple and religious race, such as the early Aryans certainly were, to stamp religious emblems and sentences on objects in daily use, and then to consecrate them as *ex voto* offerings, according to Dr. Schliemann's suggestion. The astronomical significance, which Schliemann finds in many of the whorls, is unmistakeable in most of the terra-cotta balls ; and this seems to furnish evidence that the people who made them had some acquaintance, at least, with the astronomical science of Babylonia.

The keen discussion provoked by Dr. Schliemann's novel explanation of the θέα γλαυκῶπις Ἀθήνη might be left "a pretty quarrel as it stands," † did there not appear to be a key of which neither party has made sufficient use. The symbolism, which embodied divine attributes in animal forms, belonged unquestionably to an early form of the Greek religion, as well as to the Egyptian and Assyrian.‡

---

* Had the first conclusions of Haug and Gomperz remained good, we should have had the very significant evidence that all the inscriptions were in the nature of dedications or invocations ; but of course this question must now be held in suspense.

† See Max Müller's Review of Schliemann in the *Academy*, Jan. 10th, 1874, p. 39; Schliemann's Reply, entitled 'Hera Boöpis and Athené Glaukopis,' *Ibid.* Nov. 21st, 1874, p. 563, and Max Müller's Rejoinder, *Ibid.* Nov. 24th, p. 585.

‡ On the whole subject of this symbolism see the recent work of PROFESSOR CONZE on the 'Figures of Heroes and Gods' (*Heroen- und*

The ram-headed Ammon, the hawk-headed Ra, the eagle-headed Nisroch, form exact precedents for an owl-headed Athena, a personation which may very well have passed into the slighter forms of owl-faced, owl-eyed, bright-eyed. Indeed, we see no other explanation of the constant connection of the owl with the goddess, which survived to the most perfect age of Greek sculpture. The question is not to be decided by an etymological analysis of the sense of γλαυκῶπις in the Greek writers, long after the old symbolism had been forgotten, nor even by the sense which Homer may have attached to the word in his own mind. One of the most striking characters of his language is his use of *fixed epithets ;* and he might very well have inherited the title of the tutelar goddess of the Ionian race with the rest of his stock of traditions. If γλαυκῶπις were merely a common attributive, signifying " bright-eyed," it is very remarkable that Homer should never apply it to mortal women, or to any goddess save Athena. We are expressing no opinion upon the accuracy of Schliemann's identification in every case ; but the *rudeness* of many of his " owl-faced idols " is no stumbling-block, for the oldest and rudest sacred images were held in lasting and peculiar reverence. The Ephesian image of Artemis, " which fell down from Jove," is a case parallel to what the " Palladium " of Ilium may have been.

The ethnological interpretation of the four *strata* of remains at Hissarlik is another of the questions which it would be premature to discuss ; but a passing reference

---

Götter-Gestalten). He shows that the *symbol* preceded the *image*, two things which have been confounded in the discussion. A fuller illustration may be obtained from the use of *animals* in the *armorial devices of the Greeks*, which has been recently discussed by Professor Curtius in a paper contributed to the Berlin Academy of Science. He believes that the practice came originally from *Assyria*, so that *Troy* would be on the route.

may be allowed to their very remarkable correspondence
with the traditions relating to the site. First, Homer re-
cognizes a city which preceded the Ilium of Priam, and
which had been destroyed by Hercules; and Schliemann
found a primeval city, of considerable civilization, on the
native rock, below the ruins which he regards as the
Homeric Troy. Tradition speaks of a Phrygian population,
of which the Trojans were a branch, as having apparently
displaced, and driven over into Europe, the kindred Pelasgians. Above the second stratum are the remains of a
third city, which, in the type and patterns of its terra-
cottas, instruments, and ornaments, shows a close resemblance to the second; and the link of connection is rivetted
by the inscriptions in the same character in both strata.
And so, in the Homeric poems, every reader is struck with
the common bonds of genealogy and language, traditions
and mutual intercourse, religion and manners, between the
Greeks who assail Troy and the Trojans who defend it. If
the legend of the Trojan War preserves the tradition of a
real conquest of the city by a kindred race, the very nature
of the case forbids us to accept literally the story, that the
conquerors simply sailed away again.* It is far more reasonable to regard the *ten years* of the War, and the *ten
years* of the *Return of the Chiefs* (Νόστοι) as cycles of
ethnic struggles, the details of which had been sublimed
into poetical traditions. The fact, that Schliemann traces
in the third stratum a civilization lower than in the second,
is an objection only from the point of view of our classical
prepossessions. There are not wanting indications in

---

* While writing this, we remember (though without the means of
verification at hand) that Niebuhr maintains the same view in his
' Lectures on Ancient History'; and it is confirmed by the tradition
among the Æolians of the Troad, that Agamemnon was the founder
of their colony (κτίστης).

Homer (as Curtius, among others, has pointed out) that the Trojans were more civilized and wealthy than the Greeks; and in the much earlier age, to which the conflict—if real at all—must have belonged, we may be sure that the Asiatic people had over their European kindred an advantage which we may venture to symbolize by the golden arms of Glaucus and the brazen arms of Diomed (Homer, *Iliad*, VI. 235, 236). Xanthus, the old historian of Lydia, preserves the tradition of a reflux migration of Phrygians from Europe into Asia, after the Trojan War, and says that they conquered Troy and settled in its territory. This migration is ascribed to the pressure of the barbarian Thracians; and the fourth stratum, with its traces of merely wooden buildings, and other marks of a lower stage of civilization, corresponds to that conquest of the Troad by those same barbarian Thracians, the tradition of which is preserved by Herodotus and other writers. The primitive dwellings of those races in Thrace still furnish the flint implements, which are most abundant in the fourth stratum at Hissarlik.

The extremely interesting concurrence of instruments of stone with those of copper (or bronze, see p. 361) in all the four strata at Hissarlik, may be illustrated by a case which has fallen under our notice while dismissing this sheet for press. A mound recently opened at the Bocenos, near Carnac (in the Morbihan), has disclosed the remains of a Gallic house, of the *second century* of our era, in which *flint implements* were found, intermixed with pottery of various styles, from the most primitive to the finest examples of native Gallic art, and among all these objects was a terracotta head of the *Venus Anadyomene*.* Such facts as

---

* See the *Academy*, Jan. 9th, 1875.

these furnish a caution against the too hasty application of the theory of the Ages of Stone, Bronze, and Iron.

Another illustration is worth adding of the persistence of the forms of objects in common use in the same region. (See p. 47.) Mr. Davis, in his recently published travels in Asia Minor,* describes a wooden vessel for carrying water, which he saw at Hierapolis, in Phrygia, of the very same form as the crown-handled vase-covers of terra-cotta found in such numbers by Schliemann (see pp. 25, 48, 86, 95, &c.). "They are made of a section of the pine : the inside is hollowed from below, and the bottom is closed by another piece of wood exactly fitted into it." The two drawings given by Mr. Davis closely resemble our cut, No. 51, p. 86.

Our last letter from Dr. Schliemann announced the approaching termination of his lawsuit with the Turkish Government, arising out of the dispute referred to in the 'Introduction' (p. 52). The collection has been valued by two experts; and Dr. Schliemann satisfies the demand of the Turkish Government by a payment in cash, and an engagement to continue the excavations in Troy for three or four months for the benefit of the Imperial Museum at Constantinople. We rejoice that he has not "closed the excavations at Hissarlik for ever" (see p. 356), and wait to see what new discoveries may equal or surpass those of the "Scæan Gates," the "Palace," and the "Treasure of Priam."

Meanwhile, as the use of so mythical a name as that of Troy's last king has furnished a special butt for critical scorn, it seems due to Dr. Schliemann to quote his reason for retaining it :—†

---

* ·*Anatolica;* or the Journal of a Visit to some of the ancient Ruined Cities of Caria, Phrygia, Lycia, and Pisidia. By the Rev. E. J. DAVIS, H.B.M.'s Consular Chaplain, Alexandria, 1874.' Page 101.

† The *Academy*, Nov. 7th, 1874.

"I identify with the Homeric Ilion the city second in succession from the virgin soil, because only in that city were used the Great Tower, the great Circuit Wall, the great Double Gate, and the ancient palace of the chief or king, whom I call Priam, because he is called so by the tradition of which Homer is the echo; but as soon as it is proved that Homer and the tradition were wrong, and that Troy's last king was called 'Smith,' I shall at once call him so." Those who believe Troy to be a myth and Priam a shadow as unsubstantial as the shape, whose head

"The likeness of a kingly crown had on,"

need not grudge Schliemann the satisfaction of giving the unappropriated *nominis umbra* to the owner of his very substantial Treasure. The name of Priam may possibly even yet be read on the inscriptions, as the names of the Assyrian kings have been read on theirs, or it may be an invention of the bard's; but the name of TROY can no longer be withheld from the "splendid ruins" of the great and wealthy city which stood upon its traditional site—*a city which has been sacked by enemies and burnt with fire.*

PHILIP SMITH.

HAMPSTEAD,
Christmas Eve, 1874.

Terra-cotta Tablets from the Greek Stratum (1–2 M.).

TABLE OF CONTENTS.

WORK AT HISSARLIK IN 1871.

CHAPTER I.

On the Hill of Hissarlik, October 18th, 1871.

The site of ILIUM described — Excavations in 1870 : the City Wall of Lysi-
machus — Purchase of the sité and grant of a *firman* — Arrival of Dr. and
Madame Schliemann in 1871, and beginning of the Excavations — The
Hill of HISSARLIK, the *Acropolis* of the Greek Ilium — Search for its
limits — Difficulties of the work — The great cutting on the North side —
Greek coins found — Dangers from fever 57

CHAPTER II.

On the Hill of Hissarlik, October 26th, 1871.

Number of workmen — Discoveries at 2 to 4 meters deep — Greek coins —
Remarkable terra-cottas with small stamps, probably *Ex votos* — These
cease, and are succeeded by the whorls — Bones of sharks, shells of mus-
sels and oysters, and pottery — Three Greek Inscriptions — The splendid
panoramic view from Hissarlik — The Plain of Troy and the heroic *tumuli*
— Thymbria : Mr. Frank Calvert's Museum — The mound of Chanaï
Tépé — The Scamander and its ancient bed — Valley of the Simoïs, and
Ruins of Ophrynium 64

CHAPTER III.

On the Hill of Hissarlik, November 3rd, 1871.

Puzzling transitions from the "Stone Age" to a higher civilization — The
stone age reappears in force, mixed with pottery of fine workmanship, and

CHAPTER VIII.

On the Hill of Hissarlik, May 11th, 1872.

CHAPTER IX.

On the Hill of Hissarlik, May 23rd, 1872.

CHAPTER X.

On the Hill of Hissarlik, June 18th, 1872.

CHAPTER XI.

On the Hill of Hissarlik, July 13th, 1872.

CHAPTER XII.

Pergamus of Troy, August 4th, 1872.

CHAPTER XIII.

Pergamus of Troy, August 14th, 1872.

CHAPTER XIV.

Athens, September 28th, 1872.

WORK AT HISSARLIK IN 1873.

CHAPTER XV.

Pergamus of Troy, February 22nd, 1873.

CHAPTER XXI.

Pergamus of Troy, April 16th, 1873.

CHAPTER XXII.

Pergamus of Troy, May 10th, 1873.

CHAPTER XXIII.

Troy, June 17th, 1873.

by the conflagration — A knife and a piece of a sword — Signs of the Treasure having been packed in a wooden chest — The key found — The Treasure probably left behind in an effort to escape — Other articles found near the Treasure — The thousands of gold jewels found in a silver vase — The two golden diadems — The ear-rings, bracelets, and finger-rings — The smaller jewels of gold — Analysis of the copper articles by M. Landerer — Discovery of another room in the palace containing an inscribed stone, and curious terra-cottas — Silver dishes — Greek terra-cotta figures — Great abundance of the owl-faced vases — Limited extent of Troy — Its walls traced — Poetic exaggerations of Homer — *The one great point of* TROY'S *reality established* — It was as large as the primitive Athens and Mycenæ — The wealth and power of Troy — Great height of its houses — Probable population — Troy known to Homer only by tradition — Question of a temple in Homer's time — Characteristics of the Trojan stratum of remains, and their difference from those of the lowest stratum — The former opinion on this point recalled — Layer of metallic *scoriæ* through the whole hill — Error of Strabo about the utter destruction of Troy — Part of the real Troy unfortunately destroyed in the earlier excavations ; but many Trojan houses brought to light since — The stones of Troy not used in building other cities — Trojan houses of sun-dried bricks, except the most important buildings, which are of stones and earth — Extent and results of the excavations — Advice to future explorers — Further excavations on the north side — Very curious terra-cotta vessels — Perforated vases — A terra-cotta with hieroglyphics — Heads of oxen and horses ; their probable significance — Idols of the Ilian Athena — Greek and Roman medals — Greek inscriptions — Final close of the excavations ; thanksgiving for freedom from serious accidents — Commendations of Nicolaus Saphyros Jannakis, and other assistants, and of the artist Polychronios Tempesis, and of the engineer Adolphe Laurent .. .. Page 321

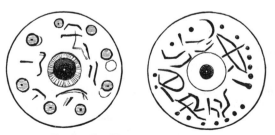

Two Inscribed Whorls (5 M. and 7 M.).

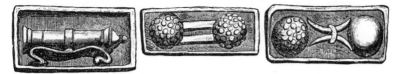

Terra-cotta Tablets from the Greek Stratum (2 M.).

LIST OF ILLUSTRATIONS.

—◆◇◆—

MAPS AND PLANS.

PLATES AND CUTS.

and Road is seen part of the Great *Tower of Ilium*, and to the right hand, next to and behind the Gate, the ruins of the *Palace of Priam*, partly overladen with later but still pre-Hellenic walls, and partly standing free. Behind, the Scæan Gate appears again, going in a direction W.N.W., then the great City Wall, and upon it, at or about the spot marked *a*, the *Treasure* was found. In the background, where the man stands, is seen a wall built of massive hewn stones, belonging to a Tower of the Greek age. Behind this Tower-wall appear the Plain of Troy, the Hellespont, the island of Imbros, and above this the mountains of Samothrace. At the right extremity of the picture, also, a part of the Plain of Troy is seen through the great cutting, over the ruins of the royal House.

PLATES XXI.–LII. LITHOGRAPHIC PLATES OF TERRA-COTTA WHORLS AND BALLS.*

(*At End of the Volume.*)

——◆◇◆——

PLATE XXI. SECTIONS OF WHORLS.

Nos. 301–308. Sections of Plain Whorls (see p. 40) (2–10 M.).

No. 309. Piece of Terra-cotta, of unknown use (see p. 219) (10 M.).

Nos. 310–316. Sections of Decorated Whorls (see p. 60) (3–11 M.).

PLATE XXII. TYPICAL PATTERNS OF WHORLS.†

No. 317. A Cross, with 4 nail-marks (7 M.).

No. 318.   Do.   with the lines double and oblique (7 M.).

No. 319.   Do.   with three arms (7 M.).

---

* The only exceptions to this description are the two terra-cottas, Pl. XXI.
No. 309, and Pl. XLVIII. No. 484, and the one on Pl. XXIV. No. 349, which links
the whorls with the round terra-cottas of the Greek strata.

† The descriptions of the patterns are partly from Dr. Schliemann's work, and
partly added by the Editor; but the chief part are from M. Burnouf's descriptions
appended to the original drawings by himself and his accomplished daughter, from
which all, from Plate XXIV. and onwards, have been engraved. These descriptions
are quoted simply for what they may be worth, as the *speculations* of so eminent
an orientalist. We have omitted some of them as too speculative. In special cases
the initial (B) is added. The material, colour, and style of work are given from
M. Burnouf's notes. Those on Plates XXI., XXII., XXIII., are engraved from the
photographs in Schliemann's Atlas.

PLATE XXIII. TYPICAL PATTERNS OF WHORLS.

* D for *double*, denotes a whorl decorated on both sides.

---

* In M. Burnouf's descriptions the 卐 is called "*le sacrifice*," or "*le saint sacrifice*."
† Where the depth is not given, we have been unable to discover the objects in the Atlas; neither the numbers nor the depths being given on the drawings.

* One of numerous examples showing the workman's *free hand*; he has not measured his spaces with any exactness.

---

* This is rather suggestive of a *teetotum*.

---

* An example of one of the rudest attempts at drawing from the *latest* pre-Hellenic stratum; some equally rude figures are scratched on a wall at Pompeii.

† This is an example of many cases, in which the pattern may be viewed quite differently, according as we start from the centre or from the circumference.

No. 480. Four quadruple Zigzags (Signs of Lightning), arranged as a Cross (see p. 160). Very beautiful black; polished; pattern very white; angles very sharp; very hard. One of the finest Trojan Whorls (10 M.).

No. 481D. Five parallel Circles of quadruple lines on the edge and both faces, probably meant for a wheel in rapid motion (comp. Plate XXIII. No. 340). " The exactly parallel circular lines were marked on the moist clay with a *comb*, as is proved by the way in which their extremities cross at the point of junction."—B.

PLATE XLVIII. VARIOUS PATTERNS.

No. 482. Three 卍 (Sacrifices) and 2 obscure Signs.—B. (Comp. Plate XXII. No. 326, and Schliemann's description, pp. 84 and 137.) Reddish; very rude; kneaded. The *axes* of the Whorl and the hole do not coincide (8½ M.).

No. 483. A 卍 and rude Figures (*Qu.*, animals or letters?). Grey; polished; very coarse (4 M.)

No. 484. A Terra-cotta Tripod. The top (in the upper figure) shews the Tree of Life (in the middle) attacked by the Caterpillar (on the right), the symbol of the Powers of Mischief. On the left is a 卍 and other Marks. Grey; polished; work rude (3 M.).

No. 485. Three concentric rows of Dots: 12 in the inner, 14 in the next, and 17 in the outer border, which is marked by a Circle and divided by straight lines. M. Burnouf explains the inner ring of dots as the 12 months of the year, and the 2 outer as referring to the days and lunations (8 M.).

PLATE XLIX. A BALL AND WHORLS.

No. 486. A Celestial Sphere, with lines marking the Zones and the Ecliptic. (The Ecliptic is not continued across the S. hemisphere, but ends at the extremities of a hole pierced through the middle of the Ball, possibly signifying the ancient belief that the nocturnal course of the Sun was subterranean.) Black; unpolished (8 M.).

No. 487. Three quintuple Rising Suns, with a Sun crossed by a 卍. Grey; polished; very regular (7 M.).

No. 488. Three Arcs, enclosing dots, and 2 卍. " The 3 stations of the Sun. The Morning and Evening Sacrifices, with their priests: the Noon has 3 priests."—B. Grey. Worn by circular friction.

No. 489. Four triple Arcs (Rising Suns) and a 卍. " The 4 quarters of the month or of the year, with the Holy Sacrifice."—B. Fine black earth (10 M.).

No. 490D. *Obv.* Three Suns and 3 卍 alternately. " The 3 stations of the Sun and the 3 Sacrifices." *Rev.* Three triple Radii. Fine black earth; polished (4 M.).

Piece of a Terra-cotta Dish, with the Owl's Face. (14 M)

AUTOBIOGRAPHICAL NOTICE

OF

DR. HENRY SCHLIEMANN.

FROM THE PREFACE TO HIS

'ITHACA, THE PELOPONNESUS, AND TROY.'

AUTOBIOGRAPHICAL NOTICE.

————◦◦————

WHEN, in the year 1832, at Kalkhorst, a village in Mecklen-burg-Schwerin, at the age of ten, I presented my father, as a Christmas gift, with a badly written Latin essay upon the principal events of the Trojan war and the adventures of Ulysses and Agamemnon, little did I think that, six-and-thirty years later, I should offer the public a work on the same subject, after having had the good fortune to see with my own eyes the scene of that war, and the country of the heroes whose names have been immortalized by Homer.

As soon as I had learnt to speak, my father related to me the great deeds of the Homeric heroes. I loved these stories; they enchanted me and transported me with the highest enthusiasm. The first impressions which a child receives abide with him during his whole life; and, though it was my lot, at the age of fourteen, to be apprenticed in the ware-house of E. Ludwig Holtz in the small town of Fürstenberg, in Mecklenburg, instead of following the scientific career for which I felt an extraordinary predisposition, I always retained the same love for the famous men of antiquity which I had conceived for them in my first childhood.

In the small shop where I was employed for five years and a half, first by Mr. Holtz and then by his successor, the excellent Mr. Th. Huckstädt, my occupation consisted in retailing herrings, butter, brandy, milk and salt, grinding potatoes for the still, sweeping the shop, and so forth. I only came into contact with the lower classes of society.

From five in the morning to eleven at night I was engaged in this work, and had not a moment free for study. Moreover I rapidly forgot the little that I had learnt in my childhood, but I did not lose the love of learning; indeed I never lost it, and, as long as I live, I shall never forget the evening when a drunken miller came into the shop. He was the son of a Protestant clergyman in a village near Teterow, and had almost concluded his studies at the Gymnasium when he was expelled on account of his bad conduct. To punish him for this, his father made him learn the trade of a miller. Dissatisfied with his lot, the young man gave himself up to drink, which however had not made him forget his Homer ; for he recited to us about one hundred lines of the poet, observing the rhythmic cadence. Although I did not understand a word, the melodious speech made a deep impression upon me, and I wept bitter tears for my unhappy fate. Thrice I got him to repeat to me those god-like verses, paying him with three glasses of brandy, which I bought with the few pence that made up my whole fortune. From that moment I never ceased to pray God that by His grace I might yet have the happiness to learn Greek.

There seemed, however, no hope of my escaping from the sad and low position in which I found myself. And yet I was released from it as if by a miracle. In lifting a cask too heavy for me, I hurt my chest ; I spat blood and was no longer able to work. In despair I went to Hamburg, where I succeeded in obtaining a situation as cabin-boy on board of a ship bound for La Guayra in Venezuela.*

On the 28th of November, 1841, we left Hamburg, but on the 12th of December we were shipwrecked in a fearful storm off the island of Texel. After innumerable dangers, the crew were saved. I regarded it as my destiny to remain in Holland, and resolved to go to Amsterdam and enlist as a soldier. But this could not be done as quickly as I had imagined, and the few florins, which I had collected as alms on the island of Texel and in Enkhuyzen, were soon spent in Amsterdam. As my means of living were entirely exhausted, I feigned illness and was taken into the hospital. From this terrible situation I was released by the kind ship-broker J. F. Wendt of Hamburg, who heard of my misfortune and sent me the proceeds of a small subscription which had been raised for me. He at the same time recommended me to the

---

* Dr. Schliemann desires us to add that this ship was the "Dorothea" (Captain Simonsen), owned by the merchants Wachsmuth and Kroog.—[ED.]

excellent Consul-General of the North German Confederation in Amsterdam, Mr. W. Hepner, who procured me a situation in the office of Mr. F. C. Quien.

In my new situation my work consisted in stamping bills of exchange and getting them cashed in the town, and in carrying letters to and from the post-office. This mechanical occupation suited me, for it left me time to think of my neglected education.

First of all I took pains to learn to write legibly, and then, in order to improve my position, I went on to the study of the modern languages. My annual salary amounted only to 800 francs (32*l.*), half of which I spent upon my studies ; on the other half I lived, miserably enough to be sure. My lodging, which cost 8 francs a month, was a wretched garret without a fire, where I shivered with cold in winter and was scorched with the heat in summer ; my breakfast consisted of rye-meal porridge, and my dinner never cost more than a penny farthing. But nothing spurs one on more to study than misery and the certain prospect of being able to release oneself from it by unremitting work. I applied myself with extraordinary diligence to the study of English. Necessity showed me a method which greatly facilitates the study of a language. This method consists in reading a great deal aloud, without making a translation ; devoting one hour every day to writing essays upon subjects that interest one, correcting these under a teacher's supervision, learning them by heart, and repeating in the next lesson what was corrected on the previous day. My memory was bad, since from my childhood it had not been exercised upon any object ; but I made use of every moment, and even stole time for study. I never went on my errands, even in the rain, without having my book in my hand and learning something by heart ; and I never waited at the post-office without reading. By such means I gradually strengthened my memory, and in half a year I had succeeded in acquiring a thorough knowledge of the English language. I then applied the same method to the study of French, the difficulties of which I overcame likewise in another six months. These persevering and ex-cessive studies had in the course of one year strengthened my memory to such a degree that the study of Dutch, Spanish, Italian, and Portuguese appeared very easy, and it did not

take me more than six weeks to write each of these languages
and to speak them fluently.   But my passion for study caused
me to neglect my mechanical occupation in the office, especially when I began to consider it beneath me.   My principals
would give me no promotion; they probably thought that a
person who shows his incapacity for the business of a servant
in an office is therefore quite worthless for any higher duties.

At last, through the intercession of my worthy friends,
L. Stoll of Mannheim and Ballauff of Bremen, I had the
good fortune to obtain a situation as correspondent and book-
keeper in the office of Messrs. B. H. Schröder and Co. in
Amsterdam, who engaged me at a salary of 1200 francs (48*l.*);
but when they saw my zeal, they paid me 2000 francs as an
encouragement.   This generosity, for which I shall ever be
grateful to them, was in fact the foundation of my prosperity;
for, as I thought that I could make myself still more useful
by a knowledge of Russian, I set to work to learn that
language also.   But the only Russian books that I could
procure were an old grammar, a lexicon, and a bad translation
of Telemachus.   In spite of all my inquiries I could not find
a teacher of Russian, for no one in Amsterdam understood a
word of the language: so I betook myself to study without
a master, and, with the help of the grammar, I learnt the
Russian letters and their pronunciation in a few days.   Then,
following my old method, I began to write short stories of my
own composition and to learn them off by heart.   As I had
no one to correct my work, it was, no doubt, very bad indeed,
but I tried at the same time to correct my faults by the
practical exercise of learning Telemachus by heart.   It occurred to me that I should make more progress if I had some
one to whom I could relate the adventures of Telemachus;
so I hired a poor Jew for 4 francs a week, who had to come
every evening for two hours to listen to my Russian recitations,
of which he did not understand a syllable.

As the ceilings of the rooms in Holland consist of single
boards, people on the ground-floor can hear what is said in
the third storey.   My recitations therefore, delivered in a loud
voice, annoyed the other tenants, who complained to the
landlord, and twice during my study of the Russian language
I was forced to change my lodgings.   But these inconve-
niences did not diminish my zeal, and in the course of six

weeks I wrote my first Russian letter to a Russian in London, and I was able to converse fluently in this language with the Russian merchants who had come to Amsterdam for the indigo auctions.

After I had concluded my study of the Russian language, I began to occupy myself seriously with the literatures of the languages which I had learnt.

In the beginning of the year 1846, my worthy principals sent me as their agent to St. Petersburg, where a year later I established a mercantile house on my own account ; but, during the first eight or nine years that I spent in Russia, I was so overwhelmed with work that I could not continue my linguistic studies, and it was not till the year 1854 that I found it possible to acquire the Swedish and Polish languages.

Great as was my wish to learn Greek, I did not venture upon its study till I had acquired a moderate fortune ; for I was afraid that this language would exercise too great a fascination upon me and estrange me from my commercial business. When, however, I could no longer restrain my desire for learning, I at last set vigorously to work at Greek in January 1856; first with Mr. N. Pappadakes, and then with Mr. Th. Vimpos of Athens, always following my old method. It did not take me more than six weeks to master the difficulties of modern Greek, and I then applied myself to the ancient language, of which in three months I learned sufficient to understand some of the ancient authors, and especially Homer, whom I read and re-read with the most lively enthusiasm.

I then occupied myself for two years exclusively with the ancient Greek literature ; and during this time I read almost all the old authors cursorily, and the Iliad and Odyssey several times.

In the year 1858 I travelled to Sweden, Denmark, Germany, Italy and Egypt, where I sailed up the Nile as far as the second cataract in Nubia. I availed myself of this opportunity to learn Arabic, and I afterwards travelled across the desert from Cairo to Jerusalem. I visited Petra, traversed the whole of Syria, and in this manner I had abundant opportunity of acquiring a practical knowledge of Arabic, the deeper study of which I afterwards continued in St. Petersburg. After leaving Syria, I visited Athens in the summer of 1859, and I was on the point of starting for the island of Ithaca when I was seized with an illness which obliged me to return to St. Petersburg.

Heaven had blessed my mercantile undertakings in a wonderful manner, so that at the end of 1863 I found myself in possession of a fortune such as my ambition had never ventured to aspire to. I therefore retired from business, in order to devote myself exclusively to the studies which have the greatest fascination for me.

In the year 1864 I was on the road to visit the native island of Ulysses and the Plain of Troy, when I allowed myself to be persuaded to visit India, China and Japan, and to travel round the world. I spent two years on this journey, and on my return in 1866 I settled in Paris, with the purpose of devoting the rest of my life to study, and especially to archæology, which has the greatest charm for me.

At last I was able to realize the dream of my whole life, and to visit at my leisure the scene of those events which had such an intense interest for me, and the country of the heroes whose adventures had delighted and comforted my childhood. I started, therefore, last summer, and visited in succession the places which still possess such living poetic memorials of antiquity.

I had not, however, the ambition of publishing a work on the subject; this I only decided upon doing when I found what errors almost all archæologists had spread about the site once occupied by the Homeric capital of Ithaca, about the stables of Eumæus, the Island of Asteris, ancient Troy, the sepulchral mounds of Batiea and of Æsyetes, the tomb of Hector, and so forth.

Apart from the hope of correcting opinions which I hold to be erroneous, I should consider myself fortunate could I aid in diffusing among the intelligent public a taste for the beautiful and noble studies which have sustained my courage during the hard trials of my life, and which will sweeten the days yet left me to live.

HENRY SCHLIEMANN.

6, *Place St.-Michel, Paris,*
   Dec. 31*st*, 1868.

INTRODUCTION.

DIAGRAM

SHEWING THE SUCCESSIVE *STRATA* OF REMAINS ON THE
HILL OF HISSARLIK.

Meters.	Feet (*abt.*)	Surface.
2		Remains of Greek Ilium.
2	6½	
2		4th Stratum.
4	13	
3		3rd Stratum.
7	23	
3		2nd Stratum. The Troy of Homer, according to Schliemann.
10	33	
4 to 6		1st Stratum.
14	46	
to	to	
16	52½	
		Native rock.

INTRODUCTION.

———◆◇◆———

CONTENTS.

The three so-called tombs of heroes also Greek — Proposed sites
at Chiplak and Akshi-Koï refuted by the absence of remains —
Modern authorities in favour of Hissarlik — Ancient types of pottery
still made in the Troad — Covers with owl-faces, and vases with
uplifted wings — Colouring materials of the pottery — The inscriptions — The author's relations with the Turkish Government —
Professor Max Müller on the owl-headed goddess — Some probable
traces of another settlement between the fourth pre-Hellenic people
and the Greek colonists.

THE present book is a sort of Diary of my excavations at
Troy, for all the memoirs of which it consists were, as the
vividness of the descriptions will prove, written down by me
on the spot while proceeding with my works.*

If my memoirs now and then contain contradictions, I
hope that these may be pardoned when it is considered that
I have here revealed a new world for archæology, that the
objects which I have brought to light by thousands are of
a kind hitherto never or but very rarely found, and that
consequently everything appeared strange and mysterious
to me. Hence I frequently ventured upon conjectures
which I was obliged to give up on mature consideration,
till I at last acquired a thorough insight, and could draw
well-founded conclusions from many actual proofs.

One of my greatest difficulties has been to make the
enormous accumulation of *débris* at Troy agree with chronology; and in this—in spite of long-searching and pondering
—I have only partially succeeded. According to Herodotus
(VII. 43) : " Xerxes in his march through the Troad, before
invading Greece (B.C. 480) arrived at the Scamander and
went up to Priam's Pergamus, as he wished to see that
citadel ; and, after having seen it, and inquired into its past
fortunes, he sacrificed 1000 oxen to the Ilian Athena, and
the Magi poured libations to the manes of the heroes."

This passage tacitly implies that at that time a Greek
colony had long since held possession of the town, and,
according to Strabo's testimony (XIII. i. 42), such a colony

---

* Each of these Memoirs forms a chapter of the Translation.

built Ilium during the dominion of the Lydians. Now, as
the commencement of the Lydian dominion dates from the
year 797 B.C., and as the Ilians seem to have been completely established there long before the arrival of Xerxes
in 480 B.C., we may fairly assume that their first settlement
in Troy took place about 700 B.C. The house-walls of
Hellenic architecture, consisting of large stones without
cement, as well as the remains of Greek household utensils,
do not, however, extend in any case to a depth of more
than two meters (6½ feet) in the excavations on the flat
surface of the hill.

As I find in Ilium no inscriptions later than those
belonging to the second century after Christ, and no coins
of a later date than Constans II. and Constantine II., but
very many belonging to these two emperors, as well as to
Constantine the Great, it may be regarded as certain that the
town began to decay even before the time of Constantine
the Great, who, as is well known, at first intended to build
Constantinople on that site; but that it remained an inhabited place till about the end of the reign of Constans II.,
that is till about A.D. 361. But the accumulation of *débris*
during this long period of 1061 years amounts only to two
meters or 6½ feet, whereas we have still to dig to a depth of
12 meters or 40 feet, and in many places even to 14 meters
or 46½ feet, below this, before reaching the native ground
which consists of shelly limestone (*Muschelkalk*). This
immense layer of *débris* from 40 to 46½ feet thick, which has
been left by the four different nations that successively inhabited the hill *before* the arrival of the Greek colony, that is
before 700 B.C., is an immensely rich *cornucopia* of the most
remarkable terra-cottas, such as have never been seen before,
and of other objects which have not the most distant resemblance to the productions of Hellenic art. The question
now forces itself upon us:—Whether this enormous mass
of ruins may not have been brought from another place to
increase the height of the hill? Such an hypothesis, as every

visitor to my excavations may convince himself at the first
glance, is perfectly impossible ; because in all the strata of
débris, from the native rock, at a depth of from 14 to 16 meters
(46 to 52½ feet) up to 4 meters (13 feet) below the surface, we
continually see remains of masonry, which rest upon strong
foundations, and are the ruins of real houses ; and, moreover,
because all the numerous large wine, water, and funereal urns
that are met with are found in an upright position. The next
question is :—But how many centuries have been required
to form a layer of *débris,* 40 and even 46½ feet thick, from
the ruins of pre-Hellenic houses, if the formation of the
uppermost one, the Greek layer of 6½ feet thick, required
1061 years? During my three years' excavations in the depths
of Troy, I have had daily and hourly opportunities of convincing myself that, from the standard of our own or of the
ancient Greek mode of life, we can form no idea of the life
and doings of the four nations which successively inhabited
this hill before the time of the Greek settlement. They
must have had a terrible time of it, otherwise we should
not find the walls of one house upon the ruined remains of
another, in continuous but *irregular* succession ; and it is
just because we can form no idea of the way in which these
nations lived and what calamities they had to endure, that
it is impossible to calculate the duration of their existence,
even approximately, from the thickness of their ruins. It is
extremely remarkable, but perfectly intelligible from the continual calamities which befel the town, that the civilization
of all the four nations constantly declined ; the terra-cottas,
which show continuous *décadence,* leave no doubt of this.

The first settlement on this hill of *Hissarlik* seems, however, to have been of the longest duration, for its ruins cover
the rock to a height of from 4 to 6 meters (13 to 20 feet).
Its houses and walls of fortification were built of stones, large
and small, joined with earth, and manifold remains of these
may be seen in my excavations. I thought last year that
these settlers were identical with the Trojans of whom

Homer sings, because I imagined that I had found among their ruins fragments of the double cup, the Homeric "δέπας ἀμφικύπελλον." From closer examination, however, it has become evident that these fragments were the remains of simple cups with a hollow stem, which can never have been used as a second cup. Moreover, I believe that in my memoirs of this year (1873) I have sufficiently proved that Aristotle (*Hist. Anim.*, IX. 40) is wrong in assigning to the Homeric "δέπας ἀμφικύπελλον" the form of a bee's cell, whence this cup has ever since been erroneously interpreted as a double cup, and that it can mean nothing but a cup with a handle on either side. Cups of such a form are *never* met with in the *débris* of the first settlement of this hill; but they frequently occur, and in great quantities, among those of the succeeding people, and also among those of the two later nations which preceded the Greek colony on the spot. The large golden cup with two handles, weighing 600 grammes (a pound and a half), which I found in the royal treasure at the depth of 28 feet in the *débris* of the second people, leaves no doubt of this fact.*

No. 1.

Fragment of *painted* pottery from the lowest stratum (16 M.).

The terra-cottas which I found on the native rock, at a depth of 14 meters (46 feet), are all of a more excellent quality than any met with in the upper strata. They are of a brilliant black, red, or brown colour, ornamented with patterns cut and filled with a white substance; the flat cups have horizontal rings on two sides, the vases have generally two perpendicular rings on each side for hanging them up with cords. Of painted terra-cottas I found only one fragment.†

---

* For this remarkable vessel see Chapter XXIII. and Plate XVII.

† But a second was found in the stratum above (see the Illustration, No. 35, at the end of the Introduction).

All that can be said of the first settlers is that they belonged to the Aryan race, as is sufficiently proved by the Aryan religious symbols met with in the strata of their ruins (among which we find the *Suastika* 卍), both upon the pieces of pottery and upon the small curious terra-cottas with a hole in the centre, which have the form of the crater of a volcano or of a *carrousel* (*i. e.* a top).*

The excavations made this year (1873) have sufficiently proved that the second nation which built a town on this hill, upon the *débris* of the first settlers (which is from 13 to 20 feet deep), are the Trojans of whom Homer sings. Their *débris* lies from 7 to 10 meters, or 23 to 33 feet, below the surface. This Trojan stratum, which, without exception, bears marks of great heat, consists mainly of red ashes of wood, which rise from 5 to 10 feet above the Great Tower of Ilium, the double Scæan Gate, and the great enclosing Wall, the construction of which Homer ascribes to Poseidon and Apollo; and they show that the town was destroyed by a fearful conflagration. How great the heat must have been is clear also from the large slabs of stone upon the road leading from the double Scæan Gate down to the Plain: for when I laid this road open a few months ago, all the slabs appeared as uninjured as if they had been put down quite recently; but after they had been exposed to the air for a few days, the slabs of the upper part of the road, to the extent of some

---

* The word by which Dr. Schliemann usually denotes these curious objects is *carrousels*, as a translation of *fusaioli*, the term applied by the Italian antiquaries to the similar objects found in the marshes about Modena. It is difficult to choose an English word, without assuming their use on the one hand, or not being specific enough on the other. *Top* and *teetotum* are objectionable on the former grounds, and *wheel* is objectionable on both. On the whole, *whorl* seems most convenient, and Dr. Schliemann gives his approval to this term. Their various shapes are shown in the Plates at the end of the volume. Those in the form of single cones, with flat bases, seem to be what Dr. Schliemann calls volcanoes (*Vulkans*), the hole representing the *crater*.—[ED.]

10 feet, which had been exposed to the heat, began to crumble away, and they have now almost disappeared, while those of the lower portion of the road, which had not been touched by the fire, have remained uninjured, and seem to be indestructible. A further proof of the terrible cata-strophe is furnished by a stratum of scoriæ of melted lead and copper, from $\frac{1}{5}$ to $1\frac{1}{5}$ of an inch thick, which extends nearly through the whole hill at a depth of from 28 to $29\frac{1}{2}$ feet. That Troy was destroyed by enemies after a bloody war is further attested by the many human bones which I found in these heaps of *débris*, and above all by the skeletons with helmets, found in the depths of the temple of Athena ;* for, as we know from Homer, all corpses were burnt and the ashes were preserved in urns. Of such urns I have found an immense number in all the pre-Hellenic strata on the hill. Lastly, the Treasure, which some member of the royal family had probably endeavoured to save during the destruction of the city, but was forced to abandon, leaves no doubt that the city was destroyed by the hands of enemies. I found this Treasure on the large enclosing wall by the side of the royal palace, at a depth of $27\frac{1}{2}$ feet, and covered with red Trojan ashes from 5 to $6\frac{1}{2}$ feet in depth, above which was a post-Trojan wall of fortification $19\frac{1}{2}$ feet high.

Trusting to the data of the Iliad, the exactness of which I used to believe in as in the Gospel itself, I imagined that *Hissarlik*, the hill which I have ransacked for three years, was the Pergamus of the city, that Troy must have had 50,000 inhabitants, and that its area must have extended over the whole space occupied by the Greek colony of Ilium.†

Notwithstanding this, I was determined to investigate the matter accurately, and I thought that I could not do so in any better way than by making borings. I accordingly began cautiously to dig at the extreme ends of the

---

* See p. 280. † See the Plan of Greek Ilium (Plan I.).

Greek Ilium; but these borings down to the native rock brought to light only walls of houses, and fragments of pottery belonging to the Greek period,—not a trace of the remains of the preceding occupants. In making these borings, therefore, I gradually came nearer to the fancied Pergamus, but without any better success; till at last as many as seven shafts, which I dug at the very foot of the hill down to the rock, produced only Greek masonry and fragments of Greek pottery. I now therefore assert most positively that Troy was limited to the small surface of this hill; that its area is accurately marked by its great surrounding wall, laid open by me in many places; that the city had no Acropolis, and that the Pergamus is a pure invention of Homer; and further that the area of Troy in post-Trojan times down to the Greek settlement was only increased so far as the hill was enlarged by the *débris* that was thrown down, but that the Ilium of the Greek colony had a much larger extent at the time of its foundation.*

Though, however, we find on the one hand that we have been deceived in regard to the size of Troy, yet on the other we must feel great satisfaction in the certainty, now at length ascertained, that Troy really existed, that the greater portion of this Troy has been brought to light by me, and that the Iliad—although on an exaggerated scale—sings of this city and of the fact of its tragic end. Homer, however, is no historian, but an epic poet, and hence we must excuse his exaggerations.

As Homer is so well informed about the topography and the climatic conditions of the Troad, there can surely be no doubt that he had himself visited Troy. But, as he was there long after its destruction, and its site had moreover been buried deep in the *débris* of the ruined town, and had for centuries been built over by a new town, Homer could

* See the Plan of Dr. Schliemann's Researches (Plan II.).

neither have seen the Great Tower of Ilium nor the Scæan
Gate, nor the great enclosing Wall, nor the palace of Priam ;
for, as every visitor to the Troad may convince himself by
my excavations, the ruins and red ashes of Troy alone—
forming a layer of from five to ten feet thick—covered all
these remains of immortal fame ; and this accumulation of
débris must have been much more considerable at the time
of Homer's visit. Homer made no excavations so as to bring
those remains to light, but he knew of them from tradition ;
for the tragic fate of Troy had for centuries been in the
mouths of all minstrels, and the interest attached to it was
so great that, as my excavations have proved, tradition
itself gave the exact truth in many details. Such, for instance, is the memory of the Scæan Gate in the Great Tower
of Ilium, and the constant use of the name Scæan Gate in
the plural, because it had to be described as double,* and
in fact it has been proved to be a double gate. According
to the lines in the Iliad (XX. 307, 308), it now seems to me
extremely probable that, at the time of Homer's visit, the
King of Troy declared that his race was descended in a
direct line from Æneas.†

Now as Homer never saw Ilium's Great Tower, nor the
Scæan Gate, and could not imagine that these buildings
lay buried deep beneath his feet, and as he probably
imagined Troy to have been very large—according to the
then existing poetical legends—and perhaps wished to

---

* The double form of an outer and inner gate, and the use of πύλαι
in the plural for a city gate, are both far too frequent to justify our
founding an argument merely on the plural form of the Σκαίαι πύλαι.—
[ED.]

† Νῦν δὲ δὴ Αἰνείαο βίη Τρώεσσιν ἀνάξει,
Καὶ παίδων παῖδες, τοί κεν μετόπισθε γένωνται.

"But o'er the Trojans shall Æneas reign,
And his sons' sons, through ages yet unborn."

This is the declaration of Poseidon to the gods, when Æneas was in
peril of his life by the sword of Achilles. (But compare p. 182).—[ED.]

describe it as still larger, we cannot be surprised that he makes Hector descend from the palace in the Pergamus and hurry through the town in order to arrive at the Scæan Gate; whereas that gate and Ilium's Great Tower, in which it stands, are in reality directly in front of the royal house. That this house is really the king's palace seems evident from its size, from the thickness of its stone walls, in contrast to those of the other houses of the town, which are built almost exclusively of unburnt bricks, and from its imposing situation upon an artificial hill directly in front of or beside the Scæan Gate, the Great Tower, and the great surrounding Wall. This is confirmed by the many splendid objects found in its ruins, especially the enormous royally ornamented vase with the picture of the owl-headed goddess Athena, the tutelary divinity of Ilium (see No. 219, p. 307); and lastly, above all other things, by the rich Treasure found close by it (Plate II.). I cannot, of course, prove that the name of this king, the owner of this treasure, was really PRIAM; but I give him this name because he is so called by Homer and in all the traditions. All that I can prove is, that the palace of the owner of this treasure, this last Trojan king, perished in the great catastrophe, which destroyed the Scæan Gate, the great surrounding Wall, and the Great Tower, and which desolated the whole city. I can prove, by the enormous quantities of red and yellow calcined Trojan ruins, from five to ten feet in height, which covered and enveloped these edifices, and by the many post-Trojan buildings, which were again erected upon these calcined heaps of ruins, that neither the palace of the owner of the Treasure, nor the Scæan Gate, nor the great surrounding Wall, nor Ilium's Great Tower, were ever again brought to light. A city, whose king possessed such a treasure, was immensely wealthy, considering the circumstances of those times; and because Troy was rich, it was powerful, had many subjects, and obtained auxiliaries from all quarters.

Last year I ascribed the building of the Great Tower of

Ilium to the first occupants of the hill; but I have long since come to the firm conviction that it is the work of the second people, the Trojans, because it is upon the north side only, within the Trojan stratum of ruins, and from 16 to 19½ feet above the native soil, that it is made of actual masonry. I have, in my letters, repeatedly drawn attention to the fact, that the terra-cottas which I found upon the Tower can only be compared with those found at a depth of from 36 to 46 feet. This, however, applies only to the beauty of the clay and the elegance of the vessels, but in no way to their types, which, as the reader may convince himself from the illustrations to this work, are utterly different from the pottery of the first settlers.

It has been hitherto thought that the occurrence of stone implements indicates the "Age of Stone." My excavations here in Troy, however, prove this opinion to be completely erroneous; for I very frequently find implements of stone even immediately below the *débris* belonging to the Greek colony, that is at a depth of 6½ feet, and they occur in very great quantities from a depth of 13 feet downwards. Those, however, in the Trojan *stratum*, from 23 to 33 feet below the surface, are in general of much better workmanship than those above. I wish to draw attention to the fact that unfortunately, when writing the present book, I made the mistake, which is now inconceivable to me, of applying the name of *wedges* to those splendidly-cut weapons and implements, the greater part of which are made of diorite, but frequently also of very hard and transparent green stone, such as are given here and in several later illustrations. They are,

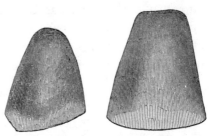

No. 2. Small Trojan Axes of Diorite (8 M.).

however, as anyone can convince himself, not wedges but

axes, and the majority of them must have been used as battle-axes. Many, to judge from their form, seem to be excellently fitted to be employed as lances, and may have been used as such. I have collected many hundreds of them. But, together with the thousands of stone implements, I found also many of copper; and the frequently discovered moulds of mica-schist for casting copper weapons and implements, as well as the many small crucibles, and small roughly made bowls, spoons, and funnels for filling the moulds, prove that this metal was much used. The strata of copper and lead scoriæ, met with at a depth of from 28 to 29½ feet, leave no doubt that this was the case. It must be observed that all the copper articles met with are of pure copper, without the admixture of any other metal.* Even the king's Treasure contained, besides other articles made of this metal, a shield with a large boss in the centre; a great caldron; a kettle or vase; a long slab with a silver vase welded on to it by the conflagration; and many fragments of other vases.†

This Treasure of the supposed mythical king Priam, of the mythical heroic age, which I discovered at a great depth in the ruins of the supposed mythical Troy, is at all events a discovery which stands alone in archæology, revealing great wealth, great civilization and a great taste for art, in an age preceding the discovery of bronze, when weapons and implements of pure copper were employed contemporaneously with enormous quantities of stone weapons and implements. This treasure further leaves no doubt that Homer must have actually seen gold and silver articles, such as he continually describes; it is, in every respect, of

---

* To this statement there are at least some exceptions. See the Analysis by M. Damour, of Lyon, at the end of the book.—[ED.]

† We omit here the Author's further enumeration of the objects composing the "King's Treasure," as they are fully described on the occasion of their wonderful discovery (Chapter XXIII.). Meanwhile the Plate opposite gives a general view of the whole.—[ED.]

PLATE II.

GENERAL VIEW OF THE TREASURE OF PRIAM. (Depth 8½ M.)

a. Key of the Treasure Chest.
b. The Golden Diadems, Fillet, Ear-rings, and Small Jewels.
c. Silver "Talents" and Vessels of Silver and Gold.
d. Silver Vases and curious Plate of Copper.
e. Weapons and Helmet-Crests of Copper or Bronze.
f. Copper Vessel.   *g.* Copper Caldron.   *h.* Copper Shield.

inestimable value to science, and will for centuries remain the object of careful investigation.

Unfortunately upon none of the articles of the Treasure do I find an inscription, or any other religious symbols, except the 100 idols of the Homeric " θεὰ γλαυκῶπις Ἀθήνη," which glitter upon the two diadems and the four ear-rings. These are, however, an irrefragable proof that the Treasure belongs to the city and to the age of which Homer sings.

Yet a written language was not wanting at that time. For instance, I found at a depth of 26 feet, in the royal palace, the vase with an inscription, of which a drawing is here given ; and I wish to call especial attention to

No. 3. (*a*). Inscribed Terra-cotta Vase from the Palace (8 M.).
(*b*). The Inscription thereon.

the fact, that of the characters occurring in it, the letter like the Greek P occurs also in the inscription on a seal, found at the depth of 23 feet ; the second and third letter to the left of this upon a whorl of terra-cotta,*

* Engraved among the lithographic plates at the end of the volume, Pl. LI., No. 496. Since the publication of Dr. Schliemann's work, many

likewise found at a depth of 23 feet; and the third letter
also upon two small funnels of terra-cotta, from a depth of

No. 4.   Inscribed Terra-cotta Seal
(7 M.).

10 feet (see p. 191). I further found
in the royal palace the excellent
engraved inscription on a piece of
red slate; but I see here only one
character resembling one of the
letters of the inscription on the
above-mentioned seal. My friend
the great Indian scholar, Emile
Burnouf, conjectures that all these
characters belong to a very ancient
Græco-Asiatic local alphabet. Professor H. Brunn, of Munich,
writes to me that he has shown these inscriptions to Professor
Haug, and that he has pointed out their relationship and con-

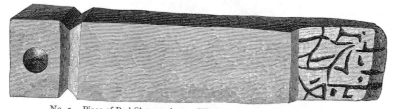

No. 5.   Piece of Red Slate, perhaps a Whetstone, with an Inscription (7 M.).

nection with the Phœnician alphabet (from which the Greek
alphabet is however derived), and has found certain analogies
between them and the inscription on the bronze table which
was found at Idalium in Cyprus, and is now in the *Cabinet
des Médailles* in Paris. Professor Brunn adds that the connection of things found at Troy with those found in Cyprus
is in no way surprising, but may be very well reconciled with
Homer, and that at all events particular attention should
be paid to this connection, for, in his opinion, Cyprus is the

---

of these Trojan inscriptions have been more certainly determined to be
real inscriptions in the *Cyprian syllabic character*, through the researches
of Dr. Martin Haug and Professor Gomperz of Vienna.   (See the
Appendix.)—[ED.]

cradle of Greek art, or, so to speak, the caldron in which Asiatic, Egyptian, and Greek ingredients were brewed together, and out of which, at a later period, Greek art came forth as the clear product.

I find in these Trojan layers of *débris* an abundance of splendid pottery, and more especially large and small cups with two handles, or with one from below in the form of a crown;* vases with rings on the sides and with holes in the same direction in the lip, for hanging them up by cords; all kinds of domestic utensils; also a beautifully ornamented flute made of bone, several pieces of other flutes, and a splendidly ornamented piece of ivory, which is part of a lyre *with only four strings.*

No. 6.   Terra-cotta Vase Cover (8 M.).

Like the first settlers on this sacred spot, the Trojans also were of the Aryan race; for I find among their remains enormous quantities of the

No. 7.   Ornamented Ivory Tube, probably a Trojan Flute (8 M.).

small articles of terra-cotta in the form of volcanoes and tops (*carrousels*), with carvings of Aryan religious symbols.

The building materials of the Trojans are of various kinds.   With but few exceptions, all the house-walls which I have uncovered are composed of unburnt sun-dried bricks, which in the heat of the conflagration have become a kind of really burnt bricks.   But the royal palace and two small buildings in the depths of the temple of

No. 8.   Piece of Ivory, belonging to a Trojan Lyre with Four Strings (about 8 M.).

---

* Dr. Schliemann has since pronounced these crown-shaped vessels to be *covers* of vases; though they may, he thinks, have been used for cups as well.   One is seen placed on the splendid vase on p. 48.—[ED]

Athena, as well as the Great Tower of Ilium, the Scæan Gate, and the great enclosing Wall, are generally composed of unhewn stones joined with earth, the less rough face of the stones being turned to the outside, so that the walls have a tolerably smooth appearance.

I thought last year, upon uncovering the Great Tower of Ilium, that it must have been at one time higher than it now is, namely 6 meters or 20 feet; but its flat-built top beside the Scæan Gate, and the *benches* (not ruins, as I formerly thought) afterwards found upon it, prove that it can never have been higher.* I would draw especial attention to the fact, that the masonry of the Scæan Gate, upon being uncovered, looked as wonderfully fresh as if it had been erected quite recently. It is quite certain that it possessed strong wooden fortifications, and probably also a wooden tower above the gateway; for otherwise it is inexplicable to me how the entrance of the Gate can have been covered to the height of 10 feet by those red Trojan woodashes, and especially how it was that there, far from the other buildings, the heat should have been so great that even the thick slabs of stone have been destroyed by it.

Homer speaks of Troy as having been destroyed by Hercules previous to the Trojan war,† and it will ever remain an enigma to us whether this information, which had been preserved by traditions down to his time, really refers to the Ilium of Priam, or to the very ancient town of the first settlers.

---

* See Plan III., p. 306.

† *Iliad*, V. 640-642, where Tlepolemus boasts of his ancestor Hercules—

> Ὅς ποτε δεῦρ' ἐλθὼν ἕνεχ' ἵππων Λαομέδοντος,
> Ἐξ οἴης σὺν νηυσὶ καὶ ἀνδράσι παυροτέροισιν,
> Ἰλίου ἐξαλάπαξε πόλιν, χήρωσε δ' ἀγυιάς.

> "With but six ships, and with a scanty band,
> The horses by Laomedon withheld
> Avenging, he o'erthrew this city, Troy,
> And made her streets a desert."

As to the chronology of Troy, we have only the general supposition of antiquity that the Trojan War occurred about B.C. 1200, and Homer's statement (*Iliad*, XX. 215-237) that Dardanus, the first Trojan King, founded Dardania, which town I agree with Virgil and Euripides in considering identical with Ilium, and that after him it was governed by his son Erichthonius, and then by his grandson Tros, by his great-grandson Ilus, and then by his son Laomedon, and by his grandson Priam. Even if we allow every one of these six kings a long reign of 33 years, we nevertheless scarcely carry the foundation of the town beyond 1400 B.C., that is 700 years before the Greek colony.

The site of Troy, which at the time of its foundation was 10 meters (about 33 feet) below the present surface, was only 7 meters (23 feet) below it after its destruction, when Ilium was again rebuilt by another people of Aryan origin; for, in the *débris* of this people, which extends to a depth of from 7 to 4 meters (23 to 13 feet) below the present surface, I find the same objects of terra-cotta with religious symbols.

On the photographic plates of the Atlas I have carefully stated the depth at which every object was found, so that it is very easy to find out which of them belong to this people.* Their pottery resembles that of the Trojans, but it is worse and coarser, and we meet with many new types. Almost all their vases have a tube on either side for hanging them up by cords. I here found, at a depth of 16½ feet, part of a lyre made of stone, with six strings; and

No. 9. Ornamented Piece of Ivory belonging to a Trojan Seven-Stringed Lyre (7 M.).

---

* This most important key to the archæological evidence collected by Dr. Schliemann has been preserved in the present translation. The depths are given in *meters* for the reasons stated in the Preface.

at a depth of 13 feet the beautifully ornamented ivory piece of another lyre, with seven strings, here shown.

The architecture of this people, as may be seen from the many house-walls which I have uncovered, was always of small stones joined with earth. Yet in two places in the depths of the temple of Athena there is a wall of sun-dried bricks, which appears to belong to this nation. Their houses were smaller, and less wood was employed in their construction than in those of the Trojans; for, although the ruins of houses lying one upon another show that several great convulsions have taken place, still we find here far fewer charred ruins than among those of the preceding people; nay, these layers of *débris* have in the majority of cases a grey or black appearance, and they contain millions of small mussel-shells, bones, fish-bones, and so forth. It is curious that in these strata certain types of terra-cottas are only found exactly at the same depth, and that, for instance, the splendid *black* cups in the form of an hour-glass, and with two large handles, are confined to a depth of 6 meters (nearly 20 feet).

During the first two years of my excavations, at the depth of from 4 to 7 meters (13 to 23 feet), I found scarcely any copper, and consequently I believed that the metal was but rarely, if at all, known to this people. This year, however, I found a number of copper nails in this stratum, as well as some knives and battle-axes, together with moulds of mica-schist for casting them, besides other weapons and implements.* Yet copper must have been rare with them; for stone implements, such as knives of silex, hammers and axes of diorite, and so forth, are found by thousands.

This people also seem to have disappeared simultaneously with the destruction of their town; for not only do I find, at a depth of from 4 meters up to 2 meters

---

* These objects resemble those from other strata, engraved in Chapter IV. and subsequently.

(13 to 6½ feet), many new types of terra-cotta vessels, but I
no longer find any remains of house-walls; nay, even single
stones are scarcely ever met with. At all events, directly
after its destruction, the town was rebuilt of wood by
another tribe of the Aryan race; for the small terra-cottas,
adorned with Aryan religious symbols, although frequently
of new types, occur in numbers in these layers of *débris*.
Walls of fortification are indeed met with in these depths,
but they had been built by the preceding people; as, for
instance, the wall 19½ feet in height, whose base is at a
depth of 5 to 6½ feet above the treasure, and which reached
to within 1¼ ft. of the surface. This *wooden Ilium* was, to
all appearance, still less fortunate than the stone town of its
predecessors; for, as is proved by the numerous calcined
layers of *débris*, it was frequently desolated by fire.
Whether these fires broke out accidentally, or were kindled
by the hands of enemies, must for ever remain a riddle to
us; but thus much is certain and evident from the terra-
cottas found at these depths, that the civilization of the
people, which had been but slight from the beginning,
continued to decrease during the perpetual misfortunes
of their town. I find, among the ruins of this nation,
lances, battle-axes, and implements, of pure copper, and
moulds for casting them; likewise a number of copper
nails, which, however—as in the case of the preceding
peoples who have inhabited this hill—are too long and thin
to have been employed for fastening wood together, and
must in all probability have been used as brooches: this
seems to be proved by two nails of this kind on the
top of which I found rows of perforated beads of gold
or *electrum* soldered upon them. These two copper
nails were, it is true, found immediately below the surface,
but they must in any case belong to the pre-Hellenic
time.

In the ruins of this people, at a depth of from 13 to
6½ feet, we also meet with stone implements, such as

hammers, splendidly polished axes and battle-axes of diorite, but considerably fewer than in the preceding stratum.

When the surface of the hill was about 2 meters (6½ feet) lower than it is now, Ilium was built by a Greek colony; and we have already endeavoured to prove that this settlement must have been founded about the year 700 B.C. From that time we find the remains of Hellenic house-walls of large hewn stones joined without cement. From about 1 meter (3¼ feet) below the surface, and upwards, there are also ruins of buildings, the stones of which are joined with cement or lime. We also meet with great numbers of copper coins of Ilium of the time of the Roman empire, from Augustus to Constans II. and Constantine II.; likewise older Ilian coins with the image of Athena, and medals of Alexandria Troas; also with some coins of Tenedos, Ophrynium and Sigeum, in some few cases at 3¼ feet, but generally at less than 20 inches below the surface. I once remarked erroneously that Byzantine coins were also met with here near the surface. But in my three years' excavations I have not found a single medal of a later date than Constans II. and Constantine II., except two bad coins belonging to a Byzantine monastery, which may have been lost by shepherds; and, as there is here not the remotest trace of Byzantine masonry or of Byzantine pottery, it may be regarded as certain that the Ilium of the Greek colony was destroyed towards the middle of the fourth century after Christ, and that no village, much less a town, has ever again been built upon its site. The wall I mentioned in my memoir of the 1st of March, 1873,* as consisting of Corinthian pillars joined with cement, and which I believed to have belonged to the Middle Ages, must be referred to the time of Constantine I. or to Constans II., when the temple of Athena was destroyed by the pious zeal of the first Christians.

---

* Chapter XVI., p. 239; comp. Chap. XV., p. 230, XVII., p. 250, XIX., p. 272.

Of the walls and fortifications of the Greek colony, almost the only portions that have been preserved are those which were apparently built by Lysimachus. The lower and prominent portion of the wall of the Tower belongs to more ancient times, probably to the beginning of the Greek colony. Of great political convulsions or catastrophes there seem now to have been but few or none at all; for the accumulation of *débris* during the long duration of the Greek colony, about 10½ centuries, amounts only to 2 meters (6½ feet).

Curiously enough, I find extremely little metal in the *débris* of the Greek colony. Half-a-dozen scythe-shaped knives, a double-edged axe, about two dozen nails, a cup, a few lances and arrows, are pretty nearly all that I discovered. I have described these objects in my memoirs as made of copper; but upon a more careful examination they have been found to be bronze, and pure copper is no longer met with in the Greek colony. The only objects of iron which I found were a key of curious shape, and a few arrows and nails, close to the surface. From Homer we know that the Trojans also possessed iron, as well as the metal which he calls κύανος, and which, even in antiquity, was translated by χάλυψ (steel). I am sure, however, that I have not discovered even a trace of this metal, either among the Trojan ruins or among those of any of the other nations which preceded the Greek colony on the hill.* Yet articles of iron and steel may have existed: I believe positively that they did exist: but they have vanished without leaving a trace of their existence; for, as we know, iron and steel become decomposed much more readily than copper. Of tin, which Homer so repeatedly mentions, I found of course no trace: this metal, as we know, is corroded very rapidly even when lying in a dry locality. Lead is found in the ruins of all the dif-

---

* It will be seen, however, from the analysis of M. Damour, that traces of iron (probably in the state of an ore) are found in one of the sling-bullets discovered by Dr. Schliemann.—[ED.]

ferent nations which have inhabited the hill; but, among those which preceded the Greek settlement, it is found principally in lumps of a hemispherical form. I find it first in general use only in the Greek colony, where it was employed as a means for uniting stones in building.

To judge from the area of the Ilium of the Greek colony,* it may have possessed 100,000 inhabitants. It must in its best days have been very rich, and the plastic art must have attained a high degree of perfection here. Accordingly the site of the town, which is covered with abundant relics of grand buildings, is strewn with fragments of excellent sculptures, and the splendid block of triglyphs —6½ feet in length and 2 feet 10 inches in height, with a *metopé* which represents Phœbus Apollo with the four horses of the Sun—is one of the most glorious masterpieces that have been preserved from the time when Greek art was in its zenith. I discovered it in the depths of the temple of Apollo, and it now adorns my garden at Athens. In describing this treasure of art in my memoir of the 18th of June, 1872,† directly after having discovered it, I made the remark that it must have belonged to the time of Lysimachus, that is to say to about the year 306 B.C. I sent a plaster cast of it to the Museum of Casts in Munich, and the Director of the Museum, Professor H. Brunn, who is certainly one of the greatest authorities in the world respecting the plastic works of antiquity, wrote me the following communication with regard to it. "Even photographs furnish no adequate means of judging of plastic works, and, in the present case, the cast alone has quite convinced me that this work must be judged much more favourably than it has been in the 'Archäologische Zeitung.' I do not venture to speak decidedly about the triglyphs: the history of the Doric style after the time of the Parthenon and the Propylæa is still utterly obscure: yet the straight cutting of the channellings can certainly be referred to pre-Roman

---

* See Plan II. at the end of the volume.   † Chapter X.

PLATE III.

BLOCK OF TRIGLYPHS, WITH METOPÉ OF THE SUN-GOD.

From the Temple of Apollo in the Ruins of Greek Ilium.

Page 32.

times. Of external criteria the halo of rays is the only one. According to the investigations of Stephani,* this first occurs about the time of Alexander the Great. For the special form of long and short rays, we have the coins of Alexander I., of Epirus and of Ceos (Carthæa), mentioned by Curtius. The most recent example that I have as yet found is the Hades vase of Canosa, in our Museum, which belongs *at latest* to the second century before Christ; hence the extreme termini for the relief would be about the end of the fourth and the middle of the second centuries. The composition, as a work of art, shows the greatest skill in solving one of the most difficult problems. For the team of four horses ought *not* to move on the surface of the relief, but to appear as if it came out of it in a half-turn. This has been attained principally by making the right hinder thigh of the horse in the fore-ground pressed back while the left foot steps forward, and moreover this same horse is slightly foreshortened, and the surface of the thigh lies deeper than the upper surface of the triglyphs, while, on the other hand, the surfaces of the withers and of the neck are higher, and the head, in con-formity with the rules of Greek reliefs, is again almost parallel with the base. For this reason there is no indication of a chariot, which has to be imagined as concealed by the foremost horse. Moreover the position of the god is half turned forwards, slightly following that of the head, and here also the arm is again strongly turned inwards, but not so as to bring the position in conflict with the rules of relief. If the encroachment of the head on the upper border of the triglyph is considered inaccurate, I find in this a very happy thought, which may remind us of the differently con-ceived pediment of the Parthenon, where only the head and shoulders of Helios rise out of the chariot still under the ocean. Helios here, so to speak, bursts forth from the gates of day and sheds the light of his glory over all. These

---

* *Nimbus und Strahlenkranz.*

are beauties peculiar only to Greek art in the fulness of its power. The execution corresponds perfectly with the excellence of the ideas, and thus I do not hesitate to place the relief nearer to the commencement than to the end of the above limited space of time. If, therefore, for other reasons, you believe it to belong to the time of Lysimachus, I, from an archæological point of view, have no objection to make against the supposition, but I rejoice to see our treasure of monuments enriched by an original from those times."

I have already proved the relationship of the four different peoples, who inhabited the site of Troy before the arrival of the Greek colony, by the small terra-cottas in the form of volcanoes and tops which are met with in quantities in all of the strata, and by the similarity of the Aryan religious symbols engraved upon them. I prove this relationship further, and above all, by the plastic representations of Athena, the owl-faced tutelary goddess of Ilium, for this representation is common to all the four nations which preceded the Greek colony. Immediately below the strata of the last, at a depth of 2 meters (6½ feet), I found this owl's face upon terra-cotta cups with a kind of

No. 10.   No. 11.   No. 12.

Terra-cotta Covers of Vases, with the Owl's Face.

No. 10.—From 3 M.   No. 11.—From 2 M.   No. 12.—From 7 M. Interesting for *depth* and *form*.

helmet, which likewise occur in all the succeeding layers of *débris* to a depth of 12 meters (39½ feet), and are of very frequent occurrence down to a depth of 9 meters (29½ feet). These cups may, as my learned friend Émile Burnouf thinks, have served only as lids to the vases which occur contemporaneously with them, and which have two upraised wings, and the breasts and abdomen of a woman, for they fit these vases perfectly. I found likewise in all the layers of *débris*, from a depth of 3 meters (nearly 10 feet) down to a depth of 10 meters (33 feet), vases with owls' faces, two upraised wings (not arms, as I formerly thought), and the two large breasts and abdomen of a woman, and even, at a depth of 6 meters (nearly 20 feet), a vase upon which the navel is ornamented with a cross and four nails. As far down as a depth of 14 meters (46 feet) I found the upper portion of a vase and the fragment of a dish adorned with owls' faces. Besides these, in all the layers of *débris*, from a depth of 6½ feet downwards, as far as the primary soil, there were found idols of very fine marble, of bone, of mica-schist, of slate, and even of ordinary

No. 13. Terra-cotta Vase, marked with an Aryan symbol (6 M.).

limestone, which are from ¼ of an inch to 7¼ inches in length, and from 0·6 of an inch to 4·8 inches in breadth. Upon a great many of these there is an owl's face, and some have even long female hair engraved upon them; many also have a woman's girdle. As upon several of the idols, upon which I find the owl's head, it is not cut, but represented in a red or black colour, I presume that this was once the case with all the idols which now possess no indications of an owl, and that the colour upon these latter has been destroyed by damp, during the course of thousands of years. Upon several idols of marble and bone there are mere indications of wings on the sides. But I also find the petrified vertebra of an antediluvian animal upon which the Trojans have carved a large owl's head. Further, at a depth of 3, 4, 6, 7, 8, 9, and 14 meters (10, 13, 20, 23, 26, 30 and 46 feet), I found twelve idols of terra-cotta, and all, with only one exception, have owls' faces

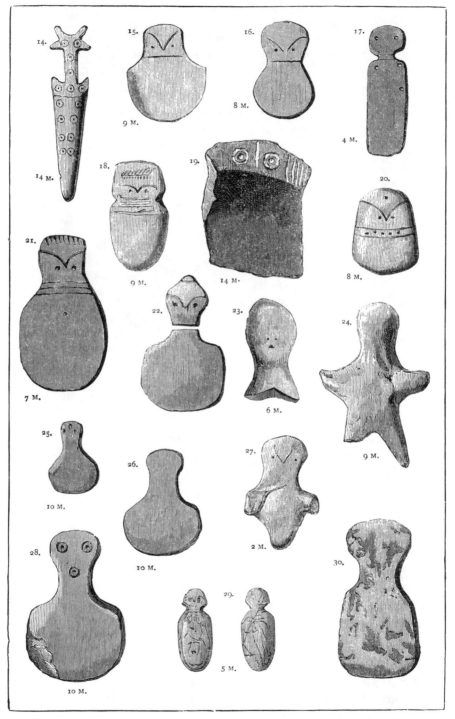

Nos. 14–30. Rude Idols found in the various Strata (2 to 14 M.).

No. 14 is of Ivory, with the same Decorations on both sides.   Nos. 15, 16, 18, 20, 25, 26, 28, are of very fine
Marble.   No. 17 is of Green Slate.   Nos. 23, 24, 27 are of Terra-cotta : and No. 19 is a Piece of a Dish.

upon them; most of them also have the two breasts of a woman, and upon the back traces of long female hair. One of these owl-headed idols has the form of a vessel, with a funnel on each side in the shape of a smaller vessel; the front part of the body of the goddess, up to the neck, is covered by a long shield, and on the back of the body there is the long female hair hanging down, like that of the Karyatides in the Acropolis of Athens. Upon several of these terra-cotta idols there are indications of wings.

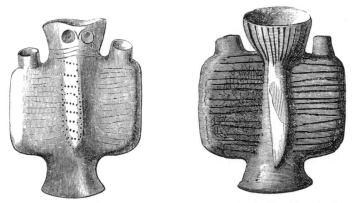

No. 31.   Remarkable Trojan Terra-cotta Vase, representing the Ilian Athena (9 M.).

These owl-faced female figures, which occur so frequently upon the cups, vases and idols, can represent but one goddess, and this goddess can be none other than Athena, *the tutelary goddess of Troy*, all the more so as Homer continually calls her " θεὰ γλαυκῶπις 'Αθήνη; " for " γλαυκῶπις " has been wrongly translated by the scholars of every century, and does not signify "with bright and sparkling eyes," but " *with the face of an owl.*" The natural conclusion, in the first place, is that Homer perfectly well knew that the owl-faced Athena was the tutelary goddess of Troy; secondly, that the locality whose depths I have ransacked for three years must be the spot "ubi Troja fuit;" and thirdly, that, in the progress of civilization, Pallas Athena received a human face, and her former owl's head was transformed into her favourite bird, the owl,

which as such is quite unknown to Homer.   At a depth
of from 4 to 9 meters (13 to 29½ feet), I also found some
vases and cups with a human face, but which have a good
deal of the owl about them.

As I did not find a trace of the owl's face among the
ruins of the Greek colony, we may regard it as certain that
it had already advanced beyond the civilization of the old
Ilians of whose town it took possession, and that it brought
the idea of the goddess with a human face with it to
Troy.

With regard to the often mentioned perforated terra-
cottas in the form of a top and the crater of a volcano,
adorned with Aryan religious symbols, it is possible that
their original form was that of a wheel, for they occur frequently in this shape upon the primary rock at a depth of
from 14 to 16 meters (46 to 52½ feet).*   In the upper layers
of *débris*, these objects in the form of wheels are indeed
rare, but the representation of the wheel in motion, effected
by the incisions being more numerous, still occurs very
frequently.†   In spite of all my searching and pondering, I
have not yet succeeded in arriving at an opinion as to what
these extremely interesting objects were used for.   As has
now become evident by the excavation of the temple of
Athena, it is only among the pre-Hellenic peoples that
they were adorned with Aryan symbols.   In the Greek
colony these occur but rarely; they are of a different form,
and they possess no trace of carved decorations; instead of
these, we find the much larger objects of terra-cotta, round,
and twice perforated, which occasionally bear the mark of
a kind of stamp.‡

Through the kindness of my friend Professor Giuseppe
G. Bianconi in Bologna, I have received the drawings of

---

* See the Sections on the Plates of Whorls.
† For examples of this type see Nos. 337, 340, 341, &c.
‡ See the Illustrations to Chapter II., p. 65.

ten similar round articles of terra-cotta in the form of the top or volcano, which are preserved in the Museum of Modena, and were found in the terramares of that district, in the lake-habitations of the stone age. To my extreme astonishment, I found that six of them possessed the same ornamental carvings which I found upon the articles of the same form here in Troy. Three of them have a circle round the central sun, a triple cross, which, as I have endeavoured minutely to explain in my sixth memoir, was the symbol of the two pieces of wood of our Aryan forefathers for producing the holy fire, and is an emblem of the highest importance. The fourth represents one of these machines for producing fire with five ends, and Indian scholars may possibly find that one of the staves represents the piece of wood called "pramantha," with which fire was generated by friction, and which the Greeks at a later time transformed into their Prometheus, who, as they imagined, stole fire from heaven. The fifth represents a somewhat different form of the fire producer of our remote ancestors; and the sixth has twelve circles round the central sun. Probably these are the twelve stations of the sun which are so frequently mentioned in the Rigvêda, and which are personified by the twelve Adityas, the sons of Adity (the Indivisible or Infinite Space), and represent the twelve signs of the Zodiac.

The same friend has also sent me drawings of eighteen similar round terra-cottas found in the graves of the cemetery in Villanova, and now in the Museum of Count Gozzadini in Bologna. As the count found an "aes rude" in one of the graves, he thinks that the cemetery, like it, belongs to the time of King Numa, that is, to about 700 years before Christ. G. de Mortillet,* however, ascribes a much greater age to the cemetery. But, at all events, fifteen of the eighteen drawings lying before

---

* 'Le Signe de la Croix,' pp. 88–89.

me have a modern appearance compared with the ten in the Museum of Modena, and compared with my small terra-cottas in the form of tops, volcanoes, and wheels, found in Troy; for not only the decorations, but the forms also of the articles are very much more elaborate. Only three of the eighteen articles show a shape and decorations like those met with in Troy. All three have the form of a top: the first has seven suns in a circle round the central sun; the second has two crosses, one of which is formed by four stars, the other by four lines. The third has five triangles and five stars in the circle round the central point. The comparison of these eighteen articles with those from Troy convinces me that Count Gozzadini is right in ascribing no greater age to the cemetery of Villanova than 700 B.C.

But besides the articles ornamented with religious symbols, we meet in Troy with thousands of terra-cottas of a similar, but in most cases more lengthened form, with no decorations whatever; at a depth of 3 metres (10 feet), they occur also in the shape of cones.* Formerly, at a depth of 10 feet, I found similar pieces in blue or green stone, which I have also recently met with frequently at a depth of from 23 to 33 feet. Among the unembellished terra-cottas of this description I find some, but scarcely more than 2 per cent., which show signs of wear, and may have been used on spindles. The pieces adorned with carvings, on the other hand, never show signs of any kind of wear, and the symbols engraved upon them are filled with white clay so as to make them more striking to the eye.† This white clay must have dis-

---

* See the Sections of Plain Whorls, Pl. XXI., Nos. 436–440.

† This statement needs considerable qualification. The notes on M. Burnouf's drawings, supplied by Dr. Schliemann for this book, frequently describe the decorated whorls as worn and rubbed, especially on the under side and at the point, in some cases " by a circular motion." All this strongly favours the hypothesis of their use for spindles.—[ED.]

appeared directly, if the pieces had been used on spindles or as coins. They cannot have been worn as amulets, on account of their size and weight: I am therefore forced to believe that they were employed as offerings, or that they were worshipped as idols of the Sun, whose image is seen in the centre.

Unfortunately, owing to the great extent of my excavations, the hurry in which they were carried on, and the hardness of the *débris*, by far the greater portion of the terra-cotta vessels found by me in the depths of Ilium were brought out more or less broken. But everything that could in any way be repaired I have restored by means of shell-lac and gypsum, and in this state they are represented in the drawings.* In all cases where I found a piece broken off and wanting, I restored it according to the model of other vessels of the same kind which I obtained in an unbroken condition; but where such models were wanting, or where I had the slightest doubt, I did not attempt to restore the articles.

The town of Ilium, upon whose site I have been digging for more than three years, boasted itself to be the successor of Troy; and as throughout antiquity the belief in the identity of its site with that of the ancient city of Priam was firmly established and not doubted by anyone, it is clear that the whole course of tradition confirms this identity. At last Strabo lifted up his voice against it; though, as he himself admits, he had never visited the Plain of Troy, and he trusted to the accounts of Demetrius of Scepsis, which were suggested by vanity. According to Strabo,† this Demetrius maintained that his native town of Scepsis had been the residence of Æneas, and he envied Ilium the honour of having been the

---

* These restorations are indicated in the engravings by light shading.

† XIII. i., p. 122, Tauchnitz edition.

metropolis of the Trojan kingdom. He therefore put forward the following view of the case :—that Ilium and its environs did not contain space enough for the great deeds of the Iliad; that the whole plain which separated the city from the sea was alluvial land, and that it was not formed until after the time of the Trojan war. As another proof that the locality of the two cities could not be the same, he adds that Achilles and Hector ran three times round Troy, whereas one could not run round Ilium on account of the continuous mountain ridge (διὰ τὴν συνεχῆ ῥάχην). For all of these reasons he says that ancient Troy must be placed on the site of the "Village of the Ilians" ('Ιλιέων κώμη), 30 stadia or 3 geographical miles from Ilium and 42 stadia from the coast, although he is obliged to admit that not the faintest trace of the city has been preserved.*

Strabo, with his peculiarly correct judgment, would assuredly have rejected all these erroneous assertions of Demetrius of Scepsis, had he himself visited the Plain of Troy, for they can easily be refuted.

I have to remark that it is quite easy to run round the site of Troy; further, that the distance from Ilium to the coast, in a straight line, is about 4 miles, while the distance in a straight line north-west to the promontory of Sigeum (and at this place tradition, as late as Strabo's time, fixed the site of the Greek encampment) amounts to about 4½ miles. For Strabo says :† "Next to Rhœteum may be seen the ruined town of Sigeum, the port of the Achæans, the Achæan camp, and the marsh or lake called Stomalimne, and the mouth of the Scamander."

In November, 1871, I made excavations upon the site of the "'Ιλιέων κώμη," the results of which completely refute the theory of Demetrius of Scepsis; for I found everywhere

---

* Strabo, XIII. i., p. 99. See the Map of the Plain of Troy.
† XIII. i., p. 103.

the primary soil at a depth of less than a foot and a half; and the continuous ridge on the one side of the site, which appeared to contain the ruins of a large town-wall, consisted of nothing but pure granulated earth, without any admixture of ruins.

In the year 1788, Lechevalier visited the plain of Troy, and was so enthusiastically in favour of the theory that the site of Homer's Troy was to be found at the village of Bunarbashi and the heights behind it, that he disdained to investigate the site of Ilium: this is evident from his work 'Voyage de la Troade' (3ᵉ éd., Paris, 1802) and from the accompanying map, in which he most absurdly calls this very ancient town " Ilium Novum," and transposes it to the other side of the Scamander, beside *Kumkaleh*, close to the sea and about 4 miles from its true position. This theory, that the site of Troy can only be looked for in the village of Bunarbashi and upon the heights behind it, was likewise maintained by the following scholars: by Rennell, ' Observations on the Topography of the Plain of Troy' (London, 1814); by P. W. Forchhammer in the ' Journal of the Royal Geographical Society,' vol. xii., 1842; by Mauduit, ' Découvertes dans la Troade' (Paris et Londres, 1840); by Welcker, 'Kleine Schriften;' by Texier; by Choiseul-Gouffrier, 'Voyage Pittoresque de la Grèce' (1820); by M. G. Nikolaïdes (Paris, 1867); and by Ernst Curtius in his lecture delivered at Berlin in November, 1871, after his journey to the Troad and Ephesus, whither he was accompanied by Professors Adler and Müllenhof, and by Dr. Hirschfeldt. But, as I have explained in detail in my work, 'Ithaque, le Péloponnèse et Troie' (Paris, 1869), this theory is in every respect in direct opposition to all the statements of the Iliad. My excavations at Bunarbashi prove, moreover, that no town can ever have stood there; for I find everywhere the pure virgin soil at a depth of less than 5 feet, and generally immediately below the surface. I have likewise proved, by my excavations on the heights behind this village, that human dwellings can never have existed there; for I found the native rock nowhere at a greater depth than a foot and a half. This is further confirmed by the sometimes pointed, sometimes abrupt, and always anomalous form of the rocks which are seen wherever they are not covered with earth. At half-an-hour's distance behind Bunarbashi there is, it is true, the site of quite a small town, encircled on two sides by precipices and on the other by the ruins of a surrounding wall, which town I formerly considered to be Scamandria; but one of the inscriptions found in the ruins of the temple of Athena in the Ilium of the Greek colony makes me now believe with certainty that the spot above Bunarbashi is not the site of Scamandria, but of Gergis. Moreover, the accumulation of *débris* there is extremely insignificant, and the naked rock protrudes not only in the small Acropolis, but also in very many places of the site of the little town. Further, in all cases where there is an accumulation of *débris*, I found fragments of Hellenic pottery, and of Hellenic pottery only, down to the primary soil. As archæology cannot allow the *most ancient* of these fragments to be any older than from 500 to 600 years before Christ, the walls of the small town—which used to be regarded as of the same age as those of Mycenæ—can certainly be no older than 500 to 600 B.C. at most.

Immediately below this little town there are three tombs of heroes, one of which has been assigned to Priam, another to Hector, because it was built entirely of small stones. The latter grave was laid open in October 1872, by Sir John Lubbock, who found it to contain nothing but painted fragments of Hellenic pottery to which the highest date that can be assigned is 300 B.C.; and these fragments tell us the age of the tomb likewise.

The late Consul J. G. von Hahn, who in May 1864, in his extensive excavations of the acropolis of Gergis

down to the primary soil, only discovered the same, and
nothing but exactly the same, fragments of Hellenic pottery
as I found there in my small excavations, writes in his
pamphlet, 'Die Ausgrabungen des Homerischen Pergamos:' "In spite of the diligent search which my com-
panions and I made on the extensive northern slope of the
Balidagh, from the foot of the acropolis (of Gergis) to the
springs of Bunarbashi, we could not discover any indication
beyond the three heroic tombs, that might have pointed to
a former human settlement, not even antique fragments of
pottery and pieces of brick,—those never-failing, and consequently imperishable, proofs of an ancient settlement.
No pillars or other masonry, no ancient square stones, no
quarry in the natural rock, no artificial levelling of the
rock; on all sides the earth was in its natural state and
had not been touched by human hands."

The erroneous theory which assigns Troy to the heights
of Bunarbashi could, in fact, never have gained ground,
had its above-named advocates employed the few hours
which they spent on the heights, and in Bunarbashi itself, in
making small holes, with the aid of even a single workman.

Clarke and Barker Webb (Paris, 1844) maintained that
Troy was situated on the hills of *Chiplak*. But unfortunately they also had not given themselves the trouble
to make excavations there; otherwise they would have
convinced themselves, with but very little trouble, that all
the hills in and around Chiplak, as far as the surrounding
Wall of Ilium, contain only the pure native soil.

H. N. Ulrichs * maintains that Troy was situated on
the hills of *Atzik-Kioï*, which in my map I have called
Eski Akshi köi. But I have examined these hills also, and
found that they consist of the pure native soil. I used a
spade in making these excavations, but a pocket-knife would
have answered the purpose.

---

* 'Rheinisches Museum,' Neue Folge, III., s. 573–608.

I cannot conceive how it is possible that the solution of
the great problem, " ubi Troja fuit "—which is surely one
of the greatest interest to the whole civilized world—should
have been treated so superficially that, after a few hours'
visit to the Plain of Troy, men have sat down at home and
written voluminous works to defend a theory, the worth-
lessness of which they would have perceived had they but
made excavations for a single hour.

I am rejoiced that I can mention with praise Dr.
Wilhelm Buchner,* Dr. G. von Eckenbrecher, † and C.
MacLaren, ‡ who, although they made no excavations,
have nevertheless in their excellent treatises proved by
many irrefutable arguments that the site of Ilium, where
I have been digging for more than three years, corresponds
with all the statements of the Iliad in regard to the site of
Troy, and that the ancient city must be looked for there
and nowhere else.

It is also with gratitude that I think of the great
German scholar, who unfortunately succumbed five years
ago to his unwearied exertions, Julius Braun, the advocate
of the theory that Homer's Troy was to be found only on
the site of Ilium, in the depths of the hill of HISSARLIK.
I most strongly recommend his excellent work, 'Die Geschichte der Kunst in ihrem Entwickelungsgang,' to all
those who are interested in whatever is true, beautiful and
sublime.

Neither can I do otherwise than gratefully mention my
honoured friend, the celebrated Sanscrit scholar and unwearied investigator Émile Burnouf, the Director of the

---

* 'Jahresbericht über das Gymnasium Fridericianum,' Schwerin,
1871 und 1872.

† 'Rheinisches Museum,' Neue Folge, 2. Jahrg., s. 1 fg.

‡ 'Dissertation on the Topography of the Trojan War.' Edinburgh,
1822. Second Edition. 'The Plain of Troy described,' &c. 1863.
Dr. Schliemann might have added the weighty authority of Mr. Grote,
'History of Greece,' vol. i., chap. xv.—[ED.]

French school in Athens, who personally, and through his many excellent works, especially the one published last year, ' La Science des Religions,' has given me several suggestions, which have enabled me to decipher many of the Trojan symbols.*

It is also with a feeling of gratitude that I think of my honoured friend, the most learned Greek whom I have ever had the pleasure of knowing, Professor Stephanos Kommanoudes, in Athens, who has supported me with his most valuable advice whenever I was in need of it. In like manner I here tender my cordial thanks to my honoured friend the Greek Consul of the Dardanelles, G. Dokos, who showed me many kindnesses during my long excavations.

I beg to draw especial attention to the fact that, in the neighbourhood of Troy, several types of very ancient pottery—like those found in my excavations at a depth of from 10 to 33 feet — have been preserved down to the present day. For instance, in the crockery-shops on the shores of the Dardanelles there are immense numbers of earthen vessels with long upright necks and the breasts of a woman, and others in the shape of animals. In spite of their gilding and other decorations, these vessels cannot, either in regard to quality or elegance of form, be compared with the Ilian terra-cottas, not even with those from a depth of 10 feet ; but still they furnish a remarkable proof of the fact that, in spite of manifold political changes, certain types of terra-cottas can continue in existence in one district for more than 3000 years.

After long and mature deliberation, I have arrived at the firm conviction that all of those vessels—met with here in great numbers at a depth of from 10 to 33 feet, and

---

* Dr. Émile Burnouf has published a very clear and interesting account of Dr. Schliemann's discoveries, in the ' Revue des Deux Mondes' for Jan. 1, 1874.—[ED.]

more especially in the Trojan layer of *débris*, at a depth of from 23 to 33 feet—which have the exact shape of a bell and a coronet beneath, so that they can only stand upon their mouth, and which I have hitherto described as cups, must necessarily, and perhaps even exclusively, have been used as *lids* to the numerous terra-cotta vases with a smooth neck and on either side two ear-shaped decorations, between which are two mighty wings, which, as they are hollowed and taper away to a point, can never have served as handles, the more so as between the ear-shaped decorations there is a small handle on either side. Now, as the latter resembles an owl's beak, and especially as this is seen between the ear-shaped ornaments, it was doubtless intended to represent the image of the owl with upraised wings on each side of the vases, which image received a noble appearance from the splendid lid with a coronet. I give a drawing of the largest vase of this type, which

No. 32. The largest of the Terra-cotta Vases found in the Royal Palace of Troy. Height 20 inches. The Cover was found near it.

was found a few days ago in the royal palace at a depth
of from 28 to 29½ feet; on the top of it I have placed
the bell-shaped lid with a coronet, which was discovered
close by and appears to have belonged to it.

My friend M. Landerer, Professor of Chemistry in
Athens, who has carefully examined the colours of the
Trojan antiquities, writes to me as follows:—" In the first
place, as to the vessels themselves, some have been turned
upon a potter's wheel, some have been moulded by the
hand. Their *ground-colour* varies according to the nature
of the *clay*. I find some of them made of black, deep-
brown, red, yellowish, and ashy-grey clay. All of these
kinds of clay, which the Trojan potters used for their ware,
consist of clay containing oxide of iron and silica (*argile
silicieuse ferrugineuse*), and, according to the stronger or
weaker mode of burning, the oxide of iron in the clay
became more or less oxidised: thus the black, brown, red,
yellow, or grey colour is explained by the oxidation of the
iron. The beautiful black gloss of the vessels found upon
the native soil, at a depth of 46 feet, does not contain any
oxide of lead, but consists of *coal-black* (*Kohlenschwarz*),*
which was melted together with the clay and penetrated into
its pores. This can be explained by the clay vessels having
been placed in slow furnaces in which resinous wood was
burnt, and where there was consequently dense smoke,
which descended upon the earthenware in the form of the
finest powder and was likewise burnt into the clay. It is
also possible, but by no means probable, that they used
a black pitch or asphalt, which was dissolved in oil of
turpentine; perhaps they used liquid pitch, and painted
the vessels with it. The burning of these would likewise
produce coal-black, which in later times was called the
Atramentum indelibile of Apelles. This is the manner in
which colour and gloss were given to Hellenic terra-cottas.

---

* As we call it, *lamp-black*, that is, tolerably pure carbon.—[ED.]

"The white colour with which the engraved decorations of the Trojan terra-cottas were filled, by means of a pointed instrument, is nothing but pure white clay. In like manner, the painting on the potsherd given above,[*] is made with white clay, and with black clay containing coal. The brilliant red colour of the large two-handled vessels ($\delta\acute{\epsilon}\pi\alpha$ $\dot{\alpha}\mu\phi\iota\kappa\acute{\upsilon}\pi\epsilon\lambda\lambda\alpha$)[†] is no peculiar colour, but merely oxide of iron, which is a component part of the clay of which the cups were made. Many of the brilliant yellow Trojan vessels, I find, are made of grey clay, and painted

No. 34. Inscription on the Vase No. 33.

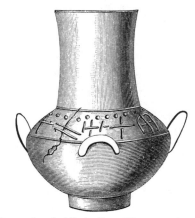

No. 33. Inscribed Trojan Vase of Terra-cotta (8¼ M.).

over with a mass of yellow clay containing oxide of iron; they were then polished with one of those sharp pieces of diorite which are so frequently met with in Troy, and afterwards burnt.

---

* See the Cut No. 1 on p. 15.
† These are the vases so often mentioned as having the form of

The large marshes lying before the site of Ἰλιέων κώμη, and discussed in my second memoir, have long since been drained, and thus the estate of Thymbria (formerly Batak) has acquired 240 acres of rich land. As might have been expected, they were not found to contain any hot springs, but only three springs of cold water.

In my twenty-second memoir I have mentioned a Trojan vase, with a row of signs running round it, which I considered to be symbolical, and therefore did not have them specially reproduced by photography. However, as my learned friend Émile Burnouf is of opinion that they form a real inscription in Chinese letters,* I give them here according to his drawing.

M. Burnouf explains them as follows:—

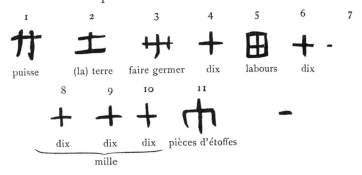

1	2	3	4	5	6	7
puisse	(la) terre	faire germer	dix	labours	dix	

8	9	10	11	
dix	dix	dix	pièces d'étoffes	

mille

and adds: " Les caractères du petit vase ne sont ni grecs ni sanscrits, ni phéniciens, ni, ni, ni—ils sont parfaitement lisibles en chinois!!! Ce vase peut être venu en Troade de l'Asie septentrional, dont tout le Nord était touranien." Characters similar to those given above frequently occur, more especially upon the perforated terra-cottas in the form of volcanoes and tops.

---

great champagne glasses (see the Cuts on pp. 85, 158, 166, 171). Dr. Schliemann also applies the name to the unique boat-shaped vessel of pure gold found in the Treasure.—[ED.]

* If M. Burnouf meant this seriously at the time, it can now only stand as a curious coincidence, interesting as one example of the tentative process of this new enquiry. (See the Appendix.)—[ED.]

As the Turkish papers have charged me in a shameful manner with having acted against the letter of the firman granted to me, in having kept the Treasure for myself instead of sharing it with the Turkish Government, I find myself obliged to explain here, in a few words, how it is that I have the most perfect right to that treasure. It was only in order to spare Safvet Pacha, the late Minister of Public Instruction, that I stated in my first memoir, that at my request, and in the interest of science, he had arranged for the portion of Hissarlik, which belonged to the two Turks in Kum-Kaleh, to be bought by the Government. But the true state of the case is this. Since my excavations here in the beginning of April 1870, I had made unceasing endeavours to buy this field, and at last, after having travelled three times to Kum-Kaleh simply with this object, I succeeded in beating the two proprietors down to the sum of 1000 francs (40*l.*) Then, in December 1870, I went to Safvet Pacha at Constantinople, and told him that, after eight months' vain endeavours, I had at last succeeded in arranging for the purchase of the principal site of Troy for 1000 francs, and that I should conclude the bargain as soon as he would grant me permission to excavate the field. He knew nothing about Troy or Homer; but I explained the matter to him briefly, and said that I hoped to find there antiquities of immense value to science. He, however, thought that I should find a great deal of gold, and therefore wished me to give him all the details I could, and then requested me to call again in eight days. When I returned to him, I heard to my horror that he had already compelled the two proprietors to sell him the field for 600 francs (24*l.*), and that I might make excavations there if I wished, but that everything I found must be given up to him. I told him in the plainest language what I thought of his odious and contemptible conduct, and declared that I would have nothing more to do with him, and that I should make no excavations.

But through Mr. Wyne McVeagh, at that time the American Consul, he repeatedly offered to let me make excavations, on condition that I should give him only one-half of the things found. At the persuasion of that gentle-man I accepted the offer, on condition that I should have the right to carry away my half out of Turkey. But the right thus conceded to me was revoked in April 1872, by a ministerial decree, in which it was said that I was not to export any part of my share of the discovered antiquities, but that I had the right to sell them in Turkey. The Turkish Government, by this new decree, broke our written contract in the fullest sense of the word, and I was released from every obligation. Hence I no longer troubled myself in the slightest degree about the contract which was broken without any fault on my part. I kept everything valuable that I found for myself, and thus saved it for science; and I feel sure that the whole civilized world will approve of my having done so. The new-discovered Trojan antiquities, and especially the Treasure, far surpass my most sanguine expectations, and fully repay me for the contemptible trick which Safvet Pacha played me, as well as for the continual and unpleasant presence of a Turkish official during my excavations, to whom I was forced to pay $4\frac{3}{4}$ francs a day.

It was by no means because I considered it to be my duty, but simply to show my friendly intentions, that I presented the Museum in Constantinople with seven large vases, from 5 to $6\frac{1}{2}$ feet in height, and with four sacks of stone implements. I have thus become the only bene-factor the Museum has ever had; for, although all firmans are granted upon the express condition that one-half of the discovered antiquities shall be given to the Museum, yet it has hitherto never received an article from anyone. The reason is that the Museum is any-thing but open to the public, and the sentry frequently refuses admittance even to its Director, so everyone knows that the antiquities sent there would be for ever lost to science.

The great Indian scholar, Max Müller of Oxford, has just written to me in regard to the owl-headed tutelary divinity of Troy. "Under all circumstances, the owl-headed idol cannot be made to explain the idea of the goddess. The ideal conception and the naming of the goddess came first; and in that name the owl's head, whatever it may mean, is figurative or ideal. In the idol the figurative intention is forgotten, just as the sun is represented with a golden hand, whereas the ideal conception of 'golden-handed' was 'spreading his golden rays.' An owl-headed deity was most likely intended for a deity of the morning or the dawn, the owl-light; to change it into a human figure with an owl's head was the work of a later and more materializing age."

I completely agree with this. But it is evident from this that the Trojans, or at least the first settlers on the hill, spoke Greek, for if they took the epithet of their goddess, "γλαυκῶπις," from the ideal conception which they formed of her and in later times changed it into an owl-headed female figure, they must necessarily have known that γλαῦξ meant *owl*, and ὠπή *face*. That the transformation took place many centuries, and probably more than 1000 years, before Homer's time, is moreover proved by owls' heads occurring on the vases and even in the monograms in the lowest strata of the predecessors of the Trojans, even at a depth of 46 feet.

I have still to draw attention to the fact, that in looking over my Trojan collection from a depth of 2 meters (6½ feet), I find 70 very pretty brilliant black or red terra-cottas, with or without engraved decorations, which, both in quality and form, have not the slightest resemblance either to the Greek or to the pre-historic earthenware. Thus it seems that just before the arrival of the Greek colony yet another tribe inhabited this hill for a short time.* These pieces of earthenware may be recognised by the two long-pointed handles of the large channelled cups, which also generally possess three or four small horns.

DR. HENRY SCHLIEMANN.

---

* These indications of a fifth pre-Hellenic settlement, if confirmed by further investigation, would seem to point to the spread of the Lydians over western Asia Minor.—ED.

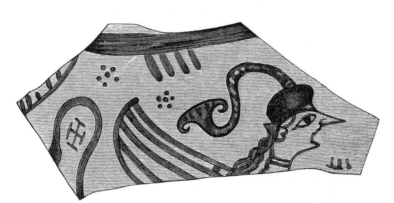

No. 35.   Fragment of a second painted Vase, from the Trojan Stratum.
(From a new Drawing.)

COMPARATIVE TABLE OF FRENCH METERS AND ENGLISH
MEASURES, EXACT AND APPROXIMATE,

M.	Inches.	Ft.	Inches.	Approximate. 1 M. = 3¼ ft.
				Feet.
1	39·3708	3	3·3708	3¼
2	78·7416	6	6·7416	6½
3	118·1124	9	10·1124	10
4	157·4832	13	1·4832	13
5	196·8540	16	4·8540	16⅓
6	236·2248	19	8·2248	19⅔
7	275·5956	22	11·5956	23
8	314·9664	26	2·9664	26¼
9	354·3372	29	6·3372	29½
10	393·7089	32	9·7080	33
11	433·0788	36	1·0788	36 (12 yds.)
12	472·4496	39	4·4496	39⅓
13	511·8204	42	7·8204	42⅔
14	551·1912	45	11·1912	46
15	590·5620	49	2·5620	49¼
16	620·9328	52	5·9328	52½
17	669·3036	55	9·3036	55¾
18	708·6744	59	0·6744	59
19	748·0452	62	4·0452	62⅓
20	787·416	65	7·4160	65⅔
30	1181·124	98	5·124	98½
40	1574·832	131	2·832	131¼
50	1968·54	164	0·54	164
100	3937·08	328	1·08	328 (109 yds.)

N.B.—The following is a convenient approximate Rule :—" To turn
Meters into *Yards*, add 1–11th to the number of Meters."

WORK AT HISSARLIK IN 1871.

CHAPTER I.

The site of ILIUM described — Excavations in 1870 : the City Wall of Lysimachus — Purchase of the site and grant of a *firman* — Arrival of Dr. and Madame Schliemann in 1871, and beginning of the Excavations — The Hill of HISSARLIK, the *Acropolis* of the Greek Ilium — Search for its limits — Difficulties of the work — The great cutting on the North side — Greek coins found — Dangers from fever.

On the Hill of Hissarlik, in the Plain of Troy,
October 18th, 1871.

IN my work 'Ithaca, the Peloponnesus, and Troy,' published in 1869, I endeavoured to prove, both by the result of my own excavations and by the statements of the Iliad, that the Homeric Troy cannot possibly have been situated on the heights of Bunarbashi, to which place most archæologists assign it. At the same time I endeavoured to explain that the site of Troy must necessarily be identical with the site of that town which, throughout all antiquity and down to its complete destruction at the end of the eighth or the beginning of the ninth century A.D.,* was called Ilium, and not until 1000 years after its disappearance— that is 1788 A.D.—was christened Ilium Novum by Le-

---

* This date refers to Dr. Schliemann's former opinion, that there were Byzantine remains at Hissarlik. He now places the final destruction of Ilium in the fourth century, on the evidence of the latest coins found there. See pp. 318, 319.—ED.

chevalier,* who, as his work proves, can never have visited his *Ilium Novum ;* for in his map he places it on the other side of the Scamander, close to *Kum-kaleh*, and therefore 4 miles from its true position.

The site of Ilium is upon a plateau lying on an average about 80 feet above the Plain, and descending very abruptly on the north side. Its north-western corner is formed by a hill about 26 feet higher still, which is about 705 feet in breadth and 984 in length,† and from its imposing situation and natural fortifications this hill of *Hissarlik* seems specially suited to be the Acropolis of the town.‡ Ever since my first visit, I never doubted that I should find the Pergamus of Priam in the depths of this hill. In an excavation which I made on its north-western corner in April 1870,§ I found among other things, at a depth of 16 feet, walls about 6½ feet thick, which, as has now been proved, belong to a bastion of the time of Lysimachus. Unfortunately I could not continue those excavations at the time, because the proprietors of the field, two Turks in Kum-Kaleh, who had their sheepfolds on the site, would only grant me permission to dig further on condition that I would at once pay them 12,000 piasters for damages,|| and in addition they wished to bind me, after the conclusion of my excavations, to put the field in order again. As this did not suit my convenience, and the two proprietors would not sell me the field at any price, I applied to his Excellency Safvet Pacha, the Minister of Public Instruction, who at my request, and in the interest of science, managed that Achmed Pacha, the Governor of the Dardanelles and the Archipelago, should receive orders from the Ministry of the Interior to have the field valued

---

* *Voyage de la Troade* (3ᵉ éd. Paris, 1802).
† See Plan I., of Greek Ilium, at the end of the volume.
‡ See the Frontispiece.
§ See Plan II., of the Excavations, at the end of the volume.
|| The Turkish *piaster* is somewhat over twopence English.

by competent persons, and to force the proprietors to sell
it to the Government at the price at which it had been
valued : it was thus obtained for 3000 piasters.

In trying to obtain the necessary firman for continuing my excavations, I met with new and great difficulties, for the Turkish Government are collecting ancient
works of art for their recently established Museum in
Constantinople, in consequence of which the Sultan no
longer grants permission for making excavations.   But
what I could not obtain in spite of three journeys to
Constantinople, I got at last through the intercession of
my valued friend, the temporary *chargé d'affaires* of the
United States to the Sublime Porte—Mr. John P. Brown,
the author of the excellent work 'Ancient and Modern
Constantinople' (London, 1868).

So on the 27th of September I arrived at the Dardanelles with my firman.   But here again I met with
difficulties, this time on the part of the before named
Achmed Pacha, who imagined that the position of the field
which I was to excavate was not accurately enough indicated in the document, and therefore would not give me
his permission for the excavations until he should receive
a more definite explanation from the Grand Vizier.   Owing
to the change of ministry which had occurred, a long time
would no doubt have elapsed before the matter was settled,
had it not occurred to Mr. Brown to apply to his Excel-
lency Kiamil-Pacha, the new Minister of Public Instruction,
who takes a lively interest in science, and at whose intercession the Grand Vizier immediately gave Achmed Pacha
the desired explanation.   This, however, again occupied
13 days, and it was only on the evening of the 10th of
October that I started with my wife from the Dardanelles
for the Plain of Troy, a journey of eight hours.   As,
according to the firman, I was to be watched by a
Turkish official, whose salary I have to pay during the
time of my excavations, Achmed Pacha assigned to me

the second secretary of his chancellary of justice, an Armenian, by name Georgios Sarkis, whom I pay 23 piasters daily.

At last, on Wednesday, the 11th of this month, I again commenced my excavations with 8 workmen, but on the following morning I was enabled to increase their number to 35, and on the 13th to 74, each of whom receives 9 piasters daily (1 franc 80 centimes). As, unfortunately, I only brought 8 wheelbarrows from France, and they cannot be obtained here, and cannot even be made in all the country round, I have to use 52 baskets for carrying away the rubbish. This work, however, proceeds but slowly and is very tiring, as the rubbish has to be carried a long way off. I therefore employ also four carts drawn by oxen, each of which again costs me 20 piasters a day. I work with great energy and spare no cost, in order, if possible, to reach the native soil before the winter rains set in, which may happen at any moment. Thus I hope finally to solve the great problem as to whether the hill of Hissarlik is—as I firmly believe—the citadel of Troy.

As it is an established fact that hills which consist of pure earth and are brought under the plough gradually disappear—that for instance, the Wartsberg, near the village of Ackershagen in Mecklenburg, which I once, as a child, considered to be the highest mountain in the world, has quite vanished in 40 years—so it is equally a fact, that hills on which, in the course of thousands of years, new buildings have been continually erected upon the ruins of former buildings, gain very considerably in circumference and height. The hill of Hissarlik furnishes the most striking proof of this. As already mentioned, it lies at the north-western end of the site of Ilium, which is distinctly indicated by the surrounding walls built by Lysimachus. In addition to the imposing situation of this hill within the circuit of the town, its present Turkish name of *Hissarlik*, "fortress" or "acropolis"—from

the word حصار (root حصر, to enclose), which has passed
from the Arabic into the Turkish—seems also to prove that
this is the Pergamus of Ilium ; that here Xerxes (in
480 B.C.) offered up 1000 oxen to the Ilian Athena ;* that
here Alexander the Great hung up his armour in the
temple of the goddess, and took away in its stead some
of the weapons dedicated therein belonging to the time
of the Trojan war, and likewise sacrificed to the Ilian
Athena.† I conjectured that this temple, the pride of the
Ilians, must have stood on the highest point of the hill,
and I therefore decided to excavate this locality down
to the native soil. But in order, at the same time, to
bring to light the most ancient of the fortifying walls of
the Pergamus, and to decide accurately how much the hill
had increased in breadth by the *débris* which had been
thrown down since the erection of those walls, I made an
immense cutting on the face of the steep northern slope,
about 66 feet from my last year's work.‡ This cutting was
made in a direction due south, and extended across the highest
plateau, and was so broad that it embraced the whole building, the foundations of which, consisting of large hewn
stones, I had already laid open last year to a depth of from
only 1 to 3 feet below the surface. According to an exact
measurement, this building, which appears to belong to the
first century after Christ, is about 59 feet in length, and
43 feet in breadth. I have of course had all these foundations removed as, being within my excavation, they were of
no use and would only have been in the way.

The difficulty of making excavations in a wilderness
like this, where everything is wanting, are immense and
they increase day by day; for, on account of the steep

---

* Herod. VII. 43.

† Strabo, XIII. 1. 8 ; Arrian, I. 11. ; Plutarch, Life of Alexander the
Great, viii.

‡ See Plan II., of the Excavations.

slope of the hill, the cutting becomes longer the deeper
I dig, and so the difficulty of removing the rubbish is always
increasing. This, moreover, cannot be thrown directly
down the slope, for it would of course only have to be
carried away again; so it has to be thrown down on the
steep side of the hill at some distance to the right and left
of the mouth of the cutting. The numbers of immense
blocks of stone also, which we continually come upon,
cause great trouble and have to be got out and removed,
which takes up a great deal of time, for at the moment
when a large block of this kind is rolled to the edge of the
slope, all of my workmen leave their own work and hurry
off to see the enormous weight roll down its steep path
with a thundering noise and settle itself at some distance
in the Plain. It is, moreover, an absolute impossibility for
me, who am the only one to preside over all, to give each
workman his right occupation, and to watch that each
does his duty. Then, for the purpose of carrying away
the rubbish, the side passages have to be kept in order,
which likewise runs away with a great deal of time, for
their inclinations have to be considerably modified at each
step that we go further down.

Notwithstanding all these difficulties the work advances
rapidly, and if I could only work on uninterruptedly for
a month, I should certainly reach a depth of more than
32 feet, in spite of the immense breadth of the cutting.

The medals hitherto discovered are all of copper, and
belong for the most part to Alexandria Troas; some also
are of Ilium, and of the first centuries before and after
Christ.

My dear wife, an Athenian lady, who is an enthusiastic
admirer of Homer, and knows almost the whole of the
'Iliad' by heart, is present at the excavations from morning
to night. I will not say anything about our mode of life
in this solitude, where everything is wanting, and where
we have to take four grains of quinine every morning as

a precaution against the pestilential malaria. All of my workmen are Greeks, from the neighbouring village of Renkoï; only on Sunday, a day on which the Greeks do not work, I employ Turks. My servant, Nikolaos Zaphyros, from Renkoï, whom I pay 30 piasters a day, is invaluable to me in paying the daily wages of the workmen, for he knows every one of them, and is honest. Unfortunately, however, he gives me no assistance in the works, as he neither possesses the gift of commanding, nor has he the slightest knowledge of what I am seeking.

I naturally have no leisure here, and I have only been able to write the above because it is raining heavily, and therefore no work can be done. On the next rainy day I shall report further on the progress of my excavations.

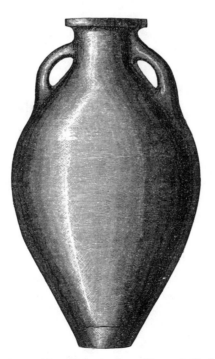

No. 36.   A large Trojan Amphora of Terra-cotta (8 M.).

CHAPTER II.

Number of workmen — Discoveries at 2 to 4 meters deep — Greek coins — Remarkable terra-cottas with small stamps, probably *Ex votos* — These cease, and are succeeded by the whorls — Bones of sharks, shells of mussels and oysters, and pottery — Three Greek Inscriptions — The splendid panoramic view from Hissarlik — The Plain of Troy and the heroic *tumuli* — Thymbria : Mr. Frank Calvert's Museum — The mound of Chanaï Tépé — The Ṣcamander and its ancient bed — Valley of the Simoïs, and ruins of Ophrynium.

On the Hill of Hissarlik, October 26th, 1871.

SINCE my report of the 18th I have continued the excavations with the utmost energy, with, on an average, 80 workmen, and I have to-day reached an average depth of 4 meters (13 feet). At a depth of 6½ feet I discovered a well, covered with a very large stone, and filled with rubbish. Its depth I have not been able to ascertain ; it belongs to the Roman period, as is proved by the cement with which the stones are joined together. Ruins of buildings, consisting of hewn stones joined or not joined by cement, I only find at about a depth of 2 meters (6½ feet). In the layers of *débris* between 2 and 4 meters deep (6½ to 13 feet), I find scarcely any stones, and to my delight the huge blocks of stone no longer occur at all. Medals belonging to Ilium and to the first and second centuries before Christ, and the first two centuries after Christ, as well as coins of Alexandria Troas and Sigeum, the age of which I do not know, were found almost immediately below the surface, and only in some few cases as deep as 1 meter (3¼ feet). By far the greater number of the Ilian coins bear the image of Minerva, of Faustina the elder, of Marcus Aurelius, of Faustina the younger, of

Commodus or of Crispina, and I found one with the following inscription: **ΦΑΥΣΤΙΝΑ ƎΚΤΩΡ ΙΛΙΕΩΝ**. As far down as 2 meters (6½ feet) I found, as during my last year's excavations in this hill, an immense number of round articles of terra-cotta, red, yellow, grey and black, with two holes, without inscriptions, but frequently with a kind of potter's stamp upon them. I cannot find in the holes of any one of these articles the slightest trace of wear by their having been used for domestic purposes, and therefore I presume that they have served as *Ex votos* for hanging up in the

Nos. 37–39.   Stamped Terra-cottas (1¼—2 M.).

temples. Upon most of those bearing a stamp I perceive in it an altar, and above the latter a bee or fly with outspread wings; upon others there is a bull, a swan, a child, or two horses. Curiously enough these articles vanish all at once at a depth of 2 meters (6½ feet), and from this depth downwards I find, in their stead, pieces that are sometimes as round as a ball, exactly the shape of

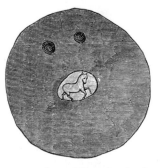

No. 40.   Stamped Terra-cotta (2 M.).

a German humming-top, sometimes in the form of hemispheres, others again in the form of cones, tops (*carrouselen*), or volcanoes. They are from ¾ of an inch to 2¼ inches high and broad, and all the different forms have a hole right through the centre; almost all of them have on one side the most

various kinds of decorations encircling the central hole.*
With the exception of a few of these objects made of blue
stone, from ¾ of an inch to 1½ inch broad, and found at a
depth of 3 meters (10 feet), they are all made of terra-cotta,
and it is quite evident that the decorations were engraved
when the clay was still in a soft state. All are of such
excellent clay, and burnt so hard, that I at first believed
them to be of stone, and only perceived my mistake after
having carefully examined them. In the depth we have
now arrived at I also find very many of those elegant round
vertebræ which form the backbone of the shark, and of
which walking-sticks are often made. The existence of these
vertebræ seems to prove that in remote antiquity this sea
contained sharks, which are now no longer met with here.
To-day I also found upon a fragment of rough pottery the
representation of a man's head with large protruding eyes,
a long nose, and a very small mouth, which seems clearly
to be of Phœnician workmanship.

I also constantly come upon immense quantities of
mussel-shells, and it seems as if the old inhabitants of Ilium
had been very fond of this shell-fish. Oyster-shells are
also found, but only seldom; on the other hand, I find
very many fragments of pottery. As far as the depth yet
reached, all the buildings which have stood upon this hill
in the course of thousands of years seem to have been
destroyed by fire; every one of them is distinctly indicated
by a layer of calcined ruins. This is at all events the
reason why I do not also find other objects, and especially
why I no longer find earthen vessels. Those I have hitherto
found uninjured are very small pots of coarse workmanship; however, the fragments of the pottery prove that
even in the time to which the ruins belong, at a depth of
4 meters (13 feet), there already existed good kitchen utensils.

---

* The various forms of the whorls are shown in the lithographed
plates at the end of the volume.

In the quadrangular building already mentioned I found, at a depth of about 5 feet, a slab of marble 25·6 inches in length, the upper part of which is 13·6 inches in breadth, and the lower part 15·36 inches. It contains the following inscription :—

Ἐπειδὴ Διαφένης Πολλέως Τημνίτης, διατρίβων παρὰ τῷ βασιλεῖ, φίλος ὢν καὶ εὔνους διατελεῖ τῷ δήμῳ, χρείας παρεχόμενος προθύμως εἰς ἃ ἄν τις αὐτὸν παρακαλῇ, δεδόχθαι τῇ βουλῇ καὶ τῷ δήμῳ ἐπαινέσαι μὲν αὐτὸν ἐπὶ τούτοις, παρακαλεῖν δὲ καὶ εἰς τὸ λοιπὸν εἶναι φιλότιμον εἰς τὰ τοῦ δήμου συμφέροντα, δεδόσθαι δὲ αὐτῷ πολιτείαν, προξενίαν, ἔγκτησιν, ἀτέλειαν ὧν καὶ οἱ πολῖται ἀτελεῖς εἰσι καὶ ἔφοδον ἐπὶ τὴν βουλὴν πρώτῳ μετὰ τὰ ἱερὰ καὶ ἄφιξιν καὶ ἐμ πολέμῳ καὶ ἐν εἰρήνῃ ἀσυλεὶ καὶ ἀσπονδεί· ἀναγράψαι δὲ τὰ δεδομένα αὐτῷ ταῦτα εἰς στήλην καὶ (ἀνα)θεῖναι ε(ἰς . . . .

The king spoken of in this inscription must have been one of the kings of Pergamus, and from the character of the writing I believe that it must be assigned to the third century before Christ.

At about the same depth, and by the side of the building, I found a second marble slab 16·5 inches in length and 13·4 inches in breadth. The inscription runs as follows :—

Ἰλιεῖς ἔδοσαν Μενελάῳ Ἀρραβαίου Ἀθηναίῳ εὐεργέτῃ γενομένῳ αὐτῶν καὶ περὶ τὴν ἐλευθερίαν ἀνδρὶ ἀγαθῷ γενομένῳ προξενίαν καὶ εὐεργεσίαν.

This second inscription, to judge from the form of the letters, appears to belong to the first century B.C. "'Ἀρραβαῖος" here occurs for the first time as an Attic name.

At the same depth, and likewise by the side of the foundations of the same building, I found a third marble slab, nearly 15 inches long and about 14 broad. Its inscription is :—

Μηνόφιλος Γλαυρίου εἶπεν· ἐπειδὴ πλείονες τῶν πολιτῶν
ἐπελθόντες ἐπὶ τὴν βουλήν φασιν Χαιρέαν τὸν τεταγμένον ἐπ'
Ἀβύδου εὔνουν τε εἶναι τῇ πόλει καὶ ἐνίοις πρεσβευομένοις
ὑπὸ τοῦ δήμου πρὸς αὐτὸν βουλόμενον τῇ πόλει χαρίζεσθαι
τὴν πᾶσαν σπουδὴν καὶ πρόνοιαν ποεῖσθαι καὶ τοῖς συναν-
τῶσιν αὐτῷ τῶν πολιτῶν φιλανθρώπως προσφέρεσθαι, ἵνα
οὖν καὶ ὁ δῆμος φαίνηται τὴν καθήκουσαν χάριν ἀποδιδοὺς
τοῖς προαιρουμένοις τὴν πό(λιν) . . . . δεδόχθαι.

This third inscription also appears to belong to the first
century B.C.

It is probable that the building in and around which I
discovered these three inscriptions was the Town-hall of
Ilium; at all events, it does not appear to have been a
temple.

The view from the hill of Hissarlik is extremely magni-
ficent.* Before me lies the glorious Plain of Troy, which,
since the recent rain, is again covered with grass and yellow
buttercups; on the north-north-west, at about an hour's
distance, it is bounded by the Hellespont. The peninsula
of Gallipoli here runs out to a point, upon which stands
a lighthouse. To the left of it is the island of Imbros,
above which rises Mount Ida of the island of Samothrace,
at present covered with snow; a little more to the west, on
the Macedonian peninsula, lies the celebrated Mount Athos,
or Monte Santo, with its monasteries, at the north-western
side of which there are still to be seen traces of that great
canal which, according to Herodotus (VII. 22-23), was
made by Xerxes, in order to avoid sailing round the stormy
Cape Athos.

Returning to the Plain of Troy, we see to the right
of it, upon a spur of the promontory of Rhœteum, the
sepulchral mound of Ajax; at the foot of the opposite
Cape of Sigeum that of Patroclus, and upon a spur of
the same cape the sepulchre of Achilles; to the left of

---

* See Plate IV.   View of the Northern part of the Plain of Troy.

the latter, on the promontory itself, is the village of Yenishehr. The Plain, which is about two hours' journey in
breadth, is thence bounded on the west by the shores of
the Ægean, which are, on an average, about 131 feet high,
and upon which we see first the sepulchral mound of
Festus, the confidential friend of Caracalla, whom the
Emperor (according to Herodian, IV.) caused to be poisoned
on his visit to Ilium, that he might be able to imitate the
funeral rites which Achilles celebrated in honour of his
friend Patroclus, as described by Homer (*Iliad*, XXIII.).
Then upon the same coast there is another sepulchral
mound, called *Udjek-Tépé*, rather more than 78½ feet in
height, which most archæologists consider to be that of the
old man Æsyetes, from which Polites, trusting to the swift-
ness of his feet, watched to see when the Greek army would
set forth from the ships.* The distance of this mound
from the Greek camp on the Hellespont is, however, fully
3½ hours, whereas at a distance of a quarter of an hour a
man cannot be seen. Polites, moreover, would not have
required to have been very swift-footed to have escaped at
a distance of 3½ hours. In short, from the passage in the
Iliad this tomb cannot possibly be identified with that of
Æsyetes, whether the site of ancient Troy be assigned to
the heights of Bunarbashi or to Ilium, where I am digging.
Between the last-named mounds we see projecting above
the high shores of the Ægean Sea the island of Tenedos.

---

* Homer, *Iliad*, II. 790–794 :—

Ἀγχοῦ δ' ἱσταμένη προσέφη πόδας ὠκέα Ἶρις·
Εἴσατο δὲ φθογγὴν υἷϊ Πριάμοιο Πολίτῃ,
Ὃς Τρώων σκοπὸς ἷζε, ποδωκείῃσι πεποιθὼς,
Τύμβῳ ἐπ' ἀκροτάτῳ Αἰσυήταο γέροντος,
Δέγμενος ὁππότε ναῦφιν ἀφορμηθεῖεν Ἀχαιοί—

" Swift Iris stood amidst them, and the voice
Assuming of Polites, Priam's son,
The Trojan scout, who, trusting to his speed,
Was posted on the summit of the mound
Of ancient Æsyetes, there to watch
Till from their ships the Grecian troops should march—"

To the south, we see the Plain of Troy, extending again
to a distance of two hours, as far as the heights of
Bunarbashi, above which rises majestically the snow-capped
Gargarus of Mount Ida, from which Jupiter witnessed the
battles between the Trojans and the Greeks.*   At half-an-
hour's distance to the left of Bunarbashi is the beautiful
estate of 5000 acres, whose name of Batak is now changed
into Thymbria, belonging to my friend Mr. Frederick
Calvert.   It deserves the change of name for more than
one reason; for not only does the river Thymbrius (now
Kemer) flow through it, but it comprises the whole site
of the ancient town of Thymbria, with its temple of
Apollo, among the ruins of which the proprietor's brother,
Mr. Frank Calvert—known for his archæological investigations — is making excavations, and has found several
valuable inscriptions; among others, an inventory of the
temple.   This estate further comprises the site of an ancient
town, which is apparently encompassed in some places by
ramparts; it is covered with fragments of pottery, and in
regard to position, distance, &c., corresponds so closely
with the statements of Strabo that it must certainly be his
" Ἰλιέων κώμη," where, agreeing with the theory of Demetrius of Scepsis, he places the Homeric Troy.   At the foot
of the hill containing the site, there are, curiously enough,
two springs, one of hot the other of cold water.†   These
springs—probably owing to their natural channels having
been stopped up for centuries by a fallen bridge—have
formed a large marsh of 240 acres, the evaporations of
which greatly contribute to the malaria of the glorious
Plain.   The marvellous circumstance that these springs are

---

* See Plate V., View of the South-eastern part of the Plain of Troy.
The word "perpetual" (*ewigem*) in reference to the snow on Ida is
omitted at the desire of the Author; who has ascertained that the summit
is clear of snow in July and August.—[ED.]

† The difference of temperature in the springs seems to have been
disproved afterwards.   (See Chapter V., p. 92.)—[ED.]

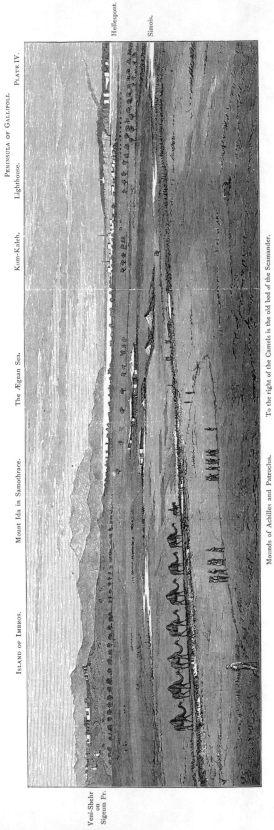

ISLAND OF IMBROS. Mount Ida in Samothrace. The Ægean Sea. Kum-Kaleh. Lighthouse.

Hellespont.

Simois.

Yeni-Shehr
on
Sigeum Pr.

Mounds of Achilles and Patroclus.   To the right of the Camels is the old bed of the Scamander.

VIEW OF THE NORTHERN PART OF THE PLAIN OF TROY, FROM THE HILL OF HISSARLIK.

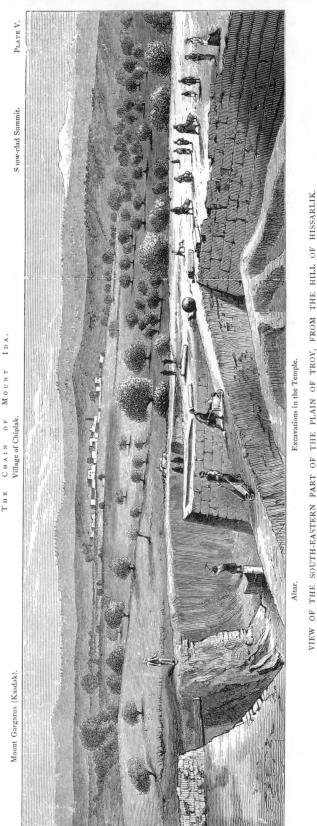

PLATE V.

Snow-clad Summit.

The Chain of Mount Ida.

Village of Chiplak.

Mount Gargarus (Kasdak).

Altar.

Excavations in the Temple.

VIEW OF THE SOUTH-EASTERN PART OF THE PLAIN OF TROY, FROM THE HILL OF HISSARLIK.

situated directly before the site of " Ἰλιέων κώμη," and that
their position corresponds so exactly with the two springs
of hot and cold water which existed in front of ancient
Troy, and in which the Trojan women used to wash their
clothes, convinces Mr. Frederick Calvert that Demetrius
of Scepsis and Strabo were right, and that he possesses the
actual site of ancient Troy.   In order to gain 240 acres
of rich land and to make the district more healthy, but
especially also in the interest of science, Mr. Calvert has
now caused the channels to be opened, and he believes, as
the incline is considerable, amounting at least to 53 feet,
and the distance from the Hellespont is three hours, that by
next summer the whole marsh will be dried up, and the
two springs, which are now 5 feet under water, will be
brought to light.*   I have in vain endeavoured to make
Mr. Calvert change his opinion, by seeking to convince
him that, according to the Iliad (II. 123-30),† Troy must
at least have had 50,000 inhabitants, whereas the site he
possesses is scarcely large enough for 10,000 ; further, that
the distance from the Ἰλιέων κώμη to the Hellespont directly
contradicts the statements of Homer, for we are told that
the Greek troops in one day twice forced their way fighting
from the camp to the town, and returned twice, fighting.
The distance of the town from the ships, therefore, in my
opinion, can at most have been that of one hour (about
3 miles).   Mr. Calvert replies that the whole Plain of Troy
is alluvial land, and that at the time of the Trojan war its
site must have been nearer the Hellespont ; but, three years
ago, in my work, 'Ithaca, the Peloponnesus, and Troy,' I
endeavoured to prove that the Plain of Troy is decidedly
not alluvial land.

---

* This work has now been done.   See ' Introduction,' p. 51.

† The ' Introduction ' has already shown how Dr. Schliemann
changed his opinion as to the magnitude of Troy.   Compare also
Chapter XXIII.   It is hard to see how the vague poetic language of the
passage cited furnishes any *data* for the computation in the text.—[ED.]

Another curiosity of this estate is, that close to the temple of Apollo there exists a round hill, called "Chanaï Tépé," about 32¾ feet in height, and 216½ feet in diameter at its base. It used to be considered a natural hill, till Mr. Frank Calvert, in the year 1856, made a cutting in it, and found upon a flat rock, 16 feet high, a circular space, enclosed by a wall 6½ feet in height. The whole of the inner space, as far as the edge of the surrounding wall, was filled with calcined bones, which the surgeons of the English fleet pronounced to be human bones. In the centre Mr. Calvert found the skeleton of a human being. The whole was covered with about 10 feet of earth.

The Plain of Troy is traversed from the south-east to the north-west by the Scamander, which is distant from Hissarlik 35 minutes' walk, and the bed of which I can recognise from here by the uninterrupted row of trees growing upon its banks. Between the Scamander and Hissarlik, at a distance of only 15 minutes from the latter, the Plain is again intersected by the river Kalifatli-Asmak, which rises in the marshes of Batak (Thymbria), and is filled with running water only in late autumn, winter, and spring; but during the hot summer months, till the end of October, it consists of an uninterrupted series of deep pools. This stream, even during the continual heavy winter rains, and in comparison with its splendid and immensely broad channel, has but a very scanty supply of water—in fact, never so much as to cover even the tenth part of the breadth of its bed. I therefore believe that its huge bed must at one time have been the bed of the Scamander; I believe this all the more, as the Simoïs still flows into the Kalifatli-Asmak at a quarter of an hour's distance north of Ilium, where I am digging.* By identifying the channel of this river, which may be traced to the Hellespont near Cape Rhœteum, with the most ancient

---

* See the Map.

bed of the Scamander, we may settle the otherwise insur-
mountable difficulties of the Homeric topography of the
Plain of Troy; for, had the Scamander occupied its
present bed at the time of the Trojan war, it would have
flowed through the Greek camp, and Homer would have
had abundant opportunity of speaking of this important
circumstance.   But as he never mentions a river in the
camp, there can, of course, have been none there.   Moreover, the Simoïs is now half-an-hour's distance from the
Scamander; whereas Homer frequently mentions the confluence of these two streams before Ilium, and most
of the battles took place in the fields between Troy, the
Scamander, and the Simoïs.   At its confluence with the
Kalifatli-Asmak, whose enormous bed must, at one time,
have belonged to the Scamander, the Simoïs has an
especially large and deep bed, which is doubtless still
the same that this stream occupied at the time of the
Trojan war.

The Kalifatli-Asmak, after its confluence with the
Scamander near the village of Kum-köi, turns to the north-
west, and flows into the sea by three arms, not very far
from the present bed of the Scamander; below the village,
however, it has quite a narrow bed, which is obviously of
recent formation.   Its old channel, on the other hand,
which was the ancient bed of the Scamander and is of an
immense breadth, proceeds direct northwards from Kum-köi:
it is now occupied by the water of the small rivulet called
In-tépé-Asmak, which I shall afterwards describe minutely,
and empties itself, as before said, into the Hellespont close
to Cape Rhœteum.

The Scamander did not take possession of its present
bed suddenly, but very gradually, probably in the course
of many centuries; for between its present channel and its
ancient one there are three enormous river-beds, likewise
leading to the Hellespont, which possess no water and
must necessarily have been successively formed by the

Scamander, as there is no other river here that could have formed them.

To the north-north-east, I overlook another plain, called Chalil-Owasi, half an hour in breadth and 1½ hour in length, which is traversed by the Simoïs and extends to the hill upon which are the mighty ruins of the ancient city of Ophrynium. The coins which have been found there leave no doubt about this. There, close to the Simoïs, was Hector's (so-called) tomb, and a grove sacred to his memory.*

---

* Lycophron's *Cassandra ;* Virgil's *Æneid*, III., 302–305 ; Strabo, XIII., 1.

No. 41.   A great mixing Vessel (κρατήρ), of Terra-cotta, with 4 Handles, about 1 ft. 5 in. high, and nearly 1 ft. 9 in. in diameter (7 M.).   (See pp. 157, 262).

CHAPTER III.

Puzzling transitions from the " Stone Age " to a higher civilization —
The stone age reappears in force, mixed with pottery of fine workmanship, and the whorls in great number — Conjectures as to their
uses : probably *Ex votos* — *Priapi* of stone and terra-cotta : their
worship brought by the primitive Aryans from Bactria — Vessels
with the owl's face — Boars' tusks — Varied implements and weapons
of stone — Hand mill-stones — Models of canoes in terra-cotta —
Whetstones — The one object of the excavations, to find TROY.

On the Hill of Hissarlik, November 3rd, 1871.

MY last communication was dated the 26th of October,
and since then I have proceeded vigorously with 80 workmen on an average. Unfortunately, however, I have lost
three days ; for on Sunday, a day on which the Greeks do
not work, I could not secure the services of any Turkish
workmen, for they are now sowing their crops; on two other
days I was hindered by heavy rains.

To my extreme surprise, on Monday, the 30th of last
month, I suddenly came upon a mass of *débris*, in which I
found an immense quantity of implements made of hard
black stone (diorite), but of a very primitive form. On the
following day, however, not a single stone implement was
found, but a small piece of silver wire and a great deal of
broken pottery of elegant workmanship, among others the
fragment of a cup with an owl's head. I therefore thought
I had again come upon the remains of a civilized people,
and that the stone implements of the previous day were the
remains of an invasion of a barbarous tribe, whose dominion
had been of but short duration. But I was mistaken, for
on the Wednesday the stone period reappeared in even

greater force, and continued throughout the whole of yester-day. To-day, unfortunately, no work can be done owing to the heavy downpour of rain.

I find much in this stone period that is quite inexplic-able to me, and I therefore consider it necessary to describe everything as minutely as possible, in the hope that one or other of my honoured colleagues will be able to give an explanation of the points which are obscure to me.

In the first place, I am astonished that here on the highest point of the hill, where, according to every suppo-sition the noblest buildings must have stood, I come upon the stone period as early as at a depth of 4½ meters (about 15 feet), whereas last year, at a distance of only 66 feet from the top of the hill, I found in my cutting, at the depth of more than 16 feet, a wall, 6½ feet thick, and by no means very ancient, and no trace of the stone period, although I carried that cutting to a depth of more than 26 feet. This probably can be explained in no other way than that the hill, at the place where the wall stands, must have been very low, and that this low position has been gradually raised by the *débris*.

Further, I do not understand how it is possible that in the present stratum and upon the whole length of my cutting (which must now be at least 184 feet) to its mouth, that is, as far as the steep declivity, I should find stone implements, which obviously prove that that part of the steep side of the hill cannot have increased in size since the stone period by rubbish thrown down from above.

Next, I cannot explain how it is possible that I should find things which, to all appearance, must have been used by the uncivilized men of the stone period, but which could not have been made with the rude implements at their disposal. Among these I may specially mention the earthen vessels found in great numbers, without decorations, it is true, and not fine, but which however are of excellent workmanship. Not one of these vessels has been turned upon a potter's wheel, and yet it appears to me that they could not have been made without the aid of some kind of machine, such as, on the other hand, could not have been produced by the rude stone implements of the period.

I am further surprised to find, in this stone period, and more frequently than ever before, those round articles with a hole in the centre, which have sometimes the form of humming-tops or whorls (*carrouselen*), sometimes of fiery mountains. In the last form they bear, on a small scale, the most striking resemblance to the colossal sepulchral mounds of this district, which latter, both on this account and also because stone implements have been found in one of them (the Chanaï Tépé) belong probably to the stone period, and therefore perhaps to an age thousands of years before the Trojan war.* At a depth of 3 meters (about 10 feet), I found one of these objects made of very fine marble: all the rest are made of excellent clay rendered very hard by burning; almost all of them have decorations, which have evidently been scratched into them when the clay was as yet unburnt, and which in very many cases have been filled with a white substance, to make them more striking to the eye. It is probable that at one time the decorations upon all of these objects were filled with that white substance, for upon many of them, where it no longer exists, I see some traces of it. Upon some of the articles of very hard black clay without decorations, some hand has endeavoured to make them after the clay had been burnt, and, when looked at through a magnifying glass, these marks leave no doubt that they have been laboriously scratched with a piece of flint.

The question then forces itself upon us: *For what were*

---

* For the further and most interesting discoveries which speedily led Dr. Schliemann to recal this conjecture, and which have affected all previous theories about the ages of stone and bronze, see the beginning of Chapter IV.

these objects used? They cannot possibly have been employed in spinning or weaving, or as weights for fishing-
nets, for they are too fine and elegant for such purposes;
neither have I as yet been able to discover any indication
that they could have been used for any handicraft. When,
therefore, I consider the perfect likeness of most of these
objects to the form of the heroic sepulchral mounds, I
am forced to believe that they, as well as those with two
holes which occurred only at a depth of 6½ feet, were used
as *Ex votos*.

Again, to my surprise, I frequently find the Priapus,
sometimes represented quite true to nature in stone or terra-
cotta, sometimes in the form of a pillar rounded off at the
top (just such as I have seen in Indian temples, but there only
about 4 inches in length). I once also found the symbol in
the form of a little pillar only about 1 inch in length, made
of splendid black marble striped with white and beautifully polished, such as is never met with in the whole of
this district. I consequently have not the slightest doubt
that the Trojan people of the stone period worshipped
Priapus as a divinity, and that, belonging to the Indo-
Germanic race, they brought this religion from Bactria;
for in India, as is well known, the god of production and
of destruction is represented and worshipped in this form.
Moreover, it is probable that these ancient Trojans are the
ancestors of the great Hellenic nation, for I repeatedly find
upon cups and vases of terra-cotta representations of the
owl's head, which is probably the great-great-grandmother
of the Athenian bird of Pallas-Athena.

With the exception of the above-mentioned piece of
silver wire and two copper nails, I have as yet found no
trace of metal in the strata of the stone period.

As in the upper strata, so in those of the stone period,
I find a great many boars' tusks, which, in the latter strata,
have without exception been pointed at the end, and have
served as implements. It is inconceivable to me how the

men of the stone period, with their imperfect weapons, were able to kill wild boars. Their lances—like all their other weapons and instruments—are, it is true, made of very hard black or green stone, but still they are so blunt that it must have required a giant's strength to kill a boar with them. Hammers and axes are met with of all sizes and in great numbers.* I likewise find very many weights of granite, also a number of hand-mills of lava, which consist of two pieces about a foot in length, oval on one side and flat on the other, between which the corn was crushed. Sometimes these mill-stones are made of granite. Knives are found in very great numbers ; all are of flint, some in the form of knife-blades, others—by far the greater majority— are jagged on one or on both sides, like saws. Needles and bodkins made of bone are of frequent occurrence, and sometimes also small bone spoons. Primitive canoes, such as I frequently saw in Ceylon, formed out of a hollowed trunk of a tree, are often met with here in miniature, made of terra-cotta, and I presume that these small vessels may have served as salt-cellars or pepper-boxes. I likewise find a number of whetstones about 4 inches in length and nearly as much in breadth, which are sometimes made of clay, sometimes of green or black slate ; further, a number of round, flat stones a little under and over two inches in diameter, painted red on one side; also many hundreds of round terra-cottas of the like size and shape, with a hole in the centre, and which have evidently been made out of fragments of pottery, and may have been used on spindles. Flat stone mortars are also met with.

I also find in my excavations a house-wall of the stone period, consisting of stones joined by clay, like the buildings which were discovered on the islands of Therasia and Thera

---

* The stone implements here described are so similar in form to the better-made objects of the same sort, exhibited in subsequent illustrations, that it seems superfluous to engrave them here.—[Ed.]

(Santorin) under three layers of volcanic ashes, forming together a height of 68 feet.

My expectations are extremely modest; I have no hope of finding plastic works of art. The single object of my excavations from the beginning was only to find Troy, whose site has been discussed by a hundred scholars in a hundred books, but which as yet no one has ever sought to bring to light by excavations. If I should not succeed in this, still I shall be perfectly contented, if by my labours I succeed only in penetrating to the deepest darkness of pre-historic times, and enriching archæology by the discovery of a few interesting features from the most ancient history of the great Hellenic race. The discovery of the stone period, instead of discouraging me, has therefore only made me the more desirous to penetrate to the place which was occupied by the first people that came here, and I still intend to reach it even if I should have to dig another 50 feet further down.

Note.—The "Stone Period" described in this chapter seems to be that of the *third stratum* upwards from the rock (4 to 7 meters, or 13 to 23 feet deep); but the description does not make this perfectly clear.— [ED.]

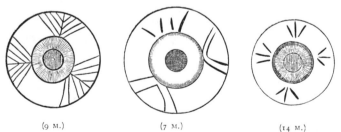

(9 M.)   (7 M.)   (14 M.)

Nos. 42–44. Terra-cotta Whorls.
No. 44 is remarkable for the *depth* at which it was found.

CHAPTER IV.

Another passage from the Stone Age to copper implements mixed with
stone — The signs of a higher civilization increase with the depth
reached — All the implements are of better workmanship — Discovery of supposed inscriptions — Further discussion of the use of
the whorls — TROY still to be reached — Fine terra-cotta vessels of
remarkable forms — Great numbers of stone weights and hand mill-
stones — Numerous house-walls — Construction of the great cutting
— Fever and quinine — Wounds and arnica.

On the Hill of Hissarlik, November 18th, 1871.

SINCE my report of the 3rd of this month I have continued my
excavations with the greatest zeal, and although interrupted
sometimes by the rain, and sometimes by Greek festivals,
and also in spite of the continually increasing difficulty in
removing the rubbish, I have now reached an average depth
of 10 meters or about 33 English feet.* Much that was inexplicable to me has now become clear, and I must first of
all correct an error made in my last report, that I had come
upon the stone period. I was deceived by the enormous
mass of stone implements of all kinds which were daily dug
up, and by the absence of any trace of metal, except two
copper nails, which I believed to have come in some way
from one of the upper strata into the deeper stratum of the
stone period. But since the 6th of this month there have

---

* This depth of 10 meters, or 33 feet, is that which Dr. Schliemann
came to regard as the *lower* limit of the ruins of the true heroic Troy.
The depth of 7 meters, or 23 feet, presently mentioned is the *upper* limit
of the same stratum. (See the Introduction and the later Memoirs.)—
[ED.]

appeared not only many nails, but also knives, lances, and battle-axes of copper of such elegant workmanship that they can have been made only by a civilized people.

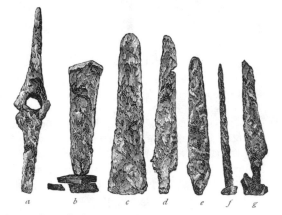

No. 45.   Copper Implements and Weapons from the Trojan stratum (8 M.).
a, Axe of an unusual form; b, c, Battle-Axes of the common form; d, e, g, Knives; f, a Nail.*

Hence I must not only recal my conjecture that I had reached the stone period, but I cannot even admit that I have reached the bronze period, for the implements and weapons which I find are too well finished. I must, moreover, draw attention to the fact, that the deeper I dig, from 7 meters (23 feet) downwards, the greater are the indications of a higher civilization. At a depth of from 4 to 7 meters (13 to 23 feet) the stone implements and weapons were of a coarse description; the knives were of flint, generally in the form of small saws, and rarely in that of a blade; but there were a very great number of sharp pieces of silex, which must likewise have served as knives. Since

No. 46.   A Mould of Mica-schist for casting Copper Implements (8 M.).

---

* These, like all the objects of copper found at Troy, are coated with verdigris and malachite.   (Letter-press to the Atlas.)

then, however, the stone implements, such as hammers and axes, are of much better workmanship; there still occur a quantity of silex·knives in the form of saws, but they are much better made than those of the upper strata, and at a depth below 23 feet double-edged knife-blades of obsidian, which are so sharp that they might serve as razors. In

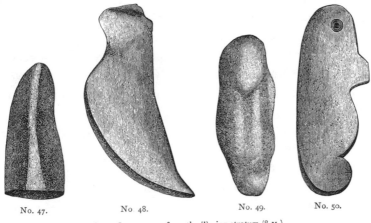

No. 47.　　No 48.　　No. 49.　　No. 50.

Stone Instruments from the Trojan stratum (8 M.).
Nos. 47, 48, 49, of Green Stone, probably Lance-Heads ; No. 50, of Diorite, use unknown.

these depths, moreover, as I have already said, we again meet with weapons and quantities of nails, knives, and implements of copper.

But what above all other circumstances seems to prove that I never reached the stone period, and that, after digging further down into the strata of rude races between 13 and 23 feet, I have again come upon the remains of a more civilized nation, are two inscriptions, one of which, found at a depth of $7\frac{1}{2}$ meters (about 25 feet), seems to be Phœnician, but consists of only about five letters, which have been scratched by a pointed instrument, into that side of a small terra-cotta disc which had been painted white, the disc being only about $2\frac{1}{3}$ inches in diameter. The letters, in any case, must have stood out very distinctly in the white colour, but the greater portion of it has disappeared, and thus two of the five written characters cannot

easily be distinguished.   I hope, however, that the inscription may nevertheless be deciphered.*

The other inscription was found at a depth of 8½ meters
(27¾ feet) upon one of those small round articles of terra-
cotta with a hole in the centre, which, from a depth of
6½ feet downwards, occur in immense numbers in the
form of the humming-top, the carrousel, and the volcano.
I have already expressed my opinion that they may have
been used as *Ex votos*, and I may now suggest whether
they might not even have been idols, and especially
whether those in the form of a volcano do not represent
Hephæstus?   This thought struck me principally from
the great resemblance between these objects and the
colossal sepulchral mounds on the Plain of Troy, which
cover the ashes of the corpses of the heroes, which were
burnt by the fire of Hephæstus.   At all events, the decorations introduced upon all of these objects—which seem
to have been executed with very great care, especially
on those made of immensely hard burnt terra-cotta—and
also the white substance with which these decorations are
filled so as to be more striking to the eye, leave no doubt
that they have served important purposes.   It was upon
one of these small articles of terra-cotta, in the form of a
top, that I found the second inscription.†   It is so admi-
rably engraved, that one is astonished to find such work
possible in terra-cotta.   As the writing runs right round
the small whorl, and is formed on both sides alike, it seems
to me, in my complete ignorance of the language, impossible to perceive with which letter it commences, or which
is the upper or lower portion of it.

* See Plate LI., No. 496.   Comp. Chapter IX., p. 138.   This is
one of the most important of the inscriptions determined to be such by
Professor Gomperz.   It has *six* characters.   (See the Appendix.)

† This is given on Plate XXII., No. 326, from the Photograph, and
more accurately from M. Burnouf's drawing on Plate XLVIII., No. 482.
Dr. Schliemann supposed that it bore an inscription ; but he afterwards
recalled the opinion. (See Chapter IX., p. 137.)—[ED.]

Upon an ordinary stone I at the same time found the character ＼ひ. I should be immensely delighted if any one were able to read these inscriptions, and thus be in a position to give an explanation about the use of these remarkable objects, about the people who made them, and about the epoch in which I found myself at the depth of from 25 to 28 feet.

When, at the time of writing my last report, I saw stone implements and weapons brought to light, and none but stone, and was forced to believe that I had penetrated into the stratum of the people belonging to the stone period, I really began to fear that the actual object of my excavations, to find here the Pergamus of Priam, had failed ; that I had already reached a period long anterior to the Trojan war, and that the colossal sepulchral mounds in the Plain of Troy were perhaps thousands of years older than the deeds of Achilles. But as I find ever more and more traces of civilization the deeper I dig, I am now perfectly convinced that I have not yet penetrated to the period of the Trojan war, and hence I am more hopeful than ever of finding the site of Troy by further excavations ; for if there ever was a Troy—and my belief in this is firm—it can only have been here, on the site of Ilium. I think that my excavations of 1868 on the heights of Bunarbashi have proved the impossibility of a city or even a village ever having stood there, except at the extreme end of Balidagh, where Consul Hahn has made excavations, but where, owing to the small space, which is limited by precipices, there can only have been a small town of 2000 inhabitants at most. Upon the site of the Ἰλιέων κώμη, which place was regarded as the site of ancient Troy by Strabo—who had never visited the Plain of Troy—in accordance with the theory of Demetrius of Scepsis, which I discussed in my report of the 26th of last month—I have, since Tuesday the 21st, employed ten workmen to lay bare a portion of the surrounding wall which seems to be indicated by a low but long rise of the ground. I do this, however, simply in the interest of science, and I am far from fancying that I shall find Troy there.

I must also add, in regard to the round articles of terra-cotta, that, after a depth of 7 meters (23 feet), those in the form of the volcano occur less frequently, and almost all are the shape of the top (*carrousel*). At this depth also, the idols of Vishnu, in the form of the Priapus, are no longer

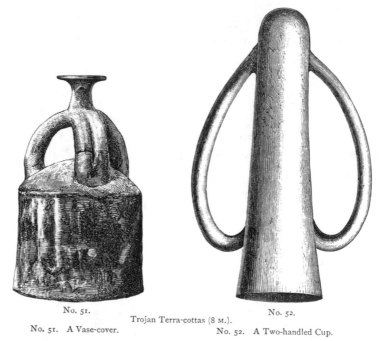

No. 51.

Trojan Terra-cottas (8 M.).

No. 52.

No. 51.   A Vase-cover.   No. 52.   A Two-handled Cup.

met with. But I still very frequently find at a depth below 23 feet the owl's head on the earthen vessels, which, although only of one colour and without any decorations, are elegant in their simplicity, and become the more elegant and finer the deeper I dig. I have to draw especial attention to the bright red cups, which are sometimes found in the form of a bell with a kind of coronet below,*

---

* These cups, as already observed, are really covers of vases, the " coronet " being the upper, instead of the under part.—[ED.]

sometimes in the shape of immense champagne-glasses
with two large handles.   In neither form can they stand
upon the lower end like the cups of the present day, but
only upon the upper part, just as we should be obliged
to set down a bell, if we used it as a drinking-cup.   I must
next mention the small pots with
three little feet, and the large ones
with a neck bent back, then the large
vessels with two handles and two
others in the form of upraised arms;
and, lastly, the very large funereal
urns, frequently more than a meter

No. 53.   Small Trojan Vase (9 M.).

(3¼ feet) in height and breadth, which are met with in such
numbers that they hinder us in our work, but which have
hitherto been so much broken that I have been unable to
save even one of them.   It is impossible to cement together

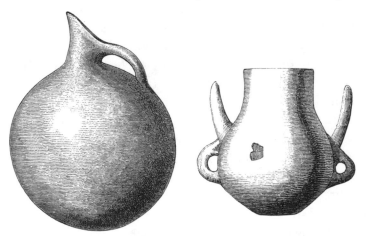

Nos. 54, 55.   Trojan Terra-cotta Vases (8 M.).

the pieces of these broken urns, as the clay is from an inch
and a half to nearly 2 inches thick.

At a depth below 6 meters (nearly 20 feet) down to
the depth of 10 meters (33 feet), we find a great many
pieces of clay an inch and a half thick, from about 4
to 5 inches in height, and from about 3 to 4 inches

in breadth, with a perforated hole, either on the broad upper side or on the narrow side, and which appear to have been used as weights; we also frequently meet with cylinders of the same clay, which are from $3\frac{1}{3}$ inches in length to $2\frac{1}{2}$ inches in breadth. The enormous quantities of stone weights and hand-mills of lava, continually brought to light, give an idea of the number of the houses, through the ruins of which I daily penetrate. I have placed great numbers of these mills and other stone implements in the niches of the walls in my excavations for the inspection of the admirers of Homer who may visit the Plain of Troy.

At a depth of from 8 to 10 meters (26 to 33 feet), I have found numerous fragments of a substance, about $2\frac{3}{4}$ inches broad and $1\frac{3}{4}$ thick, which is on the inside as hard as stone and of a resinous colour, and on the outside it has a brilliant gloss, which has evidently been produced artificially. It has clearly been poured into a mould when in a liquid state, for it is channelled on all four sides. Doubtless in the continuation of my excavations I shall obtain an explanation of how these pieces (the length of which I do not yet know, as I have hitherto only met with fragments) were made, and what they were used for.*

The numerous house-walls, the ruins of which I have daily to remove, are, at the depth of from 4 to 7 meters (13 to 23 feet), all built of ordinary unhewn stones joined with clay; and from 7 to 10 meters (23 to 33 feet) they are made of unburnt bricks, dried only in the sun. The foundations and the door-cills of these brick houses, however, consist of large stones, such as we have not met with since 2 meters ($6\frac{1}{2}$ feet) below the surface.

Lastly, as regards the inclination of the walls of my great cutting, the nature of the *débris* allowed me only in three places, each of about 49 feet in length, to make it

---

* In these the Author afterwards recognized *moulds* for casting instruments and ornaments of copper. (See Chapter IX.)—[ED.]

at an angle of 85 degrees; in all other places it is at an angle of 67½ degrees. In order to make this more clear, I may add that my walls of 33 feet high at an angle of 85 degrees deviate only about 25½ inches, but those of 67½ degrees deviate about 8½ feet from the perpendicular.

It would give me much pleasure if, in my next communication, I could report some very interesting discovery.

November 21*st.*—The heavy rainfall of yesterday and the day before, which continued till this morning, rendered it impossible to dispatch this report before the evening; for I am here living in a wilderness at eight hours' distance from the nearest post-office, that is, from the Dardanelles. I hope that the ground will have become sufficiently dry by to-morrow morning for me to proceed with my work. I intend, at all events, to continue the excavations till the appearance of winter, and then to begin again in April.

The constant warm damp weather produces a very malignant fever, and my services as a doctor are daily sought. Fortunately, I have a large stock of quinine by me, and can thus help everyone. But as I do not understand anything about medicine I should, no doubt, make great mistakes. Fortunately, however, I remember that once when I was at the point of death with a fever contracted in the marshes of Nicaragua, the excellent German physician, Tellkampf of New York, saved my life by a dose of 64 grains of quinine. Hence I give a similar quantity here, but only *in one dose* when the case is a very bad one; the quantity I generally give is four doses of 16 grains. I am also daily called upon not only to cure wounded men, but camels, donkeys, and horses. I have hitherto been successful in all cases by using tincture of arnica. I have also, thus far, cured all the fever patients who have applied for my help. Not one of them, however, has ever come to thank me; indeed, gratitude does not appear to be one of the virtues of the present Trojans.

CHAPTER V.

Interruptions from Rain — Last works of the season, 1871 — The supposed ruins of Troy reached — Great blocks of stone — Engineering
contrivances — Excavations at the " Village of the Ilians : " no traces
of habitation, and none of hot springs — Results of the excavations
thus far — Review of the objects found at various depths — Structure
of the lowest houses yet reached — Difficulties of the excavations —
The object aimed at — Growth of the Hill of Hissarlik.

On the Hill of Hissarlik, November 24th, 1871.

SINCE my last report, of the 18th and 21st instant, I have
had three days' work in spite of the continual wet weather ;
but unfortunately I find myself now compelled to cease the
excavations for the winter, intending to begin again on the
1st of April, 1872. It is not likely that winter will set in
before the middle of December, and I should gladly have
continued my work till then, in spite of the rain, especially
as I now most firmly believe that I am already among the
ruins of Troy. Since the day before yesterday, I find on
the whole extent of my excavations scarcely anything but
large stones—sometimes hewn, sometimes unhewn—and
some of them are enormous blocks. This morning, for
instance, I worked for three hours with 65 workmen in
removing a single threshold by means of ropes and rollers.

I have been obliged to abandon the two large side-
passages, when already at a depth of 23 feet, and I have
since caused all the rubbish and small stones to be brought
in baskets and wheel-barrows through the large exit-channel,
and thrown down at its end upon the sides of the steep
declivity. This channel—the walls of which have a slope
of 67½ degrees—is now, at the present depth of 33 feet,

no longer wide enough for carrying away such enormous blocks of stone, and it must first of all be made at least 13 feet wider. This is, however, a gigantic piece of work, which, owing to the daily rain, I dare not venture to begin with winter close upon me.

On account of the many huge stones, no terra-cottas were found either yesterday or on the preceding day. To day, however, during the last hour's work, I found a small pot, only about 2 inches high, with three feet; the whole of the upper portion is in the form of a globe, and is divided into five large and five small fields, changing alternately in regular succession. All of the large fields are filled with imprinted little stars. The mouth or opening is only about $\frac{1}{3}$ of an inch in diameter. I presume that this small and wonderful Trojan vessel was used by ladies for holding scented oil, which we know was applied after the bath. It cannot have been used as a lamp, for Homer, who lived 200 years after the destruction of Troy, does not as yet know of lamps. I also found this morning two copper arrow-heads, and one of those small terra-cotta "volcanoes," which for some days have been less frequently met with. Further, a small leaden plate, nearly an inch and a half in length as well as in breadth, with the character ⌐ in the centre and a hole in one corner, which leaves no doubt that the small piece used to be hung up.

Although the word γράφειν only occurs twice in Homer, and both times only signifies "to scratch into," yet I am firmly convinced that an alphabetical language was known in ancient Troy, and I cherish the hope of being able next spring to discover inscriptions and other monuments, which will leave no doubt, that, since yesterday, at the depth of 33 feet,* I have begun to uncover the ruins of the city of Troy, so long looked for theoretically and

---

* This refers to the *lowest* of the *strata*, which Dr. Schliemann long took for the ruins of the Homeric Troy.—[ED.]

now at last practically. All the objects that I find, I shall, of course, describe in the most faithful and careful manner.

My excavations at the village of the Ilians ('Ιλιέων κώμη), as was to be expected, have decidedly turned out unfavourable for Strabo and Demetrius of Scepsis; for the steep continuous elevation contains no trace of walls, and consists of coarse sand without the slightest admixture of *débris*. Neither do I believe, contrary to the assertion of the proprietor of Thymbria, my worthy friend Mr. Frederick Calvert, in the existence of a hot spring at the foot of the hill of the 'Ιλιέων κώμη, for I have now searched the whole marsh, with a thermometer in my hand, and I nowhere find, either in the stagnant or the running water, the faintest difference in temperature. Of cold springs there are certainly more than one, but it will be impossible to state how many till the marsh has been thoroughly drained; it consists at present of floating islands.

Now when I collect the result of my excavations :— I found close to the surface only, and in rare cases as far as a depth of 1 meter (3¼ feet), copper medals of Sigeum, Alexandria Troas, and Ilium—the latter belonging to the first centuries before and after Christ; then small solid round articles of terra-cotta, like lamps, with two holes, which occur in great numbers, as far as a depth of 2 meters (6½ feet). These, however, have no ornaments except the potter's stamp, in which there is sometimes an altar with a bee or fly above it, sometimes a child with its hands stretched forth, sometimes two horses, sometimes a bull or a swan. Below this depth they cease all at once.* In place of them I found, at depths of from 2 to 10 meters (6½ to 33 feet), the often described terra-cottas in the form of small volcanoes, humming-tops or whorls, which, at a depth

---

* A few, however, were afterwards found in lower strata, at 6 and even 8 meters. (See p. 295.)—[ED.]

of 3 meters only (nearly 10 feet), were frequently met with in blue stone, but were in all other cases of terra-cotta, and almost all of them with decorations.   At 6½ feet below the surface I found a Roman well, which I dug out to a depth of more than 36 feet, but which seems to be sunk down as far as the Plain.   At all depths we met with many mussel-shells, boars' tusks, and fish-bones; but the bones of sharks only at the depth of from 11 to 13 feet below the surface.   The ruins of houses built of hewn stone, joined with cement or lime, seldom extend lower than 3¼ feet, and the ruins of buildings built of large hewn stones not joined by any kind of cement, never below 6½ feet: visitors to the Plain of Troy can convince themselves of this with their own eyes, by looking at the walls of my cuttings. From a depth of 3 to 4 meters (6½ to 13 feet) downwards, we met with few or no stones; and the calcined ruins of innumerable layers of *débris* seem to prove that all of the buildings which existed there during the course of centuries were built of wood, and were destroyed by fire.   Consequently in these depths I have hitherto only found fragments of good earthenware; the only things brought out in an uninjured condition were small pots of the coarsest description.

At a depth of 4 meters (13 feet), I found a fragment of pottery with a drawing of a bust, of Phœnician workmanship.   Directly upon it were an immense quantity of stone implements and weapons of hard black stone, which continued to a depth of 7 meters (23 feet). Simultaneously with these, but extending to a depth of 10 meters (33 feet), I found elegant pottery of one colour and without any kind of ornament beyond the owl's face; small pots and vases of a larger size with three little feet; then, but only as far as a depth of 23 feet, the Priapus of terra-cotta in its natural form, and also in the form of a pillar rounded off at the top.   From 4 to 7 meters (13 to 23 feet) deep, there were a great many flint knives, the majority of which have the shape of saws, or consist only of sharp pieces, rarely in the form of blades; needles and little spoons made of bone, as well as an enormous number of terra-cotta discs with a hole through the centre; and two copper nails.　As is proved by the numerous

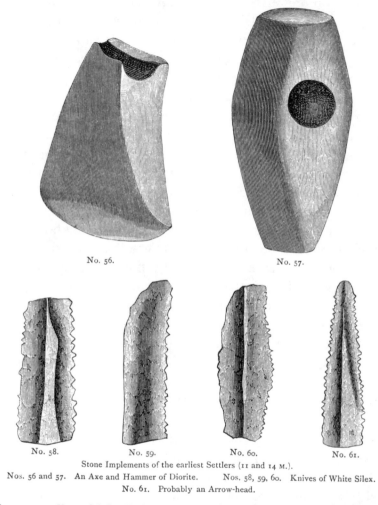

No. 56.　　　　　　　　　　No. 57.

No. 58.　　　No. 59.　　　No. 60.　　　　　　No. 61.

Stone Implements of the earliest Settlers (11 and 14 m.).

Nos. 56 and 57.　An Axe and Hammer of Diorite.　　Nos. 58, 59, 60.　Knives of White Silex.
No. 61.　Probably an Arrow-head.

house-walls which I have cut through in these depths, many of which are in the earth-wall of my excavations, the houses were built of small stones joined with earth.　From 7 to 10 meters (23 to 33 feet), I found a great many copper nails, frequently 5 inches in length, and a few lances and

battle-axes of elegant workmanship.   At every foot of earth
that we dig down, after a depth of 23 feet, we find the traces
of a much higher civilization ; stone weapons are still occasionally met with, but they are of splendid workmanship.
I found many copper knives, but also immense numbers
of flint knives, which, however, are incomparably better
made than those of the preceding strata.   We also found,
although not often, very sharp double-edged knife-blades of
obsidian, 2¾ inches in length.   The pots and vases continue

No. 62.   Small Trojan Vase of Terra-cotta, with   No. 63.   A Trojan Vase-cover of red Terra-
             Decorations (8 M.).   cotta (7 M.).

to be more elegant ; there were also bright red vase-covers in
the form of a bell with a coronet above, or like gigantic
champagne glasses with two large handles; very many
elegant vessels with or without three little feet, but with
little rings on the sides and holes in the mouth in the same
direction, so that they could not only stand, but also be
carried on a cord; likewise a number of very small vases
with three little feet.   All the terra-cottas are of a brilliant
red, yellow, green, or black colour; only the very large
urns are colourless.   From 2 to 10 meters deep (6½–33
feet) we note the complete absence of painting.   At a depth

of 7½ meters (24¾ feet) was a small terra-cotta disc with five letters, which I consider to be Phœnician; at 28 feet one of those frequently mentioned terra-cottas in the form of a top with six written characters. At the same depth, upon a stone, one letter, which to all appearance belongs to a different language; and lastly, at a depth of 10 meters, or 33 English feet, a leaden plate with one letter.

Now as regards the construction of the houses belonging to the strata at a depth of from 7 to 10 meters (23 to 33 feet), only the foundations and thresholds were composed of large stones—as anyone may convince himself by a glance at the earthen walls of my excavations. The house-walls, on the other hand, were composed of unburnt sun-dried bricks. At a depth of 10 meters (33 feet), I again found the buildings to be of stone, but of colossal proportions. Most of the stones are very large, many of them hewn, and we meet with a great many massive blocks. It appears to me that I have already brought to light several walls at this depth; but I have unfortunately not yet succeeded in arriving at an opinion as to how they were actually built and what their thickness was. The stones of the walls seem to me to have been separated from one another by a violent earthquake. I have hitherto seen no trace of any kind of cement between them, either of clay or lime.

Of the terrible difficulties of the excavations, where such large pieces of stone are met with, only those can have any idea who have been present at the work and have seen how much time and trouble it takes, especially during the present rainy weather—first to get out the small stones round one of the many immense blocks, then to dig out the block itself, to get the lever under it, to heave it up and roll it through the mud of the channel to the steep declivity.

But these difficulties only increase my desire, after so many disappointments, to reach the great goal which is at last lying before me, to prove that the Iliad is founded on facts, and that the great Greek nation must not be deprived of this crown of her glory. I shall spare no trouble and shun no expense to attain this result.

I must still draw attention to the remarkable growth of this hill. The huge square stones of the foundations of the house on the summit of the hill (where I found the inscription which appears to belong to the third century B.C.), which in its day must have been on the surface, are now in some places only 13 inches, in others only 3¼ feet below the earth. But as the colossal ruins, which I positively maintain to be those of ancient Troy, lie at a depth of 33 feet, the accumulation of *débris* on this part must have amounted to more than 30 feet during the first 1000 years, and only from 1 to 3 feet during the last 2000 years.

But, strange to say, on the north side of the hill, with its steep declivity, at the place where I am digging, the thickness of the hill has not increased in the slightest degree. For not only do the ruins of the innumerable habitations in all cases extend to the extreme edge of the declivity, but I also find up to this point the same objects that I find on the same horizontal line as far as the opposite end of my excavations. Hence it is interesting to know that the declivity of the hill on the north side was exactly as steep at the time of the Trojan war as it is now, namely, that even at that time it rose at an angle of 40 degrees.

No. 64. A stone Implement of unknown
use. Weight 472 grammes. (2 M.)

No. 65. A strange Vessel of Terra-cotta
(15 M.).

WORK AT HISSARLIK IN 1872.

CHAPTER VI.

New assistants for 1872 — Cost of the excavations — Digging of the great platform on the North — Venomous snakes — A supporting buttress on the North side of the hill — Objects discovered : little idols of fine marble—Whorls engraved with the *suastika* and — Significance of these emblems in the old Aryan religion — Their occurrence among other Aryan nations — Mentioned in old Indian literature — Illustrative quotation from Émile Burnouf.

On the Hill of Hissarlik, April 5th, 1872.

My last report was dated November 24th, 1871. On the first of this month, at 6 o'clock on the morning of a glorious day, accompanied by my wife, I resumed the excavations with 100 Greek workmen from the neighbouring villages of Renkoï, Kalifatli, and Yenishehr. Mr. John Latham, of Folkestone, the director of the railway from the Piræus to Athens, who by his excellent management brings the shareholders an annual dividend of 30 per cent., had the kindness to give me two of his best workmen, Theodorus Makrys of Mitylene, and Spiridion Demetrios of Athens, as foremen. To each of them I pay 150 fr. (6*l*.) per month, while the daily wages of the other men are but 1 fr. 80 cent. Nikolaos Zaphyros, of Renkoï, gets 6 fr., as formerly; he is of great use to me on account of his local knowledge, and serves me at once as cashier, attendant, and cook. Mr. Piat, who has undertaken the construction of the railroad from the Piræus to Lanira, has also had the kindness to let me have his engineer, Adolphe Laurent, for a month, whom I shall have to pay 500 fr. (20*l*.), and his travelling expenses. But in addition

there are other considerable expenses to be defrayed, so
that the total cost of my excavations amounts to no less
than 300 fr. (12*l.*) daily.

Now in order to be sure, in every case, of thoroughly
solving the Trojan question this year, I am having an
immense horizontal platform made on the steep northern
slope, which rises at an angle of 40 degrees, a height
of 105 feet perpendicular, and 131 feet above the level
of the sea.   The platform extends through the entire hill,
at an exact perpendicular depth of 14 meters or 46½
English feet, it has a breadth of 79 meters or 233 English feet, and embraces my last year's cutting.*   M. Laurent
calculates the mass of matter to be removed at 78,545
cubic meters (above 100,000 cubic yards): it will be less
if I should find the native soil at less than 46 feet, and
greater if I should have to make the platform still lower.
It is above all things necessary for me to reach the primary
soil, in order to make accurate investigations.   To make
the work easier, after having had the earth on the
northern declivity picked down in such a manner
that it rises perpendicularly to the height of about
8½ feet from the bottom, and after that at an angle of
50 degrees, I continue to have the *débris* of the mighty
earth wall loosened in such a manner that this angle always
remains exactly the same.   In this way I certainly work
three times more rapidly than before, when, on account of
the small breadth of the channel, I was forced to open it
on the summit of the hill in a direct horizontal direction
along its entire length.   In spite of every precaution, however, I am unable to guard my men or myself against the
stones which continually come rolling down, when the
steep wall is being picked away.   Not one of us is without
several wounds in his feet.

During the first three days of the excavations, in

* See the Frontispiece and Plan II.

digging down the slope of the hill, we came upon an immense number of poisonous snakes, and among them a remarkable quantity of the small brown vipers called *antelion* (Ἀντήλιον), which are scarcely thicker than rain worms, and which have their name from the circumstance that the person bitten by them only survives till sunset. It seems to me that, were it not for the many thousands of storks which destroy the snakes in spring and summer, the Plain of Troy would be uninhabitable, owing to the excessive numbers of these vermin.

Through the kindness of my friends, Messrs. J. Henry Schröder and Co., in London, I have obtained the best English pickaxes and spades for loosening and pulling down the rubbish, also 60 excellent wheel-barrows with iron wheels for carrying it away.

For the purpose of consolidating the buildings on the top of the hill, the whole of the steep northern slope has evidently been supported by a buttress, for I find the remains of one in several places. This buttress is however not very ancient, for it is composed of large blocks of shelly limestone, mostly hewn, and joined with lime or cement. The remains of this wall have only a slight covering of earth; but on all other places there is more or less soil, which, at the eastern end of the platform, extends to a depth of between 6½ and 10 feet. Behind the platform, as well as behind the remains of the buttress, the *débris* is as hard as stone, and consists of the ruins of houses, among which I find axes of diorite, sling-bullets of loadstone, a number of flint knives, innumerable handmills of lava, a great number of small idols of very fine marble, with or without the owl's-head and woman's girdle, weights of clay in the form of pyramids and with a hole at the point, or made of stone and in the form of balls; lastly, a great many of those small terra-cotta whorls, which have already been so frequently spoken of in my previous reports. Two pieces of this kind, with crosses on the under side, were found in the terramares of Castione and Campeggine,* and are now in the Museum of Parma. Many of these Trojan articles, and especially those in the form of volcanoes, have crosses of the most various descriptions, as may be seen in the lithographed

Nos. 66, 67, 68.   Trojan Sling-bullets of Loadstone (9 and 10 M.).

drawings.† The form ⊞ occurs especially often; upon a great many we find the sign 卐, of which there are often whole rows in a circle round the central point. In my earlier reports I never spoke of these crosses, because their meaning was utterly unknown to me.

This winter, I have read in Athens many excellent works of celebrated scholars on Indian antiquities, especially Adalbert Kuhn, *Die Herabkunft des Feuers;* Max Müller's *Essays;* Émile Burnouf, *La Science des Religions* and *Essai sur le Vêda,* as well as several works by Eugène Burnouf; and I now perceive that these crosses upon the Trojan terra-cottas are of the highest importance to archæology. I therefore consider it necessary to enter more fully into the subject, all the more so as I am now able to prove that both the ⊞ and the 卐 , which I find in Émile Burnouf's Sanscrit lexicon, under the name of "suastika," and with the meaning εὖ ἐστι, or as the sign of good wishes, were already regarded, thousands of years before

---

* Gabriel de Mortillet, *Le Signe de la Croix avant le Christianisme.*
† Plates XXI. to LII. at the end of the volume.

Christ, as religious symbols of the very greatest importance among the early progenitors of the Aryan races in Bactria and in the villages of the Oxus, at a time when Germans, Indians, Pelasgians, Celts, Persians, Slavonians and Iranians still formed one nation and spoke one language.   For I recognise at the first glance the "suastika" upon one of those three pot bottoms,* which were discovered on Bishop's Island near Königswalde on the right bank of the Oder, and have given rise to very many learned discussions, while no one recognised the mark as that exceedingly significant religious symbol of our remote ancestors.   I find a whole row of these "suastikas" all round the famous pulpit of Saint Ambrose in Milan; I find it occurring a thousand times in the catacombs of Rome.†   I find it in three rows, and thus repeated sixty times, upon an ancient Celtic funereal urn discovered in Shropham in the county of Norfolk, and now in the British Museum.‡   I find it also upon several Corinthian vases in my own collection, as well as upon two very ancient Attic vases in the possession of Professor Kusopulos at Athens, which are assigned to a date as early, at least, as 1000 years before Christ.   I likewise find it upon several ancient coins of Leucas, and in the large mosaic in the royal palace garden in Athens.   An English clergyman, the Rev. W. Brown Keer, who visited me here, assures me that he has seen the ⊓⅃ innumerable times in the most ancient Hindu temples, and especially in those of Gaïna.§   I find in the *Ramayana* that the ships of king

---

* Copied in the *Zeitschrift für Ethnologie, Organ der Berliner Gesellschaft für Anthropologie und Urgeschichte*, 1871, *Heft III*.

† Émile Burnouf, *La Science des Religions*.

‡ A. W. Franks, *Horæ ferales*, pl. 30, fig. 19.

§ The cut, for which we are indebted to Mr. Fergusson, represents the foot-print of Buddha, as carved on the Amraverti Tope, near the river Kistna.   Besides the *suastika*, repeated again and again on the heels, the cushions, and the toes, it bears the emblem of the *mystic rose*,

Rama—in which he carried his troops across the Ganges on his expedition of conquest to India and Ceylon—bore the ⊐⊔ on their prows.   Sanscrit scholars believe that this heroic epic (the *Rama-yana*) was composed at the latest 800 years before Christ, and they assign the campaign of Rama at the latest to the thirteenth or fourteenth century B.C., for, as Kiepert points out in his very interesting article in the *National ⸗ Zeitung*, the names of the products mentioned in the 2nd Book of Kings, in the

No. 69.   The Foot-print of Buddha.

reign of King Solomon, as brought by Phœnician ships from Ophir, as for example, ivory, peacocks, apes and spices, are Sanscrit words with scarcely any alteration. Hence we may surely regard it as certain, that it took at least three or four centuries before the language of the conquerors was generally introduced into the immensely large and densely peopled country of India, especially as the number of the conquerors cannot have been very large. In the myths of the Rigvêda, which were written before the expedition into Northern India (*Heptopotamia*), the Aryan population is always represented as inconsiderable in numbers.

Émile Burnouf, in his excellent work *La Science des Religions*, just published, says, "The ⊐⊔ represents the two pieces of wood which were laid cross-wise upon one

---

likewise frequently repeated (comp. the lithographed whorls, Nos. 330, 339, &c.), and the central circles show a close resemblance to some of the Trojan whorls.—[ED.]

another before the sacrificial altars in order to produce the holy fire (*Agni*), and whose ends were bent round at right angles and fastened by means of four nails, 卍, so that this wooden scaffolding might not be moved. At the point where the two pieces of wood were joined, there was a small hole, in which a third piece of wood, in the form of a lance (called *Pramantha*) was rotated by means of a cord made of cow's hair and hemp, till the fire was generated by friction. The father of the holy fire (*Agni*) is Twastri, *i. e.* the divine carpenter, who made the 卍 and the Pramantha, by the friction of which the divine child was produced. The Pramantha was afterwards transformed by the Greeks into Prometheus, who, they imagined, stole fire from heaven, so as to instil into earth-born man the bright spark of the soul. The mother of the holy fire is the divine Mâjâ, who represents the productive force in the form of a woman; every divine being has his Mâjâ. Scarcely has the weak spark escaped from its mother's lap, that is from the 卍, which is likewise called mother, and is the place where the divine Mâjâ principally dwells—when it (Agni) receives the name of child. In the Rigvêda we find hymns of heavenly beauty in praise of this new-born weak divine creature. The little child is laid upon straw; beside it is the mystic cow, that is, the milk and butter destined as the offering; before it is the holy priest of the divine Vâju, who waves the small oriental fan in the form of a flag, so as to kindle life in the little child, which is close upon expiring. Then the little child is placed upon the altar, where, through the holy "sôma" (the juice of the tree of life) poured over it, and through the purified butter, it receives a mysterious power, surpassing all comprehension of the worshippers. The child's glory shines upon all around it; angels (*dêvâs*) and men shout for joy, sing hymns in its praise, and throw themselves on their faces before it. On its left is the rising sun, on its right the full moon on the horizon, and both appear to grow

pale in the glory of the new-born god (Agni) and to worship
him.   But how did this transfiguration of Agni take place?
At the moment when one priest laid the young god upon
the altar, another poured the holy draught, the spiritual
"sôma" upon its head, and then immediately anointed it
by spreading over it the butter of the holy sacrifice.   By
being thus anointed Agni receives the name of the Anointed
(*akta*);   he has, however, grown enormously through the
combustible substances;   rich in glory he sends forth his
blazing flames;   he shines in a cloud of smoke which rises
to heaven like a pillar, and his light unites with the light
of the heavenly orbs.   The god Agni, in his splendour
and glory, reveals to man the secret things;   he teaches the
Doctors;   he is the Master of the masters, and receives the
name of Jâtavêdas, that is, he in whom wisdom is in-born.

Upon my writing to M. É. Burnouf to enquire about
the other symbol, the cross in the form ⊞, which occurs hundreds of times upon the Trojan terra-cottas,
he replied, that he knows with certainty from the
ancient scholiasts on the Rigvêda, from comparative phi-
lology, and from the *Monuments figurés*, that *Suastikas*, in
this form also, were employed in the very remotest times for
producing the holy fire.   He adds that the Greeks for a
long time generated fire by friction, and that the two lower
pieces of wood that lay at right angles across one another
were called "στανρός," which word is either derived from
the root "stri," which signifies lying upon the earth, and is
then identical with the Latin "sternere," or it is derived
from the Sanscrit word "stâvara," which means firm, solid,
immovable.   Since the Greeks had other means of producing fire, the word στανρός passed into simply in the
sense of "cross."

Other passages might be quoted from Indian scholars to
prove that from the very remotest times the 卐 and the
⊞ were the most sacred symbols of our Aryan forefathers.

In my present excavations I shall probably find a
definite explanation as to the purpose for which the
articles ornamented with such significant symbols were
used; till then I shall maintain my former opinion, that
they either served as *Ex votos* or as actual idols of
Hephæstus.

No. 70.   Large Terra-cotta Vase, with the Symbols of the Ilian Goddess (4 M.).

CHAPTER VII.

Smoking at work forbidden, and a mutiny suppressed — Progress of the
  great platform — Traces of sacrifices — Colossal blocks of stone
  belonging to great buildings — Funereal and other huge urns —
  Supposed traces of Assyrian art — Ancient undisturbed remains —
  Further discoveries of stone implements and owl-faced idols —
  Meaning of the epithet " γλαυκῶπις "—Parallel of Ἥρα βοῶπις, and
  expected discovery of ox-headed idols at Mycenæ — Vases of remarkable forms — Dangers and engineering expedients — Georgios
  Photidas — Extent of the Pergamus of Troy — Poisonous snakes,
  and the snake-weed — The whorls with the central sun, stars, the
  suastika, the *Sôma*, or Tree of Life, and sacrificial altars — The name
  of Mount Ida, probably brought from Bactria.

On the Hill of Hissarlik, April 25th, 1872.

SINCE my report of the 5th of this month I have continued
the excavations most industriously with an average of 120
workmen.   Unfortunately, however, seven of these twenty
days were lost through rainy weather and festivals, one day
also by a mutiny among my men.   I had observed that the
smoking of cigarettes interrupted the work, and I therefore
forbad smoking during working hours, but I did not gain
my point immediately, for I found that the men smoked in
secret.   I was, however, determined to carry my point, and
caused it to be proclaimed that transgressors would be
forthwith dismissed and never taken on again.   Enraged at
this, the workmen from the village of Renkoï—about 70
in number—declared that they would not work, if everyone were not allowed to smoke as much as he pleased;
they left the platform, and deterred the men from the
other villages from working by throwing stones.   The
good people had imagined that I would give in to them
at once, as I could not do without them, and that

now I could not obtain workmen enough; that moreover during the beautiful weather it was not likely that
I would sit still a whole day. But they found themselves mistaken, for I immediately sent my foreman to the
other neighbouring villages and succeeded (to the horror
of the 70 Renkoïts, who had waited the whole night at my
door) in collecting 120 workmen for the next morning
without requiring their services. My energetic measures
have at last completely humbled the Renkoïts, from whose
impudence I had very much to put up with during my last
year's excavations, and have also had a beneficial effect upon
all of my present men. Since the mutiny I have not only
been able to prohibit smoking, but even to lengthen the
day's work by one hour; for, instead of working as formerly
from half-past five in the morning to half-past five in the
evening, I now always commence at five and continue till
six in the evening. But, as before, I allow half an hour at
nine and an hour and a half in the afternoon for eating
and smoking.

According to an exact calculation of the engineer,
M. A. Laurent, in the seventeen days since the 1st of the
month I have removed about 8500 cubic meters (11,000
cubic yards) of *débris*; this is about 666 cubic yards each
day, and somewhat above $5\frac{1}{3}$ cubic yards each workman.

We have already advanced the platform 49 feet into
the hill, but to my extreme surprise I have not yet reached
the primary soil. The opinion I expressed in my report
of the 24th of November of last year, that the thickness of the hill on the north side had not increased
since the remotest times, I find confirmed as regards the
whole western end of my platform, to a breadth of 45
meters ($147\frac{1}{2}$ feet); for it is only upon the eastern portion
of it, to a breadth of 82 feet, that I found $6\frac{1}{2}$ and even
10 feet of soil; below and behind it, as far as $16\frac{1}{2}$ feet
above the platform, there is *débris* as hard as stone, which
appears to consist only of ashes of wood and animals,

the remains of the offerings presented to the Ilian Athena. I therefore feel perfectly convinced that by penetrating further into this part I shall come upon the site of the very ancient temple of the goddess. The ashes of this stratum have such a clayey appearance, that I should believe it to be the pure earth, were it not that I find it frequently to contain bones, charcoal, and small shells, occasionally also small pieces of brick. The shells are uninjured, which sufficiently proves that they cannot have been exposed to heat. In this very hard stratum of ash, at 11 feet above the platform, and 46 feet from its edge, I found a channel made of green sandstone nearly 8 inches broad and above 7 inches high, which probably once served for carrying away the blood of the animals sacrificed, and must necessarily at one time have discharged its contents down the declivity of the hill. It therefore proves that the thickness of the hill at this point has increased fully 46 feet since the destruction of the temple to which it belonged.

Upon the other 147½ feet of the platform I find everywhere, as far as to about 16½ feet high, colossal masses of large blocks of shelly limestone, often more or less hewn, but generally unhewn, which frequently lie so close one upon another that they have the appearance of actual walls. But I soon found that all of these masses of stone must of necessity belong to grand buildings which once have stood there and were destroyed by a fearful catastrophe. The buildings cannot possibly have been built of these stones without some uniting substance, and I presume that this was done with mere earth, for I find no trace of lime or cement. Between the immense masses of stone there are intermediate spaces, more or less large, consisting of very firm *débris*, often as hard as stone, in which we meet with very many bones, shells, and quantities of other remains of habitation. No traces of any kind of interesting articles were found in the whole length of the wall of *débris*, 229½ feet in length and 16¼ feet in height, except a small splendidly worked hair- or dress-pin of silver, but destroyed by rust.   To-

day, however, at a perpendicular depth of 14 meters (46 feet) I found a beautiful polished piece of mica-schist, with moulds for casting two breast-pins, and two other ornaments which are quite unknown to me—all of the most fanciful description.   I also found a funereal or water urn, unfortunately completely broken, with decorations in the form of two flat wreaths which run right round it.   The

No. 71.   A Mould of Mica-schist for casting Ornaments (14 M.).

urn must have been 5 feet high, and at least 27½ inches in breadth.   In both of the wreaths there is an uninterrupted

No. 72.   Fragment of a large Urn of Terra-cotta with Assyrian (?) Decorations, from the Lowest Stratum (14 M.).

row of cuneiform impressions, which at first sight seem to be Assyrian inscriptions; but on closer examination it is found that they are mere ornaments.   The fragments of this vase

show a thickness of about ¾ of an inch. Two other enormous urns, but completely broken, either for water, wine,
or funereal ashes, with decorations in the form of several
wreaths, forming perfect circles, were found on the 22nd
and 23rd of this month, at from 19½ to 23 feet above the
platform, and therefore, at a perpendicular depth of from
26 to 33 feet. Both must have been more than 6½ feet
high, and more than 3¼ feet in diameter, for the fragments
show a thickness of nearly 2 inches. The wreaths are
likewise in bas-relief, and show either double triangles fitting
into one another with circles, or flowers, or three rows or
sometimes one row of circles. The last decoration was also
found upon the frieze of green stone which Lord Elgin
discovered in the year 1810 in the treasury of Agamemnon
in Mycenæ, and which is now in the British Museum.
Both this frieze, and the above-mentioned urns discovered
by me in the depths of Ilium, distinctly point to Assyrian
art, and I cannot look at them without a feeling of sadness
when I think with what tears of joy and with what delight
the ever-memorable German scholar, Julius Braun, who
unfortunately succumbed three years ago to his excessive
exertions, would have welcomed their discovery; for he
was not only the great advocate of the theory that the
Homeric Troy must be only looked for below the ruins of
Ilium, but he was also the able defender of the doctrine,
that the plastic arts and a portion of the Egyptian and
Assyrian mythology had migrated to Asia Minor and
Greece, and he has shown this by thousands of irrefutable
proofs in his profound and excellent work, *Geschichte der
Kunst in ihrem Entwickelungsgange*, which I most urgently
recommend to all who are interested in art and archæology.

Both the urns found at a depth of 46 feet and those
at from 26 to 33 feet, as well as all the funereal urns and
large wine or water vessels which I formerly discovered, were
standing upright, which sufficiently proves that the colossal
masses of *débris* and ruins were gradually formed on the

spot, and could not have been brought there from another
place in order to increase the height of the hill. This is,
moreover, a pure impossibility in regard to the immense
numbers of gigantic blocks of stone, hewn and unhewn,
which frequently weigh from 1 to 2 tons.

In the strata at a depth of from 7 to 10 meters (23 to
33 feet), I found two lumps of lead of a round and con-
cave form, each weighing about two pounds; a great
number of rusted copper nails, also some knives and a
copper lance; further very many smaller and larger knives
of white and brown silex in the form of single and double-
edged saws; a number of whet-stones of green and black
slate with a hole at one end, as well as various small objects
of ivory.* In all the strata from 4 to 10 meters (13 to 33
feet) deep I found a number of hammers, axes and wedges
of diorite, which, however, are decidedly of much better
workmanship in the strata below the depth of 7 meters
(23 feet) than in the upper ones. Likewise at all depths
from 3 meters (10 feet) below the surface we find a number
of flat idols of very fine marble; upon many of them is
the owl's face and a female girdle with dots; upon one
there are in addition two female breasts.† The striking
resemblance of these owls' faces to those upon many of
the vases and covers, with a kind of helmet on the owl's
head, makes me firmly convinced that all of the idols, and
all of the helmeted owls' heads represent a goddess, and
indeed must represent one and the same goddess, all the
more so as, in fact, all the owl-faced vases with female
breasts and a navel have also generally two upraised arms:
in one case the navel is represented by a cross with four
nails.‡ The cups (covers) with owls' heads, on the other

---

* See an illustration to Chapter X. for similar ivories, still more
interesting, from their greater depth, than those mentioned in the text,
which are very imperfectly shown on the original photograph.

† See the Plate of Idols, p. 36.   ‡ See Cut, No. 13, p. 35.

hand, never have breasts or a navel, yet upon some of them I find long female hair represented at the back.*

The important question now presents itself:—*What goddess is it who is here found so repeatedly, and is, moreover, the only one to be found, upon the idols, drinking-cups and vases?* The answer is :—She must necessarily be *the tutelary goddess of Troy*, she must be *the Ilian Athena*, and this indeed perfectly agrees with the statement of Homer, who continually calls her θέα γλαυκῶπις Ἀθήνη, " the goddess Athena with the owl's face." For the epithet " γλαυκῶπις " has been wrongly trànslated by the scholars of all ages, because they could not imagine that Athena should have been represented with an owl's face. The epithet, however, consists of the two words γλαῦξ and ὠπή, and, as I can show by an immense number of proofs, the only possible literal translation is " with an owl's face "; and the usual translation " with blue, fiery or sparkling eyes " is utterly wrong. The natural conclusion is that owing to progressive civilization Athena received a human face, and her former owl's head was transformed into her favourite bird, the owl, which as such is unknown to Homer. The next conclusion is that the worship of Athena as the tutelary goddess of Troy was well known to Homer ; hence that a Troy existed, and that it was situated on the sacred spot, the depths of which I am investigating.

In like manner, when excavations shall be made in the Heræum between Argos and Mycenæ, and on the site of the very ancient temple of Hera on the island of Samos, the image of this goddess with a cow's head will doubtless be found upon idols, cups and vases; for " βοῶπις," the usual epithet of Hera in Homer, can originally have

---

* Dr. Schliemann is here speaking of the "cups" which he afterwards decided to be *covers*, which of course represent only the *head*, the *body* being on the vase.—[ED.]

signified nothing else than "with the face of an ox." But as Homer also sometimes applies the epithet βοῶπις to mortal women, it is probable that even at his time it was considered to be bad taste to represent Hera, the wife of the mightiest of all the gods, with the face of an ox, and that therefore men even at that time began to represent her with a woman's face, but with the eyes of an ox, that is, with very large eyes; consequently the common epithet of βοῶπις, which had formerly been only applied to Hera with the meaning of "with the face of an ox," now merely signified with large eyes.

Of pottery we have found a great deal during the last weeks, but unfortunately more than half of it in a broken condition. Of painting upon terra-cotta there is still no trace; most of the vessels are of a simple brilliant black, yellow, or brown colour; the very large vases on the other hand are generally colourless. Plates of ordinary manufacture I have as yet found only at a depth of from 8 to 10 meters (26 to 33 feet), and, as can be distinctly seen, they have been turned upon a potter's wheel. All the other vessels hitherto found seem, however, to have been formed by the hand alone; yet they possess a certain elegance, and excite the admiration of beholders by their strange and very curious forms. The vases with a long neck bent back, a beak-shaped mouth turned upwards, and a round protruding body *—two of which are in the British

No. 73.   Trojan Plates found on the Tower (8 M.).

---

* See Cut, No. 54, p. 86.

Museum, several of those found in Cyprus in the Museum in Constantinople, and several of those discovered beneath three layers of volcanic ashes in Thera and Therassia in the French school in Athens—are almost certainly intended to represent women, for I find the same here at a depth of from 26 to 33 feet, with two or even with three breasts, and hence I believe that those found here represent the tutelary goddess of Ilium. We also find some vases and covers with men's faces, which, however, are never without some indications of the owl; moreover, the vases with such faces always have two female breasts and a navel. I must draw especial attention to the fact that almost all of the vases with owls' faces, or with human faces and the indications of the owl, have two uplifted arms, which serve as handles, and this leads me to conjecture that they are imitations of the large idol which was placed in the very ancient temple of the Ilian divinity, which therefore must have had an

No. 74. Vase Cover with a human face. From the Trojan Stratum (8 M.).

owl's face, but a female figure, and two arms beside the head. It is very remarkable that most of the vessels which I find have been suspended by cords, as is proved by the two holes in the mouth, and the two little tubes, or holes in the handles, at the side of the vessels.

Unfortunately, many of the terra-cottas get broken when the *débris* is being loosened and falls down, for there is only one way in which I can save my men and myself from being crushed and maimed by the falling stones: this is, by keeping the lowest part of the mighty earthen wall on the perpendicular up to 16 feet (not 7 feet, as on the first five days), and the whole of the upper part at an angle of 50 degrees, by always loosening the perpendicular portion, by making shafts, and working with large iron levers in pieces of from 15 to 30 cubic metres (20 to 40 cubic yards). By thus causing the *débris* and the stones of the upper portion to be loosened with the pickaxe, the stones fall in almost a direct line over the lower perpendicular wall of 16 feet; therefore they roll at most a few paces, and there is less danger that anyone will be hurt. By this means I also have the advantage that the greatest portion of the *débris* falls down of its own accord, and what remains can be shovelled down with little trouble, whereas at first I spent half of my time in getting it down. As, however, in making shafts and in bringing down the colossal lumps of earth a certain amount of skill and caution is necessary, I have engaged a third foreman at 7 francs a day, Georgios Photidos, of Paxos, who has for seven years worked as a miner in Australia, and was there occupied principally in making tunnels. Home-sickness led him back to his native country, where, without having sufficient means of earning his daily bread, he, in youthful thoughtlessness and out of patriotism, married a poor girl of his own people who was but fifteen years old. It was only after his marriage, and in consequence of domestic cares, that he recovered his senses. He heard that I was making excavations here, and came on speculation to offer me his services. As he had assured me, when I first saw him, that my accepting his services was a question of life and death to him and his wife, I engaged him at once, the more so because I was very much in want of a miner, tunnel-maker, and pitman, such as he is. Besides acting in these capacities, he is of great use to me on Sundays and on other festivals, for he can write Greek, and he is thus able to copy my Greek reports for the newspapers and learned societies in the East; for I had hitherto found nothing more intolerable than to have to write out in Greek three times over my long reports about one and the same subject, especially as I had to take the time from my sleep. To my great regret, the excellent engineer Adolphe Laurent leaves me to-morrow, for his month is up, and he has now

to commence the construction of the railroad from the
Piræus to Lamia.   He has, however, made me a good
plan of this hill.   I must add that the Pergamus of
Priam cannot have been limited to this hill, which is,
for the most part, artificial; but that, as I endeavoured
to explain four years ago,* it must necessarily have extended a good way further south, beyond the high plateau.
But even if the Pergamus should have been confined
to this hill, it was, nevertheless, larger than the Acropolis
of Athens; for the latter covers only 50,126 square
meters (about 60,000 square yards), whereas the plateau
of this hill amounts to 64,500 square meters (about 77,400
square yards).   I must further mention that, according to
Laurent's calculation, the plateau rises 46 feet above my
platform, and that his measurements of its height (about
38 feet on the north and 39 feet on the south) applies to
those points where the steep precipice commences.   I have
just built a house with three rooms, as well as a magazine
and kitchen, which altogether cost only 1000 francs (40*l*.),
including the covering of waterproof felt; for wood is
cheap here, and a plank of about 10 feet in length, 10
inches in breadth, and 1 inch thick, may be got for 2 piasters,
or 40 centimes.   (*These houses are seen in Plates X. and
XI.*)

We still find poisonous snakes among the stones as far
down as from 33 to 36 feet, and I had hitherto been
astonished to see my workmen take hold of the reptiles
with their hands and play with them; nay, yesterday I saw
one of the men bitten twice by a viper, without seeming
to trouble himself about it.   When I expressed my horror,
he laughed, and said that he and all his comrades knew
that there were a great many snakes in this hill, and they
had therefore all drunk a decoction of the snake-weed which

---

* *Ithaque, le Péloponnèse et Troie.*   Dr. Schliemann's subsequent
change of opinion on this point is explained in subsequent chapters,
and in the Introduction.

grows in the district, and which renders the bite harmless. Of course I ordered a decoction to be brought to me, so that I also may be safe from their bites. I should, however, like to know whether this decoction would be a safeguard against the fatal effects of the bite of the hooded cobra, of which in India I have seen a man die within half an hour; if it were so, it would be a good speculation to cultivate snake-weed in India.

The frequently-discussed terra-cottas in the form of the volcano and top (*carrousel*) are continually found in immense numbers, as far as a depth of from 33 to 36 feet, and most of them have decorations, of which I always make an accurate drawing.* On comparing these drawings, I now find that all, without exception, represent the sun in the centre, and that almost the half of the other carvings show either only simple rays or rays with stars between, or round the edge; or again, three, four, six, or eight simple, double, treble, and quadruple rising suns in a circle round the edge.† Sometimes the sun is in the centre of the cross with four nails, which, according to the explanations in my sixth memoir, can evidently, and in all cases, represent only the instrument which our Aryan forefathers used for producing the holy fire (Agni), and which some Sanscrit scholars call "Arani" and others "Suastika." The rising sun must have been the most sacred object to our Aryan ancestors; for, according to Max Müller ('Essays'), out of it—that is, out of its struggle with the clouds—arose a very large portion of the gods who afterwards peopled Olympus. Upon some pieces the sun is surrounded by 40 or 50 little stars. I also found one upon which it is represented

---

* The various types of whorls spoken of here and throughout the work are delineated in the lithographic Plates at the end of the volume, and are described in the List of Illustrations.

† These "rising suns" are the arcs with their ends resting on the circumference of the whorl, as in Nos. 321–28, and many others on the Plates. M. Burnouf describes them as "stations of the sun."

in the centre, surrounded by 32 little stars and three
卍 ; another where one entire half of the circle is filled
by the rays of the sun, which, as in all cases, occupies the
central point ; on the other half are two 卍 and 18 little
stars, of which twice three (like the sword of Orion) stand in
a row; and another where even four are seen in a row. As
M. Émile Burnouf tells me, three dots in a row, in the
Persian cuneiform inscriptions, denote " royal majesty." I
do not venture to decide whether the three dots here admit
of a similar interpretation. Perhaps they point to the
majesty of the sun-god and of Agni, who was produced out
of the 卍. Upon some of these terra-cottas the sun is
even surrounded by four 卍, which again form a cross
by their position round it. Upon others, again, I find
the sun in the centre of a cross formed by four trees,
and each one of these trees has three or four large leaves.*
Indian scholars will, perhaps, find these tree-crosses to
represent the framework upon which our ancestors used
to produce the holy fire, and the repeatedly-recurring fifth
tree to be the " Pramantha." I find representations of this
same tree several times, either surrounded by circles or
standing alone, upon small terra-cotta cones of from 1½ to
2⅓ inches in diameter, which, in addition, have the most
various kinds of symbols and a number of suns and stars.
Upon a ball, found at the depth of 8 meters (26 feet),
there is a tree of this kind, surrounded by stars, opposite a
卍, beside which there is a group of nine little stars.† I
therefore venture to express the conjecture that this tree is
the tree of life, which is so frequently met with in the Assyrian
sculptures, and that it is identical with the holy Sôma-tree,
which, according to the Vêdas (see Émile Burnouf, Max
Müller, Adalbert Kuhn, and Fr. Windischmann), grows in

---

* For the type of whorls with " sôma-trees " or " trees of life " (four,
or more, or fewer), see Nos. 398, 400, 401, 404, &c.   In No. 410 the
four trees form a cross.

† Plate LII., No. 498.

heaven, and is there guarded by the Gandharvas, who belong to the primeval Aryan period, and subsequently became the Centaurs of the Greeks. Indra, the sun-god, in the form of a falcon,* stole from heaven this Sôma-tree, from which trickled the Amrita (ambrosia) which conferred immortality. Fr. Windischmann † has pointed out the existence of the Sôma-tree worship as common to the tribes of Aryans before their separation, and he therefore justly designates it an inheritance from their most ancient traditions.‡ Julius Braun§ says, in regard to this Sôma-tree: "Hermes, the rare visitor, is regaled with nectar and ambrosia. This is the food which the gods require in order to preserve their immortality. It has come to the West from Central Asia, with the whole company of the Olympian gods; for the root of this conception is the tree of life in the ancient system of Zoroaster. The fruit and sap of this tree of life bestows immortality, and the future Messiah (*Sosiosh*, in the Zend writings) will give some of it to all the faithful and make them all immortal. This hope we have seen fully expressed in the Assyrian sculptures, where the winged genii stand before the holy tree with a vessel containing the juice and fruit."

Just now two of those curious little terra-cottas, in the form of a volcano, were brought to me, upon one of which three animals with antlers are engraved in a circle round the sun;‖ upon another there are four signs (which I have hitherto not met with) in the shape of large combs with

---

* This falcon seems to be represented by rude two-legged figures on some of the whorls :—*e. g.* on Plate XLV., No. 468 (comp. p. 135).

† *Abhandlungen der K. bayerischen Akademie der Wissenschaften,* 1846, s. 127.

‡ A. Kuhn, 'Herabkunft des Feuers.'

§ *Geschichte der Kunst.*

‖ See the cut No. 75 and also on Plate XXX., No. 382. M. Burnouf describes the animal to the right as a *hare*, the symbol of the Moon, and the other two as the *antelopes*, which denote the prevailing of the two halves of the month (*quinzaines*).

long teeth, forming a cross round the sun.*   I conjecture
that these extremely remarkable hieroglyphics, which at
first sight might be imagined to be
actual letters, can by no means represent anything else than the sacrificial
altar with the flames blazing upon it.
I do not doubt moreover, that in the
continuation of the excavations I shall
find this comb-shaped sign together
with other symbols, which will confirm
my conjectures.

No. 75.   A Whorl, with three
animals (3 M.).

I must also add that the good old Trojans may perhaps
have brought with them from Bactria the name of Ida,
which they gave to the mountain which I see before me to
the south-east, covered with snow, upon which Jove and
Hera held dalliance,† and from which Jove looked down
upon Ilium and upon the battles in the Plain of Troy, for,
according to Max Müller,‡ Ida was the wife of Dyaus
(Zeus), and their son was Eros. The parents whom Sappho
ascribes to Eros—Heaven and Earth—are identical with his
Vedic parents. Heracles is called 'Ιδαῖος, from his being
identical with the Sun, and he has this name in common
with Apollo and Jove.

To-morrow the Greek Easter festival commences, during
which unfortunately there are six days on which no work is
done. Thus I shall not be able to continue the excavations until the 1st of May.

---

* See Plate XXXV., No. 414. The same symbol is seen on several
other examples.

† *Iliad*, XIV. 346–351. An English writer ought surely to use our
old-fashioned form *Jove*, which is also even philologically preferable as
the stem common to Ζεύς and *Ju*-piter (Διο = Ζεϝ = *Jov*), rather than the
somewhat pedantically sounding Ζεύς.—[ED.]

‡ *Essays*, II. 93.

CHAPTER VIII.

Hindrances through Greek festivals — Thickness of the layers of *débris* above the native rock — Date of the foundation of Troy — Impossibility of the *Bunarbashi* theory — Homeric epithets suitable to Hissarlik — Etymology of Ἴλιος, signifying probably the "fortress of the Sun " — The *Aruna* of the Egyptian records — Progress of the platform, and corresponding excavation on the south — The bulwark of Lysimachus — Ruins of great buildings — Marks of civilization increasing with the depth — Vases, and fragments of great urns — A remarkable terra-cotta — A whorl with the appearance of an inscription.

On the Hill of Hissarlik, May 11th, 1872.

SINCE my report of the 25th of last month I have only been able to have ten days' digging, owing to the various Greek festivals, for even the poorest Greek of this district would not work on a church festival even if he could earn 1000 francs in an hour. Turkish workmen were not to be had, for they are at present occupied with field work. The weather has been and still is very favourable for making excavations, as the heat during the day does not yet rise above 20° Réaumur (77° Fahrenheit) in the shade, and then it never rains here from the beginning of May till October, except during thunderstorms, and they rarely last more than half an hour at a time. Moreover, the Plain of Troy is at present still healthy; the notorious Trojan fevers do not actually begin till July, when the many stagnant waters have evaporated, and the pestilential miasma arises from the decomposition of the millions of dead frogs, and from the dried-up marshes, the ground of which cracks with the heat of the sun. My wife and I have therefore still six weeks before us, with the precaution of taking quinine to guard against fever.

I have cleared out the Roman well, which has been repeatedly mentioned, to a depth of 20 meters (65½ feet), and I find that it is walled only as far as 52½ feet below the surface of the hill, and then runs into the limestone rock which forms the native soil. I have caused Georgios Photidas to make a small tunnel in this rock from the well, and have now become quite convinced that the ground—upon which, according to Homer, the Trojan king Dardanus, who had up to that time lived at the foot of many-fountained Ida, built the town of Dardania (Troy) in the Plain*—is covered with a layer of *débris* about 16 meters, or 52½ English feet, thick. I must here remind the reader that the ruins of the Greek colony, which settled on the spot, scarcely extend to a depth of 6½ feet ; that consequently if, with Strabo (XIII. 1, 43) we suppose the establishment of this colony to have taken place under the Lydian dominion, that is about 700 B.C., and calculate the duration of the reigns of the six kings (Dardanus, Erichthonios, Tros, Ilus, Laomedon, and Priam) who, according to the Iliad (XX. 215-240), preceded the destruction of Troy, at 200 years, and thus presume the town to have been founded about 1400 years before Christ, the accumulation of *débris* must in this place have amounted to 14 meters, or 46 feet, during the first 700 years.

I am firmly convinced that, on a glance at my excavations, every one of the remaining advocates of the anti-

---

* *Iliad*, XX. 216-218 :—

Κτίσσε δὲ Δαρδανίην· ἐπεὶ οὔπω Ἴλιος ἱρὴ
'Εν πεδίῳ πεπόλιστο, πόλις μερόπων ἀνθρώπων,
'Αλλ' ἔθ' ὑπωρείας ᾤκεον πολυπίδακος Ἴδης.

" By Dardanus, of cloud-compelling Jove
  Begotten, was Dardania peopled first,
  Ere sacred Ilion, populous city of men,
  Was founded on the plain ; as yet they dwelt
  On spring-abounding Ida's lowest spurs."

quated theory that Troy is to be looked for at the back
of the Plain, upon the heights of Bunarbashi, will at once
condemn that theory, for the Acropolis and town which
once stood upon those heights, and the small area of which
is accurately defined by the ruins of the surrounding walls
and by the precipices, is scarcely large enough to have
contained a population of 2000 souls; the accumulation of
débris moreover is extremely small.   In many places, even
in the middle of the Acropolis, the naked rock protrudes,
and between the area of this small town and Bunarbashi
the ground—in some places pointed, in others abrupt, but
in all parts irregular—shows that no village, much less a
town, can ever have stood upon it.   Immediately above
Bunarbashi, and in fact wherever there was any earth at all,
I and my guide, with five workmen, made (in August
1868) a long series of borings at distances of 100 meters
(328 feet) apart, as far as the Scamander, but we found
the primary soil in all cases directly, and the rock at quite
an insignificant depth; and nowhere was there a trace of
fragments of pottery or other indications that the place
could ever have been inhabited by human beings.   Even
in Bunarbashi itself I found the primary soil at a depth of
less than 2 feet. Besides this, if Troy had been built at the
back of the Plain, upon the heights of Bunarbashi, Homer
(*Iliad*, XX. 216-218) would not have expressly said that
previous to its foundation by Dardanus it had not yet been
built in the Plain.

The primary soil of Hissarlik is indeed less than 20
meters (65½ feet) above the Plain, immediately at the foot
of the hill; but at all events the Plain itself, and especially
that part bordering upon the hill, has increased in height
considerably in the course of 31 centuries. But even
if this had not been the case, still the Troy built upon
this hill running out into the Plain would, on account
of its high and imposing position, deserve the Homeric
epithets of ὀφρυόεσσα, αἰπεινή, and ἠνεμόεσσα, especially

the latter; for one of my greatest troubles here is the continual high wind, and it cannot possibly have been otherwise in Homer's time. It is assuredly time that the
Bunarbashi theory, which stands in direct contradiction
with all the statements of the Iliad, should now at last come
to an end. The theory, in fact, would never have arisen
had its advocates, instead of spending one hour, remained a
whole day on the heights, and made investigations even
with the aid of a single workman.

As I observed in my last report, I here find the sun
represented in the centre of all the innumerable round
ornamented terra-cottas in the form of the volcano and top
(*carrousel*), and yesterday I even found one upon which the
central sun was surrounded by five other suns, each of
them with twelve rays.*

I know very well that some would derive the name of
the town of Ilium (῎Ιλιος or ῎Ιλιον) from the Sanscrit word
vilû, " fortress," and ῞Ηλιος from a lost masculine form
of Σελήνη, probably Σείριος, and the thought involuntarily forces itself upon me, when looking at the above-
mentioned terra-cottas with the five suns in a circle round
the central sun, that the image of the Sun which occurs
thousands and thousands of times must be connected with
the name of Troy, namely ῎Ιλιος, for ῎Ιλιον only occurs once
in Homer (Iliad, XV.71); he always elsewhere speaks of ῎Ιλιος,
and always uses this word as a feminine. Homer, it is true,
always says ᾽Ηέλιος instead of ῞Ηλιος, but in my opinion the
root of both is ἕλη or εἵλη, from the verb αἱρέω, the aorist
of which is εἷλον. In Germany, according to the Erasmian pronunciation εἵλη is certainly pronounced *heila*, and
εἷλον, *heilon ;* but in the modern Greek pronunciation εἵλη
is *ili* ; εἷλον, *ilon* ; and ῞Ηλιος, *ilios*. There are a number
of proofs that the Erasmian pronunciation is radically wrong,
and that the modern Greek is the correct one. Among these

---

* See Plate XXII., No. 327.

I will only mention that all the Greek words which passed over into the Russian language, when Russia embraced Christianity 900 years ago, are pronounced in Russian exactly as they still are in Greece; and moreover that those who decipher the Assyrian cuneiform inscriptions (especially, I believe, J. Oppert, in Paris), have pointed out that the Greek names, which occur in these inscriptions from the time of the Seleucidæ, are represented in the cuneiform writing exactly according to the modern Greek pronunciation. Now, if out of the word εἴλη, ἔλη, or εἴλον, there has arisen Ἥλιος and Ἥλιος, then surely by the sameness of the pronunciation there may have arisen out of one of the first three words in pre-Homeric times Ἴλιος in the feminine for πόλις Ἡλίου or Ἰλίου, signifying "Sun-castle," for the earlier meaning of πόλις was certainly castle, fortress, or acropolis, as for instance in, the Iliad, VI. 88, 257, 317, XXII. 383. Although I am well aware that Egyptian scholars have hitherto found no relationship between the hieroglyphic and Sanscrit languages, yet I cannot help mentioning that three years ago, in the Institute of France, I heard a lecture by the Vicomte de Rougé, who had found in a papyrus the names of the powers leagued against Rameses III., and among these the state of *Arouna* or *Aruna*, which he without hesitation identified with Ilium, as he thought that this was the only way in which the latter word could be rendered in the hieroglyphic language. Now, curiously enough, according to Max Müller * and Adalbert Kuhn,† the Sanscrit word *Aruna* signifies "charioteer of the sun." I leave it to Egyptian and Sanscrit scholars to judge whether and how far this may serve to confirm what I have said above.

Although since Easter I have been obliged to pay my men 1 piaster more per diem, which makes their wages 10 piasters or 2 francs a day, still I am now working with

---

* *Essays*, II. 324.   † *Herabkunft des Feuers*, p. 59.

130 men, and I firmly hope by the 1st of October to have carried my great platform through the entire hill, preserving exactly the same breadth; for while my wife and I, with 85 workmen, are busy on the platform on the north side, Georgios Photidas and 45 men have for 10 days been working towards us from a second platform on the south side.   Unfortunately, however, the slope of the hill on the south side is so slight, that we were forced to begin this work 16¼ feet below the surface, in order to have room and freedom for removing the *débris;* we have, however, given it a dip of 14°, so that it must reach the primary soil at a length of about 75 meters (246 feet).   This southern platform is under the sole direction of Georgios Photidas, for he has proved himself to be a very skilful engineer, and he works forward very quickly through his cleverly devised side terraces.   He has hitherto, however, had only light *débris* to remove, and has not yet come upon that very hard, tough, damp *débris* which I have on my platform at the depth of 10 to 16 meters (33 to 52½ feet).   To-day he has brought to light a splendid bastion, composed of large finely-hewn blocks of limestone, not joined by either cement or lime, which, however, does not seem to me to be older than the time of Lysimachus.   It is certainly very much in our way, but it is too beautiful and venerable for me to venture to lay hands upon it, so it shall be preserved.

On the south side the accumulation of *débris* from the Greek period is much more considerable than on the north side and upon the plateau; and thus far Georgios Photidas constantly finds Greek pottery and those terra-cottas with two holes at one end, which, in my excavations hitherto, ceased entirely at a depth of 2 meters (6½ feet).   The greater portion of these round articles have the potter's stamp already mentioned, representing a bee or fly with outspread wings above an altar. (*See Cuts,* Nos. 37–40, p. 65.)

I have also given the platform on the north side an inclination of 10° in a length of 66 feet, so as to be able to work forward on the primary soil, without the indescribable trouble of lowering it another 6½ feet, and of thus having to remove 4000 cubic yards of *débris*. This primary soil sufficiently proves that all those enormous masses of immense stones, generally more or less hewn, with which, as already said, I had continually to battle at a depth of from 10 to 14 meters (33 to 46 feet), are the remains of large buildings, which in the course of centuries have been erected successively upon the ruins of others. For it does not appear conceivable to me that even a large palace, were it six storeys high, could leave such colossal ruins, which, as they reach down to the rock, are nearly 20 feet in height.

For some days these masses of stone have diminished in number, but we continually find many single large blocks. Instead of the stone strata, however, we now have before us, upon the whole breadth of the platform (230 feet), and to the height of 20 feet (hence at a depth of from 10 to 16 meters, 33 to 52½ feet), a damp wall as hard as stone, composed of ashes mixed with small shells, bones, boars' tusks, &c., exactly like that which we before found at the east end. This mass is so tough, that it is only by making shafts, and breaking down the walls by means of huge iron levers, that we manage to get on at all.

The signs of a higher civilization increasing with the greater depth—which I mentioned in my last report when speaking of the large urn with Assyrian inscriptions—continue down to the native soil. Close above it I find a great quantity of fragments of brilliant black and sometimes red or brown pottery, with engraved decorations, of a quality more excellent than I have hitherto met with even in the highest strata, among the ruins of the Greek period. I also found several fragments of cups, the lower part of which likewise forms a cup, but not a large one, and hence I do not doubt that these are fragments of double cups (δέπας ἀμφικύπελλον). In Homer it indeed seems as if all double cups were made of gold or silver with a gilt rim,* but I do not doubt that there were at the same time also double cups made of clay.†

The other vessels, of which I found fragments, were made so as to be carried by strings, as is proved by the two rings projecting beside one another on either side. I also found upon the primary soil the head of a brilliant black pitcher, with a beak-shaped mouth bent back; also the fragment of a vessel painted white, but divided into

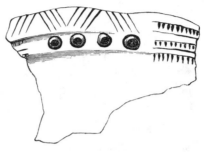

No. 76.   Fragment of a Vase of polished black Earthenware, with Pattern inlaid in White, from the Lowest Stratum (14 M.).

two compartments by black lines drawn horizontally; the upper compartment contains undulating black lines, which are perhaps meant to represent water, the lower one is filled with a row of arrow-shaped decorations, with square pointed heads, in the centre of which there is always a dot.

At the same depth I found fragments of large water or funereal urns with engraved ornaments

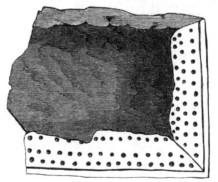

No. 77.   Fragment of Terra-cotta, perhaps part of a box, found on the primitive Rock (16 M.).

of various descriptions; also a square piece of terra-cotta painted black and ornamented all round with lines and four rows of dots filled with a white substance. As appears

---

* See, for example, *Iliad*, XI. 633–635, *Odyssey*, XV. 116, 446.

† Dr. Schliemann found afterwards that these fragments did not belong to double cups. (See Chap. XXII., p. 313, and 'Introduction,' p. 15.)

from the upper and the lower side, and from the two perforations, it must have been the setting and decoration of
a wooden jewel-casket. It is made with so much symmetry
and looks so elegant, that I at first thought it was ebony
inlaid with ivory.

At the depth of 8 meters (26 feet) I found a terra-
cotta seal an inch and a half in length, with a hole for

suspending it; there are a number of signs
upon it resembling the ancient Koppa—like
that stamped upon Corinthian coins. *

At a depth of 5 meters (16¼ feet), I found
to-day a very pretty jar with three feet, which is
evidently intended to represent a woman, probably the Ilian Athena, for it has two breasts

No. 78. A Tro-
jan Terra-cotta and a navel.
Seal (8 M.).

The snakes seem to have been enticed out
of their winter quarters by the warm weather which has set
in; for it is ten days since I have seen any.

Amid all the fatigues and troubles of the excavations
there is this among other pleasures, that time never hangs
heavy on one's hands.

---

* As the device on a seal may be presumed to be significant, and as
patterns strikingly similar to this occur on some of the whorls (*e. g.*
on Plate XLIV., No. 461), we have a strong argument for the significance
of the latter class of devices.—[ED.]

4 M.   3 M.   5 M.

No. 78*. Terra-cottas with Aryan Emblems.

CHAPTER IX.

Superstition of the Greeks about saints' days — Further engineering works — Narrow escape of six men — Ancient building on the western terrace — The ruins under this house — Old Trojan mode of building — Continued marks of higher civilization — Terra-cottas engraved with Aryan symbols : antelopes, a man in the attitude of prayer, flaming altars, hares — The symbol of the moon — Solar emblems and rotating wheels — Remarks on former supposed inscriptions—Stone moulds for casting weapons and implements — Absence of cellars, and use of colossal jars in their stead — The quarry used for the Trojan buildings — " Un Médecin malgré lui." — Blood-letting priest-doctors — Efficacy of sea-baths — Ingratitude of the peasants cured — Increasing heat.

CHAPTER X.

On the Hill of Hissarlik, May 23rd, 1872.

SINCE my report of the 11th instant there have again been, including to-day, three great and two lesser Greek church festivals, so that out of these twelve days I have in reality only had seven days of work. Poor as the people are, and gladly as they would like to work, it is impossible to persuade them to do so on feast days, even if it be the day of some most unimportant saint. Μᾶς δέρνει ὁ ἅγιος (" the saint will strike us ") is ever their reply, when I try to persuade the poor creatures to set their superstition aside for higher wages.

In order to hasten the works, I have now had terraces made at from 16 to 19 feet above the great platform on its east and west ends ; and I have also had two walls made of large blocks of stone—the intermediate spaces being filled with earth—for the purpose of removing the *débris*. The smaller wall did not seem to me to be strong enough, and I kept the workmen from it ; in fact, it did not bear the pressure, and it fell down when it was scarcely finished. Great trouble was taken with the larger and higher wall: it was built entirely of large stones, for the most part hewn, and all of us, even Georgios Photidas, thought it might last for centuries. But nevertheless on the following morning I thought it best to have a buttress of large stones erected, so as to render it impossible for the wall to fall; and six men were busy with this work when the wall suddenly fell in with a thundering crash. My fright was terrible and indescribable, for I quite believed that the six men must have been crushed by the mass of stones; to my extreme joy, however, I heard that they had all escaped directly, as if by a miracle.

In spite of every precaution, excavations in which men have to work under earthen walls of above 50 feet in perpendicular depth are always very dangerous. The call of "guarda, guarda" is not always of avail, for these words are continually heard in different places. Many stones roll down the steep walls without the workmen noticing them, and when I see the fearful danger to which we are all day exposed, I cannot but fervently thank God, on returning home in the evening, for the great blessing that another day has passed without an accident. I still think with horror of what would have become of the discovery of Ilium and of myself, had the six men been crushed by the wall which gave way; no money and no promises could have saved me; the poor widows would have torn me to pieces in their despair—for the Trojan women have this in common with all Greeks of their sex, that the husband, be he old or young, rich or poor, is everything to them; heaven and earth have but a secondary interest.

Upon the newly made western terrace, directly beside my last year's excavation, we have laid bare a portion of a large building—the walls of which are $6\frac{1}{4}$ feet thick, and consist for the most part of hewn blocks of limestone joined with clay. (*No. 24 on Plan II.*) None of the stones

seem to be more than 1 foot 9 inches long, and they are so
skilfully put together, that the wall forms a smooth surface.
This house is built upon a layer of yellow and brown ashes
and ruins, at a depth of 6 meters (20 feet), and the portion of
the walls preserved reaches up to within 10 feet below the
surface of the hill. In the house, as far as we have as yet
excavated, we found only one vase, with two breasts in front
and one breast at the side ; also a number of those frequently
mentioned round terra-cottas in the form of the volcano
and top, all of which have five or six quadruple rising
suns in a circle round the central sun.*   These objects, as
well as the depth of 6 meters (20 feet), and the architecture
of the walls described above, leave no doubt that the house
was built centuries before the foundation of the Greek
colony, the ruins of which extend only to a depth of 6½
feet. It is with a feeling of great interest that, from this
great platform, that is, at a perpendicular height of from
33 to 42 feet, I see this very ancient building (which
may have been erected 1000 years before Christ) standing
as it were in mid air. To my regret, however, it must in
any case be pulled down, to allow us to dig still deeper.
As I said before, directly below this house there is a layer of
ruins consisting of yellow and brown ashes, and next, as
far as the terrace, there are four layers more of ashes and
other *débris*, each of which represents the remains of one
house at least. Immediately above the terrace, that is 13
feet below the foundation of that very ancient house, I find
a wall about 6 feet thick, built of large blocks of limestone, the description of which I must reserve for my next
report, for a large portion of the building I have mentioned,
and immense masses of the upper strata of *débris*, as well
as the high earthen wall of the terrace (26 feet thick and 20
feet high) must be pulled down, before I can lay bare any
portion of this wall and investigate how far down it extends.

---

* See Plate XXII., No. 321.

If it reaches to or even approaches the primary soil, then I shall reverently preserve it. (See No. 25 on Plan II.) It is a very remarkable fact, that this is the first wall built of large stones that I have hitherto found at the depth of from 10 to 16 meters (33 to 52½ feet).* I cannot explain this, considering the colossal masses of loose stones which lie irregularly beside one another (especially at a depth of from 36 to 52½ feet), in any other way than by supposing that the houses of the Trojans were built of blocks of limestone joined with clay, and consequently easily destroyed. If my excavations are not interrupted by any accident, I hope, in this at all events, to make some interesting discoveries very soon, with respect to this question.

Unfortunately during the last twelve days I have not been able to pull down much of the lower firm earth-wall, for, in order to avoid fatal accidents, I have had to occupy myself especially in making and enlarging the side terraces. I have now, however, procured enormous iron levers of nearly 10 feet in length and 6 inches in circumference, and I thus hope henceforth to be able at once to break down, by means of windlasses, the hardest of the earth-walls, which are 10 feet thick, 66 broad, and from 16 to 26 feet high. In the small portion of the earth-wall pulled down during these last days, I repeatedly found the most irrefutable proofs of a higher civilization; but I will only mention one of these, a fragment of a brilliant dark grey vessel which I have at present lying before me, found at a depth of 15 meters (49 feet). It may probably have been nearly 2 feet in diameter, and it has decorations both outside and inside, which consist of engraved horizontal and undulating lines. The former are arranged in three sets in stripes of five lines, and the lowest space is adorned with eight and the following with five undulating lines, which are probably meant to represent the waves of the sea; of the

---

* That is, belonging to the lowest stratum.

next set no part has been preserved; the thickness of the clay is just $\frac{3}{5}$ of an inch.

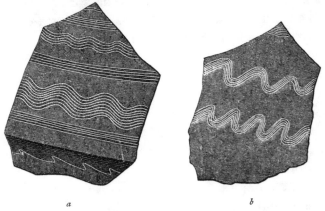

a   *b*

No. 79.   Fragment of a brilliant dark-grey Vessel, from the Lowest Stratum (15 M.).
a Inside ; *b* Outside.

In my report of the 25th of last month,* I mentioned the discovery of one of those terra-cottas upon which were engraved three animals with antlers in the circle round the central sun. Since then four others of these remarkable objects with similar engravings have been discovered. Upon one of them, found at a depth of 6 meters (20 feet), there are only two animals with antlers in the circle round the sun, and at the end of each antler, and connected with it, is an exceedingly curious sign resembling a large candle-stick or censer, which is certainly an especially important symbol, for it is repeatedly found here standing alone.† Upon a second, there is below a rough representation of a man who seems to be praying, for he has both arms raised towards heaven; this position reminds us forcibly of the two uplifted arms of the owl-faced vases; to the left is an animal with but two feet and two trees on its back.‡ Indian scholars will perhaps find that this is intended to represent the falcon, in which shape the sun-god stole the sacred sôma-tree from

---

* Chapter VII., p. 121.
† See No. 380, on Plate XXIX.   ‡ See No. 383, on Plate XXX.

heaven. Then follow two animals with two horns, probably antelopes, which are so frequently met with upon ancient Greek vases, and which in the Rigvêda are always made to draw the chariot of the winds. Upon a third terra-cotta there are three of these antelopes with one or two rows of stars above the back, which perhaps are intended to represent heaven; then five fire-machines, such as our Aryan ancestors used; lastly, a sign in zigzag, which, as already said, cannot represent anything but the flaming altar.* Upon the fourth whorl are four hares, the symbols of the moon, forming a cross round the sun. They probably represent the four seasons of the year.†

At a depth of 14 meters (46 feet) we found to-day two of those round articles of a splendidly brilliant black terra-cotta, which are only $\frac{3}{5}$ of an inch in height, but $2\frac{1}{3}$ inches in diameter, and have five triple rising suns and five stars in the circle round the central sun. All of these decorations, which are engraved, as in every other case, are filled in with a very fine white substance. When looking at these curious articles, one of which is exactly the shape of a carriage-wheel,‡ the thought involuntarily strikes me that they are symbols of the sun's chariot, which, as is well known, is symbolized in the Rigvêda by a wheel, and that all and each of these articles met with in the upper strata (although their form deviates from that of a wheel on account of their greater thickness) cannot be anything but degenerated representations of the sun's wheel. I conjecture this all the more, because not only is the sun the central

---

* Plate XXIX., No. 379. The front bears 4 ⊓ ; on the back are the emblems described, which are shown separately in detail, and of which M. Burnouf gives an elaborate description. (See List of Illustrations.)

† Plate XXVIII., No. 377 ; compare Plate XXVII., No. 367.

‡ See Plate XXII., No. 328 ; the *depth* (14 M.) deserves special notice. The *wheel-shape*, which is characteristic of the whorls in the lowest stratum, is seen at No. 314, Plate XXI.

point of all the round terra-cottas, but it is almost always surrounded by one, two, three, four or five circles, which may represent the nave of the wheel.   At a depth of 16 meters (52½ feet) we found a round terra-cotta, which is barely an inch in diameter, and a fifth of an inch thick; there are five concentric circles round the central point, and between the fourth and fifth circle oblique little lines, which are perhaps meant to denote the rotation of the wheel.

No. 80.   Whorl with pattern of a moving Wheel (16 M.).

I must here again refer to the round terra-cotta mentioned in my report of the 18th of November, 1871,* and to my regret I must now express my firm conviction that there are no letters upon it, but only symbolical signs; that for instance the upper sign (which is almost exactly the same as that upon the terra-cotta lately cited) † must positively represent a man in an attitude of prayer, and that the three signs to the left can in no case be anything but the fire-machine of our Aryan ancestors, the 卐 little or not at all changed.   The sign which then follows, and which is connected with the fourth and sixth signs, I also find, at least very similar ones, on the other, cited in the same report, but I will not venture to express an opinion as to what it may mean.‡   The sixth sign (the fifth from the figure in prayer) is very like the Phœnician letter "Nun," but in my opinion cannot be a letter, for how would it be possible to find a single Semitic letter, between Aryan religious symbols?   Its great resemblance to the zigzag sign of other examples,§ which I recognise to be lightning,

---

* Chapter IV. p. 84.   See Plate XXII., No. 326, from the Atlas of Photographs, and Plate XLVIII., No. 482, from M. Burnouf's drawings.

† Plate XXX., No. 383.

‡ Page 83, and Plate LI., No. 496.   This is one of the inscriptions examined by Professor Gomperz.   (See Appendix.)

§ See Cut, No. 81, and Plate XXVII., No. 369.   The latter is an inscription, which Professor Gomperz has discussed.   (See Appendix.)

leads me to suppose that it likewise can only represent lightning.

All the primitive symbols of the Aryan race, which I find upon the Trojan terra-cottas, must be symbols of good men, for surely only such would have been engraved upon the thousands of terra-cottas met with here. Yet these symbols remind one forcibly of the "σήματα λυγρά" and "θυμοφθόρα," which King Prœtus of Tiryns gave to Bellerophon

No. 81. Whorl with Symbols of Lightning (7. M.).

to take to his father-in-law in Lycia.*　Had he scratched a symbol of good fortune, for instance a ⌐┘, upon the folded tablet, it would assuredly have sufficed to secure him a good reception, and protection. But he gave him the symbol of death, that he might be killed.

The five [six] characters found on a small terra-cotta disc at a depth of 24 feet, and which in my report of November 18th, 1871,† I considered to be Phœnician, have unfortunately been proved not to be Phœnician, for M. Ernest Renan of Paris, to whom I sent the small disc, finds nothing Phœnician in the symbols, and maintains that I could not find anything of the kind in Troy, as it was not the custom of the Phœnicians to write upon terra-cotta, and moreover that, with the exception of the recently discovered Moabite inscription of King Mesha, no Phœnician inscription has

---

* *Iliad*, VI. 168–170 :—

Πέμπε δέ μιν Λυκίηνδε, πόρεν δ' ὅ γε σήματα λυγρά,
Γράψας ἐν πίνακι πτυκτῷ θυμοφθόρα πολλά,
Δεῖξαι δ' ἠνώγειν ᾧ πενθερῷ ὄφρ' ἀπόλοιτο.

"But to the father of his wife, the King
Of Lycia, sent him forth, with tokens charged
Of dire import, on folded tablets traced,
Which, to the monarch shown, might work his death."

† Chapter IV., pp. 83–84. Though not Phœnician, these are Cyprian letters, and they have been discussed by Professor Gomperz, who found in this very whorl his *experimentum crucis*. (See Appendix.)

ever been found belonging to a date anterior to 500
years B.C.

I may also remark, with regard to my last year's excavations, that I have now found quadrangular pieces of mica-
schist and chlorite slate, from nearly 6 inches to nearly
11 inches long, and from about 1¼ to 3½ inches thick,

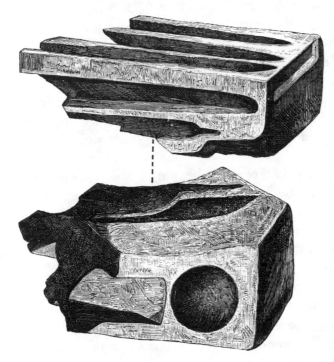

No. 82.   Two fragments of a great Mould of Mica-schist for casting Copper Weapons and
Ornaments (14 M.).

which have on all four sides, and several of them on
six sides, forms or moulds for casting weapons and instruments; and further, that the channelled pieces, spoken
of in the report of November 18th, 1871,* are nothing but
fragments of similar stone-moulds; the brilliant, glossy
appearance of the slate seems to have been produced by
simple polishing.

----

* Chapter IV., p. 87.

Of cellars, such as we have in civilized countries, I have as yet found not the slightest trace, either in the strata of the Hellenic or in those of the pre-Hellenic period; earthen vessels seem everywhere to have been used in their stead. On my southern platform, in the strata of Hellenic times, I have already had ten such vessels dug out in an uninjured condition; they are from 5¾ to 6½ feet high, and from 2 to 4½ feet in diameter, but without decorations.*   I sent seven of these jars (πίθοι) to the Museum in Constantinople.

In the strata of the pre-Hellenic period I find an immense number of these πίθοι, but I have as yet only succeeded in getting two of them out uninjured, from a depth of 26 feet; these are about 3½ feet high and 26¾ inches in diameter; they have only unimportant decorations.

In my last communication, I was able to speak of a lesser number of the blocks of stone obstructing the works upon the great platform; to-day, however, I have again unfortunately to report a considerable increase of them.

At a distance of scarcely 328 yards from my house, on the south side, and at the part of the plateau of Ilium in a direct perpendicular line below the ruined city wall, which seems to have been built by Lysimachus, I have now discovered the stone quarry, whence all those colossal masses of shelly limestone (*Muschelkalk*) were obtained, which the Trojans and their successors, down to a time after the Christian era, employed in building their houses and walls, and which have given my workmen and me such inexpressible anxiety, trouble, and labour. The entrance to the quarry, which is called by the native Greeks and Turks "lagum" ("mine" or "tunnel," from the Arabic word لغم), which has passed over into Turkish), is filled with rubbish, but, as I am assured by all the people about

---

* Some examples of these jars, still more interesting on account of the great depth at which they were found, are seen in Plate XI., p. 290.

here, it was still open only 20 years ago, and, as my excavations have proved, it was very large. The town, as seems
to be indicated by a continuous elevation extending below
the quarry, had a double surrounding wall at this point,
and this was in fact necessary, for otherwise the enemy
would have been able, with no further difficulty, to force
his way into the quarry below the town-wall, as the entrance
to the quarry was outside of the wall.

Unfortunately, without possessing the slightest knowledge of medicine, I have become celebrated here as a
physician, owing to the great quantity of quinine and tincture of arnica which I brought with me and distributed
liberally, and by means of which, in October and November
of last year, I cured all fever patients and wounds. In
consequence of this, my valuable time is now claimed in a
troublesome manner by sick people, who frequently come
from a distance of many miles, in order to be healed of
their complaints by my medicine and advice. In all the
villages of this district, the priest is the parish doctor,
and as he himself possesses no medicines, and is ignorant
of their properties, and has besides an innate dislike to
cold water and all species of washing, he never uses any
other means than bleeding, which, of course, often kills
the poor creatures. Wrinkles on either side of the lips
of children from 10 to 12 years of age show that the priest
has repeatedly bled them. Now I hate the custom of
bleeding, and am enthusiastically in favour of the cold-
water cure; hence I never bleed anyone, and I prescribe
sea-bathing for almost all diseases; this can be had here by
everyone, except myself, who have no time for it. My
ordering these baths has given rise to such confidence, nay
enthusiasm, that even women, who fancied that it would
be their death to touch their bodies with cold water, now
go joyfully into the water and take their dip. Among
others, a fortnight ago, a girl of seventeen from Neo-
Chori was brought to me; her body was covered with

ulcers, especially her face, and one terrible ulcer on the left
eye had made it quite useless. She could scarcely speak,
walk or stand, and, as her mother said, she had no appetite;
her chest had fallen in, and she coughed. I saw immediately that excessive bleeding and the consequent want
of blood had given rise to all her ailments, and therefore
I did not ask whether she had been bled, but how many
times. The answer was, the girl had taken cold, and the
parish priest had bled her seven times in one month. I
gave her a dose of castor oil, and ordered her a sea bath
every day, and that, when she had recovered sufficient
strength, her father should put her through some simple
passive gymnastic exercises—which I carefully described—
in order to expand her chest. I was quite touched when
early this morning the same girl appeared on the platform,
threw herself on the ground, kissed my dirty shoes, and
told me, with tears of joy that even the first sea bath had
given her an appetite, that all the sores had begun to heal
directly, and had now disappeared, but that the left eye was
still blind, otherwise she was perfectly well, for even the
cough had left her. I, of course, cannot cure the eye; it
seems to me to be covered with a skin which an oculist
might easily remove. The girl had come on foot from Neo-
Chori, a distance of three hours, to thank me, and I can
assure my readers that this is the first case, in the Plain of
Troy, in which I have received thanks for medicines or
medical advice; but I am not even quite sure whether it
was a feeling of pure gratitude that induced the girl to come
to me, or whether it was in the hope that by some other
means I might restore sight to the blind eye.

The heat has increased considerably during the last
few days; the thermometer stands the whole day at 25°
Réaumur (88¼° Fahrenheit) in the shade.

PLATE VI.

TROJAN BUILDINGS ON THE NORTH SIDE, AND IN THE GREAT TRENCH CUT THROUGH THE WHOLE HILL.

CHAPTER X.

A third platform dug — Traces of former excavations by the Turks —
Block of triglyphs, with bas-relief of Apollo — Fall of an earth-wall —
Plan of a trench through the whole hill — Admirable remains in the
lowest stratum but one — The plain and engraved whorls — Objects of
gold, silver, copper, and ivory — Remarkable terra-cottas — The pottery
of the *lowest stratum* quite distinct from that of the next above —
Its resemblance to the Etruscan, in quality only — Curious funereal
urns — Skeleton of a six months' embryo — Other remains in the
lowest stratum — Idols of fine marble, the sole exception to the
superior workmanship of this stratum — The houses and palaces of
the lowest stratum, of large stones joined with earth — Disappearance
of the first people with the destruction of their town.

The *second settlers*, of a different civilization — Their buildings of unburnt
brick on stone foundations — These bricks burnt by the great conflagration — Destruction of the walls of the former settlers — Live toads
coëval with Troy ! — Long duration of the second settlers — Their
Aryan descent proved by Aryan symbols — Various forms of their
pottery — Vases in the form of animals — The whorls of this stratum
— Their interesting devices — Copper weapons and implements, and
moulds for casting — Terra-cotta seals — Bracelets and ear-rings, of
silver, gold, and electrum — Pins, &c., of ivory and bone — Fragments
of a lyre — Various objects.

The *third stratum :* the remains of an Aryan race — Hardly a trace of
metal — Structure of their houses — Their stone implements and
terra-cottas coarser — Various forms of pottery — Remarkable *terra-
cotta balls* with astronomical and religious symbols — Whorls — Stone
weapons — Whetstones — Hammers and instruments of diorite —
A well belonging to this people — This third town destroyed with its
people.

The *fourth settlers :* compararively savage, but still of Aryan race —
Whorls with like emblems, but of a degenerate form — Their pottery
inferior, but with some curious forms — Idols of Athena — Articles
of copper — Few stones — Charred remains indicating wooden
buildings — Stone weights, hand-mills, and knives and saws of flint —
With this people the pre-Hellenic ages end — The stone buildings and

painted and plain terra-cottas of *Greek Ilium* — Date of the Greek
colony — Signs that the old inhabitants were not extirpated — The
whorls of very coarse clay and patterns — Well, and jars for water
and wine — Proofs of the regular succession of nations on the hill —
Reply to the arguments of M. Nikolaïdes for the site at Bunarbashi
— The Simoïs, Thymbrius, and Scamander — The tomb of Ajax at
In-Tépé — Remains in it — Temple of Ajax and town of Aianteum
— Tomb of Achilles and town of Achilleum — Tombs of Patroclus
and Antilochus — The Greek camp — The tomb of Batiea or
Myrina — Further discussion of the site.

On the Hill of Hissarlik, June 18th, 1872.

SINCE my report of the 23rd of last month I have been
excavating, with the consent of my honoured friend, Mr.
Frank Calvert, on that half of the hill which belongs to him,
on condition that I share with him the objects I may find.
Here, directly beside my large platform, and at a perpendicular depth of 40 feet below the plateau, I have laid out a
third platform about 109 feet broad, with an upper terrace
112 feet broad, and I have seventy men digging there.
Immediately beside the edge of the steep northern declivity
I found a square depression in the ground about 112 feet
long and 76 feet broad, which can only have been caused by
excavations made by the Turks hundreds of years ago,
when searching for pillars or other kinds of marble blocks
suitable for tombstones: for all of the old Turkish ceme-
teries in the Plain of Troy and its vicinity, nay even as far
as beyond Alexandria Troas, possess thousands of such
marble blocks, taken from ancient buildings. The innumerable pieces of marble, which cover the whole of Mr.
Frank Calvert's part of the plateau, leave no doubt that
the field, at least that part of it with the square depression,
has been ransacked by marble-seeking Turks.

I had scarcely begun to extend this third platform
horizontally into the hill, when I found a block of triglyphs
of Parian marble, about 6½ feet long, nearly 2 feet 10 inches
high, and nearly 22 inches thick at one end, and a little over
14 inches on the other. In the middle there is a piece of

sculpture in high relief, a little above 2 feet 10 inches long and nearly the same height, which represents Phœbus Apollo, who, in a long woman's robe with a girdle, is riding on the four immortal horses which pursue their career through the universe. Nothing is to be seen of a chariot. Above the splendid, flowing, unparted, but not long hair on the head of the god, there is seen about two-thirds of the sun's disc with ten rays $2\frac{1}{3}$ inches long, and ten others $3\frac{1}{2}$ inches long. The face of the god is very expressive, and the folds of his long robe are so exquisitely sculptured that they vividly remind one of the masterpieces in the temple of Νίκη ἄπτερος in the Acropolis of Athens. But my admiration is especially excited by the four horses, which, snorting and looking wildly forward, career through the universe with infinite power. Their anatomy is so accurately rendered that I frankly confess that I have never seen such a masterly work. On the right and left of this metopé are Doric triglyphs; there is a third triglyph on the left side of the marble block, which is nearly 22 inches thick, whereas the right side (14 inches thick) contains no sculpture. Above and below the block, iron clamps are fastened by means of lead; and from the triglyphs on the left side I presume that this metopé, together with another sculpture which has a Doric triglyph on the right side as well, adorned the propylæa of the temple. (*See Plate IV.*, p. 32.)

It is especially remarkable to find the sun-god here, for Homer knows nothing of a temple to the Sun in Troy, and later history does not say a word about the existence of such a temple. However, the image of Phœbus Apollo does not prove that the sculpture must have belonged to a temple of the Sun; in my opinion it may just as well have served as an ornament to any other temple.

As early as my report of the 11th of May,* I ventured

---

* Chapter VIII.

to express the conjecture that the image of the Sun, which
I find represented here thousands and thousands of times
upon the whorls of terra-cotta, must be regarded as the
name or the emblem of the town, that is Ἴλιος. I now
venture to express the opinion, that in like manner this
Sun-god shone in the form of a woman upon the Propylæa of the temple of the Ilian Athena as a symbol of
the Sun-city (τῆς Ἰλίου). I have heard a learned friend
express the opinion that this masterpiece belonged to
the period between Pericles and Alexander the Great,
because the Sun-god's outstretched hand is very similar
to that of Phœbus Apollo on the coins of Rhodes of the
same period. But, according to Strabo (XIII. 1), Alexander
the Great, on his visit to Ilium, found there a little temple
(εὐτελῆ ναόν) of the Ilian Athena ; and a little temple,
of course, cannot have possessed such excellent works of
plastic art. Besides this, the head of the Sun-god appears
to me to have so much of the Alexandrian style, that I
must adhere to history and believe that this work of art
belongs to the time of Lysimachus, who, according to
Strabo (XIII. 1), after the death of Alexander the Great,
built here the new temple of the Ilian Athena, which
Alexander had promised to the town of Ilium after the
subjugation of the Persian Empire.*

The discovery of this work of art upon the steep
declivity of the hill—whereas it must necessarily have
stood on the opposite side above the entrance to the

---

* For a further description and discussion of this splendid relief, see
the Introduction, pp. 32–34. An acute critic has suggested to us that the
metopé is a sculpture of the best age of Greek art, before or about the time
of Alexander, inserted in a Doric frieze of late debased work, as is proved
by the difference of styles, and by the evident fact that the metopé was
originally too large for the space between the triglyphs. The temple to
which it belonged, in Dr. Schliemann's final opinion, was a temple of
Apollo, which he discovered later (comp. Chap. XIV., p. 223, and
Chap. XVII., p. 257).—[ED.]

temple—can only be explained by the fact that the Turks who came here in search of monumental pillars despised this sculpture because it represented living creatures, the imitation of which is strictly forbidden in the Koran.

Beneath the ruins of this temple I hope to discover the remains of that little temple which Alexander the Great found here. I do not, however, think it likely that I shall discover in its depths the old Trojan temple in which Hecuba caused the priestess Theano to lay her costly robes on the knees of Athena.* To judge from the *débris* of the ashes of animal sacrifices, which is as hard as stone, and which gives me such exceedingly great trouble along an extent of 82 feet at the eastern end of my large platform, the area of the very ancient temple cannot possibly be identical with the one built by Lysimachus; it must certainly be somewhat more to the west, and must commence somewhere near its western end.

After my report of the 23rd of last month, I began to loosen the lower earthen wall, which is as hard as stone, by means of those immense iron levers which I have already described. However, I was unfortunate; for, after having worked for three hours with 40 men and with the huge levers and windlasses in loosening an earthen wall 16 feet high, 16 broad and 10 thick, which had been already prepared by shafts and mines, only just succeeded after the strongest chains had given way several times, when the adjoining earth-wall fell of its own accord, and buried Georgios Photidas and a workman who were engaged in the

---

* *Iliad*, VI. 302-304 :—

'Η δ' ἄρα πέπλον ἑλοῦσα Θεανὼ καλλιπάρῃος
Θῆκεν Ἀθηναίης ἐπὶ γούνασιν ἠϋκόμοιο,
Εὐχομένη δ' ἠρᾶτο Διὸς κούρῃ μεγάλοιο.

" But fair Theano took the robe and placed
   On Pallas' knees, and to the heavenly maid,
   Daughter of Jove, she thus addressed her prayer."

lower excavations, believing that they were perfectly safe under thick logs of wood 23 inches high and 10 thick, which were covered with planks 3 inches thick. All of us naturally thought that the two men must have been crushed beneath the enormous mass of 100 cubic yards of stone and earth, which had dashed the thick planks to pieces. Our fright was terrible, but without losing a moment we set to work to rescue the unfortunate men. We had scarcely begun when we heard them moaning beneath the weight of earth, for the logs had only been upset, and, lying lengthwise, they still partly supported the vault, so that the men had breathing space left. But their release could not be effected without the greatest danger, owing to several large gaps in the cracked earthen wall, and the men had to be cut out. I myself cut out Georgios Photidas with my knife; the other man was cut out by my men.

In consequence of this accident, I have decided in the first place to cut a trench 98 feet broad at the top and 65 below, commencing at the platform, which is to be carried along the primary soil through the entire hill, and not to cut through the other portion of the great platform until this is finished; for I shall then be in a position to judge how we can best accomplish the former work. I am having the whole length of this trench commenced at the same time on a breadth of 98 feet, and I hope thus to have it ready in two months. In digging this trench I found that, at about 69 feet from the steep side of the hill, the primary soil gradually rises about 2 meters (6½ feet), and as the cutting must necessarily follow the primary soil, I have from this point again had the *débris* thrown upon the great platform, and have thus formed an embankment 65½ feet broad and 6½ feet high, as far as the steep slope.

Were it not for the splendid terra-cottas which I find exclusively upon the primary soil and as far as 6½ feet above it, I could swear that, at a depth of from 8 meters down to exactly 10 meters (26 to 33 feet), I am among the ruins of the Homeric Troy.*   For at this depth I have again found, as I found last year, a thousand wonderful objects; whereas I find comparatively little in the lowest stratum, the removal of which gives me such unspeakable trouble.   We daily find some of the whorls of very fine terra-cotta, and it is curious that those which have no decorations at all, are always of the ordinary shape and size of small tops or like the craters of volcanoes, while almost all those possessing decorations are flat and in the form of a wheel.†   Metals, at least gold, silver and copper, were known to the Trojans, for I found a copper knife highly gilded, a silver hair-pin, and a number of copper nails at a depth of 14 meters (46 feet); and at a depth of 16 meters (52½ feet) several copper nails from 4 to 6¼ inches in length.   There must have been also copper weapons and tools for work, though I have as yet not found any; but I found many small instruments for use as pins; also a number of ivory needles, likewise a small ivory plate, almost the shape of a playing-card, with six little stars or small suns, also a curious piece of ivory covered with the same decorations, in the form of a paper-knife, and a still more curious one in the form of an exceedingly neat dagger.‡   The ornaments on both sides of this dagger seem certainly to represent the Ilian Athena with the owl's head.   We also discovered some ivory and copper rings, likewise a pair of bracelets of copper.   One-edged or double-edged knives of white silex in the form of saws, from above 1¾ inch to nearly 2 inches in length, were found in quantities; also many hand millstones of lava about 13 inches long, and 6⅔ inches broad, in the form of an egg cut in half longitudinally.   All of the terra-

---

* The reader should bear in mind that Dr. Schliemann finally came back to this opinion.   It is not "*second* thoughts" (say the authors of 'Guesses at Truth'), but *first* and *third* thoughts, that are "best."—[ED.]

† Compare the sections shown on Plate XXI.

‡ See No. 14, on page 36.

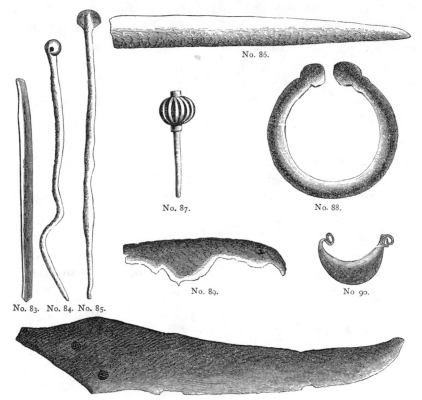

No. 91.

Objects of Metal from the Lowest Stratum (11–15 M.).

No. 83. A real Copper Nail.   Nos. 84, 85. Copper Dress-Pins (too long and thin for nails).
No. 86. A *gilt* Copper Knife.   No. 87. A Silver Dress-Pin.   No. 88. A Copper Bracelet.
Nos. 89, 91. Copper Knives.   No. 90. A Silver Crescent.

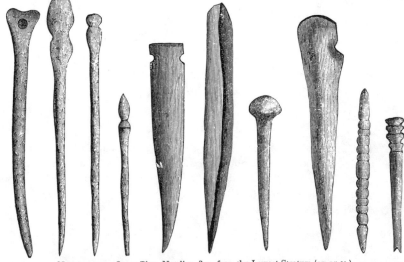

Nos. 92–101.. Ivory Pins, Needles, &c., from the Lowest Stratum (11–15 M.).

Nos, 102, 103.   Hand Mill-stones of Lava from Lowest Stratum (14–16 M.).

No. 104.   A splendid Vase with Suspension-rings, from the Lowest Stratum (15 M.).

cottas were brought out in a broken condition; however, I have got all or almost all the pieces of a number of vases and of several jars, so that I can restore them. I must specially mention a large yellowish bowl 13⅓ inches high and nearly 17 inches broad, which in addition to a handle has three large curled ram's horns; then a black vase with a round bottom, with two rings on either side for hanging it up; a beautiful red vase with four handles; also a very fine red cup: further, an exceedingly curious red vessel in the form of two jugs with long per--

No. 105.   Singular Double Vase from the
lowest Stratum (13–14 M.).

fectly upright beak-shaped mouths, the two jugs being connected with each other at the bulge, as well as by a handle; further, a brilliant

No. 106.   Black Vase of Terra-cotta from the
lowest Stratum (14 or 15 M.).

black vase, 9½ inches high, with rings on the sides for hanging it up, and a very wide neck in the form of a chimney; the lower portion of the vase is ornamented with signs in the form of lightning, the upper part with dots. Of a pair of brilliant black Trojan deep plates I have so nearly all the pieces, as to be able to put them together; these plates are very remarkable, for on two sides at the edge they have long horizontal rings for suspension by strings; the large dishes have such rings very large. I have the fragments of several black double cups, but not enough of any one to restore it.

Unfortunately, the tremendous weights of stone in the lowest stratum have broken or crushed to pieces all the terra-cottas; but all the splendid earthen vessels that I have been able to save bear witness of wealth and art, and it is easily seen at a first glance that they were made by a people quite distinct from the one to which the next stratum belongs (at the depth of from 7 to 10 meters, 23 to 33 feet). I must draw especial attention to the great similarity in the quality of the terra-cotta of the black Trojan vessels to that of the vessels found in the Etruscan tombs; but their forms and decorations are wholly different. In those found here the patterns have always been engraved upon the clay when it was still in a soft state. Most of the Trojan terra-cottas are indestructible by moisture; some of them, however, have become limp by damp, and I found,

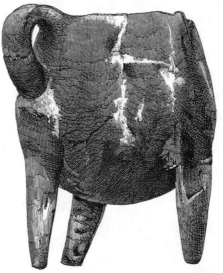

No. 107.   Funereal Urn of Stone, found on the Primary Rock, with Human Ashes in it (15½ M.).

for instance, upon the primary soil at a depth of 15½ meters (51 feet), in a small private burial-ground, formed and protected by three stones 25½ inches long and 18 inches broad, two vessels of a very remarkable form with three long feet and filled with human ashes. The vessels had suffered so from moisture that in spite of every care and precaution I could not get them out without breaking them completely. I have, however, collected all the pieces of both vessels, and shall be able to restore them. In one of them I found among the human ashes the bones of an embryo of six months, a fact which I can only explain by the mother's having died in pregnancy and having been burnt, while the bones of the embryo, being surrounded by the membrane which enclosed it, were protected and remained uninjured. Yet it seems wonderful that these small bones should have been preserved, for the bones of the mother are burnt to ashes and I found only small fragments of them. I have most carefully collected the bones of the Trojan embryo, and shall have the little skeleton restored by a skilful surgeon. The celebrated Doctor Aretaios, of Athens, has just written to me that the preservation of the bones of the embryo is only possible on the supposition that the mother had brought forth the child and then died, that her body was burnt and the unburnt embryo was put into the funereal urn with her ashes, where I found it.

In the deepest strata we also meet with simple black cups, resembling our drinking-glasses; likewise black cups (vase-covers) with a handle below, so that they can only stand upon their mouth. I also find on the primary soil weights made of granite, the exact specific weights of which I shall state in a separate table;* hammers and axes, as well as a number of large and small wedges of diorite, of splendid workmanship; sometimes also small beautifully-cut instruments in the form of wedges, made of very beautiful transparent green stone.† Besides these, we come upon quantities of round black and red terra-cotta discs, generally nearly 2 inches in diameter, with a hole in the centre; and stone quoits (δίσκοι), about 6 inches in diameter, with a hole in the centre for throwing them. Further, a number of idols of very fine marble, which form the only exception to the rule that at an increasing depth the objects are of

---

* At the end of the volume, pp. 359, 360.

† Dr. Schliemann afterwards pronounced these "wedges" to be battle-axes. See Introduction, p. 21.

much better workmanship than those above. In fact, the idols met with in the Trojan [pre-Trojan] strata of *débris*

No. 108. *a,* Hand Millstone of Lava (15 M.). *b,* Brilliant black Dish with side Rings for hanging it up (14 M.). *c, c, c, c,* Small decorated Rings of Terra-cotta (10–14 M.).

from 2 to 4 meters (6½ to 13 feet) above the primary soil, that is, at a depth of from 12 to 14 meters (39¼ to 46 feet), are so coarsely wrought, as may be seen from the drawings (on page 36), that one might be inclined to believe that they were the very first attempts of an uncivilized people at making plastic representations of a deity. There was only one mutilated idol of terra-cotta found among these ruins, a drawing of which I give; all the others are of very fine marble. I must also mention another Priapus, of fine marble, which was discovered at a depth of 13 meters (42½ feet).

No. 109.
Rude Terra-cotta Idol (14 M.).

In these depths we likewise find many bones of animals, boars' tusks, small shells, horns of the buffalo, ram, and stag, as well as the vertebræ of the shark.

The houses and palaces, in which the splendid terra-cottas were used, were large and spacious, for to them belong all those mighty heaps of large stones hewn and unhewn, which cover them to the height of from 13 to 20 feet.

These houses and palaces were easily destroyed, for the stones were only joined with earth, and when the walls fell everything in the houses was crushed to pieces by the immense blocks of stone. The primitive Trojan people disappeared simultaneously with the destruction of their town, for in none of the succeeding layers of *débris* do we find the style of architecture to consist of large blocks of stone joined with earth; in none do we find the terra-cottas—with the exception of the round articles in the form of tops and volcanoes—to possess any resemblance with the excellent and artistic earthenware of the people of Priam.*

Upon the site of the destroyed city new settlers, of a different civilization, manners and customs, built a new town; but only the foundation of their houses consisted of stones joined with clay; all of the house-walls were built of unburnt bricks. Many such walls may be seen at a depth of from 7 to 10 meters (23 to 33 feet) in the earthen sides of my excavations; they have been preserved through the very fact that the houses were burnt out, and the walls of unburnt bricks, through the great heat, received a sort of brick-crust, or became actually burnt bricks.

In my memoir of the 23rd of last month, I spoke of a stone wall, found at a depth of 33 feet, which I hoped would extend down to the primary soil. Unfortunately, however, it proved to be merely the foundation of a house belonging to the immediate successors of the ancient Trojans, and these foundations only extended to a depth of 1¾ foot.

The remains of the ruined walls belonging to ancient Troy had, of course, to be levelled by the new settlers, whose mode of life and style of architecture were entirely different. This explains how it is that, with the exception of a small wall in the northern entrance of my large trench, I have hitherto not been able to point out a single wall

---

* Here, as well as in what goes before, Dr. Schliemann writes on the supposition, which he afterwards abandoned, that the remains in the lowest stratum are those of the Trojans of the Iliad.—[ED.]

belonging to ancient Troy ; and that, until now, I have only been able to present archæology with a few splendid urns, vases, pots, plates, and dishes, and with but one bowl (*crater*). (See Cut, No. 41, p. 74.) Yet I have found thousands of fragments of other excellent vessels, the sad memorials of a people whose fame is immortal.

I cannot conclude the description of the lowest stratum without mentioning that among the huge blocks of stone, at a depth of from 12 to 16 meters (39½ to 52½ feet), I found two toads; and at a depth of 39½ feet a small but very poisonous snake, with a scutiform head. The snake may have found its way down from above; but this is an impossibility in the case of the large toads —they must have spent 3000 years in these depths. It is very interesting to find in the ruins of Troy living creatures from the time of Hector and Andromache, even though these creatures are but toads.*

I must also draw attention to the fact that I have found the ⊓ twice on fragments of pottery, one of which was discovered at a depth of 16 meters (52½ feet), the other at 14 meters (46 feet). The primitive Trojans, therefore, belonged to the Aryan race, which is further sufficiently proved by the symbols on the round terra-cottas.

No. 110.

Fragment of Pottery, with the *Suastika*, from the lowest Stratum (14 M.).

The existence of the nation which succeeded the Trojans was likewise of a long duration, for all the layers of *débris* at the depth of from 10 to 7 meters (33 to 23 feet) belong to it. They also were of Aryan descent, for they possessed innumerable Aryan religious symbols. I think I have proved that several of the

---

* We believe that naturalists are now agreed that such appearances of toads imprisoned for long periods are deceptive. Into what depths cannot a tadpole (whether literal or metaphorical) wriggle himself down ?—[ED.]

symbols were common to our ancestors at a time when Germans, Pelasgians, Hindoos, Persians, Celts, and Greeks still formed one nation. I found no trace of a double cup among this people, but instead of it, those curious cups (vase-covers) which have a coronet below in place of a handle; then those brilliant red fanciful goblets, in the form of immense champagne-glasses, with two mighty handles on the sides: they are round

Nos. 111, 112. Double-handed Vases of Terra-cotta, from the Trojan Stratum (9 m.).

below, so that they also can only stand on their mouths. Further, those small covers, from about 4 to 4¾ inches high, with owls' faces, with a kind of helmet on the lower end, furnished with a high button or tuft, which is, no doubt, intended to represent the crest of a helmet and served as a handle. This cup likewise can only stand on its mouth.* Further, all those splendid vessels of burnt earthenware—as, for instance, funereal, water, or wine urns, 5 feet high and from 1¾ to 3¼ feet in

---

* This description itself suggests an inversion of the so-called "cup," which is, in fact, a vase-cover. For its form see No. 74, on p. 115.—[Ed.]

diameter; also smaller funereal urns, plates, dishes, and vases, of exceedingly fanciful forms, and from about 8 to 10 inches in height, with the owl's face of the tutelary goddess of Troy, two female breasts, and a navel, besides the two upraised arms on each side of the head, which served as handles; further, all of those vessels with a beak-shaped

mouth, bent back, and either short or long. Most of these vessels are round below, so that they cannot stand; others have three feet; others, again, are flat-bottomed. The neck of many is so much bent backwards that it resembles a swan or a goose. To this class also belong all of those globular and egg-shaped vessels, small and large, with or without a neck like a chimney, which have a short ring on either side, and a hole in the same direction in the lip, through which was passed the string for suspending them; many have in addition three little feet. All

No. 113. A Trojan Vase in Terra-cotta of a very remarkable form (8 M.).

are of uniform colour, either brown, yellow, red, or black; some have rows of leaves or twigs as decorations. I also meet with very curious vases, in the shape of animals, with three feet. The mouth of the vessel is in the tail, which is upright and very thick, and which is connected with the back by a handle. Upon one of these last-mentioned vases there are decorations, consisting of three engraved stripes of three lines each. I formerly found the Priapus only at a depth of 7 meters (23 feet); but a short time ago I found one at a depth of 13 meters (42½ feet). I now find it again at 8 meters (26 feet) that is, among the ruins of the nation of which I am at present speaking.   In these strata we also meet with an

immense quantity of those round terra-cottas (the whorls), which, it is true, deviate from the wheel-shape of the articles found on the primary soil owing to their greater thickness, and are also not of such excellently-burnt clay as those ; but, as anyone may convince himself by examining the drawings,

No. 114.   Engraved Terra-cotta Vessel in the form of a Pig (or Hedgehog ?).   7 M.

they are embellished with uncommonly beautiful and in-genious symbolical signs.   Among these the Sun-god always occupies the most prominent position ; but the fire-machine of our primeval ancestors, the holy sacrificial altar with blazing flames, the holy sôma-tree or tree of life, and the *rosa mystica*, are also very frequently met with here. This mystic rose, which occurs very often in the Byzantine sculptures, and the name of which, as is well known, is employed to designate the Holy Virgin in the Roman Catholic Litanies, is a very ancient Aryan religious symbol, as yet, unfortunately, unexplained.*   It is very ancient, because I find it at a depth of from 7 to 10 meters (23 to 33 feet) in the strata of the successors to the Trojans, which must belong to a period about 1200 years before Christ.†

The sign which resembles the Phœnician letter " Nun " I found represented sixteen times ‡ upon one of those round

---

* See Plate XXIII., No. 339 ; Plate XLVII., No. 478.

† According to Dr. Schliemann's later view these " successors to the Trojans " were, as we have seen, the Trojans themselves.—[ED.]

‡ The drawing, Plate XLVII., No. 480, shows the sign 20 times in 5 groups of 4 each.   This seems to be a similar type to the one described, but from a lesser depth.—[ED.]

terra-cottas from a depth of 8 meters (26 feet); for these signs
stand in groups of four, and by their position form a cross
round the sun, or, if my present supposition is right, round
the nave of the wheel representing the chariot of the sun.
I also find the symbol of lightning in all the higher strata
up to 10 feet below the surface. In all the strata, from a
depth of 33 feet up to 1¾ feet below the surface, I find
engravings of the sun with its rays innumerable times upon
the round terra-cottas, exactly as it is represented on the
head of the Sun-god on the metopé which I discovered
when excavating the temple; but more frequently still in
circles of three, four, five, six or eight double, treble or
quadruple rising suns, and in by far the greater number of
cases it stands in the centre of four treble rising suns, which
form a cross round it. Hundreds of times I find the sun
surrounded by stars in the centre of a double or treble
cross, which has a large dot on every one of the four ends.
These dots probably denote the four nails which fixed the
wooden frame by which the holy fire was prepared. At the
depth of from 10 to 7 meters (33 to 23 feet) I also found
although more rarely, five mystic roses in a circle round
the sun.   One with signs, which may
probably prove to be not merely symbols,
but actual letters, I found at a depth of 7
meters (23 feet).* I have still to mention
those round articles from the same depth,
which have three mystic roses and two
sheaves of sun-rays in the circle round the

No. 115.
Inscribed Whorl (7 M.).

sun.   Further, from a depth of 9 meters (29½ feet) I have
several round pieces, upon which there are 14 crooked
sheaves of three sun-rays each, resembling the sails of a
windmill, which radiate in all directions from the sun, while
the compartments between the sheaves of rays are filled
with stars. This representation must indicate the rotation

---

* The inscription, which Professor Gomperz has pointed out, is identical with that on Pl. LI., No. 496. (See pp. 83–84 and Appendix.)—[ED.]

of the wheel in the course of the sun's chariot in the heavens, that is, if the supposition I before ventured to make, that the round objects represent the wheel, is correct. Another, found at the same depth, has on one side three holy sacrificial altars covered with flames, and a group of stars; on the other side three similar altars, and a suastika forming a cross round the sun.* There also occur some with only four curved sheaves of rays, or two ⌐⌐ and two flaming altars in a cross round the sun; there is again another upon which two crosses stand opposite each other, and all the rest of the space round the sun (or round the nave of the wheel) is filled with stars. All the whorls met with at a depth of from 10 to 7 meters (33 to 23 feet) are made of clay, for the most part of black or red clay, and as hard as stone, which, in comparison with that of the whorls in the higher strata, is distinguished by its fineness. We also find in these strata some whorls made of lead or fine marble, but they have no decorations.

In the strata of the same nation I found also copper battle-axes, lances, arrows, knives, and implements of different kinds, as well as a number of moulds of schist and chlorite slate for casting these and many other objects, some being of forms quite unknown to me. Seals of terra-cotta, with crosses and other ornaments, are not peculiar to these strata, but occur also at a depth of from 33 feet as far up as 1¾ feet below the surface. We have also brought to light hand mill-stones of lava, which are oval on one side and flat on the other, and some also of granite; large and small hammers, axes, and balls with a hole through the centre; further, mortars and pestles of diorite, and weights of granite; quoits made of granite and other kinds of stone, with

No. 116.
Terra-cotta Seal
(1 M.).

---

* The types here described will be found on the Lithographs.

a hole through the centre for throwing them. Sling-bullets
made of loadstone, and great quantities of knives made
of white or yellow silex in the form of saws, sometimes
also knives of volcanic glass and lances of diorite are met

No. 117.   A Trojan Hand Mill-stone of Lava (10 M.).

No. 118.
A Piece of Granite, perhaps used, by means
of a wooden Handle, as an upper Mill-
stone (10 M.).

No. 119.
A massive Hammer of Diorite
(10 M.).

No. 120.
Piece of Granite, probably
used as a Pestle.   From
the lowest Stratum (11–
16 M.).

with among the ruins of this people, but all these instruments are much better finished than in the strata above a
depth of 7 meters (23 feet).

I likewise find in these strata numerous idols of very
fine marble, and upon a number of them are engraved the

owl's face of the Ilian Athena and her girdle. At a depth of 8 meters (26 feet) we discovered a terra-cotta idol of the same tutelary goddess; four horizontal strokes on the neck

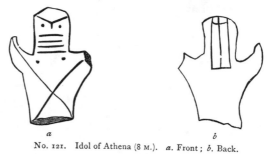

No. 121. Idol of Athena (8 m.). *a.* Front; *b.* Back.

seem to denote her armour; only one of the arms has been preserved, which is in an upright position; two lines proceeding from the arms and crossing each other over the body give her a warlike appearance; her breasts are indicated by two points; her long hair is distinctly marked at the back of the head.

At a depth of 9½ meters (30½ feet) among the yellow ashes of a house which was destroyed by fire, I found a large lump of thick wire, which I believed to be copper wire, and therefore laid carelessly upon my table; but when the lump was knocked down accidentally, a silver wire, which held the packet together, broke, and out fell three bracelets, one of which is simple, the second double, and the third treble: within the last is a very artistic ornament and an ear-ring formed of six wires, and these things must have been welded to the bracelet by the heat of the conflagration, for it cannot possibly have been worn on the arm as it is now.* The packet further contained a very pretty gold ear-ring, which has three rows of little stars on both sides; then two bunches of ear-rings of various forms, most of which are of silver and terminate in five leaves. But the packet also contained several ear-rings of the same form

---

* Similar jewels are depicted among the articles of the Treasure (Chapter XXIII., Plate XX.).

made of electrum (ἤλεκτρον) : three of the ear-rings I know positively to be of electrum; there are, however, probably several others of electrum among the two bunches which I dare not attempt to loosen for fear of breaking the silver ear-rings which have suffered very much from rust.

According to Pliny (*H. N.* XXXIII. 23), and Pausanias (V. 12, § 6) electrum was an artificial compound of metals, four parts of gold and one of silver. The most ancient Lydian coins are likewise made of electrum.

At the same depth I not unfrequently find balls of serpentine or porphyry of nearly 2 inches in diameter, and with a hole through the centre. Besides these we find spoons made of bone or terra-cotta, and great quantities of instruments of ivory and bone for use as pins. I also found a

Nos. 122, 123, 124.   Balls of fine red Agate ; from the Trojan Stratum (9 M.).

very artistically carved piece of ebony, which is certainly part of a musical stringed instrument. I must also mention having found, not only in these depths, but also up to 6 meters (20 feet) below the surface, round pieces of terra-cotta with a hole running longitudinally through them, 2¾ inches long and 2⅓ inches broad; and also pieces of terra-cotta from 2¾ to nearly 4 inches broad, flat below and rounded off at the top, with two holes at the edge of the broad surface, or with only one hole above running through from the side. All of these articles have probably served as weights. In all of the strata we discovered a number of the vertebræ of sharks, boars' tusks, antlers, and great quantities of the shells of small sea-mussels, of which the Trojans and their successors at all times must have been very fond.

I now come to the strata of *débris* at a depth of from
7 to 4 meters (23 to 13 feet), which are evidently also the
remains of a people of the Aryan race, who took possession
of the town built upon the ruins of Troy, and who destroyed
it and extirpated the inhabitants; for in these strata of
10 feet thick I find no trace of metal beyond two nails and
a small piece of silver wire, and the structure of the houses
is entirely different. All the house-walls consist of small
stones joined with clay; in the larger buildings the stones
are more or less hewn, but in the smaller they are altogether rough. Visitors to the Plain of Troy can see in
the earthen walls of my excavations, at these depths, a
number of larger or smaller house-walls of this description. Among others are the
remains of those huge walls 6¼
feet thick, of which I spoke in
my report of the 23rd of last
month. The foundations lie at
a depth of 20 feet, and they

No. 125.
A curious Terra-cotta Cup (4 M.).

No. 126.
Terra-cotta Pitcher of a frequent form
(6 M.).

extend to within 10 feet below the present surface;* for
as, with the exception of excavating the temple, I only

---

* Chapter IX., pp. 132–3.

intend to make the trench through the hill 98 feet broad above, it has not been necessary to pull down the building entirely.

In these strata (at a depth of from 23 to 13 feet) not only are all the stone implements much rougher, but all

No. 127.
A small Terra-cotta Vase, with two Handles and three feet (6 M.)

No. 128.
Terra-cotta Vase of a frequent form (6 M.).

the terra-cottas also are of a coarser quality.   Still it cannot be denied that with all their simplicity they possess a certain elegance, and I must especially mention the very pretty black or red vases in the form of hour glasses with two large handles, the red ones being nearly 4 inches high, the black ones 5½ inches high; the small jars in the form of cups with large handles, the larger jars with one or two handles; but above all the frequently occurring covers with the owl's face of the tutelary goddess of Troy, which are, it is true, almost like those from a depth of from 30 to 23 feet in size, but considerably inferior in quality.

The terra-cotta balls found in these strata are especially remarkable, owing to their most varied symbols. I will describe two of these, found at a depth of 5 meters (16½ feet). The surface of the one is divided by lines into eight equal parts;* in one of these is a sun with ten rays, of which only four are straight, all of the others seem to represent religious symbols. One ray has the form of the Phœnician letter "Nun," and must denote lightning;

---

* See Plate LI., No. 493. M. Burnouf's drawings, from which our engraving is taken, seem to differ from Dr. Schliemann's description in a few of the minuter details.—[ED.]

another ray has the form of a serpent; another again the form of the numeral III.; a fourth is the shape of a sign-post; and the remaining two in the form of fishing-hooks; beside the sun is a star. In the next division is a tree with eight branches, a quadrangle with two stars, and a triangle with four stars. The third field contains a tree with twelve branches; a circle with a star; and, beside and above a stroke, twelve stars, one of which has a dot in the centre. The twelve little stars may possibly denote the twelve signs of the zodiac, which, being the twelve stations of the sun, are personified in the Rigvêda by the twelve Adityas, sons of Aditi, the indivisible and infinite space. The fourth field contains a tree with only six branches, a triangle with three compartments, in one of which is a stroke, and also two squares. The fifth field has again a sun with six crooked rays and one straight ray. The sixth field has five divisions: in the first there are five, in the second four, and in the third seven little stars; the fourth division contains a sign resembling the numeral II., together with three stars; in the fifth division there is a simple cross. In the seventh field is a tree with ten branches. In the eighth field there is a figure like a serpent, and a star.

Upon the second terra-cotta ball there is a sun with thirteen straight rays; further there are, between two 卍, three groups of three stars each, and four straight lines; lastly, below the sun three similar lines and three stars.* We also frequently find in these strata terra-cotta balls completely covered with stars; likewise an immense number of the round terra-cottas in the form of tops and volcanoes, more than half of which are adorned with the most various symbolical signs. We have also discovered here many weapons of diorite and hard green stone, as well as a number of whetstones of black and

---

* On Plate L., No. 491, this ball is represented from M. Burnouf's drawings, showing six different faces.

green slate with a hole at one end.*   The use of these whetstones is not very clear to me, for, as I have already said,
in the depths of from 7 to 4 meters (23 to 13 feet) I have
found no trace of any metal beyond the two nails and the
piece of silver wire.   However, we came upon a few fragments of moulds for casting instruments, and hence it is
probable that copper was known.   In any case, however,
it was rare and costly, for otherwise I should not have
found such colossal masses of stone instruments.

I found in these depths a large number of curious
large vases, and among them several beautiful urns with
the owl's head of the Ilian Athena, her two female breasts,
navel, and the two upraised arms beside the head.   Upon
one of the navels is a cross and four holes, which are
doubtless intended to represent the four nails employed by
our Aryan ancestors to fasten the two pieces of wood
which were laid crosswise for producing the holy fire.†
In these strata I also discovered a number of those
cups in the form of champagne-glasses with two handles,
which however, as may be seen from the drawings,
become clumsier, smaller, and inferior in quality at
every yard the higher we ascend.   Cups with coronets
below (vase-covers) also occur, like-
wise many small red jars with three
feet and two handles, and several
hundreds of uncoloured jars, with
a handle from nearly 4 to 4¾ inches
high.   There are also enormous
masses of large clumsy hammers
and other instruments of diorite ; I also found a Priapus of
diorite, which is above 12½ inches high and 7¾ inches thick.

No. 129.
Terra-cotta Vase of a form frequent at the depth of 3–5 M.

There is a well belonging to this nation, built of good
hewn stones cemented with clay ; its opening is at a depth

---

* See No. 5, p. 24.—[ED.]   Perhaps they were used to polish the
terra-cotta vases.
† See No. 13, p. 35.

of 13 feet. I have had it cleared out almost as far as the
primary soil; one wall of this well is still to be seen on
the left side of the northern entrance of my great cutting.
Hand mill-stones of lava are also found in immense numbers
in these strata.

A new epoch in the history of Ilium commenced when
the accumulation of *débris* on this hill had reached a height
of 4 meters (13 feet) below its present surface; for the town
was again destroyed, and the inhabitants killed or driven
out by a wretched tribe, which certainly must likewise have
belonged to the Aryan race, for upon the round terra-cottas
I still very frequently find the tree of life and the simple
and double cross with the four nails. In these depths,
however, the form of the whorls degenerates; they become
more elongated and pointed; I also find many in the
form of cones about $1\frac{1}{5}$ inch to $1\frac{1}{2}$ inch in height, which

No. 130.   Terra-cotta Vessel (4 M.).

No. 131.   A small Terra-cotta Vase with
two Rings for suspension (2 M.).

never occur in the lower strata; most of them are without
decorations. Of pottery much less is found, and all of it
is much more inartistic than that in the preceding strata.
However, an exceedingly fanciful goblet, found at a depth
of 13 feet, deserves to be specially mentioned; its body,
which rests upon three little feet, is a tube, out of which
three small cups stand up. We still frequently meet with
cups (vase-covers) bearing the owl's face of the Ilian Athena,
and a kind of helmet, but they continue to become more
and more rude.* In like manner the cups in the form of

---

* Compare these with Cut No. 74 on p. 115.

champagne-glasses continue to be inferior in quality, they are always smaller and coarser, and are now only about 5 inches high, whereas at a depth of 33 feet they were 12⅔ inches high. Several vases with female breasts, navel, and upraised arms, occur at a depth of 4

Nos. 132, 133. Owl-faced Vase-covers (3 M.).   The second is of an unusual form.

Nos. 134, 135. Two-handled Cups from the upper Stratum (2 M.).

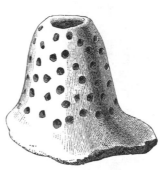

No. 136. Terra-cotta Vase (2 M.).   No. 137. Perforated Terra-cotta (2 M.).

meters (13 feet), one at a depth of 2½ meters (about 8 feet). Small red vases in the form of hour-glasses with a handle are still frequently met with; two were found at as small a depth as 2 meters (6½ feet). A very great number of

small ordinary jars were found at a depth of 4 and
3 meters (13 to 9¾ feet), but they almost entirely cease
to be found at 2 meters (6½ feet) below the surface. At

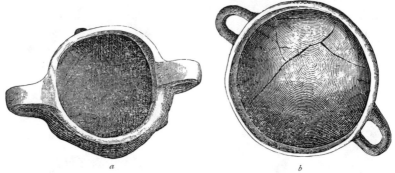

Nos. 138, 139.   Deep Plates (*pateræ*) with Rings for suspension, placed (*a*) vertically or (*b*) horizontally (1 and 2 M.).

the depths of 4, 3, and even 2½ meters (13, 9¾, and 8 feet)
I also found very many idols of the Ilian Athena, made ot
fine marble; upon several there are engravings of her owl's
head and girdle.

   At a depth of 3 meters (10 feet) I also found a terra-
cotta idol, which represents this same goddess with the owl's
face and two enormous eyes; she has two female breasts,

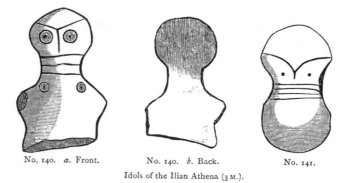

No. 140. *a*. Front.   No. 140. *b*. Back.   No. 141.
Idols of the Ilian Athena (3 M.).

and long hair hanging down behind. Three horizontal
lines on the neck seem to denote armour. At the same
depth I also found a small and splendid sacrificial basin of
terra-cotta, with three feet; in the basin there are engraved

a suastika, a tree with twenty-four branches, and a cater-pillar.*

Copper was known to this people, for I discovered here knives, lances, and nails made of this metal. The form of the nails is often curious, for occasionally I find them with two heads, one beside the other, sometimes with no head at all, but merely two pointed ends, so that a kind of head had to be made by bending over about $\frac{2}{5}$ of an inch at one of the ends. Another proof of their knowledge of metals is furnished by the moulds in mica-schist.

We find scarcely any stones in these strata, and the masses of charred ruins and wood-ashes leave no doubt that all the buildings of this tribe were made of wood. I find in these strata of 6½ feet thick some few stone weights, also a couple of hand-mills of lava, but otherwise no imple-ments of stone except knives of silex in the form of saws, which seem often to have been made with great care. Thus, for instance, at a depth of 6½ feet I found a saw made of silex 4¾ inches in length and 1·3 in breadth, which was so exquisitely

No. 142. Mould in Mica-schist for casting some unknown ob-ject (2¼ M.).

made that I at first thought it must be a comb. The upper portion of the saw bore the clearest marks of having been encased in wood.

With the people to whom these strata belonged—from 4 to 2 meters (13 to 6½ feet) below the surface—the pre-Hellenic ages end, for henceforward we see many ruined walls of Greek buildings, of beautifully hewn stones laid together without cement, and in the uppermost layer of all even the ruins of house-walls, in which the stones are joined

---

* See Plate XLVIII., No. 484.

with lime or cement.   Moreover, the painted and unpainted terra-cottas, occasionally found at a depth of 2 meters (6½ feet), leave no doubt that a Greek colony took possession of Ilium when the surface of this hill was still that much lower than it is now.   It is impossible to determine exactly when this new colonization took place, but it must certainly have been much earlier than the visit of Xerxes reported by Herodotus (VII. 43), which took place 480 years before Christ.   According to Strabo (XIII. 1. 42) the town was built under Lydian dominion, and hence this event may have taken place about 700 B.C., for the commencement of the Lydian dominion is assigned to the year 797 B.C.   Fluted jars, which archæologists believe to belong to a period 200 years anterior to Christ, are found immediately below the surface, at a depth of from 1¾ to 3¼ feet. The Greek colony does not appear by any means to have at all extirpated the inhabitants of Ilium, for I still find a great deal of pre-Hellenic pottery at a depth of 6½ and even of 5 feet.   At all events those round lamp-shaped terra-cottas with a potter's stamp and two holes at the edge, found as far down as 6½ feet, seem to me to be of Greek manufacture. The round articles with one hole through the centre, without or with decorations representing the sun and its rays, or the sun with stars, or four double or treble rising suns forming a cross, or even the sun in the centre of a simple or double cross, occur in numbers as far up as a depth of 3¼ feet; but in these uppermost strata the quality of the clay of which these articles are made is very bad, and the symbolical signs are very coarsely and inartistically engraved.   My wife, who is enthusiastic about the discovery of Ilium, and who helps me assiduously in the excavations, found, in a cutting which she and her maid had opened close to our house, the same round terra-cottas, with or without decorations, even quite close to the surface.   How these exceedingly remarkable objects, which are adorned with the most ancient religious symbols of the Aryan race, can have continued to be used

for more than 1000 years by the four tribes which successively held possession of Ilium, and even by the civilized
Greek colony, is to me a problem as inexplicable as the
purpose for which they were used.   If, as I now conjecture,
they represent the wheel, which in the Rigvêda is the symbol
of the sun's chariot, they were probably used as *Ex votos*, or
they were worshipped as idols of the sun-god, Phœbus Apollo.
But why are there such enormous numbers of them?

The well, which I last year discovered at a depth of
6½ feet, built of hewn stones with cement, belongs of course
to the Greek colony; so also do all those enormous water
and wine urns (πίθοι), which I met with in the uppermost strata.   I find all of these colossal urns, as well as all
those met with in the deeper strata, standing upright, which
is the best proof, if indeed any were needed, that the
mighty masses of *débris* cannot have been brought here
from another place, but that they were formed graduallÿ in
the course of thousands of years, and that the conquerors
and destroyers of Ilium, or at least the new settlers after its
conquest and destruction, never had the same manners and
customs as their predecessors.   Consequently, for many
centuries, houses with walls built of unburnt bricks stood
upon the mighty heaps of stone, from 13 to 20 feet thick,
belonging to the enormous buildings of the primitive
Trojans; again, for centuries, houses built of stones joined
with clay were erected upon the ruins of houses of brick;
for another long period, upon the ruins of these stone
houses wooden houses were erected; and lastly, upon the
charred ruins of the latter were established the buildings
of the Greek colony, which at first consisted of large hewn
stones joined with clay or cement.   It can thus no longer
seem astonishing that these masses of ruins, covering the
primary soil, have a thickness of from 14 to 16 meters
(46 to 52½ feet) at the least.

I take this opportunity of giving a translation of the
answer I made to an article published by M. G. Nikolaïdes

in No. 181 of the Greek newspaper ' Ἐφημερὶς Συζητήσεων,' in which the author endeavours to prove that I am giving myself unnecessary trouble, and that the site of Troy is not to be found here, but on the heights of Bunarbashi.*

" M. Nikolaïdes maintains that the site of Troy cannot be discovered by means of excavations or other proofs, but solely from the Iliad. He is right, if he supposes that Ilium is only a picture of Homer's imagination, as the City of the Birds was but a fancy of Aristophanes. If, however, he believes that a Troy actually existed, then his assertion appears most strange. He thereupon says that Troy was situated on the heights of Bunarbashi, for that at the foot of them are the two springs beside which Hector was killed. This is, however, a great mistake, for the number of springs there is forty, and not two, which is sufficiently clear from the Turkish name of the district of the springs, 'Kirkgiös' (40 eyes or springs). My excavations in 1868, on the heights of Bunarbashi, which I everywhere opened down to the primary soil, also suffice to prove that no village, much less a town, has ever stood there. This is further shown by the shape of the rocks, sometimes pointed, sometimes steep, and in all cases very irregular. At the end of the heights, at a distance of 11½ miles from the Hellespont, there are, it is true, the ruins of a small town, but its area is so very insignificant, that it cannot possibly have possessed more than 2000 inhabitants, whereas, according to the indications of the Iliad, the Homeric Ilium must have had over 50,000. In addition to this, the small town is four hours distant, and the 40 springs are 3½ hours distant, from the Hellespont; and such distances entirely contradict the statements of the Iliad, according to which the Greeks forced their way fighting, four times in

---

* We do not feel it right to spoil the unity of the following disquisition by striking out the few repetitions of arguments urged in other parts of the work.—[ED.]

one day, across the land which lay between the naval camp and the walls of Troy.

"M. Nikolaïdes's map of the Plain of Troy may give rise to errors; for he applies the name of Simoïs to the river which flows through the south-eastern portion of the Plain, whereas this river is the Thymbrius, as Mr. Frank Calvert has proved. In his excavations on the banks of that river, Mr. Calvert found the ruins of the temple of the Thymbrian Apollo, about which there cannot be the slightest doubt, owing to the long inscription which contains the inventory of the temple. Then on the map of M. Nikolaïdes I find no indication whatever of the much larger river Doumbrek-Su, which flows through the north-eastern portion of the Plain of Troy, and passed close by the ancient town of Ophrynium, near which was Hector's tomb and a grove dedicated to him.[*] Throughout all antiquity, this river was called the Simoïs, as is also proved by Virgil (*Æn.* III. 302, 305). The map of M. Nikolaïdes equally ignores the river which flows from south to north through the Plain, the Kalifatli-Asmak, with its enormously broad bed, which must certainly at one time have been occupied by the Scamander, and into which the Simoïs still flows to the north of Ilium. The Scamander has altered its course several times, as is proved by the three large river-beds between it and the bed of the Kalifatli-Asmak. But even these three ancient river-beds are not given in the map of M. Nikolaïdes.

"In complete opposition to all the traditions of antiquity, the map recognises the tomb of Achilles in the conical sepulchral mound of In-Tépé, which stands on a hill at the foot of the promontory of Rhœteum, and which, from time immemorial, has been regarded as the tomb of Ajax. During an excavation of this hill, in 1788, an

---

[*] Strabo, XIII. i. p. 103; Lycophron, *Cassandra*, 1208. See further, on the Simoïs, Note A, p. 358.

arched passage was found, about 3¾ feet high, and built of
bricks; as well as the ruins of a small temple.   According
to Strabo (XIII. 1. p. 103), the temple contained the statue
of Ajax, which Mark Antony took away and presented to
Cleopatra.   Augustus gave it back to the inhabitants of
the town of Rhœteum, which was situated near the tomb.
According to Philostratus (*Heroica*, I.), the temple, which
stood over the grave, was repaired by the Emperor Hadrian,
and according to Pliny (*H. N.*, V. 33), the town of Aianteum was at one time situated close to the tomb.   On the
other hand, throughout antiquity, the tomb of Achilles was
believed to be the sepulchral mound on an elevation at the
foot of the promontory of Sigeum, close to the Hellespont,
and its position corresponds perfectly with Homer's description.*

"The field situated directly south of this tomb, and
which is covered with fragments of pottery, is doubtless the
site of the ancient town of Achilleum, which, according to
Strabo (XIII. 1. p. 110), was built by the Mitylenæans, who
were for many years at war with the Athenians, while the
latter held Sigeum, and which was destroyed simultaneously
with Sigeum by the people of Ilium.   Pliny (*H. N.*, V. 33)
confirms the disappearance of Achilleum.   The Ilians here
brought offerings to the dead, not only on the tomb of
Achilles, but also upon the neighbouring tombs of Patroclus and Antilochus.†   Alexander the Great offered sacri-

---

* *Odyssey*, XXIV. 80–81 :

> Ἀμφ' αὐτοῖσι δ' ἔπειτα μέγαν καὶ ἀμύμονα τύμβον
> Χεύαμεν Ἀργείων ἱερὸς στρατὸς αἰχμητάων,
> Ἀκτῇ ἐπὶ προυχούσῃ, ἐπὶ πλατεῖ Ἑλλησπόντῳ,
> Ὡς κεν τηλεφανὴς ἐκ ποντόφιν ἀνδράσιν εἴη
> Τοῖς, οἳ νῦν γεγάασι, καὶ οἳ μετόπισθεν ἔσονται.

"We the holy army of the spear-throwing Argives, then raised round these
(bones) a great and honourable tomb on the projecting shore of the broad Hellespont,
so that it might be seen from the sea by the men who are now born and who shall be
hereafter."—Dr. Schliemann's translation.

† Strabo, XIII. 1.

PLATE VII.

A.—MOUND OF IN-TÉPÉ,

The traditional Tomb of Ajax, with the Ruins of his Temple.

B.—MOUND CALLED THE TOMB OF ACHILLES.

fices here in the temple of Achilles.* Caracalla also, accompanied by his army, offered sacrifices to the manes of Achilles, and held games around the tomb.† Homer never says anything about a river in the Greek camp, which probably extended along the whole shore between Cape Sigeum and the Scamander, which at that time occupied the ancient bed of the Kalifatli-Asmak. But the latter, below the village of Kumköi, is at all events identical with the large bed of the small stream In-tépé-Asmak, which flows into the Hellespont near Cape Rhœteum.

"M. Nikolaïdes further quotes the following lines from the Iliad (II. 811–815) :—

> Ἔστι δέ τις προπάροιθε πόλιος αἰπεῖα κολώνη,
> Ἐν πεδίῳ ἀπάνευθε, περίδρομος ἔνθα καὶ ἔνθα,
> Τὴν ἤτοι ἄνδρες Βατίειαν κικλήσκουσιν,
> Ἀθάνατοι δέ τε σῆμα πολυσκάρθμοιο Μυρίνης.
> Ἔνθα τότε Τρῶές τε διέκριθεν ἠδ' ἐπίκουροι.

> ' Before the city stands a lofty mound,
>   Each way encircled by the open plain ;
>   Men call it Batiea ; but the Gods
>   The tomb of swift Myrina ; mustered there
>   The Trojans and Allies their troops arrayed.'

M. Nikolaïdes gathers from this, that in front of Ilium there was a very high hill, upon which the Trojan army of 50,000 men were marshalled in battle-array. I, however, do not interpret the above lines by supposing that the mound of Batiea was large and spacious, nor that 50,000 were marshalled upon it in battle-array. On the contrary, when Homer uses the word 'αἰπύς' for height, he always means 'steep and lofty,' and upon a steep and lofty height 50,000 Trojans could not possibly have been marshalled. Moreover, the poet expressly says that the steep hill is called by the gods the tomb of the nimble-limbed Myrina,

---

* Plutarch, 'Life of Alexander the Great'; Cicero, pro Archia, 10 ; Ælian, V. H., 12, 7.

† Dio Cassius, LXXVII.

while 'Batiea,' the name which men gave the hill, can signify only 'the tomb of Batiea.' For, according to Apollodorus (iii. 12), Batiea was the daughter of the Trojan King Teucer, and married Dardanus, who had immigrated from Samothrace, and who eventually became the founder of Troy.*   Myrina was one of the Amazons who had undertaken the campaign against Troy.†   Homer can never have wished us to believe that 50,000 warriors were marshalled upon a steep and lofty tumulus, upon whose summit scarcely ten men could stand; he only wished to indicate the locality where the Trojan army was assembled; they were therefore marshalled round or beside the tumulus.

"M. Nikolaïdes goes on to say, that such a hill still exists in front of Bunarbashi, whereas there is no hill whatever, not even a mound, before Ilium Novum.   My answer to this is that in front of the heights of Bunarbashi there are none of those conical tumuli called 'σήματα' by Homer, that however there must have been one in front of Hissarlik, where I am digging, but it has disappeared, as do all earthen mounds when they are brought under the plough.‡   Thus, for instance, M. Nikolaïdes, during his one day's residence in the Plain of Troy in the year 1867, still found the tumulus of Antilochus near the Scamander, for he speaks of it in his work published in the same year.   I, too, saw the same tumulus in August, 1868, but even then it had considerably decreased in size, for it had just begun to be ploughed over, and now it has long since disappeared.

"M. Nikolaïdes says that I am excavating in New Ilium. My answer is that the city, whose depths I am investigating, was throughout antiquity, nay from the time of its foundation to that of its destruction, always simply called Ilium, and that no one ever called it New Ilium, for everyone

---

* *Iliad*, XX. 215–218.
† Herodotus, I. 27 ; *Iliad*, III. 189–190 ; Strabo, XIII. 3.
‡ But see further on this point, Chapter XI., pp. 197–8.—[Ed.]

believed that the city stood on the site of the Homeric Ilium, and that it was identical with it.   The only person who ever doubted its identity with Ilium, the city of Priam, was Demetrius of Scepsis, who maintained that the famous old city had stood on the site of the village of the Ilians (Ἰλιέων κώμη), which lies 30 stadia (3 geog. miles) to the south-east.   This opinion was afterwards shared by Strabo, who however, as he himself admits, had never visited the Plain of Troy; hence he too calls the town 'τὸ σημερινὸν Ἴλιον,' to distinguish it from the Homeric Ilium.   My last year's excavations on the site of the Ἰλιέων κώμη have, however, proved that the continuous elevation on one side of it, which appeared to contain the ruins of great town walls, contains in reality nothing but mere earth.   Wherever I investigated the site of the ancient village, I always found the primary soil at a very inconsiderable depth, and nowhere the slightest trace of a town ever having stood there.   Hence Demetrius of Scepsis and Strabo, who adopted his theory, were greatly mistaken. The town of Ilium was only named Ilium Novum about 1000 years after its complete destruction; in fact this name was only given to it in the year 1788 by Lechevalier, the author of the theory that the Homeric Ilium stood on the heights of Bunarbashi.   Unfortunately, however, as his work and map of the Plain of Troy prove, Lechevalier only knew of the town from hearsay; he had never taken the trouble to come here himself, and hence he has committed the exceedingly ludicrous mistake, in his map, of placing his New Ilium 4¼ miles from Hissarlik, on the other side of the Scamander, near Kum-kaleh.

" I wonder where M. Nikolaïdes obtained the information that the city which he calls Ilium Novum was founded by Astypalæus in the sixth century B.C.   It seems that he simply read in Strabo (XIII. 602), that the Astypalæans, living in Rhœteum, built on the Simoïs the town of Polion (which name passed over into Polisma), which, as it had no natural fortifications, was soon destroyed, and that he has changed this statement of Strabo's by making the Astypalæans build Ilium Novum in the sixth century B.C. In the following sentence Strabo says that the town (Ilium) arose under the dominion of the Lydians, which began in 797 B.C. Whence can M. Nikolaïdes have obtained the information that the foundation of the town was made in the sixth century?

"M. Nikolaïdes further says that Homer certainly saw the successors of Æneas ruling in Troy, else he could not have put the prophecy of that dynasty into the mouth of Poseidon.* I also entertained the same opinion, until my excavations proved it to be erroneous, and showed undoubtedly that Troy was completely destroyed, and rebuilt by another people.

"As a further proof that the site of the Homeric Ilium was on the heights of Bunarbashi, M. Nikolaïdes says that the Trojans placed a scout on the tumulus of Æsyetes, to watch when the Achæans would march forth from their ships, and he thinks that, on account of the short distance from the Hellespont, this watching would have been superfluous and unreasonable if, as I say, Troy had stood on the site of Ilium, which M. Nikolaïdes calls Ilium Novum. I am astonished at this remark of M. Nikolaïdes, for, as he can see from his own map of the Plain of Troy, the distance from hence to the Hellespont is nearly four miles, or 1½ hour's walk, whereas no human eye can recognise men at a distance of 1 mile, much less at a distance of four. M. Nikolaïdes, however, believes the tumulus of Æsyetes to be the mound called Udjek-Tépé, which is 8 miles or 3½ hours' journey from the Hellespont. But at such a distance the human eye could scarcely see the largest ships, and could in no case recognise men.

---

* *Iliad*, XX. 307–308, quoted in the Introduction, p. 19.

" In like manner, the assertion of M. Nikolaïdes, that there is no spring whatever near Hissarlik, is utterly wrong. It would be unfortunate for me if this were true, for I have constantly to provide my 130 workmen with fresh water to drink; but, thank God, close to my excavations, immediately below the ruins of the town-wall, there are two beautiful springs, one of which is even a double one. M. Nikolaïdes is also wrong in his assertion that the Scamander does not flow, and never has flowed, between Hissarlik and the Hellespont; for, as already stated, the Scamander must at one time have occupied the large and splendid bed of the Kalifatli-Asmak, which runs into the Hellespont near Cape Rhœteum, and which is not given in the map of M. Nikolaïdes.

" Lastly, he is completely wrong in his statement that the hill of Hissarlik, where I am digging, lies at the extreme north-eastern end of the Plain of Troy; for, as everyone may see by a glance at the map, the Plain extends still further to the north-east an hour and a half in length and half an hour in breadth, and only ends at the foot of the heights of Renkoï and the ancient city of Ophrynium.

" It will be easily understood that, being engaged with my superhuman works, I have not a moment to spare, and therefore I cannot waste my precious time with idle talk. I beg M. Nikolaïdes to come to Troy, and to convince himself with his own eyes that, in refuting his erroneous statements, I have described all I see here before me with the most perfect truth."

CHAPTER XI.

Increase of men and machinery and cost on the works : but slow progress — Continued hurricane on " the windy Ilium " (Ἴλιος ἠνεμόεσσα)
— The great platform proves too high — New cutting — Excavation
of the temple — Objects found — Greek statuettes in terra-cotta —
Many whorls with ⊓⊔ and suns — Wheel-shaped whorls with simple
patterns in the lowest strata — Terra-cotta balls with suns and stars—
Use of the whorls as amulets or coins discussed — Little bowls,
probably lamps — Other articles of pottery — Funnels — A terra-
cotta bell — Various beautiful terra-cottas — Attempts at forgery
by the workmen — Mode of naming the men — The springs in front
of Ilium — Question of Homer's hot and cold spring — Course of
the Simoïs — The tomb of Batiea or Myrina identified with the
Pacha Tépé — Theatre of Lysimachus — Heat and wind — Plague
of insects and scorpions — Konstantinos Kolobos, a native genius
without feet.

On the Hill of Hissarlik, July 13th, 1872.

My last report was dated the 18th of June. As the great
extent of my excavations renders it necessary for me
to work with no less than 120 men, I have already been
obliged, on account of the harvest season, to increase the
daily wages to 12 piasters since the 1st of June; but even
this would not have enabled me to collect the requisite
number of men, had not Mr. Max Müller, the German
Consul in Gallipoli, had the kindness to send me 40 workmen from that place. In consequence of this, even during
the busiest harvest season, I have always had from 120 to
130 workmen, and now that the harvest is over, I have
constantly 150. To facilitate the works, I have procured,
through the kindness of the English Consul in Constantinople, Mr. Charles Cookson, 10 " man-carts," which

are drawn by two men and pushed by a third. The same
gentleman also sent me 20 wheel-barrows, so that I now
work with 10 man-carts and 88 wheel-barrows. In addition to these I keep six more carts with horses, each of
which costs 5 francs a day, so that the total cost of my
excavations amounts to more than 400 francs (16*l.*) a
day. Besides battering-rams, chains, and windlasses, my
implements consist of 24 large iron levers, 108 spades, and
103 pickaxes, all of the best English manufacture. From
sunrise to sunset all are busily at work, for I have three
capital foremen, and my wife and I are always present at
the works. But for all this I do not think that I now
remove more than 400 cubic yards of *débris* in a day, for
the distance is always increasing, and in several places it
is already more than 262 feet. Besides this, the continual
hurricane from the north, which drives the dust into
our eyes and blinds us, is exceedingly disturbing. This
perpetual high wind is perhaps explained by the fact that
the Sea of Marmora, with the Black Sea behind it, is connected with the Ægean Sea by a strait comparatively so
narrow. Now, as such perpetual high winds are unknown
in any other part of the world, Homer must have lived in
the Plain of Troy, otherwise he would not have so often
given to his Ἴλιος the appropriate epithet of " ἠνεμόεσσα "
(the "windy" or "stormy"), which he gives to no other
place.

As I have already said, at a perpendicular depth of 12
meters (39½ feet) below the summit of the hill (on the
site of what is probably the temple built by Lysimachus)
I have dug a platform, 102 feet broad below and 112 feet
wide at the top: it already extends to a length of 82 feet.
But to my great alarm I find that I have made it at least
5 meters (16½ feet) too high; for, in spite of the great
depth and the great distance from the declivity of the hill,
I am here still in the *débris* of the Greek colony, whereas
on the northern declivity of the hill I generally reached the

ruins of the preceding people at a depth of less than 6½ feet. To make the whole platform 16½ feet lower would be a gigantic piece of work, for which I have no patience at present, on account of the advanced season of the year. But in order as soon as possible to find out what lies hidden in the depths of this temple, I have contented myself with making a cutting 26 feet broad above and 13 feet wide below, exactly 16¼ feet below the platform and in the centre of it. This cutting I am having dug out at the same time from below and on two terraces, so it advances rapidly.

Since the discovery of the Sun-god with the four horses, many blocks of marble with representations of suns and flowers have been found, but no sculptures of any importance. As yet very few other objects have been brought to light from the excavation of the temple; only a few round terra-cottas with the usual decoration of the central sun surrounded by three, four, or five triple or quadruple rising suns; knives of silex in the form of saws, a few pretty figures in terra-cotta, among which is a priestess with very expressive Assyrian features, with a dress of a brilliant red and green colour, and a red cloth round her head; also a small bowl, the lower end of which represents the head of a mouse. The mouse, it is well known, is a creature inspired by the vapours of the earth, and, as the symbol of wisdom, was sacred to Apollo. According to Strabo (XIII. p. 613) Apollo is said to have caused mice to show the Teucrians, who migrated from Crete, the place where they were to settle. However, the bowl with the head of a mouse is no more a proof that the temple built here by Lysimachus was dedicated to Apollo than is the metopé representing the Sun-god with four horses.

In the other parts of my excavations, since my last report, we have again brought to light an immense number of round terra-cottas, and among them, from a depth of from 4 to 10 meters (13 to 33 feet), a remarkable number with three, four, or five 卐 round the central sun.* One, from a depth of 23 feet,† shows the central sun surrounded by six suns, through each of which a 卐 passes; upon another, found at a depth of 33 feet, the central sun has 12 trees instead of rays;‡ upon a third, brought from a depth of 16½ feet, the sun has seven rays in the form of fishing-hooks, one in the form of the figure three and two in the shape of the Phœnician letter Nun, then follow 12 sheaves of rays, in each of which are four little stars; upon a fourth terra-cotta, which I found at a depth of 16½ feet, there are four rising suns and a tree in the circle round the sun.§ I very frequently find between the rising suns three or four rows of three dots running towards the central sun, ‖ which, as already said, according to É. Burnouf, denote "royal majesty" in the Persian cuneiform inscriptions. It is certain that this symbol is here also intended to glorify the Sun-god. At a depth of from 7 to 10 meters (23 to 33 feet) we also find round terra-cottas, upon which the entire surface round the sun is filled with little stars, and in addition only one 卐.

During the last few days we have also found, in the strata next above the primary soil, at a depth of from 46 to 36 feet, a number of round brilliant black terra-cottas of exquisite workmanship; most of them much flatter than those occurring in the higher strata, and resembling a wheel; many are in the shape of large flat buttons.¶ But we also meet with some in the form of tops and volcanoes, which differ from those found in the higher strata only by the fineness of the terra-cotta and by their better workmanship. The decorations on these very ancient articles are, however, generally much simpler than

---

* See the Plates of Whorls, Nos. 350, 351, 352, 356, 357, 359, &c.
† Plate XXVI., No. 362.   M. Burnouf calls these "the 6 bi-monthly sacrifices."
‡ Plate XXXIII., No. 402.   § Plate XXXIV., No. 403.
‖ Plate XXII., No. 320.   ¶ See the Sections on Plate XXI.

those met with above a depth of 10 meters (33 feet), and
are mostly confined to the representation of the sun with
its rays, or with stars between the latter, or of the sun in
the centre of a simple cross, or in the middle of four or
five double or treble rising suns. At a depth of 6 meters
(20 feet) we again found a round terra-cotta in the form of
a volcano, upon which are engraved three antelopes in the
circle round the sun.

At a depth of from 5 to 8 meters (16½ to 26 feet) a
number of terra-cotta balls were found, the surface of
each being divided into eight fields; these contain a great
many small suns and stars, either enclosed by circles or
standing alone. Most of the balls, however, are without
divisions and covered with stars; upon some I find the ⊐⊔
and the tree of life, which, as already said, upon a terra-
cotta ball found at a depth of 26 feet, had stars between
its branches.

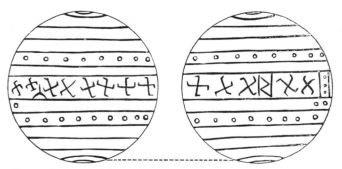

No. 143.   Terra-cotta Ball, representing apparently the climates of the globe (8 m.).*

Among the thousands and thousands of round terra-
cottas in the form of the volcano, the top, or the wheel,

---

* In the ball here depicted there is no mistaking the significance of
the line of ⊐⊔, the symbols of fire, as denoting the torrid zone. The
three dots are, according to M. Burnouf, the symbol of royal majesty
therein residing. The two rows of dots parallel to the torrid zone may
possibly represent the inhabited regions of the temperate zones, according to the oriental theory followed by Plato.—[Ed.]

which are found here from the surface down to a depth of
from 14 and 16 meters (46 to 53 feet)—that is, from the
end of the Greek colony down to the ruined strata of the
first inhabitants, I have not yet found a single one with
symbolical signs, upon which I could discover the slightest
trace that it had been used for any domestic purpose.*   On
the other hand, among those which have no decorations I
find a few, perhaps two in a hundred, of those in the form
of volcanoes, the upper surfaces of which show distinct
traces of rubbing, as if from having been used on the
spinning-wheel or loom.   That these articles, which are
frequently covered with the finest and most artistic engravings, should have served as weights for fishing-nets, is
utterly inconceivable, for, apart from all other reasons
opposed to such a supposition, pieces of terra-cotta have
not the requisite weight, and of course are directly spoilt
by being used in water.

M. É. Burnouf writes to me, that these exceedingly
remarkable objects were either worn by the Trojans
and their successors as amulets, or must have been
used as coins.   Both of these suppositions, however, seem
to me to be impossible.   For amulets they are much
too large and heavy, for they are from above 1 inch to
nearly 2 inches, and some even $2\frac{1}{3}$ inches, in diameter,
and from $\frac{3}{8}$ of an inch to nearly 2 inches high; moreover, it would be most uncomfortable to wear even a
single one of these heavy pieces on the neck or breast.
That they were used as coins appears to me inconceivable,
on account of the religious symbols; moreover, if they had
been so used, they would show traces of wear from their
continual transfer.   The white substance with which the
engravings are filled seems also to contradict their having
been used as coins; for in their constant passage from
hand to hand it would have soon disappeared.   Lastly,

---

* See the qualification of this statement on p. 40.

such an use is inconsistent with the fact that they also occur
in the strata of the Greek colony, in which I find a number
of copper and some silver coins of Ilium.   However, the
latter belong for the most part to the time of the Roman
emperors, and I cannot say with certainty that they reach
back beyond our Christian era.   There are, however, coins
of Sigeum, which probably belong to the second century
before Christ, for in Strabo's time this town was already
destroyed.

At a depth of 14 meters (46 feet) I find, among
other curious objects, small round bowls only 1¾ inch in
diameter; some of them have, on the edge of the bottom,
four little feet with a perforated hole, and in the centre a

No. 144.   Small Terra-cotta Vessel from the lowest Stratum, with four perforated feet, and one
foot in the middle (14 M.).*

fifth little foot without a hole.   Other bowls of the same
size have four little feet, only two of which have a perforated hole.   My conjecture is that all of these small
bowls, which could both stand and be hung up, were
used by the ancient Trojans as lamps.   Among the ruins
of the three succeeding nations I find no trace of lamps,
and only at a depth of less than a meter (3¼ feet) do I
find Greek λύχνοι.

At the depth of 2 meters (6½ feet) I found, among
the ruins of a house, a great quantity of very small
bowls, only 3–4ths of an inch high and 2–5ths of an

---

* In the Atlas, Dr. Schliemann describes this and another such as
Trojan lamps, but adds that they may be only vase covers.

inch broad, together with their small lids; their use is unknown to me.   At all depths below 4 meters (13 feet) I find the small flat saucers of from nearly 2 inches to above 3 inches in diameter, with two holes opposite each other; from 4 to 7 meters (13 to 23 feet) they are coarse, but from 7 to 10 meters (23 to 33 feet) they are finer, and from 13 to 14 meters (42½ to 46 feet) they are very fine.   I am completely ignorant as to what they can have been used for.   At all these depths I also find funnels from 2¾ to above 3 inches long, the broad end of which is only a little above an inch in diameter.   In the upper strata they are made of very coarse clay, but at an increasing depth they gradually become better, and at a depth

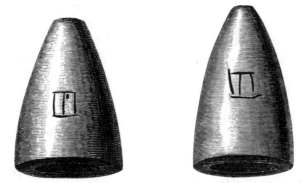

Nos. 145, 146.   Two little Funnels of Terra-cotta, inscribed with Cyprian Letters (3 m.).

of 46 feet they are made of very good terra-cotta.   It is extremely remarkable, however, that these curious and very "unpractical" funnels were kept in use in an entirely unchanged pattern by all the tribes which inhabited Ilium from the foundation of the city to before the Greek colony. I also find, in the second and third strata, terra-cottas in the form of the primitive canoes which were made of the hollowed trunk of a tree.   From 4 to 7 meters (13 to 23 feet) they are coarse, and about 4 inches long; at a depth of from 7 to 10 meters (23 to 33 feet) they are finer, and from 1½ to 2¾ inches long.   They may have been used as salt-cellars or pepper-boxes; I found several with flat lids.

These vessels cease to be found in the lowest stratum. Miniature vases and pots, between 1 and 2 inches high, are frequently found in all the strata from a depth of from 10 to 33 feet; at a depth of from 46 to 52½ feet only three miniature pots were discovered; one is not quite an inch high. At a depth of 5 meters (16½ feet) we found a perfectly closed earthen vessel with a handle, which seems to have been used as a bell, for there are pieces of metal inside of it which ring when it is shaken.

No. 147. A Trojan Humming-top (7 M.).

No. 148.   Terra-cotta Bell, or Clapper, or Rattle (5 M., 7 in the Photograph.).

Of cups (vase-covers) with owls' heads and helmets, since my last report two have been brought out from a depth of 10 and 11 feet, two from 16 feet, and one from 26 feet. The first are made of bad terra-cotta and are inartistic; those from a depth of 16 feet are much better finished and of a better clay; while that from 26 feet (8 meters) is so beautiful, that one is inclined to say that it represents the actual portrait of the goddess with the owl's face.* During these last few days we have found a number of those splendid red cups in the form of large champagne-glasses, without a foot, but with two enormous handles, one of which was 10½ inches high; but I have already found one 12½ inches in height. From a depth of from 26 to 33 feet we have also brought out many small pots with three little feet, with rings at the sides and holes in the mouth for hanging up, and with pretty engraved decorations. Upon the whole, we have

---

* The one meant seems to be that engraved on p. 115 (No. 74).

met with many beautiful terra-cottas from all the strata
during the last few days.

I have still to describe one of those very pretty vases
which occur abundantly at the depth of from 7 to 10
meters (23 to 33 feet), and have either two closed handles,
or, in place of them, two handles with perforated holes,
and also two holes in the mouth in the same direction;
thus they could stand or be hung up by means of strings
drawn through the four holes. They have in most cases
decorations all round them, which generally consist, above
and below, of three parallel lines drawn round them horizontally; between these there are 24 perpendicular lines, which
likewise run parallel; the spaces formed by the latter are
filled alternately with three or six little stars.* At a depth
of from 7 to 10 meters (23 to 33 feet) we also meet,
although seldom, with vases having cuneiform decorations.
I must, however, remind the reader that all the decorations
met with here, at a depth of from 33 feet up to 6½ feet,
have always been more or less artistically engraved upon
the terra-cottas when they were still soft and unburnt,
that all of the vases have a uniform colour (though the
ordinary pots are in most cases uncoloured), and that we
have never found a trace of painting in these depths, with
the exception of a curious box in the form of a band-box,
found at a depth of 8 meters (26 feet), which has three
feet as well as holes for hanging it up. It is adorned
on all sides with red decorations on a yellow ground,
and on its lid there is a large ᛭ or a very similar symbol
of the Maya, the fire-machine of our Aryan forefathers.

In the lowest stratum also, at the depth of 52½ feet,
I found only the one fragment, already described, of
a vase with an actual painting.† All of the other vessels
found in these strata, even the round terra-cottas in the
form of wheels, volcanoes, or tops, are of a brilliant

---

* See Cut, No. 149, p. 199.   † See Cut, No. 1, p. 15.

black, red or brown colour, and the decorations are artistically engraved and filled with a white substance, so as to be more striking to the eye.

As every object belonging to the dark night of the pre-Hellenic times, and bearing traces of human skill in art, is to me a page of history, I am, above all things, obliged to take care that nothing escapes me. I therefore pay my workmen a reward of 10 paras (5 centimes, or a half-penny) for every object that is of the slightest value to me; for instance, for every round terra-cotta with religious symbols. And, incredible as it may seem, in spite of the enormous quantities of these articles that are discovered, my workmen have occasionally attempted to make decorations on the unornamented articles, in order to obtain the reward; the sun with its rays is the special object of their industry. I, of course, detect the forged symbols at once, and always punish the forger by deducting 2 piasters from his day's wages; but, owing to the constant change of workmen, forgery is still attempted from time to time.

As I cannot remember the names of the men engaged in my numerous works, I give each a name of my own invention according to their more or less pious, military or learned appearance: dervish, monk, pilgrim, corporal, doctor, schoolmaster, and so forth. As soon as I have given a man such a name, the good fellow is called so by all as long as he is with me. I have accordingly a number of Doctors, not one of whom can either read or write.

Yesterday, at a depth of 13 meters (43½ feet), between the stones of the oldest city, I again came upon two toads, which hopped off as soon as they found themselves free.

In my last report I did not state the exact number of springs in front of Ilium. I have now visited all the springs myself, and measured their distance from my excavations, and I can give the following account of them. The first spring, which is situated directly below the ruins of the ancient town-wall, is exactly 365 meters (399 yards)

from my excavations; its water has a temperature of
16° Celsius (60·8° Fahrenheit).   It is enclosed to a height
of 6½ feet by a wall of large stones joined with cement,
9¼ feet in breadth, and in front of it there are two stone
troughs for watering cattle.   The second spring, which
is likewise still below the ruins of the ancient town-wall,
is exactly 725 meters (793 yards) distant from my excavations.   It has a similar enclosure of large stones, 7
feet high and 5 feet broad, and has the same temperature.
But it is out of repair, and the water no longer runs
through the stone pipe in the enclosure, but along the
ground before it reaches the pipe.   The double spring
spoken of in my last report is exactly 945 meters (1033
yards) from my excavations.   It consists of two distinct
springs, which run out through two stone pipes lying
beside each other in the enclosure composed of large
stones joined with earth, which rises to a height of 7
feet and is 23 feet broad; its temperature is 17° Celsius
(62·6° Fahrenheit).   In front of these two springs there
are six stone troughs, which are placed in such a
manner that the superfluous water always runs from the
first trough through all the others.   It is extremely
probable that these are the two springs mentioned by
Homer, beside which Hector was killed.*   When the poet

---

* *Iliad*, XXII. 145–156 :—

> Οἱ δὲ παρὰ σκοπιὴν καὶ ἐρινεὸν ἠνεμόεντα
> Τείχεος αἰὲν ὑπὲκ κατ' ἀμαξιτὸν ἐσσεύοντο,
> Κρουνὼ δ' ἵκανον καλλιρρόω, ἔνθα τε πηγαὶ
> Δοιαὶ ἀναΐσσουσι Σκαμάνδρου δινήεντος.
> Ἡ μὲν γάρ θ' ὕδατι λιαρῷ ῥέει, ἀμφὶ δὲ καπνὸς
> Γίγνεται ἐξ αὐτῆς ὡς εἰ πυρὸς αἰθομένοιο·
> Ἡ δ' ἑτέρη θέρεϊ προρέει εἰκυῖα χαλάζῃ
> Ἢ χιόνι ψυχρῇ ἢ ἐξ ὕδατος κρυστάλλῳ.
> Ἔνθα δ' ἐπ' αὐτάων πλυνοὶ εὐρέες ἐγγὺς ἔασιν
> Καλοὶ λαΐνεοι, ὅθι εἵματα σιγαλόεντα
> Πλύνεσκον Τρώων ἄλοχοι καλαί τε θύγατρες
> Τὸ πρὶν ἐπ' εἰρήνης, πρὶν ἐλθεῖν υἷας Ἀχαιῶν.

"They" (Hector and Achilles, in flight and pursuit)
"They by the watch-tower, and beneath the wall   [Where

describes the one as boiling hot, the other as cold as ice,
this is probably to be understood in a metaphorical sense ;
for the water of both these springs runs into the neighbouring Simoïs, and thence into the Kalifatli-Asmak, whose
enormous bed was at one time occupied by the Scamander ;
the latter, however, as is well known, comes from Mount
Ida from a hot and a cold spring.

I remarked in my last memoir that the Doumbrek-Su
(Simoïs) still flows past the north of Ilium into the former
channel of the Scamander, and I afterwards said that one
of its arms flowed into the sea near Cape Rhœteum.   This
remark requires some explanation.   The sources of the
Simoïs lie at a distance of eight hours from Hissarlik ;
and, as far down as the neighbouring village of Chalil-Koï,
though its water is drawn off into four different channels
for turning mills, its great bed has always an abundance of water even during the hottest summer weather.
At Chalil-Koï, however, it divides itself into two arms ; one
of which, after it has turned a mill, flows into the Plain in a
north-westerly direction, forms an immense marsh, and parts
into two branches, one of which again falls into the other
arm, which flows in a westerly direction from Chalil-Koï,
and then empties itself directly into the Kalifatli-Asmak,
the ancient bed of the Scamander.   The other arm of the
Simoïs, which flowed in a north-westerly direction from
Chalil-Koï, after it has received a tributary from the Kalifatli-Asmak by means of an artificial canal, turns direct

---

Where stood the wind-beat fig-tree, raced amain
Along the public road, until they reached
The fairly-flowing founts, whence issued forth,
From double source, Scamander's eddying streams.
One with hot current flows, and from beneath,
As from a furnace, clouds of steam arise ;
'Mid Summer's heat the other rises cold
As hail, or snow, or water crystallized ;
Beside the fountains stood the washing-troughs
Of well-wrought stone, where erst the wives of Troy
And daughters fair their choicest garments washed,
In peaceful times, ere came the sons of Greece."

north, and, under the name of In-tépé-Asmak, falls into
the Hellespont through an enormously broad bed, which
certainly was at one time occupied by the Kalifatli-Asmak,
and in remote antiquity by the Scamander, and is close to
the sepulchral mound of Ajax, which is called In-tépé.   I
must draw attention to the fact that the name of Ajax
(Αἴας, gen. Αἴαντος) can even be recognised in the Turkish
name (*In*-tépé: *Tépé* signifies " hill.")

In returning to the article by M. Nikolaïdes, I can now
also refute his assertion that near Ilium, where I am digging,
there is no hill which can be regarded as the one described
by Homer as the tomb of Batiea or the Amazon Myrina.*

Strabo (XIII. i. p. 109) quotes the lines already cited
from the Iliad † (II. 790–794) as an argument against
the identity of Ilium with the Ilium of Priam, and adds:
"If Troy had stood on the site of the Ilium of that
day, Polites would have been better able to watch the
movements of the Greeks in the ships from the summit of
the Pergamus than from the tumulus of Æsyetes, which
lies on the road to Alexandria Troas, 5 stadia (half a
geographical mile) from Ilium."

Strabo is perfectly right in saying that the Greek camp
must have been more readily seen from the summit of
the Pergamus than from a sepulchral mound on the road
to Alexandria Troas, 5 stadia from Ilium; for Alexandria
Troas lies to the south-west of Ilium, and the road to it,
which is distinctly marked by the ford of the Scamander at
its entrance into the valley, goes direct south as far as
Bunarbashi, whereas the Hellespont and the Greek camp
were north of Ilium.   But to the south of Ilium, exactly in
the direction where the road to Alexandria Troas must have
been, I see before me a tumulus 33 feet high and 131 yards
in circumference, and, according to an exact measurement

---

* See *Iliad*, II. 811–815, quoted above, p. 179.
† Chapter II., p. 69.

which I have made, 1017 yards from the southern city
wall. This, therefore, must necessarily be the sepulchral
mound of which Strabo writes; but he has evidently been
deceived in regard to its identity with the tumulus of
Æsyetes by Demetrius of Scepsis, who wished to prove
the situation of this mound to be in a straight line between
the Greek camp and the village of the Ilians ('Ιλιέων κώμη),
and the latter to be the site of Troy. The tumulus of
Æsyetes was probably situated in the present village of
Kum-Koï, not far from the confluence of the Scamander
and the Simoïs, for the remains of an heroic tumulus several
feet in height are still to be seen there.

The mound now before me is in front of Troy, but
somewhat to the side of the Plain, and this position corresponds perfectly with the statements which Homer gives us
of the position of the monument of Batiea or the Amazon
Myrina : " προπάροιθε πόλιος " and " ἐν πεδίῳ ἀπάνευθε."
This tumulus is now called Pacha-Tépé.

We may form an idea of what a large population Ilium
possessed at the time of Lysimachus, among other signs,
from the enormous dimensions of the theatre which he
built ; it is beside the Pergamus where I am digging, and its
stage is 197 feet in breadth.

The heat during the day, which is 32° Celsius (89·6°
Fahrenheit), is not felt at all, owing to the constant wind,
and the nights are cool and refreshing.

Our greatest plague here, after the incessant and intolerable hurricane, is from the immense numbers of insects
and vermin of all kinds ; we especially dread the scorpions
and the so-called Σαραντοπόδια (literally " with forty feet "—
a kind of centipede), which frequently fall down from the
ceiling of the rooms upon or beside us, and whose bite is
said to be fatal.

I cannot conclude without mentioning an exceedingly
remarkable person, Konstantinos Kolobos, the owner of a
shop in the village of Neo-Chorion in the Plain of Troy,

who, although born without feet, has nevertheless made a considerable fortune in a retail business. But his talents are not confined to business; they include a knowledge of languages; and although Kolobos has grown up among the rough and ignorant village lads and has never had a master, yet by self-tuition he has succeeded in acquiring the Italian and French languages, and writes and speaks both of them perfectly. He is also wonderfully expert in ancient Greek, from having several times copied and learnt by heart a large etymological dictionary, as well as from having read all the classic authors, and he can repeat whole rhapsodies from the Iliad by heart. What a pity it is that such a genius has to spend his days in a wretched village in the Troad, useless to the world, and in the constant company of the most uneducated and ignorant people, all of whom gaze at him in admiration, but none of whom understand him!

No. 149.   A Trojan decorated Vase of Terra-cotta (7 M.).

CHAPTER XII.

Discovery of an ancient wall on the northern slope — Discovery of a
Tower on the south side — Its position and construction — It is
Homer's *Great Tower of Ilium* — Manner of building with stones
and earth — A Greek inscription — Remarkable medal of the age of
Commodus — Whorls found just below the surface — Terra-cottas
found at small depths — Various objects found at the various depths
— A skeleton, with ornaments of gold, which have been exposed to
a great heat — Paucity of human remains, as the Trojans burnt their
dead — No trace of pillars — Naming of the site as " Ilium " and the
" Pergamus of Troy."

Pergamus of Troy, August 4th, 1872.

Referring to my report of the 13th of last month, I am
glad now to be able to mention that, in excavating the
depths of the temple, I found a wall 10 feet high and 6½
feet thick, which, however, has at one time been much
higher, as the quantity of stones lying beside it seem to
prove.   It is at a distance of 131 feet from the declivity of
the hill, and at a perpendicular depth of 34 feet.*   This
wall is composed of large stones joined with earth, and, as
is attested by the layers of *débris* which extend in an
oblique direction below it, it was built originally upon the
steep slope of the hill.   Hence, since the erection of the
wall, the hill at this point has increased 131 feet in breadth
and 44¼ feet in height by the accumulation of *débris*.   I
have not yet been able to ascertain whether this wall was
the foundation of an ancient Trojan temple, or whether it
belongs to the enclosing wall which, says Homer,† was
built by Poseidon and Apollo.   In the latter case, it would

---

* See Plan II.   † *Iliad*, VII. 452–453.

PLATE VIII.

Page 200.

THE GREAT TOWER OF ILIUM.
Seen from the S.E.

The top is 8 M. (26 ft.) below the surface of the Hill: the foundation is on the rock
14 M. (46 ft.) deep: the height of the Tower is 20 feet.

appear strange that it is only 6½ feet thick, and was never higher than 16½ feet, for it must be remembered that the hill has a steep incline on the north side, and that it is very precipitous at this part especially.

Below the wall I found five of those splendid, brilliant black flat Trojan terra-cottas, which are so like a wheel, that they can be distinguished at a glance from all the others. One has six suns in the circle round the central sun; another has four stars forming a cross round the sun; a third has three double rising suns in the circle round the central sun; a fourth has four rising suns with five lines, forming a cross round the sun; a fifth has three triple rising suns round the sun. I also found below the wall a number of fragments of black Trojan vessels which are directly recognised by their fineness, and by the long single or double rings on the sides.

The wall proceeds from west to east, and consequently obstructs my path, and I cannot remove the *débris* from behind it without considerably widening my trench, which would be a gigantic piece of work between the enormous earthen walls. In continuing my trench in a horizontal direction I have arrived at exactly 6½ feet below this wall. It is very interesting from a perpendicular depth of 15½ meters, or 51⅓ feet, to see this mass of primeval Trojan masonry in a depth of 13½ to 10½ meters (44¼ to 34 feet), and the wall beside it which was built by Lysimachus, and is almost immediately below the surface, standing as it were in mid air.

On the south side of the hill where, on account of the slight natural slope, I had to make my great trench with an inclination of 14 degrees, I discovered, at a distance of 197 feet from the declivity, a Tower, 12 meters or 40 feet thick, which likewise obstructs my path, and appears to extend to a great length.* I am busily engaged in making

---

* The Tower is marked No. 4, and is also named, on Plan II.

large excavations to the right and left of it, in order to lay
bare the whole; for, independently of the mighty interest
attached to this Tower, I must necessarily dig a channel to
allow the waters of the winter rains to run off, as they would
otherwise rush violently down from my platform (197 feet
in length, and with a considerable slope) against the Tower
and injure it.   I have uncovered the Tower on the north
and south sides along the whole breadth of my trench, and
have convinced myself that it is built on the rock at a
depth of 14 meters or 46½ feet.

An elevated mass of calcareous earth, 65½ feet broad
and 16½ feet high, rests upon the north side of the Tower,
and is evidently composed of the rubbish which had to be
removed in order to level the rock for building the Tower
upon it.   I have of course pierced this hillock, and have
convinced myself that the north side of the Tower, 16½ feet
above the rock, does not consist of masonry, but of large
blocks of stone lying loosely one upon another, and that only
the upper part, about a yard high, consists of actual masonry.
This hillock, having the form of a rampart, thus serves to
consolidate the north side of the Tower, and renders it possible to ascend to the top without steps.   The south side
of the Tower, looking out upon the Plain, consists of very
solid masonry, composed of blocks of limestone joined with
earth, some of the stones being hewn, others not.   This
south side of the Tower rises from the rock at an angle
of 75 degrees.

None but those who have been present at these works
can have any idea of the enormous difficulties connected
with making excavations 46½ feet deep on the right and
left of the Tower, where the *débris* has to be carried off to
a distance of more than 262 feet.   At this great distance
it is very fatiguing to work with wheel-barrows and man-
carts; so I now keep seven carts drawn by horses, which I
find a very great relief.

The Tower is at present only 6 meters (20 feet high),

but the nature of its surface, and the masses of stones lying on both sides, seem to prove that it was at one time much higher.* For the preservation of what remains we have only to thank the ruins of Troy, which entirely covered the Tower as it now stands. It is probable that after the destruction of Troy much more of it remained standing, and that the part which rose above the ruins of the town was destroyed by the successors of the Trojans, who possessed neither walls nor fortifications. The western part of the Tower, so far as it is yet uncovered, is only from 121 to 124 feet distant from the steep western slope of the hill; and, considering the enormous accumulation of *débris*, I believe that the Tower once stood on the western edge of the Acropolis, where its situation would be most interesting and imposing; for its top would have commanded, not only a view of the whole Plain of Troy, but of the sea with the islands of Tenedos, Imbros, and Samothrace. There is not a more sublime situation in the area of Troy than this, and I therefore presume that it is the "Great Tower of Ilium" which Andromache ascended because "she had heard that the Trojans were hard pressed and that the power of the Achæans was great."† After having been buried for thirty-one centuries, and after successive nations have built their houses and palaces high above its summit during thousands of years, this Tower has now again been brought to light, and commands a view, if not of the whole Plain, at least of the northern part and of the Hellespont. May this sacred and sublime monument of Greek heroism for ever

---

* This opinion was changed afterwards. See Chapter XXII., p. 318. —[ED.]

† *Iliad*, VI. 386, 387 :—

'Αλλ' ἐπὶ πύργον ἔβη μέγαν 'Ιλίου, οὕνεκ' ἄκουσεν
Τείρεσθαι Τρῶας, μέγα δὲ κράτος εἶναι 'Αχαιῶν.

"But to the height of Ilion's topmost tower
Andromache is gone ; since tidings came
The Trojan force was overmatched, and great
The Grecian strength."

attract the eyes of those who sail through the Hellespont!
May it become a place to which the enquiring youth of all
future generations shall make pilgrimage and fan their enthusiasm for knowledge, and above all for the noble language
and literature of Greece! May it be an inducement speedily
and completely to lay bare the walls of Troy, which must
necessarily be connected with this Tower and most probably
also with the wall laid open by me on the north side, to
uncover which is now a very easy matter.

The expenses of excavating Ilium are, however, too great
for private means, and I hope that a company will be
formed, or that some government will decide to continue
my excavations, so that I may proceed to the excavation of
the acropolis of Mycenæ. Meanwhile I shall continue the
excavations at my own expense, but I shall in future confine
myself to gradually uncovering the large surrounding walls,
which are sure to be in a more or less good state of preservation at a great depth below the city wall built by
Lysimachus.

Before I had seen even the smallest ruins of walls belonging to Ilium, I repeatedly maintained in my reports
that the whole city was built, as it is now proved by the
Wall and the Tower to have been, of stones joined with
earth. That this style of building, if not more ancient, is
at least just as ancient as the so-called cyclopean, is proved
by the walls and houses of Thera (Santorin) and Therassia,
which are built in the same way, and which, as is well
known, were discovered beneath three layers of volcanic
ashes 68 feet thick. These ashes were, however, thrown
up by a central volcano, which must have been at least
3800 feet high, and which, as is generally supposed, sank
into the sea at latest 1500 years before Christ.

Upon the site of the temple I found, at a depth of
6½ feet, a block of marble 5¼ feet high, and 2¾ feet both
in breadth and thickness; it weighs about 50 tons, and
contains the following inscription :—

ΗΒΟΥΛΗΚΑΙΟΔΗΜΟ
ΙΛΙΕΩΝΕΤΙΜΗΣΑΝΑΥ
ΚΛΑΥΔΙΟΝΚΑΙΚΙΝΑΙ
ΑΙΟΝΚΥΖΙΚΗΝΟΝΑ
5 ΤΑΛΟΓΙΣΤΗΝΥΠΟΤΟ
ΟΤΑΤΟΥΑΥΤΟΚΡΑΤΟΡΟ
ΣΑΡΟΣΤΙΤΟΥΑΙΛΙΟΥΑΔ
ΝΟΥΑΝΤΩΝΙΟΥΣΕΒΑ
ΕΥΣΕΒΟΥΣΚ..ΙΠΟΛΛ
10 ΜΕΓΑΛΑΤΗΙΠ..ΛΕΙΚΑΤΟ
ΣΑΝΤΑΚΑΙΓ..϶ΑΣΧΟΝΤ
ΤΕΤΗΛΟΓΙΣΤ..ΙΑΚΑΙΣΥ
ΓΟΡΙΑΙΣΑΝΔ...ΠΑΣΗΣΤ
ΑΞΙΟΝΑΡΕΤΗ..ΕΝΕΚΕΝΚ
15 ΕΥΝΟΙΑΣΤΗΣΠΡΟΣΤΗ
ΠΟΛΙΝ

The first name occurring in this inscription, of which
the syllable **ΑΥ** is preserved, is probably **ΑΥΛΟΣ**. **ΚΑΙΚΙΝΑΙ**,
must certainly be the family-name, and must indicate the
Latin ablative. Whether the other name, of which **ΑΙΟΝ**
remains, is intended for **ΓΑΙΟΝ**, I do not venture positively
to maintain, but I consider it to be probable. For the
inscription, which I read as follows, is written in bad Greek,
especially towards the end: Ἡ βουλὴ καὶ ὁ δῆμος Ἰλιέων
ἐτίμησαν Αὖλον Κλαύδιον Καικινᾷ Γάϊον Κυζικηνὸν ἄρχοντα
λογιστὴν ὑπὸ τοῦ θειοτάτου αὐτοκράτορος Καίσαρος Τίτου
Αἰλίου Ἀδριανοῦ Ἀντωνίου Σεβαστοῦ Εὐσεβοῦς καὶ πολλὰ
καὶ μεγάλα τῇ πόλει κατορθώσαντα καὶ παράσχοντά τε τῇ
λογιστείᾳ καὶ συνηγορίαις ἄνδρα πάσης τιμῆς ἄξιον ἀρετῆς
ἕνεκεν καὶ εὐνοίας τῆς πρὸς τὴν πόλιν.

The Emperor mentioned in this inscription is of course
Antoninus Pius, whose reign began in the year 138 A.D.,
and who died in 161 A.D.; it is merely by an error that
he is here called Antonius. He got the name of Hadrian
from his adoptive father, the Emperor Hadrian, and took

the name of Ælius after the death of Hadrian's first adopted son, Ælius Cæsar.

Upon the upper end of the block of marble there are two foot-marks, the one considerably in advance of the other. Each of them being $15\frac{1}{3}$ inches long, they leave no doubt that upon this block the colossal statue of the Cyzicene, who is praised in the inscription, stood in the attitude of an orator. In the hinder foot there is a square hole, $1\frac{4}{5}$ inch square, in which was placed the iron rod for fixing the statue. To judge from the size of the foot-marks, the statue must have been more than 8 feet high, and, as the marble block is $5\frac{1}{4}$ feet in height, the whole must have been at least $13\frac{1}{4}$ feet high, and hence we may conclude that the temple in which this work of art stood was very spacious.

The excavations to the right and left of the Tower have unfortunately to be made from above, which makes the work slower, but gives me the advantage of being able again to state with great accuracy at what depths the various objects are found. Generally the ruins of the Greek period extend to a depth of 2 meters ($6\frac{1}{2}$ feet), but there are places where the remains of the pre-Hellenic period commence at less than 1 meter ($3\frac{1}{4}$ feet), and this is the case on the east of the Tower, where at even $3\frac{1}{4}$ feet below the surface I found a seal made of clay with a tree and two stars. At the same depth I found one straight and three crooked copper knives, as well as a large double-edged axe and several other instruments of the same metal. Almost immediately on the surface I found, among other coins, an exceedingly remarkable medal, such as I believe has never before been met with; on one side it has the portrait of the Emperor Commodus (here written **ΚΟΜΟΔΟΣ**); upon the other there is a figure in armour, armed with two lances (probably Minerva) standing upon the fore part of a ship, which ends in an extremely well-wrought head of a gazelle; in a semi-circle round it is the word **ΕΛΑΙΟΥΣΙΩΝ**. The medal therefore comes from the very small island of Elæusa, on the coast of Cilicia, and it proves the remarkable fact that this small island, which now scarcely possesses any inhabitants, was anciently so populous that it struck its own coins.

The frequently discussed whorls of terra-cotta, bearing simple or double crosses with the marks of four nails, or having three, four, or five double rising suns in the circle round the central sun, are met with to the east of the Tower quite close below the surface, that is, at a depth of not quite a foot. At a depth of 1 meter (3¼ feet) I found a small whorl, upon which the *Rosa mystica*, with its four petals, forms a cross round the sun. At as small a depth as 2 meters (6½ feet) I discovered a small and coarsely made cup, with the owl's face of the Ilian tutelary goddess, also very clumsy goblets in the form of champagne-glasses with two handles; at a depth of 3 meters (10 feet) small saucers with three little feet, which are adorned with ⊐⊔ and trees of life. I also found at the same depth small terra-cotta volcanoes and tops with the ⊐⊔, and a great number of them at a depth of 4 meters (13 feet). At the latter depth I found, when excavating the west side of the Tower, an extremely curious cup, nearly 8 inches high, in the form of a Mecklenburg roll (*Pluten-semmel*), with four divisions, but round and furnished with two enormous handles; it has a rounded foot, so that it can only stand on its mouth. In the same place I found a curious vase, with little rings on the sides for suspension by strings, and a little spout in the bulge, so that the fluid poured into the vase would run out again directly. Vases with such tubes in the bulge, but without rings at the sides, are very frequently met with. Further, at a depth of 4 meters (13 feet) I found goblets in the form of champagne-glasses, with two large handles; also a curious little terra-cotta volcano with four ⊐⊔, the symbol of lightning, and two sacrificial altars covered with flames. At a depth of 5 meters (16½ feet)

I found several such pieces with extremely interesting symbolical signs; one of them had a very fine engraving of the flaming altar and the tree of life. In the same stratum I found a neat little vase with three feet, two handles, and prettily engraved decorations; lastly, a number of small knives made of silex, in the form of saws. At a depth of 6 meters (20 feet) we found a vessel, a little more than 9 inches long, which is exactly in the shape of an animal; it has three feet, a tail, and an upright neck, which is connected with the back by a large handle. At a depth of 7 meters (23 feet) I found a very pretty vase, with the owl's head of the tutelary goddess of Troy, her two

female breasts and navel; the two arms are raised by the side of the head, and served as handles. From the same depth we brought out a curious saw made of bone; from a depth of 8 meters (26 feet), idols with the image of the Ilian Athena, with her girdle, made of

No. 150. Terra-cotta Vase (7 M.).

very fine marble; at the same depth some of those earthen funnels which I have already frequently mentioned, also several terra-cotta balls covered with

engravings of little stars. I also discovered during the last few days, at depths of from 8 to 11 meters (26 to 36 feet) a number of large vases and vessels of various forms, with two, three, and four handles, and, besides these, at 10 meters (33 feet) deep, a vessel in the form of an animal, with three feet

No. 151.   Terra-cotta Vase in the form of an Animal, from the Trojan Stratum (10 M.).

and a tail; a horn, which projects from the upright neck and serves as a handle, connects the head with the end of the back. This vessel is not unlike a locomotive engine.

The day before yesterday, at the depth of 14 meters (46 feet), we met with a great number of interesting things; for instance, the neck of a brilliant red vase with the owl's head, which has two enormously large eyes; then a brilliant brown vessel, 8⅔ inches long, 7 inches high, and nearly

No. 152.   Terra-cotta Vessel in the shape of a Pig, from the Lowest Stratum (14 M.).

6 inches thick, in the form of a sow, with a projecting but closed head of excellent workmanship, and with three feet; the orifice of the vessel is in the tail, which is connected with the back by a handle.   Further, a lance and several instruments, as well as a number of copper nails, and needles of ivory for embroidering.   In the ashes of the same house, which has evidently been burnt, I also found, at a depth of 13 meters (42½ feet), a tolerably well preserved skeleton of a

woman, of which I think I have collected nearly all the bones; the skull especially is in a good state of preservation, but has unfortunately been broken in our excavations; however, I can easily put it together again; the mouth is somewhat protruding, and shows good but astonishingly small teeth.   By the side of the

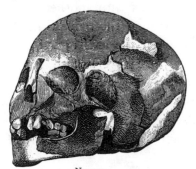

No. 153.

Skull of a Woman, found near some gold ornaments in the Lowest Stratum (13 M.).

skeleton I found a finger-ring,

three ear-rings, and a dress-pin of pure gold. The latter
is perfectly simple, and has a round head; two of the ear-
rings are of quite a primitive kind, and consist of simple
gold wire 0·058 of an inch thick; as does also the third
ear-ring, which, however, is much more finely wrought
and ends in a leaf, which is formed of six gold wires of
equal thickness, riveted together.* The finger-ring is made
of three gold wires 0·115 of an inch thick. All of these
objects bear evidence of having been exposed to great heat.
The Trojan woman must, however, have also worn other
ornaments, for by the side of the skeleton I collected several
gold beads only 0·039 of an inch large, and also a very
thin oval ring only a quarter of an inch in length. Even
the colour of the bones leaves no doubt that the lady was
overtaken by fire and burnt alive. With the exception of
the skeleton of the embryo of six months which was found
in a vase upon the primary soil, this is the only human
skeleton I have ever met with in any of the pre-Hellenic
strata on this hill.† As we know from Homer, all corpses
were burnt, and the ashes were placed in urns, of which I
have found great numbers in the ruins of all the nations
which inhabited this hill before the time of the Greek colony.
The bones, however, were always burnt to ashes; at most I
have occasionally discovered a whole tooth, in no case have
I ever met with another entire bone in the urns.

Among the remains of the same Trojan house, and not
far from the skeleton, I found the fragment of a yellow
cup (vase-cover), with a very expressive man's face; the
nose is long and somewhat aquiline. In addition to this I
found there seven of the round terra-cottas in the shape
of a flat top. Among these was one $2\frac{1}{3}$ inches in diameter,
which has the exact form of a wheel; in the circle round

---

* Similar rings are shown among the articles of the Treasure
(Chapter XXIII., Plate XX).

† Others, even more interesting, were found later (Chapter XX., pp.
279–80).

the nave it has five rising suns.   As usual, these decorations are engraved and filled with a white substance.

Of pillars I have as yet found no trace in Troy; hence if there existed real pillars, they must in all cases have been of wood.   Moreover, the word "κίων" is never met with in the Iliad, and only in the Odyssey.   In a house at a depth of 39¼ feet, I found a prettily carved and very hard piece of limestone in the form of a crescent, with a round hole 1½ inch deep, and I conjecture that it may have been used as the support for a door.

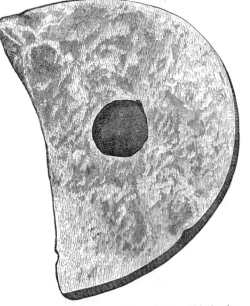

In conclusion, I flatter myself with the hope that, as a reward for my enormous expenses and all my privations, annoyances, and sufferings in this wilderness, but above all for my important disco-veries, the civilized world will acknow-ledge my right to

No. 154.   Block of Limestone, with a socket, in which the pivot of a door may have turned (12 M.).

re-christen this sacred locality; and in the name of the divine Homer I baptize it with that name of immortal renown, which fills the heart of everyone with joy and enthusiasm: I give it the name of "Troy" and "Ilium," and I call the Acropolis, where I am writing these lines, by the name of the "*Pergamus of Troy.*" *

---

* This last name was afterwards recalled by Dr. Schliemann, and that of "Ilium" or "Troy" confined to the Hill of Hissarlik.   See Chapter XXIII., p. 343; and Introduction, p. 18.

CHAPTER XIII.

Pergamus of Troy, August 14th, 1872.

SINCE my report of the 4th of this month I have continued
the excavations with the utmost energy, but I am now
compelled to stop the works this evening, for my three
foremen and my servant, who is also my cashier, have
been seized by the malignant marsh-fever, and my wife and
I are so unwell that we are quite unable to undertake the
sole direction throughout the day in the terrible heat of
the sun. We shall therefore leave our two wooden houses
and all our machines and implements in charge of a watchman, and to-morrow we shall return to Athens.

The admirers of Homer, on visiting the Pergamus of
Troy, will find that I have not only laid bare the Tower on
the south side, along the whole breadth of my trench, down
to the rock upon which it stands, at a depth of 14 meters
or 46½ feet, but that by my excavations on the east and
west I have uncovered it considerably further, without
having found its end. On the contrary, upon the east
side, where it is 40 feet broad, and seems even to be
broader still, I found the ruins of a second storey, of which,

however, as far as I can at present judge, four broad steps have been preserved.* On the western side it is only 9 meters or 30 feet in breadth, and on this side there extends to the north an enormous wall, the thickness of which I have not been able to ascertain. The fact of my not having been able to carry these new excavations down to the primary soil, but only to a depth of 11 meters (36½ feet) is owing to the brittle nature of the walls of rubbish and ruins round about the Tower, which, as any-one may convince himself, consist of red ashes and of stones calcined by the heat, and which threatened at any moment to fall in and bury my workmen.

Upon the Tower, and more especially in the long oval depression on the top of it, and upon the steps I found two copper Trojan lances, several arrow-heads in the primitive form of thick pegs, from above 1 inch to nearly 2 inches long, which were fastened at the end of the shaft; further, an arrow-head 2½ inches in length, made of silex, and in the form of a pointed double-edged saw; then several copper and silver nails with round heads, which may have served as clothes-pins; further, great quantities of bones, masses of fragments of Trojan pottery of a brilliant red and black, and a number of vases and pots more or less well preserved. Among them is a pretty brilliant red vase nearly 10 inches high, filled with the bones of a sea-fish. This vase (found in an urn, which was unfortunately broken to pieces) has two small handles, and on two sides an ornament in the form of the Greek letter *Lambda*, but with circular ends.† Three other vases

---

* Respecting these steps, which are marked No. 6, on Plan II., and *c* on Plan III., p. 306, see further in Chapter XXII., p. 318, where the idea of an upper storey is rejected.—[ED.]

† The cut represents a vase of this type, with the upper part joined on by Dr. Schliemann, who remarks that it is doubtful whether the owl's face belongs to this vase, as the Ilian goddess is in no other case repre-sented on vases without the breasts and abdomen. (Description in the Atlas of Photographs.)

of a similar form, and with exactly the same decorations, were found upon the Tower. Two other vases of the same form, and with very similar decorations, were found at depths of 26 and 20 feet. I also found upon the Tower an exceedingly curious vessel nearly 6 inches in length, exactly the shape of a mole, and with three feet; it can also be placed

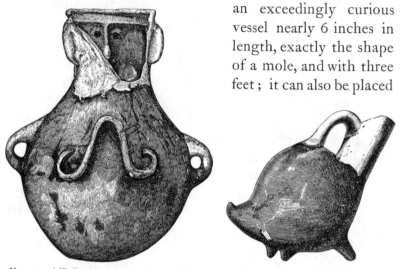

No. 155. A Trojan Terra-cotta Vase, with an Ornament like the Greek *Lambda* (8 M.).

No. 156. Curious Terra-cotta Vessel in the shape of a Mole (Tower: 7 or 8 M.).

so that the snout of the animal is lowest and serves as a foot; the orifice is in the tail, which a large handle connects with the back. I also found there a splendid Trojan vase, of a brilliant black colour, 15¾ inches high, which was unfortunately completely broken, but I have all the pieces of it, and consequently shall be able to restore it. Besides these, a Trojan pot, and a globular vessel with the above-mentioned decoration of a rounded lambda. I likewise saved, in an almost perfect condition, an exceedingly interesting red jug, above 9 inches high, quite round below and with a neck more bent backwards than I have ever found it in such vessels. I further found there a Priapus and a very pretty bird's egg made of fine marble, many small terra-cotta whorls with the usual symbols of double and treble crosses, six suns, four or five double or treble rising suns, or stars, in the circle round

the central sun; also one article where four ⊓⊔ form a
cross round the sun, and the rest of the space is filled

with stars. Fur-
ther, a few small
vessels with suspen-
sion rings were
found also on the
Tower, as well as
25 very ordinary
earthen plates,
which have been
turned by the pot-
ter, whereas all the
other articles ap-
pear to have been
made by the hand
without a potter's
wheel; about half
of the plates were
got out unin-
jured.

No. 157.   A Trojan Dish with side Rings, and Plates turned
by the Potter (Tower: 7 M.).

In digging to
the left and right
of the Tower, a number of other interesting objects have
been found since my last report; for instance, at a depth
of 2 meters (6½ feet), a number of very neat although ordinary vessels with small rings on the sides and holes in the
mouth for hanging them up, which have hitherto only been
met with much further down; at a depth of 3 meters (10
feet) a small cover, with the owl's face and helmet of the
Ilian Athena, of very good manufacture; then, at a depth
of 11½ feet, a small terra-cotta whorl with three stags in
the circle round the sun. At a depth of from 5 to 6 meters
(16½ to 20 feet), I found a great number of small knives
of silex in the form of saws. At a depth of 10 meters
(33 feet) I discovered a very curious instrument of brilliant

yellow terra-cotta, a drawing of which I give. It is quite inexplicable to me for what purpose it can have been used; it is almost in the shape of a shield, and by the side of the handle which is ornamented with a tree, it has a cavity for putting the hand in. As it is made of terra-cotta it cannot, of course, have been used as a shield.*

After having had no rain here for four months, to-day, curiously enough, just after stopping the works, we have had a thunderstorm accompanied by a tremendous downpour of rain, and I regret extremely not to have been able to make a channel for leading off the rain-water from the Tower as far as the western declivity of the hill. But such a channel would need to be 50 feet deep and as many broad, otherwise its walls, consisting of calcined ruins and loose red ashes, would fall in. I should therefore have to remove 5000 cubic meters (6000 cubic yards) of *débris*, and such a gigantic piece of work I cannot now undertake.

In stopping the excavations for this year, and in looking back upon the fearful dangers to which we have continually been exposed since the 1st of April, between the gigantic layers of ruins, I cannot but fervently thank God for His great mercy, that not only has no life been lost, but that none of us has even been seriously hurt.

Now, as regards the result of my excavations, every-one must admit that I have solved a great historical problem, and that I have solved it by the discovery of a high civilization and immense buildings upon the primary soil, in the depths of an ancient town, which throughout antiquity was called Ilium and declared itself to be the successor of Troy, the site of which was regarded as identical with the site of the Homeric Ilium by the whole civilized world of that time. The situation of this town not only corresponds perfectly with all the statements of the Iliad, but also with all the traditions handed down to

* See Plate XXI., No. 309.

us by later authors; and, moreover, neither in the Plain of
Troy, nor in its vicinity, is there any other place which
could in the slightest degree be made to correspond with
them.   To regard the heights of Bunarbashi as the site
of Troy, contradicts, in every respect, all the statements of
Homer and of tradition.   My excavations of Bunarbashi,
as well as the form of the rocks, prove that those heights,
as far as the three sepulchral mounds, can never have been
inhabited by men.   As I have already said, behind those
tumuli there are the ruins of a very small town, the area of
which, surrounded on two sides by the ruins of an enclosing
wall, and on the other side by precipices, is so insignificant,
that at most it can have only possessed 2000 inhabitants.
The enclosing wall of its small Acropolis is scarcely a foot
thick, and the gate scarcely 3¼ feet wide.   The accumulation
of *débris* is not worth mentioning, for in many places the
naked flat rocks are seen on the ground of the Acropolis.
Here in Ilium, however, the proportions are very different.
The area of the Greek city, which is indicated by the surrounding wall built by Lysimachus, is large enough for a
population of more than 100,000 souls; and that the number
of the inhabitants was actually as large is proved by the
stage of the theatre, which is 200 feet in breadth.   Here the
surrounding wall of Lysimachus is 6½ feet thick, whereas
the wall which runs out from the Tower at a great depth
below the other seems to be five times as thick, and Homer
assuredly ascribed the erection of the walls of Troy to
Poseidon and Apollo on account of their enormous proportions.*   Then, as regards the accumulation of *débris*,
here in the Pergamus there is no place where it amounts
to less than 14 meters, or 46½ feet, and in many places it is
even much more considerable.   Thus, for instance, on my
great platform, I only reached the primary soil at a depth

---

* According to Mr. Gladstone's theory, these masses of masonry,
and the tradition ascribing them to Poseidon and Apollo, are signs of
Phœnician influence.—[ED.]

of 16 meters, or 53⅓ feet, and in the depths of the temple, on the adjacent field, belonging to Mr. Frank Calvert, I have not yet reached it at a depth of 15½ meters, or 51⅔ feet. Such an accumulation of ruins has never as yet been discovered in any other part of the world, except occasionally in the rocky valleys of Jerusalem; where, however, it has only begun to accumulate since the destruction of the city by Titus, and hence is scarcely more than 1800 years old.* Here in Troy the remains of the Greek period cease entirely at a depth of ½, 1, or 2 meters, and thence, down to the primary soil, we find in regular succession the mighty layers of ruins belonging to four very ancient nations.

In like manner, as regards the more than a hundred thousand objects which I have brought to light, and which were used by those very ancient tribes, I venture to say that I have revealed a new world to archæology; for, in order to give but one instance, I have here found many thousands of those wheels, volcanoes, or tops (*carrousels*) of terra-cotta with the most various Aryan religious symbols.

If, as it seems, neither the Trojans nor any of the three succeeding peoples possessed a written language, we must, as far as possible, replace it by the "*monuments figurés*" which I have discovered.† As already said, I

---

* This statement is hardly accurate. The greatest depth of *débris* discovered by the officers of the Palestine Exploration Fund at Jerusalem was not in the valleys, but on the Eastern slope of Mount Moriah. The accumulation reached from the foot of the wall down the slope to the bed of the Kedron, and beyond it some distance up the slope of the Mount of Olives. The usual depth at the wall was 60 or 70 feet, but at the north end it reached as much as 120, owing to the descent of the original ground at that spot. The masons' marks on the lowest courses of the stones, reached by sinking shafts through these great depths, seemed to show a date nearer that of Solomon than of Titus.—[Ed.]

† We leave this, like other such passages, as landmarks of the rapid progress made in the discoveries opened up by Dr. Schliemann.—[Ed.]

make a drawing in my diary each evening of every one of
the objects which have been found during the day, and
more especially of the pictorial symbols, with the greatest
exactness. By comparing the innumerable symbols I have
succeeded in deciphering some of them, and I hope that
my learned colleagues will succeed in explaining the rest.
Archæology shall on no account lose any one of my discoveries; every article which can have any interest for
the learned world shall be photographed, or copied by a
skilful draughtsman, and published in the Appendix to this
work; and by the side of every article I shall state the
depth in which I discovered it.

No. 158. A curious Trojan Jug of Terra-cotta (8 м.).

CHAPTER XIV.

Return to Troy to take plans and photographs — Damage to retaining walls — The unfaithfulness of the watchman — Stones carried off for a neighbouring church and houses — Injury by rain — Works for security during the winter — Opening up of a retaining wall on the side of the hill, probably built to support the temple of Athena — Supposed *débris* of that temple — Drain belonging to it — Doric style of the temple proved by the block of Triglyphs — Temple of Apollo also on the Pergamus.

Athens, September 28th, 1872.

I WROTE my last memoir on the 14th of last month, and on the 10th of this month, accompanied by my wife and Sisilas the land-surveyor, I returned to Troy in order to make a new plan of the Pergamus, which contains the most exact picture of my excavations, as well as of the depth in which the remains of immortal fame were discovered by me. I also took the photographer Siebrecht from the Dardanelles with me, in order to have photographs taken of my excavations, of two of the four springs situated on the north side of Ilium, of Ilium's Great Tower and the Plain of Troy, as well as of the Hellespont as seen from this monument.

To my horror, upon arriving there, I found that the watchman whom I had left in charge had been faithless, and that an immense number of large hewn stones dug out of my excavations, with which I had erected walls in several places in order to prevent the winter rains from washing away the *débris* which we had pulled down, had been carried off. The man excused himself by saying that the stones had been used for a good purpose, namely for the construction of a belfry in the Christian village of Yenishehr, and for building houses in the Turkish village of Chiplak. I, of course, packed him off directly, and engaged in his place a watchman whom I armed with a musket. He had the reputation of being honest, and his physical strength will inspire the pilferers of the stones with respect. What vexed me most was, that these thieves had even laid their hands upon the splendid bastion of the time of Lysimachus, which I had uncovered on the south side of the hill; they had made off with two large stones from it, and the bastion would assuredly have vanished entirely had I been away a week longer.

I also regret to see that the downpour of rain on the 14th of August has filled the great cutting, which I made on the south side of the Tower, in order to bring the Tower to light down as far as the rock upon which it is built, with *débris* to a height of 2 meters (6½ feet). So, immediately upon my arrival, I engaged 20 workmen, 10 of whom are busy in clearing the south side of the Tower as far as the primary soil, in wheeling away the *débris*, and in building in front of the cutting a wall of large blocks of stone, through which the rain-water can escape, but not the *débris* that may be washed down.

I have now had an opportunity of convincing myself that the rain does not harm the Tower, for it disappears directly to the right and left of it in the loose *débris*. Of the other ten workmen, six are occupied in repairing the walls which have been destroyed or injured by wanton hands, while the other four are working in order to lay bare as far as possible an exceedingly remarkable wall, which rises at an angle of 40 degrees at the depth of 15½ meters (50½ feet) and at 43½ yards from the edge of the hill, on the site of the temple, exactly 6½ feet *below* the Trojan wall which I there brought to light. (See p. 200.) As I have before remarked, the strata of *débris*, which run obliquely to the north below that Trojan wall, prove that it was built upon the steep slope of the hill, and this is an additional and infallible proof that the buttress, which is erected 6½ feet below it, can have served no other purpose than for consolidating and strengthening the ground of the declivity so effectually that buildings of an enormous weight might be erected upon the summit without danger. Now as I have never hitherto found buttresses of this kind for consolidating the declivity of the hill among the strata of the pre-Hellenic period, although there was no lack of grand buildings in the Pergamus of Troy (as is proved by the colossal masses of hewn and unhewn stones from 16½ to 20 feet high, mixed with charred *débris*, with which I had to struggle upon my great platform), I positively believe that the above-mentioned buttress was erected to support the site of a temple of great sanctity. I believe this all the more, as the buttress here forms a curve and appears to protect the whole of the north-eastern corner of the hill, which was the extreme end of the Pergamus and perfectly corresponds with Homer's statement about the position of the temple of Athena, " on the summit of the city " (ἐν πόλει ἄκρῃ : *Iliad*, VI. 297). I have no doubt that in ascending from this buttress I shall find the ruins of that ancient temple at a distance of less than 10 meters (33 feet). But in order to penetrate further, I must first of all pull down the Trojan wall, 10 feet high and 6½ feet thick, which I have already frequently mentioned, and remove the enormous masses of *débris;* this work must be deferred till the 1st of February, for I am now too ill and tired to attempt it. The discovery of the very ancient temple of Athena at the north-eastern corner would, moreover solve the great problem—whence arises the colossal accumulation of *débris*, which here covers the declivity with a crust as hard as stone, 131 feet in thickness, and which caused me so much trouble, not only in this excavation, but also at the eastern end of my platform, along an extent of more than 80 feet. It will be found that this enormous crust has arisen solely from the remains of the sacrifices offered to the Ilian Athena.

I had not noticed this buttress at the time of my departure on the 15th of August, and I have now only discovered it because the rain has laid bare two of its stones. It is built of blocks of shelly limestone (*Muschelkalk*), from about a foot to 2 feet 2 inches long and broad, joined with earth, and it probably covered the whole north-eastern corner of the hill from the bottom to the top. I presume that the drain of green sandstone, nearly 8 inches broad and about 7 inches high, which I spoke of in my report of the 25th of April, belongs to the very ancient temple of Athena; it will be remembered that I found it at about $11\frac{1}{2}$ feet above my great platform, and at a distance of 46 feet from the edge of the declivity.

The block of triglyphs with the Sun-god and the four horses, which I found here, proves that the temple which it adorned was built in the Doric style; and, as the Doric is confessedly the oldest style of architecture, the ancient temple of the Ilian Athena was doubtless in that style. We know, however, from the Iliad* that there was also a temple of Apollo in the Pergamus. It probably stood at the south-eastern corner of the hill, for at the foot of it may be seen, in a small excavation, a wall composed of splendid Corinthian pillars joined by means of cement. It is probable that these pillars belong to a temple of Apollo of the time of Lysimachus. In excavating the Tower further to the east, I hope to find the site of this temple, and in its depths the ruins of the very ancient temple of Apollo.

If the Trojans possessed an alphabetical language, I shall probably find inscriptions in the ruins of the two temples. I am, however, no longer sanguine in regard to this, as I have hitherto found no trace of writing in the colossal strata of the four tribes which preceded the Greek colony.†

---

* *Iliad*, VII. 83 and IV. 508.; see pp. 145–6, 257.

† See note (†), p. 218.

WORK AT HISSARLIK IN 1873.

—◦◇◦—

CHAPTER XV.

Return to Hissarlik in 1873 — Interruptions by holydays and weather
— Strong cold north winds — Importance of good overseers — An
artist taken to draw the objects found — Want of workmen — Excavations on the site of the Temple — Blocks of Greek sculptured
marble — Great increase of the hill to the east — Further portions
of the great Trojan wall — Traces of fire — A terra-cotta hippopotamus, a sign of intercourse with Egypt — Idols and owl-faced
vases — Vases of very curious forms — Whorls — Sling-bullets of
copper and stone — Piece of ornamented ivory belonging to a
musical instrument — New cutting from S.E. to N.W. — Walls
close below the surface — Wall of Lysimachus — Monograms on
the stones — An inscription in honour of Caius Cæsar — Patronage
of Ilium by the Julii as the descendants of Æneas — Good wine of
the Troad.

Pergamus of Troy, February 22nd, 1873.

I RETURNED here on the 31st of January with my wife, in
order to continue the excavations, but we have been
repeatedly interrupted by Greek church festivals, thunderstorms, and also by the excessive cold, so that I can scarcely
reckon that I have had as yet more than eight good days'
work. Last autumn, by the side of my two wooden houses,
I had a house built for myself of stones from the old Trojan
buildings, the walls of which were 2 feet thick, but I was
compelled to let my foremen occupy it, for they were not
sufficiently provided with clothes and wrappers, and would
have perished through the great cold. My poor wife and
I have therefore suffered very much, for the strong icy

north wind* blew with such violence through the chinks of our house-walls which were made of planks, that we were not even able to light our lamps of an evening; and although we had fire on the hearth, yet the thermometer showed 4 degrees of cold (Réaumur = 23° Fahrenheit), and the water standing near the hearth froze in solid masses. During the day we could to some degree bear the cold by working in the excavations, but of an evening we had nothing to keep us warm except our enthusiasm for the great work of discovering Troy. Fortunately this extreme cold lasted only four days, from the 16th to the 19th of this month, and since then we have had glorious weather.

Besides Georgios Photidas, who was with me during the excavations of last year, I have as foremen Georgios Barba Tsirogiannis (a sea-captain from Chalcis in Euboea), and an Albanese from Salamis, whom, however, I shall shortly send back on account of his uselessness, and get two other foremen from the Piræus in his stead. A good foreman is more useful to me than ten common workmen, but I find that the gift of command is rarely met with except among seamen.

I have also brought with me an artist, that I may have the objects found copied immediately in Indian ink, and the drawings multiplied in Athens by means of photography. This will, however, render it impossible for me to state the depths at which the objects were found upon distinct plates, as I have hitherto done. The articles discovered in the different depths are now mixed together, but in each case the depth, as well as the relative size, is stated in meters, in addition to the number in the catalogue.

Workmen are at present not so easily to be had as before; for a merchant from Smyrna residing here has engaged 150 men to gather a medicinal root, which is here called γλυκόριζα, out of which liquorice-juice is pre-

---

* This recals to mind Homer's frequent mention of the blasts of Boreas.—[ED.]

pared. The German word *lakritze*, the French *lacorice*, and the English *liquorice*, are evidently corruptions of γλυκόριζα. Now, as the men employed by the Smyrna merchant work the ground at a certain price by square measure, they earn from 12 to 23 piasters (2 frcs. 40 cent. to 4 frcs. 60 cent.) daily; whereas I can give them only 9 piasters (1 frc. 80 cent.) during the present short days. At Easter I can offer them 10 piasters, and after the 1st of June 12 piasters. As the roots are dug up in the neighbourhood of Renkoï, it is principally the people of this village that are engaged in the work; and for carrying on my excavations I have to apply to the villages of Kafatli-Asmak, Yenishehr, and Neo-Chori, which are situated in and round about the Plain of Troy. If the weather is dry, I can count upon obtaining after to-morrow 120 workmen every day.

On the north side of the hill, at a distance of 131 feet from the declivity and at a depth of 51 feet, the wall of white stones, which rises at an angle of 40 degrees, 6½ feet below the Trojan wall, seems, as I have said, to mark the site of the Greek temple of Athena. Here I am having five terraces made on two sides simultaneously, and the *débris* carried away in man-carts and wheel-barrows. In the north-eastern excavations this *débris*, from the surface to a depth of 10 feet, consists of black earth, mixed with splinters of marble; and among them I find very many large and beautifully-sculptured blocks of marble, which evidently belong to the temple of the time of Lysimachus, which stood here, but are of no further value to archæology. The removal of these blocks, the weight of which is often nearly two tons, gives me the greatest trouble. The site of the temple is indeed indicated distinctly enough by the existence of these large marble blocks in the Doric style, but of the sanctuary itself there is not one stone in its place. A depression in the earth, 112 feet long and 76 feet broad, seems to prove that the place has been ransacked hundreds of years ago by Turks seeking stones suitable for sepulchral monuments; they have also, curiously enough, carried off all the foundations. Below the layer of *débris*, 10 feet thick, which descends at an angle of from 50 to 60 degrees, there is an accumulation of ashes, covering with a crust of 13½ feet thick the buttress previously mentioned, which distinctly marks the former declivity of the hill. The declivity at this point is rounded off towards the east; and—as is proved by the fact that the buttress itself (as well as the layers of *débris* that lie above it) turns in the same direction, and that the strata of *débris* which lie above it also extend out to the east—the *eastern* declivity at one time likewise commenced at this point, whereas its present position is 262½ feet distant from it. The hill of the Pergamus has therefore increased 262½ feet in an eastern direction since the buttress was built. I do not believe that there is a second hill in the world whose increase in size, during thousands of years, can in the remotest degree be compared with this enormous growth.

Except those small round terra-cottas in the form of volcanoes and tops, with the usual decorations, and some more or less broken pottery, nothing has as yet been discovered in this excavation. The other cutting— which I opened to reach the supposed site of the very ancient temple of Athena—is at the east end of my large platform, upon which I am again throwing the greater part of the *débris* which is being dug down there, because to remove it beyond the platform would be too difficult. In the mean time I have only had this cutting made 42½ feet broad, but I intend to widen it as soon as I find any prospect of advantage to archæology from doing so. In the lower terrace of this cutting I find the continuation of that Trojan wall which also shows itself in the more eastern cutting. This wall is here only 3¼ feet high, but the stones lying below it leave no doubt that it was at one time much higher. Every visitor to the Troad confirms

my observation of the remarkable fact, that this wall con-
tinues on the two sides of my large cutting through the
entire hill, to the right and left of the entrance, at a depth
of 39½ feet.   If this wall belongs to a time preceding the
Trojan wall (as to which I can entertain no doubt, owing
to its great depth), yet the mighty ruins beneath it, as well
as the pavement of white pebbles lying below it, at a depth
of 1¾ foot in my large cutting, prove that it must have been
built a long time after the *first* destruction of the city.
But the real object of the wall here and further to the
west is utterly inexplicable to me, for it is built above and
through the ruins of mighty buildings.

The strata of *débris* in this cutting all lie horizontally,
which leaves no doubt that they have been gradually
formed in the course of time.   Their composition proves
that most of the houses which stood here were destroyed
by fire.   But there are also several thick strata here, in
which we find thousands of shells in a state of good preservation, which proves that they at least cannot have
belonged to buildings destroyed by fire.

Among the interesting objects discovered in this
excavation, I must espe-
cially mention a brilliant
red terra-cotta hippo-
potamus, found at a
depth of 23 feet.   It is
hollow, and has a ring on
the left side, and there-
fore may have served as
a vessel.   The existence of

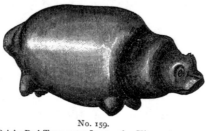

No. 159.
Bright Red Terra-cotta Image of a Hippopotamus
(7 M.).

the figure of a hippopotamus here at a depth of 23 feet
is extremely remarkable, nay, astonishing; for this animal,
as is well known, is not met with even in Upper Egypt, and
occurs only in the rivers of the interior of Africa.   It is,
however, probable that hippopotami existed in Upper Egypt
in ancient times; for, according to Herodotus (II. 71),

they were worshipped as sacred animals at the Egyptian town of Papremis. At all events, Troy must have been commercially connected with Egypt; but even so, it is still an enigma, how the animal was so well known here as to have been made of clay in a form quite faithful to nature.

Of idols of marble, it is only during these few days that we have found eight, only two of which had the engraved owl's head of the Ilian Athena. Of vases with owl's faces, two female breasts, and two upraised arms, I have found only one, at a depth of 15 meters (49¼ feet), and at a depth of 7 meters (23 feet) the upper portion of another, upon which the stump of one of the arms may still be recognised. At a depth of 10 feet we found two vases, with two female breasts and an immense navel, which are doubtless also intended to represent the tutelary goddess of Troy. Lastly, of vase-covers with an owl's face and helmet, the first found was at a depth of 1 meter (3¼ feet), having a double handle in the form of a coronet; another, found at a depth of 3 meters (26 feet), has a simple handle. Among the other terra-cotta vessels I must specially mention an exceedingly remarkable cup in the form of a bugle-horn with three feet, which was found at a depth of 3 meters (10 feet); also a vessel with

No. 160.
Remarkable Terra-cotta Vessel, in the shape of a Bugle, with three feet (3 M.).

No. 161.
Terra-cotta Vessel with three feet, a handle, and two ears (5 M.).

but two feet, which, however, as is proved by the broken places on the right side, has been attached to some other vessel of a similar form and description ; this double vessel had a ring on either side for suspension by strings. Of the other earthenware I can only mention a small curious vase which has three long feet, one handle, and two others in the form of ears.

The round articles of terra-cotta in the form of vol- canoes and humming-tops, with symbolical decorations, were met with in great quantities, as they always are. Four sling- bullets were discovered, one of which, made of copper, was brought out from a depth of 49 feet, one of alabaster from 23 feet, and two of diorite from a depth of from 20 to 23 feet. At a depth of 4 meters (13 feet) I found a splendidly ornamented flat piece of ivory, which must evidently have been part of a musical instrument.* Lastly, at the depth of 1 meter (3¼ feet) there was a fragment of a female statue of fine marble, executed in a masterly style. It not improbably represents the tutelary goddess of Ilium, whose temple, as we know, stood in the Pergamus.

Simultaneously with these excavations I had 22 men working in a north-westerly direction, from the south- eastern corner of the Acropolis, in order to lay bare the Great Tower still further on that side, an operation that has become impossible to effect from my great trench. But as the hill at this point has only a very gradual slope I was compelled to make the new cutting with a con- siderable slope, which renders the carting-off of the *débris* much more troublesome, but is absolutely necessary, to enable us to reach the requisite depth of 26 feet for arriving at the Tower. At the very commencement of this cutting, at a foot below the surface, I came upon two enormous walls, each of which is 10 feet thick. The first seems to belong to the Middle Ages,† and consists

---

* See Cut, No. 9, p. 27.

† Dr. Schliemann afterwards assigned these Corinthian pillars to the time of Constantine. (See Chapter XXII., p. 320, and Introduction, p. 30.—[ED.]

of large blocks of Corinthian pillars joined by cement
and of other marble blocks taken from ancient buildings. The second wall, which follows immediately, must
certainly belong to the town-wall built by Lysimachus,
which was 40 stadia long.* It is composed of large and
beautifully hewn blocks of limestone, which are laid one
upon another without any kind of cement, and which generally bear a monogram. As the letter is not always the
same, and as for instance upon one stone there is a **Σ**, and
upon another an **Y** or a **Δ**, I presume that they are the
initials of the different builders. In the first wall I found
a marble slab nearly a foot thick, 32½ inches broad, and
3½ feet long, with the following inscription :—

ΗΒΟΥΛΗΚΑΙΟΔΗΜΟΣ
ΓΑΙΟΝΚΑΙΣΑΡΑΤΟΝΥΙΟΝΤΟΥΣΕΒΑΣ
ΤΟΥΤΟΝΣΥΝΓΕΝΗΚΑΙΠΑΤΡΩΝΑΚΑΙΕΥ
ΕΡΓΕΤΗΝΤΗΣΠΟΛΕΩΣ

'Η βουλὴ καὶ ὁ δῆμος
Γάϊον Καίσαρα τὸν υἱὸν τοῦ Σεβαστοῦ τὸν συνγενῆ καὶ πατρῶνα καὶ εὐ-
εργέτην τῆς πόλεως.

The person praised in this inscription can by no means
have been the Emperor Caligula, for in that case the title
αὐτοκράτωρ would have been added. But as this word is
wanting, the person meant is certainly Caius Cæsar, the
son of Vipsanius Agrippa and of Julia, the daughter of
Octavianus. He had a brother called Lucius. Both were
adopted by Augustus, and owing to this adoption they
received the title of " υἱὸς τοῦ Σεβαστοῦ," and both were
selected by Augustus as his successors. Caius Cæsar, born
in the year 20 B.C., was adopted at the age of three years.
He took part in the Trojan games, which Augustus

* Strabo, XIII., pp. 100, 101, Tauchnitz edition.

instituted at the dedication of the temple of Marcellus. At the age of fifteen he was appointed Consul, and when nineteen he was made Governor of Asia. During his administration there he became involved in a war with Phraates the king of Armenia, was wounded, and died in the year 4 after Christ, on the 21st of February, at the age of 24.* As in the inscription he is called the kinsman, the benefactor, and the patron of Ilium, it is probable that he often came here during his administration; at all events, he took great interest in the city, and lavished favours upon it. The family of the Julii always attached great importance to their descent from Iülus (or Ascanius) the son of Æneas; and the sole political object of Virgil's Æneid was to prove and glorify their genealogy. This explains the favours which the Julii lavished upon Ilium, and their hatred against the Greeks because they destroyed Troy, and also because they had espoused the cause of Mark Antony.

An *oka* of wine, which contains about two ordinary wine-bottles, last year cost 1¼ piaster (25 centimes); now it costs 2 piasters (40 centimes) the oka; but it is of a most excellent quality, and I prefer it to any French wine.

No. 162. Terra-cotta Image of a Pig, curiously marked with Stars (4 M.).

---

* Velleius Paterculus, II. 102.

CHAPTER XVI.

Increased number of workmen — Further uncovering of the great buttress — Traces of a supposed small temple — Objects found on its
site — Terra-cotta serpents' heads : · great importance attached to
the serpent — Stone implements : hammers of a peculiar form —
Copper implements : a sickle — Progress of the works at the south-
east corner — Remains of an aqueduct from the Thymbrius —Large
jars, used for cellars — Ruins of the Greek temple of Athena —
Two important inscriptions discussed — Relations of the Greek
Syrian Kings Antiochus I. and III. to Ilium.

Pergamus of Troy, March 1st, 1873.

SINCE Monday morning, the 24th of last month, I have
succeeded in increasing the number of my workmen to 158,
and as throughout this week we have had splendid weather,
I have been able to accomplish a good stroke of work in
the six days, in spite of the many hindrances and difficulties
which I had at first to struggle against. Since the 1st of
February I have succeeded in removing more than 11,000
cubic yards of *débris* from the site of the temple. To-day,
at last, I have had the pleasure of uncovering a large portion of that buttress, composed of large unhewn white
stones, which at one time covered the entire north-eastern
corner of the declivity, whereas, in consequence of its
increase in size during the course of many centuries by the
ashes of the sacrificed animals, the present declivity of the
hill is 131 feet distant from it to the north, and 262½ feet
distant to the east. To my surprise I found that this
buttress reaches to within 26 feet of the surface, and thus, as
the primary soil is elsewhere always at from 46 to 52½ feet
below the surface, it must have covered an isolated hill
from 20 to 26 feet high, at the north-east end of the

Pergamus, where at one time there doubtless stood a small temple. Of this sanctuary, however, I find nothing but red wood-ashes, mixed with the fragments of brilliant black Trojan earthenware, and an enormous number of unhewn stones, which seem to have been exposed to a fearful heat, but no trace of sculpture: the building must therefore have been very small. I have broken through the buttress of this temple-hill at a breadth of 13 feet, in order to examine the ground at its foundation. I dug it away to a depth of 5 feet, and found that it consists of the virgin soil, which is of a greenish colour. Upon the site of the small and very ancient temple, which is indicated by the buttress, I find in two places pure granular sand, which appears to extend very far down, for after excavating it to a depth of 6½ feet I did not reach the end of the stratum. Whether this hill consists entirely, or but partially, of earth and sand, I cannot say, and must leave it undecided, for I should have to remove thousands more of cubic yards of rubbish. Among

No. 163. One of the largest marble Idols, found in the Trojan Stratum (8 M.).

the *débris* of the temple we found a few, but exceedingly interesting objects, for instance, the largest marble idol that has hitherto been found, which is 5¼ inches long and 3 inches broad. Further, the lid of a pot, which is divided into twelve fields by roughly engraved lines. Ten of the fields are ornamented with little stars, one with two signs of lightning, and another with six lines. There was also a small idol of terra-cotta with the owl's head of the Ilian tutelary goddess, with two arms and long hair hanging down at the back of the head; but it is so roughly made that, for instance, the eyes of the goddess are above the eyebrows. I also found among the *débris* of the temple a vase with the owl's face, two female breasts and a large navel; of the face only one eye and an ear is preserved. I must draw especial

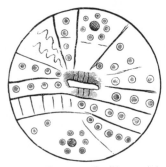

No. 164. Terra-cotta Pot-lid, engraved with symbolical marks (6 M.).

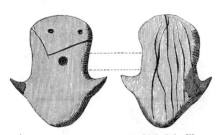

No. 165. A curious Terra-cotta Idol of the Ilian Athena (7 M.).

attention to the fact that both upon the vases with owls' heads two female breasts and a navel, and upon all of the others without the owl's face and adorned only with two female breasts and a navel, the latter is always ten times larger than the breasts. I therefore presume that the navel had some important significance, all the more so as it is frequently decorated with a cross, and in one case even with a cross and the marks of a nail at each of the four ends of the cross.* We also discovered among the ruins of the small and very ancient building some pretty wedges (battle-axes), and a number of very rude hammers made of diorite; besides a quantity of those small red and black terra-cotta whorls, with the usual engravings of four or five ⊞, or of three, four, or five triple rising suns in the circle round the central sun, or with other extremely strange decorations.

At a depth of 7 to 8 meters (23 to 26 feet), we also came upon a number of vases having engraved decorations, and with three feet or without feet, but generally with rings at the sides and holes in the mouth for suspension by strings; also goblets in the form of a circular tube, with a long spout at the side for drinking out of, which is always

---

* See Cut, No. 13, p. 35.

connected with the other side of the tube by a handle; further, smaller or larger jars with a mouth completely bent

No. 166.   Pretty Terra-cotta Jug, with the neck bent back (7 M.).

backwards; small terra-cotta funnels; very curious little sling-bullets made of diorite, from only $\frac{3}{4}$ of an inch to above 1 inch long. The most remarkable of all the objects found this year is, however, an idol of very hard black stone above $2\frac{1}{2}$ inches long and broad, discovered at a depth of 9 meters ($29\frac{1}{2}$ feet). The head, hands, and feet have the form of hemispheres, and the head is only recognised by several horizontal lines engraved below it, which seem to indicate necklaces. In the centre of the

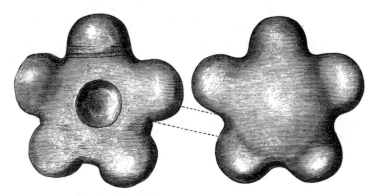

No. 167.   Remarkable Trojan Idol of Black Stone (7 M.).

belly is a navel, which is as large as the head, but, instead of protruding as in the case of the vases, it is indicated by a circular depression. The back of the middle of the body is arched, and has the appearance of a shield, so that in looking at the idol one is involuntarily led to believe that it represents Mars, the god of war.

At a depth of from 4 to 7 meters (13 to 23 feet) we also met with fragments of terra-cotta serpents, whose heads are sometimes represented with horns. The latter must

certainly be a very ancient and significant symbol of the
greatest importance, for even now there is a superstition
that the horns of serpents, by merely coming in contact
with the human body, cure a number of diseases, and
especially epilepsy ; also that by dipping them in milk the

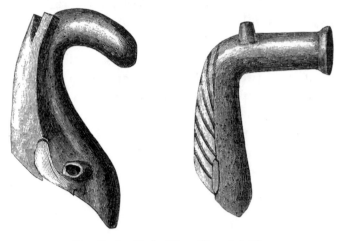

Nos. 168, 169.   Heads of Horned Serpents (4 M.).

latter is instantly turned into cheese, and other notions of
the same sort.   On account of the many wholesome and
useful effects attributed to the horns of serpents, they are regarded as immensely valuable, and on my return here at the end of
January one of my last year's workmen was
accused by a jealous comrade of having
found two serpents' horns in an urn at a
depth of 52½ feet, and of having made off
with them.   All my assurances that there
are no such things as serpents' horns could
not convince the men, and they still believe

No. 170.   A Serpent's
Head, with horns on
both sides, and very
large eyes (6 M.).

that their comrade has robbed me of a great treasure.
The serpents' heads not ornamented with horns generally
represent the poisonous asp; above the mouth they have
a number of dots, and the head and back are divided

by cross lines into sections which are filled with dots.*
These flat serpents' heads have on the opposite side lines

running longitudinally like female hair. We also found terra-cotta cones an inch and a half high, with three holes not pierced right through. At a depth of from $3\frac{1}{4}$ to $6\frac{1}{2}$ feet we have discovered several more terra-cotta vases without the owl's

No. 171. Head of an Asp in Terra-cotta (both sides) (4 M.).

face, but with two female breasts and a large navel, and with two small upright handles in the form of arms. In all the strata below 13 feet we meet with quantities of implements of diorite, and quoits of granite, sometimes also of hard limestone. Hammers and wedges (battle-axes) of diorite and of green stone were also found, in most cases very prettily wrought. The hammers do not all possess a perforated hole; upon many there is only a cavity on both sides, about $\frac{1}{5}$ to $\frac{2}{5}$ of an inch deep.

Of metals, copper only was met with. To-day we found a copper sickle $5\frac{1}{2}$ inches long; of copper weapons we have to-day for the first time found two lances at a depth of 23 feet, and an arrow-head at 4 meters (13 feet) deep. We find numbers of long, thin copper nails with a round head, or with the point only bent round. I now also find them repeatedly at a depth of from 5 to 6 meters ($16\frac{1}{2}$ to 20 feet), whereas since the commencement of my excavations in the year 1871, I only found two nails as far down as this.†

---

* The serpents' heads, found so frequently among the ruins of Troy, cannot but recal to mind the superstitious regard of Homer's Trojans for the reptile as a symbol, and their terror when a half-killed serpent was dropped by the bird of Jove amidst their ranks (*Iliad*, XII. 208, 209) :—

Τρῶες δ' ἐρρίγησαν, ὅπως ἴδον αἰόλον ὄφιν
Κείμενον ἐν μέσσοισι, Διὸς τέρας αἰγιόχοιο.

"The Trojans, shuddering, in their midst beheld
The spotted serpent, dire portent of Jove."

† That is, in the strata of the *third* dwellers on the hill.

I am now also vigorously carrying forward the cutting
which I made on the south-eastern corner of the Pergamus,
for uncovering the eastern portion of the Great Tower
as far as my last year's cutting, to a length of 315 feet
and a breadth of from 65½ to 78¾ feet.   The work
advances rapidly, as this excavation is near the southern
declivity of the hill, and the rubbish has therefore not
far to be carted off.   I have made eight side passages
for removing it.   Experience has taught me that it is
far more profitable not to have any special men for
loading the wheel-barrows, but to let every workman fill
his own barrow.   Experience has also shown me that much
precious time is lost in breaking down the earthen walls
with the long iron levers driven in by a ram, and that
it is much more profitable and less dangerous to the
workmen always to keep the earthen walls at an angle
of 55 degrees, to dig as occasion requires, and to cut
away the rubbish from below with broad pickaxes.   In
this new excavation I find four earthen pipes, from 18¾
to 22¼ inches long, and from 6½ to 11¾ inches thick,
laid together for conducting water, which was brought
from a distance of 1½ German mile (about 7 English
miles) from the upper Thymbrius.   This river is now
called the Kemar, from the Greek word καμάρα (vault),
because an aqueduct of the Roman period crosses its lower
course by a large arch.   This aqueduct formerly supplied
Ilium with drinking water from the upper portion of the
river.   But the Pergamus required special aqueducts, for
it lies higher than the city.

In this excavation I find an immense number of large
earthen wine-jars (πίθοι) from 1 to 2 meters (3¼ to 6½ feet)
high, and 29½ inches across, as well as a number of fragments of Corinthian pillars and other splendidly sculptured
blocks of marble.   All of these marble blocks must
certainly have belonged to those grand buildings whose
southern wall I have already laid bare to a length of

285½ feet. It is composed of small stones joined with a great quantity of cement as hard as stone, and rests upon large well hewn blocks of limestone. The direction of this wall, and hence of the whole building, is E.S.E. by E.

Three inscriptions, which I found among its ruins, and in one of which it is said that they were set up in the "ἱερόν," that is, in the temple, leave no doubt that this was the temple of the Ilian Athena, the "πολιοῦχος θεά," for it is only this sanctuary that could have been called simply "τὸ ἱερόν," on account of its size and importance, which surpassed that of all the other temples of Ilium. Moreover the position of the building, which is turned towards the rising sun, corresponds exactly with the position of the Parthenon and all the other temples of Athena. From the very commencement of my excavations I have searched for this important sanctuary, and have pulled down more than 130,000 cubic yards of *débris* from the most beautiful parts of the Pergamus in order to find it; and I now discover it exactly where I should have least expected to come upon it. I have sought for this *new* temple, which was probably built by Lysimachus, because I believed, and still believe, that in its depths I shall find the ruins of the primeval temple of Athena, and I am more likely here than anywhere to find something to throw light upon Troy. Of the inscriptions found here, as mentioned above, one is written upon a marble slab in the form of a tombstone, 5¼ feet long, 17½ inches broad, and 5¾ inches thick, and runs as follows :—

```
ΜΕΛΕΑΓΡΟΣΙΛΙΕΩΝΤΗΙΒΟΥΛΗΙΚΑΙΤΩΙΔΗΜΩΙΧΑΙ
ΡΕΙΝΑΠΕΔΩΚΕΝΗΜΙΝΑΡΙΣΤΟΔΙΚΙΔΗΣΟΑΣΣΙΟΣΕΠΙ
ΣΤΟΛΑΣΠΑΡΑΤΟΥΒΑΣΙΛΕΩΣΑΝΤΙΟΧΟΥΩΝΤΑΝΤΙΓΡΑ
ΦΑΥΜΙΝΥΠΟΓΕΓΡΑΦΑΜΕΝΕΝΕΤΥΧΕΝΔΗΜΙΝΚΑΙΑΥ
5    ΤΟΣΦΑΜΕΝΟΣΠΟΛΛΩΝΑΥΤΩΙΚΑΙΕΤΕΡΩΝΔΙΑΛΕ
ΓΟΜΕΝΩΝΚΑΙΣΤΕΦΑΝΟΝΔΙΔΟΝΤΩΝΩΣΠΕΡΚΑΙΗ
ΜΕΙΣΠΑΡΑΚΟΛΟΥΘΟΥΜΕΝΔΙΑΤΟΚΑΙΠΡΕΣΒΕΥΣΑΙΑ
ΠΟΤΩΝΠΟΛΕΩΝΤΙΝΑΣΠΡΟΣΗΜΑΣΒΟΥΛΕΣΘΑΙΤΗΝ
ΧΩΡΑΝΤΗΝΔΕΔΟΜΕΝΗΝΑΥΤΩΙΥΠΟΤΟΥΒΑΣΙΛΕΩΣΑΝ
```

10 ΤΙΟΧΟΥΚΑΙΔΙΑΤΟΙΕΡΟΝΚΑΙΔΙΑΤΗΝΠΡΟΣΥΜΑΣΕΥΝΟΙ
ΑΝΠΡΟΣΕΝΕΓΚΑΣΘΑΙΠΡΟΣΤΗΝΥΜΕΤΕΡΑΝΠΟΛΙΝΑ
ΜΕΝΟΥΝΑΞΙΟΙΓΕΝΕΣΘΑΙΑΥΤΩΙΠΑΡΑΤΗΣΠΟΛΕΩΣΑΥ
ΤΟΣΥΜΙΝΔΗΛΩΣΕΙΚΑΛΩΣΔΑΝΠΟΗΣΑΙΤΕΨΗΦΙΣΑΜΕ
ΝΟΙΤΕΠΑΝΤΑΤΑΦΙΛΑΝΘΡΩΠΑΑΥΤΩΙΚΑΙΚΑΘΟΤΙΑΝ
15 ΣΥΓΧΩΡΗΣΗΙΤΗΝΑΝΑΓΡΑΦΗΝΠΟΗΣΑΜΕΝΟΙΚΑΙΣΤΗ
ΛΩΣΑΝΤΕΣΚΑΙΔΕΝΤΕΣΕΙΣΤΟΙΕΡΟΝΙΝΑΜΕΝΗΙΥΜΙΝ
ΒΕΒΑΙΩΣΕΙΣΠΑΝΤΑΤΟΓΧΡΟΝΟΝΤΑΣΥΙΧΩΡΗΘΕΝΤΑ
ΕΡΡΩΣΘΕ　　　　ΒΑΣΙΛΕΥΣΑΝΤΙΟΧΟΣΜΕΛΕΑ
ΓΡΩΙΧΑΙΡΕΙΝΔΕΔΩΚΑΜΕΝΑΡΙΣΤΟΔΙΚΙΔΗΙΤΩΙΑΣΣΙΩΙ
20 ΓΗΣΕΡΓΑΣΙΜΟΥΠΛΕΘΡΑΔΙΣΧΙΛΙΑΠΡΟΣΕΝΕΓΚΑΣΘΑΙ
ΠΡΟΣΤΗΝΙΛΙΕΩΝΠΟΛΙΝΗΣΚΗΨΙΩΝΣΥΟΥΝΣΥΝΤΑΞΟΝ
ΠΛΡΑΔΕΙΞΑΙΑΡΙΣΤΟΔΙΚΙΔΗΙΑΠΟΤΗΣΟΜΟΡΟΥΣΗΣΤΗΙ
ΓΕΡΓΙΘΙΑΙΗΤΗΙΣΚΗΨΙΑΙΟΥΑΝΔΟΚΙΜΑΖΗΙΣΤΑΔΙΣΧΙΛΙΑ
ΠΛΕΘΡΑΤΗΣΓΗΣΚΑΙΠΡΟΣΟΡΙΣΑΙΕΙΣΤΗΝΙΛΙΕΩΝΗΤΗΝ
25 ΣΚΗΨΙΩΝ　　ΕΡΡΩΣΟ　　ΒΑΣΙΛΕΥΣΑΝΤΙΟΧΟΣΜΕΛΕ
ΑΓΡΩΙΧΑΙΡΕΙΝΕΝΕΤΥΧΕΝΗΜΙΝΑΡΙΣΤΟΔΙΚΙΔΗΣΟ
ΑΣΣΙΟΣΑΞΙΩΝΔΟΥΝΑΙΑΥΤΩΙΗΜΑΣΕΝΤΗΙΕΦΕΛΛΗΣ
ΠΟΝΤΟΥΣΑΤΡΑΠΕΙΑΙΤΗΝΠΕΤΡΑΝΗΜΠΡΟΤΕΡΟΝ
ΕΙΧΕΝΜΕΛΕΑΓΡΟΣΚΑΙΤΗΣΧΩΡΑΣΤΗΣΠΕΤΡΙΔΟΣ
30 ΕΡΓΑΣΙΜΟΥΠΕΘΡΑΧΙΛΙΑΠΕΝΤΑΚΟΣΙΑΚΑΙΑΛΛΑ
ΓΗΣΠΛΕΘΡΑΛΙΣΧΙΛΙΑΕΡΓΑΣΙΜΟΥΑΠΟΤΗΣΟΜΟ
ΡΟΥΣΗΣΤΗΙΠΡΟΤΕΡΟΝΔΟΘΕΙΣΗΙΑΥΤΩΙΜΕΡΙΔΙΩΙ
ΚΑΙΗΜΕΙΣΤΗΝΤΕΠΕΤΡΑΝΔΕΔΩΚΑΜΕΝΑΥΤΩΙΕΙ
ΜΗΔΕΔΟΤΑΙΑΛΛΩΙΠΡΟΤΕΡΟΝΚΑΙΤΗΓΧΩΡΑΝΤΗΝ
35 ΠΡΟΣΤΗΙΠΕΤΡΑΙΚΑΙΑΛΛΑΓΗΣΠΛΕΘΡΑΔΙΣΧΙΛΙΑ
ΕΡΓΑΣΙΜΟΥΔΙΑΤΟΦΙΛΟΝΟΝΤΑΗΜΕΤΕΡΟΝΠΑΡΕΣ
ΧΗΣΘΑΙΗΜΙΝΤΑΣΚΑΤΑΥΤΟΝΧΡΕΙΑΣΜΕΤΑΠΑΣΗΣ
ΕΥΝΟΙΑΣΚΑΙΠΡΟΘΥΜΙΑΣΣΥΟΥΝΕΠΙΣΚΕΨΑΜΕΝΟΣ
ΕΙΜΗΔΕΔΟΤΑΙΑΛΛΩΙΠΡΟΤΕΡΟΝΑΥΤΗΗΜΕΡΙΣΠΑ
40 ΡΑΔΕΙΞΟΝΑΥΤΗΝΚΑΙΤΗΝΠΡΟΣΑΥΤΗΙΧΩΡΑΝΑΡΙΣ
ΤΟΔΙΚΙΚΙΔΗΙΚΑΙΑΠΟΤΗΣΒΑΣΙΛΙΚΗΣΧΩΡΑΣΤΗΣΟΜΟ
ΡΟΥΣΗΣΤΗΙΠΡΟΤΕΡΟΝΛΕΛΟΜΕΝΗΙΧΩΡΑΙΑΡΙΣΤΟΔΙ
ΚΙΔΗΙΣΥΝΤΑΞΟΝΚΑΤΑΜΕΤΡΗΣΑΙΚΑΙΠΑΡΑΔΕΙΞΑΙ
ΑΥΤΩΙΠΛΕΘΡΑΔΙΣΧΙΛΙΑΚΑΙΕΑΣΑΙΑΥΤΩΙΠΡΟΣΕΝΕΓ
45 ΚΑΣΘΑΙΠΡΟΣΗΝΑΜΒΟΥΛΗΤΑΙΠΟΛΙΝΤΩΝΕΝΤΗΙΧΩΡΑΙ
ΤΕΚΑΙΣΥΜΜΑΧΙΑΙΟΙΔΕΒΑΣΙΛΙΚΟΙΛΑΟΙΟΙΕΚΤΟΥΤΟ
ΠΟΥΕΝΩΙΕΣΤΙΝΗΠΕΤΡΑΕΑΜΒΟΥΛΩΝΤΑΙΟΙΚΕΙΝΕΝΤΗΙ
ΠΕΤΡΑΙΑΣΦΑΛΕΙΑΣΕΝΕΚΕΣΥΝΤΕΤΑΧΑΜΕΝΑΡΙΣΤΟ
ΤΟΔΙΚΙΔΗΙΕΑΝΑΥΤΟΥΣΟΙΚΕΙΝ　　　ΕΡΡΩΣΟ
50 ΒΑΣΙΛΕΥΣΑΝΤΙΟΧΟΣΜΕΛΕΑΓΡΩΙΧΑΙΡΕΙΝΕΝΕΤΥΧΕΝΗΙ
ΜΙΝΑΡΙΣΤΟΔΙΚΙΔΗΣΦΑΜΕΝΟΣΠΕΤΡΑΝΤΟΧΩΡΙΟΝΚΑΙΤΗΜ
ΧΩΡΑΝΤΗΝΣΥΓΚΥΡΟΥΣΑΗΠΕΡΙΣΠΡΟΤΕΡΟΝΕΓΡΑΨΑΜΕΝ
ΔΙΔΟΝΤΕΣΑΥΤΩΙΟΥΔΕΤΙΚΑΙΝΥΝΠΑΡΕΙΛΗΦΕΝΑΙΔΙΑΤΟΑΘΗ
ΝΑΙΩΙΤΩΙΕΠΙΤΟΥΝΑΥΣΤΑΘΜΟΥΕΠΙΚΕΧΩΡΗΣΘΑΙΚΑΙΗΞΙ

55 ΩΣΕΝΑΝΤΙΜΕΝΤΗΣΠΕΤΡΙΤΙΔΟΣΧΩΡΑΣΠΑΡΑΔΕΙΧΘΗΝΑΙ
ΑΥΤΩΙΤΑΙΣΑΠΛΕΘΡΑΣΥΓΧΩΡΗΘΗΝΑΙΔΕΚΑΙΑΛΛΑΠΛΕ
ΘΡΑΔΙΣΧΙΛΙΑΠΡΟΣΕΝΕΓΚΑΣΘΑΙΠΡΟΣΗΝΑΜΒΟΥΛΗΤΑΙ
ΤΩΜΠΟΛΕΩΝΤΩΝΕΝΤΗΙΗΜΕΤΕΡΑΙΣΥΜΜΑΧΙΑΙΚΑΘΑ
ΠΕΡΚΑΙΠΡΟΤΕΡΟΝΕΓΡΑΨΑΜΕΝΟΡΩΝΤΕΣΟΥΝΑΥΤΟΝ
60 ΕΥΝΟΥΝΟΝΤΑΚΑΙΠΡΟΘΥΜΟΝΕΙΣΤΑΗΜΕΤΕΡΑΠΡΑΓΜΑ
ΤΑΒΟΥΛΟΜΕΘΑΠΟΛΥΩΡΕΙΝΤΑΝΘΡΩΠΟΥΚΑΙΠΕΡΙ
ΤΟΥΤΩΝΣΥΓΚΕΧΩΡΗΚΑΜΕΝΦΗΣΙΝΔΕΕΙΝΑΙΤΗΣ
ΠΕΤΡΙΤΙΔΟΣΧΩΡΑΣΤΑΣΥΓΧΩΡΗΘΕΝΤΑΑΥΤΩΙ
ΠΛΕΘΡΑΧΙΛΙΑΠΕΝΤΑΚΟΣΙΑΣΥΝΤΑΞΟΝΟΥΝΚΑΤΑ
65 ΜΕΤΡΗΣΑΙΑΡΙΣΤΟΔΙΚΙΔΗΙΚΑΙΠΑΡΑΔΕΙΞΑΙΓΗΣ
ΕΡΓΑΣΙΜΟΥΤΑΤΕΔΙΣΧΙΛΙΑΚΑΙΠΕΝΤΑΚΟΣΙΑΠΛΕ
ΘΡΑΚΑΙΑΝΤΙΤΩΝΠΕΡΙΤΗΝΠΕΤΡΑΝΑΛΛΑΕΡΓΑ
ΣΙΜΟΥΧΙΛΙΑΠΕΝΤΑΚΟΣΙΑΑΠΟΤΗΣΒΑΣΙΛΙΚΗΣΧΩ
ΡΑΣΤΗΣΣΥΝΟΡΙΖΟΥΣΗΣΤΗΙΕΝΑΡΧΗΙΔΟΘΕΙΣΗΙ
70 ΑΥΤΩΙΠΑΡΗΜΩΝΕΑΣΑΙΔΕΚΑΙΠΡΟΣΕΝΕΓΚΑΣΘΑΙ
ΤΗΝΧΩΡΑΝΑΡΙΣΤΟΔΙΚΙΔΗΝΠΡΟΣΗΝΑΝΒΟΥΛΗΤΑΙ
ΠΟΛΙΝΤΩΝΕΝΤΗΙΗΜΕΤΕΡΑΙΣΥΜΜΑΧΙΑΙΚΑΘΑ
ΠΕΡΚΑΙΕΝΤΗΙΠΡΟΤΕΡΟΝΕΠΙΣΤΟΛΗΙΕΓΡΑΨΑ
ΜΕΝ ΕΡΡΩΣΟ

Μελέαγρος Ἰλιέων τῆι βουλῆι καὶ τῶι δήμωι χαίρειν. Ἀπέδωκεν ἡμῖν Ἀριστοδικίδης ὁ Ἄσσιος ἐπι-
στολὰς παρὰ τοῦ βασιλέως Ἀντιόχου, ὧν τἀντίγρα-
φα ὑμῖν ὑπογεγράφαμεν· ἐνέτυχεν δ᾽ ἡμῖν καὶ α(ὐ)-
5 τὸς φάμενος, πολλῶν αὐτῶι καὶ ἑτέρων, διαλε-
γομένων καὶ στέφανον διδόντων, ὥσπερ καὶ ἡ-
μεῖς παρακολουθοῦμεν διὰ τὸ καὶ πρεσβεῦσαι ἀ-
πὸ τῶν πόλεων τινὰς πρὸς ἡμᾶς, βούλεσθαι τὴν
χώραν τὴν δεδομένην αὐτῶι ὑπὸ τοῦ βασιλέως Ἀν-
10 τιόχου καὶ διὰ τὸ ἱερὸν καὶ διὰ τὴν πρὸς ὑμᾶς εὔνοι-
αν προσενέγκασθαι πρὸς τὴν ὑμετέραν πόλιν. ᾝΑ
μὲν οὖν ἀξιοῖ γενέσθαι αὐτῶι παρὰ τῆς πόλεως, αὐ-
τὸς ὑμῖν δηλώσει· καλῶς δ᾽ ἂν ποήσαιτε ψηφισάμε-
νοί τε πάντα τὰ φιλάνθρωπα αὐτῶι καὶ καθ᾽ ὅτι ἂν
συγχωρήσηι τὴν ἀναγραφὴν ποησάμενοι καὶ στη-
15 λώσαντες καὶ θέντες εἰς τὸ ἱερὸν, ἵνα μένηι ὑμῖν
βεβαίως εἰς πάντα τὸγ χρόνον τὰ συγχωρηθέντα.
ἔρρωσθε.   Βασιλεὺς Ἀντίοχος Μελεά-
γρωι χαίρειν.   Δεδώκαμεν Ἀριστοδικίδηι τῶι Ἀσσίωι

20 γῆς ἐργασίμου πλέθρα δισχίλια προσενέγκασθαι
πρὸς τὴν Ἰλιέων πόλιν ἢ Σκηψίων. Σὺ οὖν σύνταξον
παραδεῖξαι Ἀριστοδικίδηι ἀπὸ τῆς ὁμορούσης τῆι
Γεργιθίαι ἢ τῆι Σκηψίαι, οὗ ἂν δοκιμάζηις τὰ δισχίλια
πλέθρα τῆς γῆς καὶ προσορίσαι εἰς τὴν Ἰλιέων ἢ τὴν
25 Σκηψίων.   ἔρρωσο.   Βασιλεὺς Ἀντίοχος Μελεάγρωι χαίρειν.   Ἐνέτυχεν ἡμῖν Ἀριστοδικίδης ὁ
Ἄσσιος ἀξιῶν δοῦναι αὐτῶι ἡμᾶς ἐν τῆι ἐφ᾽ Ἑλλησ-
πόντου σατραπείαι τὴν Πέτραν, ἣμ πρότερον
εἶχεν Μελέαγρος καὶ τῆς χώρας τῆς Πετρίδος
30 ἐργασίμου πέθρα*¹ χίλια πεντακόσια καὶ ἄλλα
γῆς πλέθρα δισχίλια ἐργασίμου ἀπὸ τῆς ὁμορούσης τῆι πρότερον δοθείσηι αὐτῶι μεριδίωι (;)
καὶ ἡμεῖς τήν τε Πέτραν δεδώκαμεν αὐτῶι, εἰ
μὴ δέδοται ἄλλωι πρότερον καὶ τὴγ χώραν τὴν
35 πρὸς τῆι Πέτραι καὶ ἄλλα γῆς πλέθρα δισχίλια
ἐργασίμου, διὰ τὸ φίλον ὄντα ἡμέτερον παρεσ-
χῆσθαι ἡμῖν τὰς καθ᾽ αὐτὸν χρείας μετὰ πάση (ς)
εὐνοίας καὶ προθυμίας.   Σὺ οὖν ἐπισκεψάμενος
εἰ μὴ δέδοται ἄλλωι πρότερον αὕτη ἡ μερίς (;), πα-
40 ράδειξον αὐτὴν καὶ τὴν πρὸς αὐτῆι χώραν Ἀρισ-
τοδικικίδηι*² καὶ ἀπὸ τῆς βασιλικῆς χώρας τῆς ὁμορούσης τῆι πρότερον δεδομένηι χώραι Ἀριστοδικίδηι σύνταξον καταμετρῆσαι καὶ παραδεῖξαι
αὐτῶι πλέθρα δισχίλια καὶ ἐᾶσαι αὐτῶι προσενέγ-
45 κασθαι πρὸς ἣν ἂμ βούληται πόλιν τῶν ἐν τῆι χώραι
τε καὶ συμμαχίαι· οἱ δὲ βασιλικοὶ λαοὶ οἱ ἐκ τοῦ τό-
που, ἐν ὧι ἐστὶν ἡ Πέτρα, ἐὰμ βούλωνται οἰκεῖν ἐν τῆ (ι)
Πέτραι ἀσφαλείας ἔνεκε, συντετάχαμεν Ἀριστο-
τοδικίδηι*³ ἐᾶν αὐτοὺς οἰκεῖν.   ἔρρωσο.
50 Βασιλεὺς Ἀντίοχος Μελεάγρωι χαίρειν. Ἐνέτυχεν ἡ-
μῖν Ἀριστοδικίδης, φάμενος Πέτραν τὸ χωρίον καὶ τὴ (γ)
χώραν τὴν συγκυροῦσαν, περὶ ἧς πρότερον ἐγράψαμεν
διδόντες αὐτῶι, οὐδ᾽ ἔτι καὶ νῦν παρειληφέναι, διὰ τὸ Ἀθη-
ναίωι τῶι ἐπὶ τοῦ ναυστάθμου ἐπικεχωρῆσθαι, καὶ ἠξί

---

*¹ sic.   *² sic.   *³ sic.

55 ωσεν ἀντὶ μὲν τῆς Πετρίτιδος χώρας παραδειχθῆνα(ι)
αὐτῶι τὰ ἴσα πλέθρα, συγχωρηθῆναι δὲ καὶ ἄλλα πλέθρα δισχίλια προσενέγκασθαι πρὸς ἣν ἂμ βούληται
τῶμ πόλεων τῶν ἐν τῆι ἡμετέραι συμμαχίαι, καθάπερ καὶ πρότερον ἐγράψαμεν. Ὁρῶντες οὖν αὐτὸν
60 εὔνουν ὄντα καὶ πρόθυμον εἰς τὰ ἡμέτερα πράγμα-
τα, βουλόμεθα πολυωρεῖν τἀνθρώπου, καὶ περὶ
τούτων συγκεχωρήκαμεν. Φησὶν δὲ εἶναι τῆς
Πετρίτιδος χώρας τὰ συγχωρηθέντα αὐτῶι
πλέθρα χίλια πεντακόσια. Σύνταξον οὖν κατα-
65 μετρῆσαι Ἀριστοδικίδηι καὶ παραδεῖξαι γῆς
ἐργασίμου τά τε δισχίλια καὶ πεντακόσια πλέθρα καὶ ἀντὶ τῶν περὶ τὴν Πέτραν ἄλλα ἐργασίμου χίλια πεντακόσια ἀπὸ τῆς βασιλικῆς χώρας τῆς συνοριζούσης τῆι ἐν ἀρχῆι δοθείσηι
70 αὐτῶι παρ' ἡμῶν· ἐᾶσαι δὲ καὶ προσενέγκασθαι
τὴν χώραν Ἀριστοδικίδην πρὸς ἣν ἂν βούληται
πόλιν τῶν ἐν τῆι ἡμετέραι συμμαχίαι, καθάπερ καὶ ἐν τῆι πρότερον ἐπιστολῆι ἐγράψαμεν. ἔρρωσο.

This inscription, the great historical value of which
cannot be denied, seems certainly to belong to the third
century B.C., judging from the subject as well as from the
form of the letters, for the king Antiochus repeatedly
mentioned must either be Antiochus I., surnamed Soter
(281 to 260 B.C.), or Antiochus III., the Great (222 to
186). Polybius, who was born in 210 or 200 B.C., and
died in 122 B.C., in his History (XXVIII. 1, and XXXI. 21)
speaks indeed of a Meleager who lived in his time, and
was an ambassador of Antiochus Epiphanes, who reigned
from 174 to 164, and it is quite possible that this Meleager
afterwards became satrap of the satrapy of the Hellespont,
and that, in this office, he wrote to the Ilians the first
letter of this inscription. But in the first letter of Antiochus to his satrap Meleager, he gives him the option

of assigning to Aristodicides the 2000 plethra of land,
either from the district bordering upon the territory of
Gergis or upon that of Scepsis. The town of Gergis,
however, according to Strabo, was destroyed by king
Attalus I. of Pergamus, who reigned from 241 to 197 B.C.,
and who transplanted the inhabitants to the neighbourhood
of the sources of the Caïcus in Mysia. These sources,
however, as Strabo himself says, are situated very far from
Mount Ida, and hence also from Ilium. Two thousand
plethra of land at such a distance could not have been
of any use to the Ilians; consequently, it is impossible to
believe that the inscription can be speaking of the new
town of Gergitha, which was rising to importance at the
sources of the Caïcus. I now perfectly agree with Mr.
Frank Calvert,[*] and with Consul von Hahn,[†] that the site
of Gergis is indicated by the ruins of the small town and
acropolis at the extreme end of the heights behind Bunarbashi, which was only a short time ago regarded by most
archæologists as the site of the Homeric Troy. This
site of Gergis, in a direct line between Ilium and Scepsis,
the ruins of which are to be seen further away on the
heights of Mount Ida, agrees perfectly with the inscription. Livy (XXXV. 43) gives an account of the visit
of Antiochus III, the Great. I also find in the 'Corpus
Inscriptionum Græcarum,' No. 3596, that the latter
had a general called Meleager, who may subsequently
have become satrap of the Hellespont. On the other
hand, Chishull, in his 'Antiquitates Asiaticæ,' says that
Antiochus I., Soter, on an expedition with his fleet against
the King of Bithynia, stopped at the town of Sigeum,
which lay near Ilium, and that the king went up to Ilium
with the queen, who was his wife and sister, and with the
great dignitaries and his suite. There is, indeed, nothing
said of the brilliant reception which was there prepared

---

[*] *Archæological Journal*, vol. xxi. 1864.
[†] *Die Ausgrabungen auf der homerischen Pergamos*, s. 24.

for him, but there is an account of the reception which
was arranged for him in Sigeum. The Sigeans lavished
servile flattery upon him, and not only did they send
ambassadors to congratulate him, but the Senate also
passed a decree, in which they praised the king's actions
to the skies, and proclaimed that public prayers should be
offered up to the Ilian Athena, to Apollo (who was regarded
as his ancestor), to the goddess of Victory and to other
deities, for his and his consort's welfare; that the priestesses
and priests, the senators and all the magistrates of the
town should carry wreaths, and that all the citizens and all
the strangers settled or temporarily residing in Sigeum
should publicly extol the virtues and the bravery of the great
king; further, that a gold equestrian statue of the king,
standing on a pedestal of white marble, should be erected in
the temple of Athena in Sigeum, and that it should bear the
inscription : " The Sigeans have erected this statue to King
Antiochus, the son of Seleucus, for the devotion he has shown
to the temple, and because he is the benefactor and the saviour
of the people; this mark of honour is to be proclaimed in
the popular assemblies and at the public games." However,
in this wilderness it is impossible for me to find out from
which ancient classic writer this episode has been taken.

It is very probable that a similar reception awaited
Antiochus I. in Ilium, so that he kept the city in good
remembrance. That he cherished kindly feelings towards
the Ilians is proved also by the inscription No. 3595 in
the 'Corpus Inscriptionum Græcarum.' But whether it
is he or Antiochus the Great that is referred to in the
inscription I do not venture to decide.

Aristodicides, of Assos, who is frequently mentioned in
the inscription, is utterly unknown, and this name occurs
here for the first time; the name of the place Petra also,
which is mentioned several times in the inscription, is quite
unknown; it must have been situated in this neighbourhood, but all my endeavours to discover it in the modern

Turkish names of the localities, or by other means, have
been made in vain.

The other inscription runs as follows:—

```
                              ΩΝΙΟΥΤΟΥΕΥΔ
            ΟΣΜΕΝ               ΟΥΚΑΜΕΝΑΧΟΣΓΛΑΥΚΟ
ΕΠΕΓΡΑΨΑΜΕΝΕΙΣΣΤΗΛΗΝΚΑΤΑΤΟΝΝΟΜΟΝΕΡΓΟΦΙΛΟΝΠΑΤΡΟΣΟΥ
ΧΡΗΜΑΤΙΣΖΗΕΖΗΜΙΩΜΕΝΟΝΥΠΟΤΩΝΠΡΟΤΑΝΕΩΝΤΩΝΠΕΡΙΔΙΟ
ΦΑΝΗΝΗΓΗΣΙΔΗΜΟΥΟΦΙΛΟΝΤΑΤΟΥΣΚΑΤΑΤΟΝΝΟΜΟΝΣΤΑΤΗΡΑΣΔΥΟ
ΚΑΙΜΗΝΟΓΕΝΗΝΜΝΗΣΑΡΧΟΥΚΑΙΑΡΤΕΜΙΔΩΡΟΝΦΑΝΙΑΚΑΙΔΙΟΜΗΔΗΝ
ΑΠΟΛΛΩΝΙΟΥΕΖΗΜΙΩΜΕΝΟΥΣΥΠΟΤΩΝΠΡΥΤΑΝΕΩΝΤΩΝΠΕΡΙΔΙΟΦΑΝΗΝ
ΗΓΗΣΙΔΗΜΟΥΥΠΟΗΜΕΡΑΣΤΡΕΙΣΟΦΙΛΟΝΤΑΣΕΚΑΣΤΟΝΑΥΤΩΝΣΤΑΤΗΡΑΣΔΥΟ
ΜΗΝΟΔΟΤΟΝΜΗΝΟΔΟΤΟΥΚΑΙΗΡΑΚΛΕΙΔΗΝΚΑΙΜΗΝΟΔΟΤΟΝΤΟΥΣΗΡΑΚΛΕΙ
ΔΟΥΕΖΗΜΙΩΜΕΝΟΥΣΥΠΟΤΩΝΠΕΡΙΦΑΙΝΩΝΑΚΤΑΕΥΔΗΜΟΥΠΡΥΤΑ
ΝΕΩΝΟΦΙΛΟΝΤΑΕΚΑΣΤΟΝΑΥΤΩΝΣΤΑΤΗΡΑΣΔΥΟ
ΑΡΤΕΜΙΔΩΡΟΝΜΗΝΟΦΑΝΤΟΥΕΖΗΜΙΩΜΕΝΟΝΥΠΟΤΩΝΝΟ
ΜΟΦΥΛΑΚΩΝΤΩΝΠΕΡΙΙΠΠΑΡΧΟΝΗΓΗΣΙΔΗΜΟΥΦΙΛΟΝ
ΤΑΣΤΑΤΗΡΑΣΔΥΟ
```

```
 . . . . . . . . . . . . . . . . . . . . . . . .
 . . . . . . . . . . . . . . . . ωνίου τοῦ Εὐδ . . . .
 . . . . . . οσμεν . . . . . . . . ουκαμεναχος γλαυκο . .
ἐπεγράψαμεν εἰς στήλην κατὰ τὸν νόμον Ἐργόφιλον Πατρόσου (;)
Χρήματις*¹ ζη*² ἐζημιωμένον ὑπὸ τῶν προτάνεων*³ τῶν περὶ Διο-
φάνην Ἡγησιδήμου, ὁ(φ)ίλοντα τοὺς κατ(ὰ) τὸν νόμον στατῆρας δύο
καὶ Μηνογένην Μνησ(άρχ;)ου καὶ Ἀρτεμίδωρον Φανία καὶ Διομήδην
Ἀπολλωνίου, ἐζημιωμένους ὑπὸ τῶν πρυτάνεων τῶν περὶ Διοφά(νην)
Ἡγησιδήμου ὑπὸ ἡμέρας τρεῖς ὀφίλοντας ἕκαστον αὐτῶν στατῆρας δύο.
Μηνόδοτον Μηνοδότου καὶ Ἡρακλείδην καὶ Μηνόδοτον τοὺς Ἡρακλεί-
δου ἐζημιωμένους ὑπὸ τῶν περὶ Φαινώνακτα Εὐδήμου πρυτά-
νεων, ὀφείλοντα ἕκαστον αὐτῶν στατῆρας δύο.
Ἀρτεμίδωρον Μηνοφάντον ἐζημιωμένον ὑπὸ τῶν νο-
μοφυλάκων τῶν περὶ Ἵππαρχον Ἡγησιδήμου, ὀφίλον-
τα στατῆρας δύο.
```

In the inscription quoted in the 'Corpus Inscriptionum
Græcarum' under No. 3604, which is admitted to belong
to the time of Augustus Octavianus, Hipparchus is mentioned as a member of the Ilian Council, and as on line 13
the same name occurs with the same attribute, I do not
hesitate to maintain that the above inscription belongs to
the same period.

---

*¹ sic.   *² sic.   *³ sic.

CHAPTER XVII.

Spring weather in the Plain of Troy — The Greek Temple of Athena — Numerous fragments of sculpture — Reservoir of the temple — Excavation of the Tower — Difficulties of the work — Further discoveries of walls — Stone implements at small depths — Important distinction between the plain and decorated whorls — Greek and Roman coins — Absence of iron — Copper nails : their peculiar forms : probably dress and hair pins : some with heads and beads of gold and electrum — Original height of the Tower — Discovery of a Greek house — Various types of whorls — Further remarks on the Greek bas-relief — It belonged to the temple of Apollo — Stones from the excavations used for building in the villages around — Fever.

Pergamus of Troy, March 15th, 1873.

SINCE my report of the 1st of this month I have continued the excavations with great zeal, favoured by glorious weather and an abundance of workmen. The nights are cold, and the thermometer still frequently falls to freezing point towards morning, whereas during the day the heat of the sun is already beginning to be troublesome, the thermometer often showing 18° Réaumur (72½° Fahrenheit) in the shade at midday. The leaves of the trees are only now beginning to sprout, while the Plain is already covered with spring flowers.* For the last fortnight we have heard the croaking of millions of frogs in the surrounding marshes, and during the last eight days the storks have returned. One of the discomforts of our life in this

---

* Compare Homer's picture of the marshalling of the Greek forces : *Iliad*, II. 467-8 :—

Ἔσταν δ᾽ ἐν λειμῶνι Σκαμανδρίῳ ἀνθεμόεντι
Μυρίοι, ὅσσα τε φύλλα καὶ ἄνθεα γίγνεται ὥρῃ.

" Upon *Scamander's flowery mead* they stood
Unnumbered as *the vernal leaves and flowers*."—[ED.]

wilderness is the hideous shrieking of the innumerable owls which build their nests in the holes of the walls of my excavations; their shrieks sound mysterious and horrible, and are especially unendurable at night.

I have proceeded with the excavation of the site of the Temple of Athena with the greatest energy. The foundations of this sanctuary nowhere extend deeper than 2 meters (6½ feet), and generally only to 1 meter (3¼ feet). The floor, which consists of large slabs of sandstone, and which rests upon double layers of large hewn blocks of the same stone, is frequently covered only with a foot, and never with more than 3¼ feet, of vegetable soil; this explains the total absence of entire sculptures. For whatever sculptures there were in or upon the temple could not sink into the ground on the summit of the hill, and they therefore remained lying on the surface for many centuries, till they were destroyed by religious zeal or wantonness. This, and this alone, explains the enormous mass of fragments of statues which cover the entire hill.

I find, however, a great number of large sculptured blocks of marble in the Corinthian style which are difficult to destroy, and the removal of which causes me great trouble and loss of time. As the Tower, which I partly uncovered last year, extends directly below the temple at a great depth, and as I wish at all events to lay bare its entire breadth, I shall leave only the ruins of the north and south walls of the temple standing, and break away all the rest, except a reservoir, 27 feet long and 26 feet broad, which is in the sanctuary, and is built of blocks of limestone laid together without cement or lime, and the walls of which have a thickness of 8 feet. The four aqueducts mentioned in my last report empty themselves into the reservoir. I shall leave it standing in order to give visitors to the Troad a faint idea of the trouble which I have to take in removing all the stones of a temple which is about 288 feet long and 72½ feet broad. But what is even much more difficult

than the removal of the stones, is the carrying off of the
débris, for as the excavation is made on the flat earth, this
can only be effected by side paths, which become steeper
the deeper we dig.   However, I only wish to uncover the
top of the ruined Tower, for to bring it to light down to
the primary soil is a piece of work to which my patience
is unequal.   This new large cutting, therefore, only requires a depth of 26 feet, and on the western end I have
given it a breadth of 78¾ feet.   By this means I hope to
reach the ancient and highly important monument on the
north side in two or three days.   As soon as this is done, I
shall have an upper and a lower terrace made for facilitating
the removal of the rubbish, and shall thus in a month from
to-day be able to finish the entire excavation of the Tower
as far as its eastern end, which I came upon yesterday in
my steep cutting at the south-eastern corner of the Pergamus, and of which I have laid open a breadth of 13 feet.
This eastern side of the Tower, thus brought to light, runs
down at an angle of 60 degrees, and has the same appearance as the ancient buttress which I uncovered at the north
side of the Pergamus.   As I did not at first think that it
was the Tower, I had the first layer of stones broken off,
but I soon found a piece of masonry composed of large
stones joined with earth.   In consequence of this I have
entirely stopped the works in this cutting, which already
extended to a length of 111½ feet, and in spite of its small
breadth was one of the most difficult works in Troy.   For,
as already said, I had first to break through a wall 10 feet
thick, consisting of large blocks of marble, but principally
of Corinthian pillars joined with lime (see p. 239); then the
wall of Lysimachus, which was also 10 feet thick, and built of
large hewn stones.   The large drums of pillars had to be
rolled up the steep path and then carried off; the large hewn
stones had to be broken with hammers and then removed in
wheel-barrows.   In addition to this, as the visitors to the
Pergamus may see in the walls of this cutting, we had to cut

through two Trojan walls, the first of which is 5¼ feet thick, and the second 10 feet ; both consist of stones joined with earth. The first of these walls is directly below a portion of the western wall of the comparatively modern Temple of Athena, and as—according to my pocket compass— it runs due E.S.E.½E., I at first thought that it might belong to the ancient diminutive temple of the Ilian tutelary goddess, which Alexander the Great * found here. But nothing further has appeared which could help to prove this. The second wall, 10 feet thick, is extremely inter- esting, for it is built of large unhewn blocks of shelly lime- stone (*Muschelkalk*), and on the top of it is a wall of small stones joined with earth. It evidently belongs to a much later age, but was in any case built long before the arrival of the Greek colony in Ilium. But even the lower wall of large stones was not built till the Tower of Ilium had formed a heap of *débris* 20 feet high ; it must therefore have been built centuries after the erection of the Tower. This *débris* consists of ashes mixed with bones and small shells, and on account of its dampness and toughness is just as difficult to break down as damp limestone rock. In it I found many fragments of those Trojan vessels, which are of a brilliant red or black colour, both outside and inside, but nothing else of any interest. Above the Tower, at the east side of the Pergamus, there is nothing but yellow wood-ashes and a great number of stones. In fact, down to the present depth of 4½ meters (14¼ feet) below the surface, that is, from 7 to 10 feet below the foundations of the temple of Athena, I find nothing but yellow wood-ashes, and among these an immense number of enormous earthen jars (πίθοι) from 3¼ to 6½ feet long, and pointed below, which must have served not only as wine and water jars, but as cellars for keeping provisions, for there are no walled cellars.

Stone implements, such as I found in my former exca- vations only below a depth of 13 feet (with the exception

---

* Plutarch, *Life of Alexander*, viii.   Comp. p. 146.

of the few knives of silex), are met with here in great
numbers at as small a depth as 6½ feet, that is, directly
below the Temple of Athena; those most frequently found
are clumsy hammers of diorite, but occasionally also hammers of the same or of green stone very prettily worked;
some of them have a wide hole at both sides and a narrow
one in the middle, and I cannot understand how a handle
could have been fixed into them. The best finished
instrument is always the wedge,* which is of diorite or
of hard green stone, sometimes also of white silex, and
occurs in all sizes from about ¾ of an inch to above
5 inches in length. This instrument is always of such
exquisite workmanship and so well polished, that it is really
astonishing how it was possible, with the miserable means
at the disposal of those times, to make anything of such an
excellent quality, for a modern artist with the best instruments could not possibly make better ones. The knives of
silex, which I found last year in such great quantities, are
as yet but rarely met with in this excavation. As stone
implements do not occur elsewhere before reaching a depth
of 4 meters (13 feet), it is probable that the numbers of
stone implements met with here, as early as at a depth of
2 meters (6½ feet) on the site of the temple, belong to the
débris which was dug up when the large reservoir was constructed, for it appears to extend pretty far down, and its
foundations may perhaps reach down to the Tower.

As, even in the temple itself, I find exclusively the
round terra-cottas in the form of cones and *without* decorations, while, on the other hand, below the foundations of
the temple I meet with great quantities of them in the form
of volcanoes and tops, with the most various Aryan religious
symbols, I am now of the opinion *that all those bearing
such Aryan symbols must belong to the tribes which preceded the Greek colony on this site.*

---

* As elsewhere, the wedges here spoken of are what the Author
afterwards decided to be axes, and especially battle-axes.—[ED.]

Of moulds of mica-schist I have only found two, one of which was used on all the six sides for casting weapons and instruments, the other for casting headless nails, and has two round holes, not perforated, for what purpose I do not know.*

While speaking of implements, I must mention a very remarkable hammer of bone, found at a depth of 3 meters (10 feet), which is covered with little engraved stars.

We again met with several marble idols, with the engraved owl's face of the Ilian Athena and her girdle with dots; also a very pretty marble idol without the owl's head, but with two small arms extended horizontally. The only terra-cottas with owls' heads that have been met with, since my last report, are two cups (vase-covers).

I find very many copper coins of Ilium and Alexandria Troas, and Roman ones from the time of Augustus to Constantine the Great, especially the latter, directly below the surface, and at most down to a meter ($3\frac{1}{4}$ feet) deep. Iron I do not find at all, not even in the temple, but a number of copper nails, which, however, I begin to think could not have been used for driving into wood; for this purpose they seem to be far too long and thin. The usual length of the nails occurring below $6\frac{1}{2}$ feet is from about 4 to above 6 inches, with a thickness of $\frac{1}{5}$ of an inch, and I do not think that it would be possible to drive such a nail even into very soft wood. Besides this, most of the nails have no head at all, others two heads, and many have two pointed ends, one of which is bent round so as to form a head. Thick copper nails suitable for driving into wood are very rarely met with; I have only found two in two years. I am therefore induced to believe that all the nails which I find in the strata of the nations preceding the Greeks have been used only as dress or hair pins. This

---

* An engraving of a similar mould, found on the Tower, is given in Chapter XVIII., No. 175, p. 261.

belief is confirmed by a copper nail, about 5 inches long,
with a head of the usual form, and the fragment of a similar
nail, which were found only 3 inches below the surface, in
a small groove, which my men had made round their reed-
hut to allow the rain-water to run off. On the head of the
nail there is a small gold ball, and then there follows downwards on the nail a row of eighteen similar little gold balls.
At the end of this row there is a second row of nine gold
balls of like size. The rows of the little balls are in the
form of necklaces, and cover a third part of the nail. The
fragment of the other nail is still more remarkable, for it
shows a string of little balls which form a perfect bow;
they are made of the alloy which in antiquity was called
electrum (ἤλεκτρον), consisting of three parts of gold and
one part of silver; below the bow, in a horizontal direction,
there is a row of little balls, which are probably intended
to represent the string. The little balls are firmly soldered
to both of the nails. In addition to this I must also mention that the silver nails so frequently met with are generally of the same form and size as the copper ones, and can
certainly never have been used for driving into wood.

On the west side of the Great Tower, which I laid bare
last year, I am likewise making an excavation 47 feet long
and 48 feet broad, so as to bring to light more of this side,
and to see how the walls of Ilium are connected with it. It
is worth a journey round the world to see this Tower, whose
site was at all events so high, that it not only commanded
a view of the Plain, but also of the plateau lying to the
south of it, whereas its summit now lies a great many feet
below the level of the plateau. According to this it seems
that the accumulation of *débris* on the site of the city is as
large as it is in the Pergamus.*

---

* It is perhaps unnecessary to remind the reader again how the
Author afterwards gave up the idea of this distinction between the city
and its Pergamus.—[ED.]

In the western excavation, already mentioned, I found the ruins of a very large house of the Greek period. It extended to the depth of 6½ feet, and must have belonged to a rich man, for the floors of the rooms are made of large red slabs splendidly polished. In it I found two small and very pretty female heads of terra-cotta, as well as two extremely remarkable pieces of hard brittle black stone, like glass, in the form of mushrooms, but with a tube running through the centre. The heads of the two pieces have decorations similar to those on the round terra-cottas in the form of humming-tops and volcanoes, and I therefore believe that both pieces belong to the pre-Hellenic period.

Below the foundations of the Greek house I found, at the depth of 3 and 4 meters (9¾ to 13 feet), many of the whorls with the usual decorations of four, five, or six double or treble rising suns; or four flaming altars; or four *Rosæ mysticæ ;* or four or five ⊓ in the circle around the central sun. I likewise found, at a depth of 10 feet, one of these articles, upon which there is a very rude and inartistic engraving of the Ilian Athena, with the owl's head and outstretched arms. By the side of this representation there are two crosses, and at the four ends of each are the marks of the nails with which our forefathers fastened the two pieces of wood which were laid crosswise for igniting the holy fire. In the same circle with the image of the goddess there are two symbols of light-

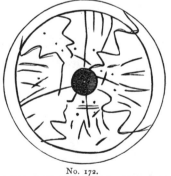

No. 172.
A Whorl with rude Symbols of the Owl's Face, Suastika, and lightning (3 M.).

ning. A faithful drawing of this terra-cotta is given in the cut.

Of the earthenware found in this excavation there is one piece especially deserving of attention. This is a vessel in the form of a helmet, with a round hole at the bottom ; it may have served as a kind of funnel.

As has been already said, the splendid block of tri- glyphs representing Phœbus Apollo with the four horses of the Sun, which I discovered last July, must, as the triglyph on the left side proves, have stood over the entrance of the temple, probably on its propylæa, and must have had another block of triglyphs of the same size on its right side. It would be of the greatest interest to archæology if I should find the second block of triglyphs, which, as happened with the other block, has probably been thrown from the summit of the hill down the steep declivity. I have also previously expressed the opinion, that the block of triglyphs which I saved had been thrown down by fanatical Turks because it represented living creatures, which is strictly prohibited in the Koran. How- ever, the locality has not been inhabited at all since the ninth century, and the labourers of the distant Turkish villages cannot possibly have given themselves the trouble of rolling down from the hill such tremendous weights from mere religious zeal. Besides this, the good state in which the sculpture has been preserved proves that it cannot possibly have stood upon the top of the hill up to the time of the Turkish invasion, and this leads me to suppose that it was thrown down by the early Christians more than a thousand years before, very likely even in the fourth century A.D. ; for it is well known, that all sculptures of heathen gods which were difficult to destroy they simply hurled from the top of the hills upon which they stood. That this is the only true explanation is also confirmed by the covering of earth, 3¼ feet thick, which enveloped the sculpture on the declivity of the hill. According to the average accumulation of the soil in this locality, the forma- tion of such a covering would be impossible in the course of three or four centuries : it would have required more than a thousand years.

It is now quite certain that the Doric temple, which at one time stood on the north side, and in the depths of which I have so long been working, was the sanctuary of Apollo; and that the block of Doric triglyphs so frequently mentioned belonged to this temple of Apollo, and to none other; since Ilium's great temple, which I am now investigating, could only have been dedicated to the tutelary goddess of Ilium, Athena, for in the great inscription quoted in my last report it is simply called " τὸ ἱερόν."

In order to try to find the second block of triglyphs, I have since yesterday set 25 men to work upwards from the foot of the hill at the point where the Phœbus Apollo was found, over a breadth of 59 feet, to remove the *débris* which unfortunately I had thrown down the declivity last year, and which forms a covering of 23 feet in thickness; and then to dig away the whole steep side of the hill to a depth of 4½ feet from the bottom upwards.

As soon as I have workmen to spare, I shall also employ thirty to make a deep cutting into the theatre, the stage of which, as already said, is 197 feet broad; this cutting I intend to make 33 feet broad and 148 feet long; for, in a small opening which I made there last year, I found a number of fragments of broken statues, and it is quite possible that some, which might be of the greatest interest to archæology, escaped the zeal of the early Christians.

The many thousands of stones which I bring out of the depths of Ilium have induced the inhabitants of the surrounding villages to erect buildings which might be called grand for the inhabitants of this wilderness. Among others, they are at present building with my Ilian stones a mosque and a minaret in the wretched Turkish village of Chiplak, and a church-tower in the Christian village of Yenishehr. A number of two-wheeled carts, drawn by oxen, are always standing by the side of my excavations, ready to receive the stones which can be of any use as soon as they have been brought to the surface; but the religious zeal of these good people is not great enough for them to offer to help me in the terrible work of breaking the large, splendidly hewn blocks so as to make them more convenient to remove.

Although spring is only just commencing, there is already a great deal of malignant fever in consequence of the mild winter, and the poor people of the neighbourhood are already daily beginning to make large claims upon my stock of quinine.

I found myself obliged to raise the men's wages to 10 piasters or 2 francs, eight days ago.

No. 173.   Splendid Trojan Vase of Terra-cotta, representing the tutelary Goddess of Ilium,
θεὰ γλαυκῶπις Ἀθήνη.   The cover forms the helmet.   (8 m.)

PLATE IX.

Altar and Reservoir.

UPPER PART OF THE BUILDINGS DISCOVERED IN THE DEPTHS OF THE TEMPLE OF ATHENA.

Page 259.

CHAPTER XVIII.

Weather and progress of the work — The lion-headed handle of a sceptre — Lions formerly in the Troad — Various objects found — Pottery — Implements of stone and copper — Whorls — Balls curiously decorated — Fragments of musical instruments — Remains of house-walls — The storks of the Troad.

Pergamus of Troy, March 22nd, 1873.

DURING this last week we have again had constant splendid weather, and, with 150 men on an average, I have got through a good piece of work. On the north side of the excavation on the site of the Temple of Athena, I have already reached a depth of 26 feet, and have laid bare the Tower in several places. The space to be dug down is now divided into four terraces, and I am having the lowest terrace, which forms the surface of the Tower, worked with especially great energy. As the paths are getting both steeper and longer, the men with the wheel-barrows have now to stop and rest half-way, so the work proceeds more slowly every day. Still I hope that I shall bring to light the whole breadth of the Tower in the eastern direction in three weeks, but the western side in a week and a half. The only part of the interior of the Temple of Athena which I have left standing is the reservoir built of large white stones without cement, which, owing to my excavations, will in a few days be 26 feet above the Tower, and will have a very pretty appearance. It is only by excavating the west side of that part of the Great Tower which I uncovered last year, that I shall be able to judge in what direction the walls run out from it, and what my next work will be. The most remarkable of the objects

found this week is certainly a large knob belonging to
a stick, of the purest and finest crystal, and in the form

No. 174.

A Lion-Headed Sceptre-handle of
the finest crystal: found on the
Tower (8 M.).

of a very beautifully wrought lion's
head; it was discovered upon the
Tower at a depth of 26 feet. It
must have been the ornament of a
Trojan's staff or sceptre (σκῆπτρον),
for I found it among those brilliant
red and black fragments of pot-
tery, which only occur at a depth of from 36 to 46
feet, except upon the Tower. Not only this lion's head,
but the illustrations drawn from the lion, which occur
repeatedly in the Iliad, make it seem extremely probable
that in remote antiquity lions existed in this neighbourhood. Homer could not possibly have described so excellently the characteristics of this animal, had he not
had frequent opportunity of watching them, and his geographical knowledge of southern countries is too slight for
us to suppose that he had visited them, and had there
become intimately acquainted with the characteristics of
the lion. Not far from the lion's head I found a splendidly
cut hexagon of the purest crystal, as well as a small
pyramid, 1½ inch long and broad, and 1⅔ inch high, made
of black, white and blue streaked marble, such as is not
found in this district; the hole which runs through the
centre of the pyramid is filled with lead.

I also found upon the Tower a very primitive marble
idol, 7½ inches in length, 3⅓ inches broad, and 1⅕ inch
thick; also a very fine copper lance; further, a large
mould of mica-schist for casting twelve different weapons
and instruments, as well as a beautiful sling-bullet made of
loadstone. In the higher strata, and in fact at a depth of
4 meters (13 feet), the most curious article certainly is an idol
of the Trojan tutelary goddess made of slate, such as has
never hitherto been found. It shows the owl's face, two
breasts and a navel, and long hair at the back of the head;

two horizontal lines on the neck, which are joined by small
cross lines, seem to denote armour.   Marble idols without
the owl's face, but otherwise of exactly the same form as
those with the owl's face, are met with in numbers in all
the strata between 3 and 8 meters deep (10 to 26 feet).   I
likewise found long, thin copper nails with round heads at
the thick end, or without heads, but with the end bent round,
which I now perceive can only be breast or hair pins, and

No. 175.   A Mould of Mica-schist, for casting various metal Instruments (Tower, 8 M.).

not actual nails for driving into wood.   I find them also
in quantities in the strata of this excavation between 4
and 7 meters deep (13 to 23 feet), and I must therefore
decidedly pronounce that the people to whom these strata
of ruins belong were acquainted with copper.

A strange instrument of copper, almost in the shape of a

No. 176.   A curious Instrument of Copper (3 M.).

No. 177.   A perforated and grooved piece
of Mica-schist, probably for supporting a
Spit.   Found on the Tower (8 M.).

horse's bit, but with two pointed hooks, was found at a depth of 10 feet. Besides this, we met with two somewhat crooked copper knives, at from 13 to 16½ feet down, as well as a small but very fine knife, in the form of a saw, made of a shell. Stone instruments are continually met with here in great numbers in all of the strata between 2 and 8 meters deep (6½ to 26 feet), whereas in my excavations of 1871 and 1872 I only found them below a depth of 13 feet. Two beautiful stone lances, one of diorite, the other of hard green stone, were found, the one at 20 feet down, the other at 11½ feet. During this week, I also found very many knives of silex in the form of saws or of sharp blades, with one or two edges; further, a very prettily cut piece of mica-schist with a perforated hole and a groove on the upper side, which may have been fastened to a fireplace and have served for turning a spit.

No 178. A large Terra-cotta Vase, with two large Handles and two small Handles or Rings (5 M.).

I have observed that the terra-cottas here generally

occur in great numbers only in and below those strata of
débris which are mixed with enormous quantities of small
shells, and which usually commence at a depth of 13 feet,
but sometimes not till 20 feet.   However, every now and
then we come upon beautiful terra-cottas above these
shell strata; and thus, for instance, in the great cutting,
directly in front of my door, we found, at a depth of
10 feet, several large and splendid vessels, among which
was an extremely elegant black vase, in the shape of a soup-
tureen, and at a depth of 11½ feet two mixing-bowls, the
smaller one of which has two, the larger one four, handles;
the larger mixing-bowl is two feet high, and its orifice is
as much in diameter.   (See Cut, No. 41, p. 74.)   At a
depth of 16½ feet I found an extremely curious large vase,
which has two large handles at the top and two small ones
at the sides.   Various other vases of extremely curious forms
were discovered at a depth of from 13 to 26 feet; of them
I will only mention one large brilliant black vase with two
female breasts and two handles, by the side of which are
the stumps of the upraised arms which ornamented this
vessel.   The upper part of it, which, as is proved by the
arms and breasts, was ornamented with the owl's head of
the Ilian Athena, is unfortunately wanting.   It is strange
that this vase has no navel.

Of the large and brilliant red goblets in the form
of huge champagne-glasses, with two immense handles,
we met with many in a more or less broken condition
at a depth of from 6 to 8 meters (20 to 26 feet); among
them is an enormous goblet 15¾ inches long, of which
I have been able to collect all the fragments and shall
therefore be able to restore it.   (See No. 112, p. 158.)

I found, at a depth of from 23 to 26 feet, quantities of
earthen plates, some of which are of a brilliant red colour,
but most of them are uncoloured.   At a depth of 20 feet
I found a fragment of pottery with a cross, at the four
ends of which are dots, which can only indicate the

nails by means of which it was fastened. Small terra-cotta
whorls, with Aryan religious symbols, were again found in
great numbers ; several of them have decorations not
hitherto met with. Of terra-cotta balls we have found
three during these last days, two of them are very remarkable. One hemisphere of the first has nineteen figures
like the Greek letter Rho (P) in a circle round it, and ten
of the same figures in a line through the middle point,

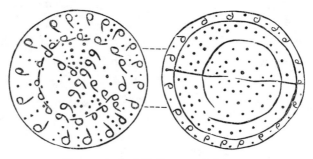

No. 179. A remarkable Terra-cotta Ball (6 M.).

also a number of little stars ; the other hemisphere is
entirely filled with little stars. The second ball has a
half moon on the one hemisphere and large stars on
the other.

Among the remarkable objects found during the week,

No. 180. A finely engraved Ivory Tube,
probably part of a Flute. Found on
the Tower (8 M.).

I must also mention a splendidly
ornamented piece of ivory, from a
depth of 8 meters (26 feet), which
is almost the shape of a flute,
and may have been used as
such ; further, a flat bone, which
has one hole at the one end and three at the other,
and seems certainly to have belonged to a musical instrument.

I sometimes find here house-walls built of stones joined
with mere earth, which must certainly have been erected
long before the Greek settlement, but which rise to
within a meter (3¼ feet) of the surface; in fact in the

great cutting in front of my house, I have pierced through two such walls 6½ feet thick, which here formed the corner of a house, and which reach up to within a foot of the surface; they appear to extend pretty far down, and in my next letter I shall be able to give more details about them.

Although the Pergamus, whose depths I have been ransacking, borders directly upon the marshes formed by the Simoïs, in which there are always hundreds of storks, yet none of them ever settle down here. Upon one of my wooden houses and upon the stone one I had two comfortable nests made for them, but although there are sometimes twelve storks' nests upon one roof in some of the surrounding Turkish villages, yet none will settle on mine; it is probably too cold and stormy for the little storks on "Ἴλιος ἠνεμόεσσα."

No. 181. Knob for a Stick, of fine marble (3 M.).

No. 182. Bone handle of a Trojan's Staff or Sceptre, σκῆπτρον (7 M.).*

---

* A handle such as this, or as that shown at p. 260 (No. 174), seems well suited for the long *leaning-staff* (σκῆπτρον, from σκήπτομαι, "to lean upon") which, in Homer, is the symbol of royal authority, and with which Ulysses beat Thersites. (*Iliad*, II. 46, 265, *et passim*.)—[ED.]

CHAPTER XIX.

Splendid vases found on the Tower — Other articles — Human skull, bones, and ashes, found in an urn — New types of whorls — Greek votive discs of diorite — Moulds of mica-schist — The smaller quantity of copper than of stone implements explained — Discussion of the objection, that stone implements are not mentioned by Homer — Reply to Mr. Calvert's article — Flint knives found in the Acropolis of Athens— A narrow escape from fire.

Pergamus of Troy, March 29th, 1873.

SINCE my report of the 22nd of this month I have unfortunately made little or no progress, for most of the villagers are trimming their vineyards during this week ; and besides this, we have been tormented by a horrible icy-cold high north wind, which yesterday and to-day rendered it impossible to carry on the works.

But in spite of this, during the week we have found at a depth of 8 meters (26 feet), and upon the Tower, a great number of splendid vases of the most remarkable form ; they are indeed all in a more or less broken condition, but they can easily be mended, as I have all the pieces. Those especially deserving of being mentioned are a brilliant black vase with two large female breasts, a large navel, and with two mighty upraised arms (No. 183) ; further, a vase 33¾ inches high, in a good state of preservation ; a large mixing bowl (κρατήρ) with two handles, and a smaller vase, round below, with four handles of two different forms. Among the smaller vessels there are, especially deserving of attention, a brilliant black cup cover, with a handle in the form of a coronet, and a brilliant red cover, with a very curious human face, in which the features of the owl cannot be mistaken. (Nos. 184, 185, p. 268.) Of the other articles,

I can only mention a little plate of gold in the form of an arrow-head, with a small hole at the lower end (No. 186); an ivory tube with very curious decorations (No. 187); and a well-preserved skull with neat little teeth, which I discovered, together with a few bones and a quantity of human ashes, in a vase (unfortunately broken) 27½ inches high and broad, at a depth of 26 feet, upon the Tower. This is the first time that I have found such well-preserved

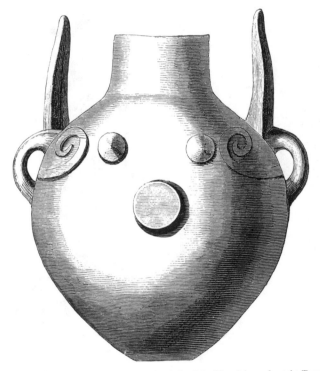

No. 183.   A brilliant Black Vase, with the Symbols of the Ilian Athena, from the Tower (8 M.).

human bones and even a skull in an urn. Funereal urns, indeed, we dig out daily, but the bodies are always completely burnt to ashes; and, with the exception of the skeleton (already described) of an embryo found in a vase at a depth of 51 feet upon the primary rock, I have hitherto never found an entire bone in a funereal urn. The vase in which I found the skull is made of that excellent Trojan terra-cotta which I find only at a depth of from 36 to 46 and 52½ feet, except upon the Tower; the skull must have belonged to a Trojan woman, for it is too delicate to have been the skull of a man. In the same urn I also found a copper hair or dress pin. Upon the Tower we also met with two marble idols without owls' faces, one of which is 6 inches long, the other 6⅓ inches. We likewise discovered quantities of terra-cotta whorls with symbolical decora-

No. 184. Vase-cover with Handle in shape of a Coronet (8 M.).

No. 185. Vase-cover with a Human Face: found on the Tower (8 M.).

No. 186. Flat piece of Gold, in the Form of an Arrow-head: from the Tower (8 M.).

No. 187. Prettily decorated Tube of Ivory. From the Tower (8 M.).

tions, twelve of which are of types not previously found. One is the form of a shirt stud,* 1⅓ inch high and 1⅕ inch broad, with the never-failing perforated hole and an engraved flower, the four petals of which form a cross round the central point; in three of the petals there

---

* See a similar example in Chapter XX., p. 286.

are very large dots, which may denote suns or moons;
upon another, in the form of a top, there are six trees in
the circle, the top and the foot of which are alternately
directed to the central sun.*

I have already repeatedly mentioned the terra-cotta
discs, between 1 and 2 inches in diameter, thick in the
middle and cut smooth on one side, in the shape of a Greek
lamp; they always have at one side two very small perforated holes, and frequently a round or oval potter's stamp,
in which one can recognise either an altar and a bee with
outspread wings, or a swan, an ox, a horse, a man, or something of the kind.   I have also said that these discs must
have belonged to the Greek colony, for I generally find them
quite close to the surface as far down as 3¼ feet and rarely
below 6½ feet, and besides this the fine and almost micro-
scopical figures in the stamp show a Greek style of art.†
The small holes at the sides leave no doubt that the articles
have been used as votive offerings to be hung up in the
temples or beside the idols.   These discs, which have
hitherto only occurred in terra-cotta, I have this week
found at a depth of 1 meter (3¼ feet), made of diorite with
two holes on one side, which, however, are not perforated;
owing to the hardness of the substance it was no doubt
found difficult to make the two perforations.

During the last few days we have again found upon
the Tower, at a depth of 8 meters (26 feet), a mould of
mica-schist, 11 inches long, upon five sides of which there
are forms for casting twelve lances, knives, and extremely
curious implements, the use of which is a puzzle to me.

The many stone moulds for casting weapons, knives,
and implements, which are met with here, sufficiently prove
that Troy possessed a number of copper weapons, knives,
and instruments.   It is, however, quite natural that I should
find comparatively few of them, for the copper implements

---

* Plate XXXIV., No. 404.   † See p. 65.

could of course easily be melted down and re-cast, and it must not even be supposed that I shall find any except those which were lost in the tumult of battle, or were preserved amidst the destruction of the city.   Therefore the fact that I find immensely larger numbers of silex knives than of copper knives, and by far more axes and hammers of stone than of copper, by no means proves that at the time of the Trojan war there were more stone than copper instruments.   Stone lances are, moreover, very rarely met with; this year I found only two of which I know positively that they are lances; the one was discovered at a depth of $11\frac{1}{2}$ feet, the other at 20 feet deep.

Mr. Frank Calvert of the Dardanelles, who wishes to convince me by the hippopotamus which I found at a depth of 23 feet, that the *débris* at this depth belongs to a period when hippopotami inhabited the rivers of the Troad, has expressed the opinion, in his article in the *Levant Herald* of the 25th of January, 1873, that Homer would necessarily have mentioned stone knives and instruments if they had existed in Troy, and that, as he speaks of none, there could have been none; consequently, that none of the ruined strata which I have cut through, containing stone implements, can belong to the Homeric Troy, and that the stratum directly following the Greek ruins, which extend as far down as $6\frac{1}{2}$ feet, must be more than 1000 years older than the Trojan war.

If Mr. Calvert had taken the trouble to look into Homer, he would have found that the word 'hammer' ($\dot{\rho}\alpha\iota\sigma\tau\dot{\eta}\rho$) occurs only once (*Iliad*, XVIII. 477), and that is in the hand of Hephæstus. It is, indeed, not said of what material the hammer was made; the fire-god, however, would probably have had none other than a copper hammer. Mr. Calvert also does not appear to have ever seen a silex knife, for otherwise he would know that they are almost always only from $1\frac{1}{2}$ to $2\frac{1}{2}$, and rarely 3, inches long; and moreover, with but few exceptions, they are made in the form of saws. I have here only once met with a saw of this kind 5 inches in length.

In Homer there is *not one* opportunity where such small saw-knives could have been mentioned, nor is it as yet altogether clear to me what they can have been used for.* Homer's heroes carry their copper knives beside their swords, and generally use them for killing the sacrificial animal, for which purpose, of course, flint knives from 1½ to 3 inches long would not have been appropriate; but those long copper knives, the size of which is accurately indicated by the stone moulds in which they were cast, would have been very suitable. In the Iliad (XVIII. 597), we see Hephæstus making youths with golden cutlasses upon the shield of Achilles.

Mr. Calvert believes that the fact of Homer's not mentioning either the small flint saws or stone knives is a proof against the identity of Hissarlik with the site of Troy. I, however, should find it surprising, and so assuredly would all scholars and admirers of Homer, if the Homeric heroes had appeared armed with silex saws from 1½ to 3 inches in length; for a hero, especially in an epic poem, can only carry and achieve something heroic. If the Homeric hero requires a stone weapon, he does not feel in his pocket for a silex saw from 1½ to 3 inches long, but he takes the first huge stone he meets with, such as two of the strongest men from among the people could not have raised from the earth on to a cart by means of levers; but the hero carries it in his hand with the same ease with which a shepherd would carry the fleece of a ram, and flings the rock with infinite force against the gate of the enemy, splinters the panels to shivers, and shatters the double hinges and the bars; the gate flies open, and the stone falls with a mighty crash into the hostile camp.†

---

* May they have been for flaying the sacrificed animals, a sharp flint being better for this purpose than a copper knife, and perhaps also being preferred to metal as less contaminated by human labour?—[Ed.]

† *Iliad*, XII. 445-462.

Upon another occasion, another hero uses a stone weapon. He, too, does not look for a small silex saw, but takes an immense block of stone, which two men from among the people would have been unable to lift, and hurls it against his opponent.* Mr. Calvert's excavations in the Pergamus were confined to two small cuttings which still exist, and he is wrong in saying that I have continued his excavations. As my plans of the Pergamus prove, my excavations of 1870, 1871, and up to the middle of June, 1872, were made exclusively on the Turkish portion of the Pergamus; and it was only in June that I began to excavate the site of the temple of Apollo upon Mr. Calvert's land, because a depression in the ground, 111½ feet long and 75½ feet broad, had betrayed the site to me. My friend's two small cuttings by no means gave any idea of the existence of such a temple.

I have never, as Mr. Calvert says, found the native rock at a depth of 67 feet. I found it at a depth of 16 meters (or 52¾ feet) upon my large platform, and at a depth of 14 meters (or 46⅕ feet) in my great cutting, in the Roman well, and upon the south side of the Tower. In Mr. Calvert's field, however, I found the primary soil only in the hill covered by the very ancient buttress, which has been repeatedly described.

Examining Mr. Calvert's article further, I assure my readers that, with the exception of the wall which I have already described as consisting of Corinthian pillars taken from the temple of Athena, I have never come upon any Byzantine ruins here; † that all the Byzantine coins I found were but a few inches below the surface; and that the ruins and the *débris* of the Greek colony, as anyone may convince himself from the earthen walls of my excavations, rarely extend below 2 meters (6½ feet). Mr. Calvert's statement, that I also find stone implements, perforated

---

* *Iliad*, V. 302-310.

† Nor are even these now considered to be Byzantine ; see Chapter XXII., p. 320, and Introduction, p. 30.—[ED.]

cylinders, grinding-mills, and masses of shells, immediately below these ruins, is incorrect; for in not one of my excavations have I hitherto found these things at less than 4 meters (13 feet) deep, and if I now find them immediately below the foundations of the Temple of Athena, I explain this by assuming that the *débris* which was dug out of the great excavation for the reservoir of the temple was used for increasing the elevation of the site of the sanctuary. Mr. Calvert is also wrong in his statement that the larger bones were all broken to get at the marrow; on the contrary, we very rarely meet with broken bones. He is again incorrect in stating that I find small articles of bronze, as well as ornaments in gold and silver filigree work.   I have never as yet found bronze here, but in all cases copper; and never have I found ornaments of gold or silver filigree work.   The ornaments represented in the drawings are of pure gold, or electrum, or silver, or copper.   His statement is also erroneous, that I occasionally find engraved representations of fish-bones upon vessels.   It is true that I often find vessels round which rows of cuneiform decorations are engraved; but these are never connected with one another, and therefore have no resemblance at all to fish-bones.   Further, Mr. Calvert is mistaken in his assertion that in the depths of this hill there are house-walls composed of unhewn stones laid roughly one on the top of the other. The architect is not yet born, who could construct house-walls of such stones without some kind of cement.   The walls of clay do not, as Mr. Calvert's statement would lead one to believe, consist of *one* mass of clay, but of sun-dried bricks; and I assure my readers that I have never yet, as Mr. Calvert erroneously maintains, found the impressions of long rushes, which indicate the use of thatch-work.   My learned friend is also completely wrong in his statement that the floors of some of the houses have been glazed, and that the regularity of the levellings and the flatness of these floors prove that the glaze is not the result of accident; further, that one of these glazed floors has a length of 20 feet. I would give a great deal if this were true, for such a Trojan marvel would attract thousands desirous of information. Unfortunately, however, such glazed floors exist only in Mr. Calvert's own imagination. My friend is as completely mistaken in his reports about the Great Tower, which he describes as consisting of two walls, which meet at a sharp angle and diverge to a distance of 40 feet, the space between them being as yet unexplored. It is only the southern wall of this building that rises at an angle of 75 degrees: on the north side, as it was sufficiently supported by the mound $65\frac{1}{2}$ feet broad which rested against it, it had above it only a small perpendicular wall, $3\frac{1}{4}$ feet high and broad; whereas the southern wall, which inclines at an angle of 15 degrees, is $6\frac{1}{2}$ feet thick. The whole of the inner space between the two walls consists of stones laid loosely upon one another. The perpendicular height of the Tower above the primary rock is not 15 feet, as Mr. Calvert says, but exactly 20 feet. The terra-cotta discs with two small holes, which, according to Mr. Calvert, I find here at all depths, I have in reality always found only close to the surface, as far down as $3\frac{1}{4}$ feet, and rarely as far down as $6\frac{1}{2}$ feet. I further assure my readers that I know nothing about the large perforated cylinders, which Mr. Calvert says I find in great quantities, and frequently with half their diameter entirely in the clay of the walls. The largest of the terra-cotta cylinders which I have discovered here are only 4 inches long, and never have I seen one of these cylinders in a house-wall.

In conclusion, I must positively deny Mr. Calvert's assertion that stone implements, although met with in the same stratum with articles made of different metals and with splendid earthenware, argue a primeval and prehistoric age. Small knives and saws of silex are, for

instance, found in numbers in the Acropolis of Athens,
and they appear to have been used up to a very late
period. A rude pre-historic people could by no means
have made the beautiful terra-cottas which are found here
immediately below the ruins of the Greek colony, and still
less could they have manufactured the splendid pottery
which shows such a high degree of artistic taste, and which
I meet with here at a great depth.

The life in this wilderness is not without danger, and
last night, for instance, my wife and I and the foreman
Photidas had the narrowest escape of being burnt alive.
In the bedroom on the north side of the wooden house
which we are inhabiting, we had had a small fireplace
made, and, owing to the terrible cold which has again set in
during the last six days, we have lighted a fire in it daily.
But the stones of the fireplace rest merely upon the boards
of the floor, and, whether it was owing to a crevice in the
cement joining the stones, or by some other means, the
floor took fire, and when I accidentally awoke this morning
at 3 o'clock, it was burning over a space of two yards long
by a yard broad. The room was filled with dense smoke,
and the north wall was just beginning to catch fire; a few
seconds would have sufficed to burn a hole into it, and
the whole house would then have been in flames in less
than a minute, for a fearful north wind was blowing from
that side. In my fright I did not lose my presence of
mind. I poured the contents of a bath upon the burning
north wall, and thus in a moment stopped the fire in that
direction. Our cries awoke Photidas, who was asleep in the
adjoining room, and he called the other foremen from the
stone house to our assistance. In the greatest haste they
fetched hammers, iron levers and pickaxes; the floor was
broken up, torn to pieces, and quantities of damp earth
thrown upon it, for we had no water. But, as the lower beams
were burning in many places, a quarter of an hour elapsed
before we got the fire under and all danger was at an end.

CHAPTER XX.

Discovery of a large house upon the Tower — Marks of a great conflagration — Primitive Altar : its very remarkable position — Ruins of the Temple of Athena — A small cellar — Skeletons of warriors with copper helmets and a lance — Structure of the helmet-crests — Terra-cottas — A crucible with copper still in it — Other objects — Extreme fineness of the engravings on the whorls — Pottery — Stone implements — Copper pins and other objects.

Pergamus of Troy, April 5th, 1873.

AMIDST cold but glorious spring weather most favourable for the workmen, who now number 150 on the average, I have this week continued the excavations with the greatest energy and with good results.

The most interesting object that I have discovered here in these three years is certainly a house which I brought to light this week, and of which eight rooms have already been laid open; it stands upon the Great Tower, at a depth of 7 and 8 meters (23 to 26 feet), directly below the Greek Temple of Athena. Its walls consist of small stones cemented with earth, and they appear to belong to different epochs; for, while some of them rest directly upon the stones of the Tower, others were not built till the Tower was covered with 8 inches, and in several cases even with $3\frac{1}{4}$ feet, of *débris*. These walls also show differences in thickness; one of them is $4\frac{1}{4}$ feet, others are only $25\frac{1}{2}$ inches, and others again not more than $19\frac{2}{3}$ inches thick. Several of these walls are 10 feet high, and on some of them may be seen large remnants of the coatings of clay, painted yellow or white. Only in one large room, the dimensions of which, however, cannot be exactly ascertained, have I as yet found an actual floor of unhewn slabs of limestone, the smooth sides of which are turned outside. Black marks, the result of fire, upon the lower portion of the walls of the other rooms which have as yet been excavated, leave no doubt that their floors were of wood, and were destroyed by fire. In one room there is a wall in the form of a semicircle, which has been burnt as black as coal. All the rooms as yet laid open, and not resting directly upon the Tower, have been excavated down to the same level; and I find, without exception, that the *débris* below them consists of red or yellow ashes and burnt ruins. Above these, even in the rooms themselves, I found nothing but either red or yellow wood-ashes, mixed with bricks that had been dried in the sun and subsequently burnt by the conflagration, or black *débris*, the remains of furniture, mixed with masses of small shells: in proof of this there are the many remains which are still hanging on the walls. In several rooms I found red jars (πίθοι) from 7 to 8 feet high, some of which I leave *in situ*. Above the house, and as far as the foundations of the temple, I found nothing but red and yellow wood-ashes. (See Plate X., opposite p. 287.)

To the east side of the house is a sacrificial Altar of a very primitive description, which is turned to the north-west by west, and consists of a slab of slate granite about $5\frac{1}{4}$ feet long, and $5\frac{1}{2}$ feet broad. The upper part of the stone is cut into the form of a crescent, probably for killing upon it the animal which was intended for sacrifice. About 4 feet below the sacrificial altar I found a channel made of slabs of green slate, which probably served to carry off the blood. Strangely enough this Altar does not stand on the Tower itself, but $3\frac{1}{4}$ feet above it, upon bricks or lumps of earth which had been dried in the sun, and which have been actually burnt by the conflagration, but nevertheless have no stability. The altar was surrounded by an enormous quantity of

the remains of bricks of this description, as well as by
red and yellow wood-ashes, to a height of 10 feet. Of
course I leave the altar *in situ,* so that visitors to the Troad
may convince themselves by the nature of its pedestal and
of the *débris* of the earthen wall, beside which it stands,
of the correctness of all these statements, which might
otherwise appear too incredible. The remarkable sub-

No. 188.   Great Altar for Sacrifices, found in the depths of the Temple of Athena ($\frac{1}{23}$ of the real size).

structure of this sacrificial altar, the curious *débris* in
which it was buried, the preservation of the great house,
which has evidently been burnt, and the walls of which
were built at different epochs, and lastly, the fact that
its spaces were filled with heterogeneous *débris* and with
colossal jars—all this is a puzzle to me. I confine myself,
therefore, to stating the facts merely, and refrain from
expressing any kind of conjecture.

Above the house, in the south-western wall of this excavation, are the ruins of the southern wall of the Temple of
Athena.   They are 5¼ feet high, and consist of large white

blocks of limestone. Their great breadth gives them an imposing appearance, and this is further increased by the great reservoir of the temple, the walls of which are directly to the east of the altar, and 4¼ feet high. Above the very ancient house, and below the southern wall of the temple, may be seen the ruins of a small round cellar, 3½ feet in diameter and about 2½ feet high, which stands below the foundations, and must, therefore, be older than the temple. It is built of chalk and stones, but the inner side has been painted over with a kind of varnish or glaze, and has a glossy appearance. This small cellar was filled with fragments of Greek terra-cottas, among which, however, I found six small vases, almost uninjured.

This very ancient house, with its small rooms, as it stands, is very like a Pompeian house; it cannot, indeed, be at all compared with the houses of Pompeii in regard to architecture or decoration, but it surpasses them in peculiarity.

No. 189. Copper Lance of a Trojan Warrior, found beside his Skeleton (7 M.).

By the side of the house, as well as in its larger apartments, I have found great quantities of human bones, but as yet only *two entire skeletons*, which must be those of *warriors*, for they were found at a depth of 7 meters (23 feet), with *copper helmets upon their heads*. Beside one of the skeletons I found *a large lance*, a drawing of which I give. The one skull is uninjured, and I add a faithful drawing of it; the other is somewhat broken, but I hope soon to have the pieces joined with cement. Both of the skulls are large, but remarkably narrow. Unfortunately both helmets were broken; however, I hope to be able to put one of the two together when I return to Athens.

The upper portions of both helmets have, however, been well preserved; and these parts form the "φάλος," or

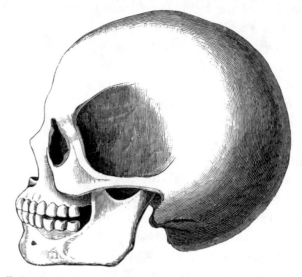

No. 190. Skull of a Trojan Warrior, belonging to one of the two Skeletons found in the House on the Tower (7 M.). It is long, but narrow.

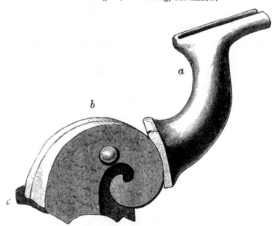

No. 191. (a) The upper and (b) lower pieces of a Trojan Helmet-crest (φάλος) placed together. (c.) A small piece of the Helmet remains adhering to the lower part of the Crest (7 M.). A pin, fastened to the front of the part (b), goes into the hollow base of (a), and supports it. (See the figures on p. 334.)

ridge, in which the "λόφος ἵππουρις," or horse-hair plume, so frequently mentioned in the Iliad, was fixed." *   In both

* Homer's *Iliad*, III. 362; IV. 459; VI. 9; XIII. 132; XVI. 216.

cases the φάλος consists of two pieces. The large copper ring found beside the helmet had been attached to it, in what manner I do not know. Two days later, when I found the second helmet, I perceived from the manner in which the lower portion was fixed to the helmet that the pieces must be put together as shown in the drawing. Through the lower portion of each helmet runs a copper nail, which has a round head and its other end simply bent round. As to the place into which the λόφος ἵππουρις was inserted and fixed there can be no doubt, for the opening at the top of the ridge can have served no other purpose. By the side of the second helmet also, I found the fragment of a copper ring similar to that found beside the first helmet.*

No. 192.   Great Copper Ring, found near the Helmet-crest (7 M.).

In some of the rooms I found no terra-cottas at all, but in others enormous quantities of splendid black, red, and brown vases, pots, and jars of all sizes, and of most

---

* Few coincidences have struck us more than the comparison of these helmet-crests with the frequent allusions in Homer, especially where " Hector of the dancing helmet-crest " (κορυθαίολος Ἕκτωρ), takes off the helmet that frightened his child (*Iliad*, VI. 469, foll.) :—

> Ταρβήσας χαλκόν τε ἰδὲ λόφον ἱππιοχαίτην
> Δεινὸν ἀπ' ἀκροτάτης κόρυθος νεύοντα νοήσας.

> " Scared by the brazen helm and horse-hair plume,
> That nodded, fearful, on the warrior's crest."

No such plumed helmets are found among the remains of " prehistoric " barbarous races. The skeletons, with the helmets and lances beside them, bear striking witness to a city taken by storm. In Homer, the Trojans under the command of " the crested Hector " are " valiant with lances " (μεμαότες ἐγχείῃσιν, *Iliad*, II. 816–818).—[ED.]

fanciful shapes; but unfortunately in hewing down the hard *débris* most of them were broken, and I shall not be able

No. 193.   An elegant bright-red Vase of Terra-cotta, decorated with branches and signs of lightning, with holes in the handles and lips, for cords to hang it up by.   Found on the Tower (8 M.).

No. 194.   Terra-cotta Vase.   Found on the Tower (8 M.).

to have them repaired till I return to Athens.   I wish to draw attention to the elegance of the red jars with necks bent back, two ears, and three breasts; as well as to the black or red vases ornamented with engraved branches of trees, with three feet and two small and two large upraised handles as arms; also to the terra-cotta goblets, which are occasionally the form of champagne-glasses, sometimes also in the shape of a soup-tureen with two handles.

The most interesting of the terra-cottas found this week, and the most important to arcnæology, are these:—the beautiful red vase-cover with the owl's face and helmet of the Ilian Athena, which was found in a large red urn at a depth of 8 meters (27 feet):—then two vases, likewise adorned with the owl's head of the tutelary goddess of Troy, but also with two breasts, a large navel, and two upraised arms. One of these vases was found upon the Tower, the other above it, at a depth of 4 meters (13 feet).

No. 195.   Profile of a Vase-cover, with the Owl's Face and Helmet of Athena, in brilliant red Terra-cotta. Found in an urn on the Tower (8 M.).

Among the other very remarkable terra-cottas found in one of

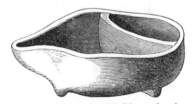

No. 196.   An Earthenware Crucible on four feet, *still containing some copper*. Found on the Tower (7 M.).

the rooms of the subterranean house, at a depth of 7 meters (23 feet), there is a crucible with four feet, in which some copper is still to be seen; also a small brilliant black funnel. I also found in the house, at the depth of 7 and 8 meters (23 to 26 feet), several idols of ordinary stone or of marble; one also of bone, upon which are seen the two arms of the goddess; it is only upon one of the marble idols, and upon one of those of stone, that I find the two eyes. This week we met with only one idol of ordinary stone with a rude engraving of the owl's face; it was discovered at a depth of 4 meters (13 feet). I must remark that the idols of common stone are always very roughly made.

Of the small terra-cotta whorls, both with and without symbolical engravings, we this week again met with 251 pieces; of these, however, only 31 had symbolical figures which I have not yet found. Several of the engraved decorations on these articles have been executed with a fineness which is truly astonishing, and more especially those which are engraved upon brilliantly black wheel-shaped pieces: they are so fine that I could only distinguish them through a magnifying glass.

At a depth of 6 and 8 meters (20 to 26 feet) we again met with very many ordinary plates, which had been turned

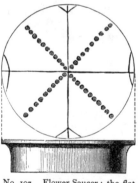

No. 197. Flower Saucer; the flat bottom ornamented. Found on the Tower (8 M.).

on a potter's wheel. At the same depth, and in the above-mentioned house, we found a curious vessel, exactly in the shape of a saucer to a flower-pot, ornamented with four triangles and two large crosses, one of which is formed by large dots, the other by lines. Several curious moulds were also found this week, one of which is of coarse terra-cotta for casting eight copper bars; the other moulds are made of mica-schist, and one was for casting an object in the form of a leaf with three long thorns on either side; the other mould shows three uniform furrows for casting oblong rings. This week we found only fragments of stone moulds for casting weapons and instruments. At a depth of from 10 to 26 feet we also discovered 27 small silex knives like saws, and six very pretty knife-blades made of black obsidian, which are sharp enough to serve as razors. We have found no copper knives this week, but, on the other hand, four copper dress or hair pins, from $2\frac{1}{3}$ to above 5 inches long; also thirteen needles for knitting or embroidering; likewise sixteen large bodkins made of stag-horn, and a number of pointed boars' tusks. Among the stone implements found during the week, there are two very pretty hammers of diorite and a very neat perforated prop of mica-schist with a small furrow at the top, for turning a spit, and other such things. (See No. 177, p. 261.)

In returning to the terra-cottas I must mention a square article, the upper part of which gradually becomes narrower and thinner: on the front side there are two small depres-sions in the form of eyes, and on one side it is perforated. I add a drawing of this curious article, the use of which is

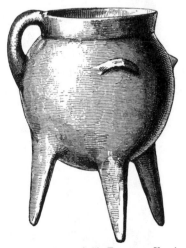

No. 198. A piece of Terra-cotta, with two holes slightly sunk in front like eyes, and a hole perforated from side to side (8 M.).

No. 199. A remarkable Terra-cotta Vessel on three long feet, with a handle and two small ears (7 M.).

quite unknown to me. I may mention further a curious pot found in the house, at a depth of 7 meters (23 feet), with three feet, two small ears, and one handle; also those neat cups with one handle and three feet, which are

repeatedly met with in the same house. At a depth of 3 meters (10 feet) we discovered a bright red polished little box, from the under side of which two small perforated rings project. The pattern on the bottom represents the sun with its rays; in the centre of the sun's disc is a cross, which ends in four small circles, and these are probably intended to represent the heads of the nails which fastened the two crossed staves employed to produce the holy fire. In every one of the four spaces formed by the cross there is a ⊓, one of which is represented by dots.

No. 200. A beautiful bright-red Terra-cotta Box (or Vase-cover?), decorated with a + four ⊔, and a halo of solar rays (3 M.).

We also again met with one of those small perforated terra-cottas, consisting of two connected balls, and which somewhat resemble our shirt-studs; the upper part of the article in question shows three simple rising suns and six stars; the lower part represents three triple rising suns, and three stars in the circle round the central point.

During the week we have met with only one terra-cotta ball; it shows an encircling jagged streak and five small streaks, which may denote suns or moons.

Nos. 201, 202.   Little Decorated Whorls, of a remarkable shape (6 M.).

Plate X.

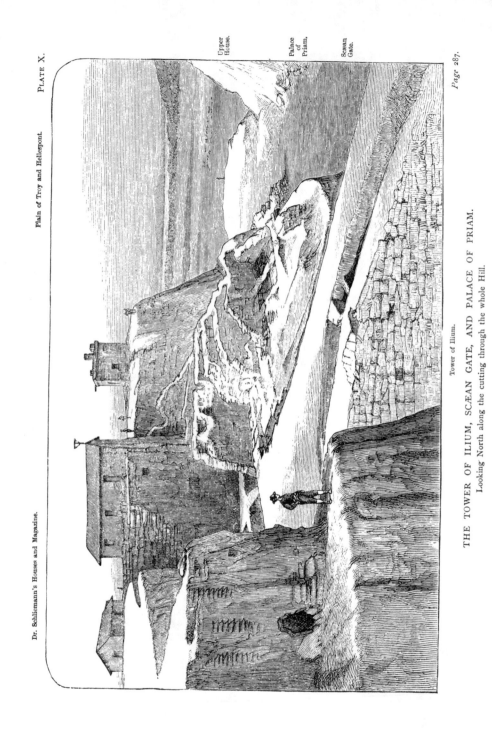

Plain of Troy and Hellespont.

Dr. Schliemann's Houses and Magazine.

Upper House.

Palace of Priam.

Scæan Gate.

Tower of Ilium.

THE TOWER OF ILIUM, SCÆAN GATE, AND PALACE OF PRIAM.

Looking North along the cutting through the whole Hill.

CHAPTER XXI.

Pergamus of Troy, April 16th, 1873.

SINCE my report of the 5th of this month I have had, on an average, 160 workmen, and have brought many won-derful things to light, among which I may especially men-tion a street of the Pergamus, which was discovered close to my house, at a depth of 30 feet, in the Great Tower. It is 17¼ feet broad, and is paved with stone flags, from 4¼ to 5 feet long, and from 35 inches to 4½ feet broad. It runs down very abruptly in a due south-western direction towards the Plain. I have as yet only been able to lay bare a length of 10 meters (33⅓ feet). It leads, without doubt, to the Scæan Gate, the position of which appears to be accurately indicated, on the west side at the foot of the hill, by the direction of the wall and by the formation of the ground; it cannot be more than 492 feet distant from the Tower. To the right and left of the street there is an enclosure 28½ inches broad and 11 feet long. The slope of the street is so great that, while on the north-east side, as far as it is there uncovered, it is only 30 feet below the surface of the hill, yet at a distance of 33 feet it already lies as low as 37 feet.*

This beautifully paved street leads me to conjecture that a grand building must at one time have stood at the top of it, at a short distance on the north-east side; and therefore, seven days ago, when the street was discovered, I immediately set 100 men to dig down the north-eastern ground lying in front of it; this cutting I have made 78½ feet long, 78½ feet broad, and 33 feet deep. The removal of these 7600 cubic yards of huge masses of hard *débris* and stones is rendered much easier by the fact that it joins my last year's great cutting, which runs quite horizontally from the northern declivity as far as the Tower, and is therefore very well adapted for the use of man-carts. In order to extract from this excavation all the objects of the greatest use to archæology, I am having the walls made perpendicular, as in fact I have had them made in almost all of the other cuttings. As the work of removing this gigantic block of earth is carried on both from above and from below, I confidently hope to have finished it in twenty days' work.

In this great bank of earth there are three curious walls, built one above another, of small stones joined with earth. They have been built at very different periods, and even the uppermost and latest of the three, as is clear from the material, must be considerably older than the foundation of the Greek colony about the year 700 B.C. This uppermost wall is about 5 feet thick, built up from a depth of 11½ feet to within 1¾ foot of the surface, a circumstance which I do not at all understand; for, as the ruins of the Greek colony reach down to the depth of 6½ feet, the wall must, for many centuries, have stood high above the earth. Still the Greeks may have used it as a foundation for a building, and it may thus have been preserved. Below

---

* Compare Plan II. with the whole of the following description.

this wall there is a stratum of earth 11½ inches thick; and
then comes the second wall, projecting about 11½ inches,
and 6½ feet high; and this again rests upon another and
much older wall. The last runs in an oblique line in a
south-western direction parallel with the Tower-road, and
furnishes a second proof that the surface of the hill, which
is now quite horizontal here, did not slope down very
abruptly towards the Plain at this part.

Thus the opinion which I have previously expressed,
that only the first inhabitants of this hill had walls and
fortifications, is now proved to be erroneous. For these
three walls, which at one time stood at the edge of the
declivity, and the three which I cut through at the south-
east side of the hill, can only have been walls of fortification, and they evidently belong to the various tribes who
inhabited this locality after the destruction of the first
nation up to the foundation of the Greek colony.

As my further excavations have shown, at a depth of
8 meters (26 feet), immediately below the Temple of Athena,
and at a distance of 131 feet from the above-mentioned
street, a large wall runs out from the Tower in a southern
direction. I have had 6½ feet of this wall laid bare to the
south. But how far it extends in this direction cannot be
ascertained without making new and enormous excavations.
It is also impossible for me to ascertain its breadth without
breaking down the curious pre-Hellenic house. It also
appears to me that the Tower ends here, for in my investigations at the foot of that ancient house I no longer found
any trace of it. Instead of it I came upon very ancient
houses, the walls of which, still partially covered with a
coating of clay and white colour, all bearing traces of a
terrible conflagration, which has so completely destroyed
everything that was in the rooms, that we only occasionally find charred fragments of pottery among the red
wood-ashes with which the spaces are filled. Curiously
enough we again find, below these very ancient houses, other

house-walls which must certainly be older; and these too show indications of having been exposed to a terrible heat. In fact, the labyrinth of very ancient house-walls, built one above another, and found in the depths of the Temple of Athena erected by Lysimachus, is unique, and presents the archæologist with the richest materials for his investigations. But what is most inexplicable to me about this labyrinth of walls is a wall of fortification, 11¾ feet high, running through it from W.N.W. to E.S.E. This is likewise built of stone joined with earth, and is 6 feet broad at the top and 12 feet broad at the foot: it does not stand directly upon the primary rock, and was not built till the rock had gradually become covered with a layer of earth 1¾ foot in thickness. It appears therefore to be somewhat less ancient than the Great Tower, which stands directly upon the primary rock. Running parallel with this wall of fortification, only 2½ feet from it and at the same depth, there is a wall 2 feet high, which is likewise built of stones joined with earth.

The room at the greatest depth which I have excavated is 10 feet high and 11¼ feet broad; but it may have been higher; its length I have not yet ascertained. One of the compartments of the uppermost houses, below the Temple of Athena and belonging to the pre-Hellenic period, appears to have been used as a wine-merchant's cellar or as a maga-zine, for in it there are nine enormous earthen jars (πίθοι) of various forms, about 5¾ feet high and 4¾ feet across, their mouths being from 29½ to 35¼ inches broad.* Each of these earthen jars has four handles, 3¾ inches broad, and the clay of which they are made has the enormous thick-ness of 2¼ inches. Upon the south side of these jars I found a wall 26 feet in extent and 10 feet high, built of sun-dried bricks, which, however, had become really

---

* See Plate XI. B. Six of the jars are shown, and a seventh (broken) lies outside of the cut to the right. The two largest of all are out of view, on the other side of the wall of the magazine, but one of them is seen in the view on Plate XI. A, in the left-hand bottom corner.

PLATE XI.

Reservoir.   Altar.

A.—THE EXCAVATIONS IN THE TEMPLE OF ATHENA.

From the East.

B.—THE MAGAZINE, WITH ITS COLOSSAL JARS,   *Page* 290.

In the depths of the Temple of Athena.

burnt bricks through the conflagration.   This wall, which likewise appears to me to be a fortification and very thick, I have had broken down to the perpendicular line of the foundations of the Temple of Athena.

I am in great fear lest the Turks should make off with the large stone altar, the upper part of which forms a crescent, to use it for building a minaret in the village of Chiplak ; therefore, without moving it from its place, I shall have it carefully split in two, so that it will be useless for building purposes.   This stone and its pedestal are daubed over with a white crust of clay, which upon the pedestal is nearly an inch thick.

I have continued the excavation on the south-east side of the Pergamus, and I have found that the great wall, which I regarded as a continuation of the Tower, is part of a very ancient and large wall of enclosure.

Since my last report we have not found any kind of interesting antiquities worth mentioning on the whole of the east side of the Tower; but in the large new excavation to the north-east of the Tower-road we have discovered a great quantity of exceedingly curious articles.   The ruins of the Greek colony here extend exactly to a depth of 6½ feet, and there I found a fragment of pottery with painted Egyptian hieroglyphics, of which I give a drawing.   Three other pieces of pottery were found at a depth of 10 feet. One of these represents an owl's face, a ᛋ and the impressions of the four nails for fixing it ; the second fragment has a ᛋ in which each of the four ends again terminates in a square ; the third fragment represents a wheel

No. 203.   Fragment of a Terra-cotta Vase, with Egyptian hieroglyphics, from the bottom of the Greek Stratum (2 M.).

in a state of rotation.   At a depth of 6½ feet we also came upon a terra-cotta idol with the owl's face and the upraised arms, which are broken off, but appear to have been longer.   This

idol, like all the others, has a human figure : the owl's beak
and eyes project from the head and have been carefully
wrought; there are indications of hair on the forehead,
and two lines on the neck seem to denote armour.   At the
same depth I found the bottom of a dish, upon which there
is a representation in high relief of two youths embracing
and kissing each other; this is a most masterly piece of
work.   At a depth of 5 feet we found the upper portion
of a vase with a pretty owl's head; the rim of the mouth
forms a kind of helmet.   A little deeper than a foot we met
with a good-looking head of a man in terra-cotta; at 2
meters (6½ feet) down, a Greek lamp with a foot 2¾ inches
long, and at the same depth some very pretty vases and
jugs, and ·a terra-cotta flattened on one side, with two
perforated holes and a stamp, in which there is a very
pretty picture of the head and shoulders of a woman.   At
a depth of 3 and 4 meters (10 and 13 feet) were twelve
marble idols without owls' faces; upon one of these idols
there are four horizontal lines on the neck; further, at a
depth of 10 feet, a fragment of a serpent with two horns;

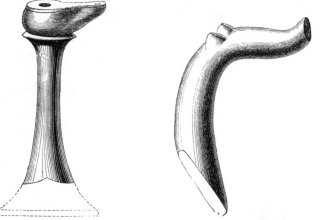

No. 204   A Greek Lamp on a tall foot (2 M.).   No. 205.   Fragment of a two-horned Serpent
                                                                        (κεράστης), in Terra-cotta (3 M.).

at a depth of 16½ feet, a piece of diorite in the form of
a bell, beautifully polished, and twice perforated; at the

same depth, a quantity of beautiful terra-cotta vases and jugs, prettily ornamented, ivory needles for knitting or embroidering, and a very neat perforated terra-cotta cylinder 1¼ inch long, covered with engraved symbolical

No. 206. Terra-cotta Cylinder, 1¼ in. long, with Symbolical Signs (5 m.).

signs.   But the most curious article, found at a depth of 5 meters (16½ feet), is an idol of the Ilian Athena with an owl's head, which is rounded off in front and at the back; the eyes are very large and beautiful, but the beak is small and roughly made; on the neck there is a cross line, and above it ten upright lines, which are probably intended to denote armour; the whole of the rest of the body is covered with lines, in which, more especially on the back, the bird's feathers are unmistakable; and there is a peculiar ornament on the abdomen.   This idol, like all the others, has a human figure.*

At a depth of 6 meters (20 feet) I found two splendid brilliant red vases with representations of the Ilian Athena with the owl's head, a kind of helmet, two upraised arms, two breasts, and the large circular prominent elevation on the abdomen.†   At the same depth I found an idol of the usual form, made of bone; and upon a handle of black terra-cotta, which has probably belonged to a large cup, the head of an ox, executed in high relief with great skill;‡ this involuntarily reminds one of Homer's Βοῶπις πότνια Ἥρη ("Our Lady Hera, with the head [or eyes] of a cow"). Among many other remarkable terra-cotta vessels, at this depth, I also found a small but really splendidly ornamented vase, the surface of which is divided into fourteen alter-

---

* See No. 29, p. 36.   † No. 207, p. 294.
‡ No. 208, pp. 294. Respecting such an impersonation of the goddess Hera, see pp. 113, 114, 353.

nate compartments, larger and smaller.* In each of the larger compartments there are three circles of little stars and a star in the centre; in each of the smaller compartments there are triple zigzag lines; this vase has little holes in the small handles for hanging it up by a string. Among the other curious articles from this depth there is a silex saw, 4 inches long and $1\frac{3}{4}$ inch broad, also one of those round, twice perforated terra-cottas flattened on one side and with a large stamp which represents a swan and an antelope. A

No. 207.   Terra-cotta Vase with helmeted image of the Ilian Athena (6 M.).

No. 208. Fragment of a large Cup-handle in black Terra-cotta; head that of an Ox (6 M.).

No. 209. A finely decorated little Vase of Terra-cotta (6 M.).

similar terra-cotta, the stamp upon which represents the head of a warrior with a helmet, was found at a depth of 8 meters (26 feet). These two are the first terra-cottas of

---

* No. 209, on this page.

this kind which I have hitherto discovered below a depth
of 2 meters (6½ feet).

No. 210. Terra-cotta Disc stamped with a
Swan and an Antelope (6 M.).
Remarkable for the depth.

No. 211. Terra-cotta Disc pierced with two holes,
and stamped with the Head of a War-
rior. Remarkable for the depth (8 M.).

At a depth of 7 meters (23 feet) I found a
small tripod with a projecting owl's face, also a
pretty red terra-cotta cup (cover) with the owl's
face of the Ilian Athena and her helmet; a knife
and a long copper instrument; a piece of bone
3¼ inches long, ornamented with very artistically
engraved symbolical signs, and among other
exceedingly curious terra-cottas, the handle of a
cup with a cross and the marks of the four
nails for fixing it; further, a fragment the upper
portion of a large urn, which is ornamented with
three encircling stripes: the upper and lower
stripes consist of peculiarly interwoven crooked
lines; the middle one contains small circles, in
each of which is a cross.

No. 212.
A piece of Bone,
curiously en-
graved (7 M.).

At a depth of 8 meters (26 feet) we discovered a
marble idol with the owl's head of the tutelary goddess
of Ilium, and a brilliant red terra-cotta idol of the same
goddess, which, curiously enough, has on its head a small,
but very pretty vase with two handles; the owl's face of
this last-mentioned idol has enormous eyes, and is very
expressive. Of terra-cotta vases and dishes we found an
especially large number in these depths. I can, however,
only give drawings of a few of them, for most were brought
out in a broken condition, and I cannot have them re-

paired till I return to Athens.   Of those terra-cottas which
were got out unharmed, a small vase with two holes in

the mouth, for being hung up by a
cord, is especially deserving of attention; it is surrounded by figures in
the shape of hearts with crosses; then
saucer-shaped pots with large handles;
other little pots in the form of salt-
cellars, and several vases round at the
bottom with three feet or without feet;
terra-cotta scoops in the form of cups
with large handles; then a large terra-
cotta lid with a handle; it is of a
very curious shape, and weighs 730

No. 213. Fragment of a Trojan
Idol of bright-red Terra-
cotta (6 M.).

grammes.   We also found several implements of copper.

At a depth of 9 meters (29½ feet) we found a copper
lance and a dozen very large vases, brown and black.

Nos. 214, 215. Terra-cotta Cups or Scoops (7 M.).   No. 216. Vase Cover in Terra-cotta (8 M.).

At the same depth I found a pretty brilliant brown cup
in the form of a flower-pot, with two large handles.   At a
depth of 26 and 29½ feet I have found, since the 5th of
the month, eleven beautiful sling-bullets of loadstone and

two of porphyry. We met with very few stone implements, only two beautiful axes of diorite, at the depths of
29½ and 33 feet. At the latter depth I again found one of
the brush-handles of terra-cotta, which
are often found, and some vases with
three feet and rings at the sides for
hanging them up.

During the last eleven days I
have collected 991 of the terra-cotta
whorls, 581 of which have symbolical
signs, but only 79 have engravings
which are new to me. Long thin
copper nails with rounded heads,
which must have been used as dress or

No. 217. Terra-cotta Handle of a Trojan Brush, with the holes in which the bristles have been fixed (10 M.).

hair pins, were met with at all depths. During these eleven
days I have found 20 exquisitely polished axes of diorite.

At a depth of 1 meter (3¼ feet), we yesterday found
in the Temple of Athena, beside an inscribed pedestal of
black slate, 3 feet 8 inches high and 20¾ inches broad,
the statue of a man, of fine white marble, nearly 4 feet
high. As is proved by the inscription, it was made by
Pytheas of Argos, and was erected by the Ilians in honour
of Metrodorus, the son of Themistagoras, of whom it is a
representation. The figure was in the position of an orator,
as is proved by the footmarks on the pedestal. The head
and the feet are unfortunately wanting.

The inscriptions run as follows:—

ΟΔΗΜΟΣΟΙΛΙΕΙΩΝ
ΜΗΤΡΟΔΩΡΟΝΘΕΜΙΣΤΑΓΟΡΟΥ

And lower down, on the same side of the pedestal—

ΠΥΘΕΑΣΑΡΓΕΙΟΣΕΠΟΙΗΣΕ

Ὁ δῆμος ὁ Ἰλιείων
Μητρόδωρον Θεμισταγόρου
Πυθέας Ἀργεῖος ἐποίησε.

There were in antiquity many men named Metrodorus,

but only two of them were especially celebrated, and both were natives of Asia Minor. The one, born in Lampsacus, was a pupil of Epicurus ;* the other, a native of Scepsis, was a philosopher, orator, and statesman, and was held in high esteem by Mithridates VII., Eupator,† who afterwards had him put to death in a horrible manner.‡ The name of the father of this Metrodorus of Scepsis is unknown, and whether he was called Themistagoras, or otherwise, is uncertain ; but it is extremely probable that the inscription and the statue were raised in honour of the Scepsian orator, philosopher, and statesman. I find no mention whatever of the sculptor Pytheas of Argos. Only one Pytheas, a silver-chaser, is named by Pliny,§ as being a contemporary of Pompey the Great : Pliny, however, does not state his birth-place. Another Pytheas was a wall painter and a native of Achaia. Neither of these can therefore be the Argive sculptor who made the statue and put his name on the pedestal. But as my learned and much esteemed friend, Professor Stephanos Kummanudes of Athens, has remarked, it is not astonishing that the name of an insignificant sculptor should be forgotten, seeing that the names of so many great kings are lost.

In the same part of the Temple of Athena we found the fragment of a marble slab, which has evidently been very long, with the inscription given on the opposite page.

The Proconsul Caius Claudius Nero, the son of Publius, who is praised in the above inscription, ruled over the province of Asia from 674 to 675 after the foundation of Rome. Hence he lived at the time of Cicero, who mentions him in his orations against Verres.||

The Pœmanenians (Ποιμανηνοί) are the inhabitants of the fortress of Pœmanenon, to the south of Cyzicus.¶

---

* Strabo, XIII. p. 589.   † Strabo, XIII. p. 609.
‡ Plutarch, *Life of Lucullus.*   § *Hist. Nat.,* XXXV. 12, s. 55.
|| Waddington, *Fastes des Provinces Asiatiques de l'Empire Romain.*
Paris, 1872, pp. 43–44.   ¶ Pape-Benseler, *Lexikon der Eigennamen.*

To judge from the form and thickness of the stone, this inscription must have been very long and have contained more than 70 lines. But even the fragment is of historical value, and all the more as we know for certain that it comes down to us from the year 80 B.C.

ΕΠΕΙΤΟΥΑΝΘΥΠΑΤΟΥΓΑΙΟΥΚΛΑΥΔΙΟΥΠΟΠΛΙΟΥΥΙΟΥΝΕΡΩΝΟΣΕΠΙΤΑΞΑΝΤΟΣ
ΤΟΙΣΠΟΙΜΑΝΗΝΩΝΑΡΧΟΥΣΙΝΕΞΑΠΟΣΤΕΙΛΑΙΠΡΟΣΗΜΑΣΕΙΣΠΑΡΑΦΥΛΑΚΗΝ
ΤΗΣΠΟΛΕΩΣΣΤΡΑΤΙΩΤΑΣΚΑΙΕΠΑΥΤΩΝΗΓΕΜΟΝΑΣΠΟΙΜΑΝΗΝΩΝ
ΟΝΤΕΣΗΜΩΝΦΙΛΟΙΚΑΙΕΥΝΟΩΣΔΙΑΚΕΙΜΕΝΟΙΠΡΟΣΤΟΝΔΗΜΟΝΗΜΩΝ
5 ΕΞΑΠΕΣΤΕΙΛΑΝΤΟΥΣΤΕΣΤΡΑΤΙΩΤΑΣΚΑΙΕΠΑΥΤΩΝΗΓΕΜΟΝΑΝΙΚ
ΔΡΟΝΜΗΝΟΦΙΛΟΥΥΙΟΣΚΑΙΠΑΡΑΓΕΝΟΜΕΝΟΣΕΙΣΤΗΝΠΟΛΙΝΗΜΩΝ
ΤΕΕΝΔΗΜΙΑΝΠΟΙΕΙΤΑΙΚΑΛΗΝΚΑΙΕΥΣΧΗΜΟΝΑΚΑΙΑΞΙΩΣ
ΡΟΥΔΗΜΟΥΚΑΙΤΗΣΕΑΥΤΟΥΠΑΤΡΙΔΟΣΤΗΝΤΕΤΩΝ
ΕΑΥΤΩΙΝΕΑΝΙΣΚΩΝΕΝΔΗΜΙΑΝΕΥΤ...ΟΝΠ
10 ΤΟΝΚΑΘΑΠΕΡΕΠΙΒΑΛΛΕΙΑΝΔΡ
ΧΕΙΡΙΣΜΕΝΗΝΕΑΤΩΙΠΙ
ΤΗΝΥΠΕΡΤΗΣΦΥΛΑΚ
ΕΙΣΦΕΡΕΤΑΙΣΠΟΥΔ
ΕΚΚΑΙΝΩΝΟΥΔΕΙ
15 ΜΟΝΚΑΙ

ἐπεὶ τοῦ ἀνθυπάτου Γαΐου Κλαυδίου Ποπλίου υἱοῦ Νέρωνος ἐπιτάξαντος
τοῖς Ποιμανηνῶν ἄρχουσιν ἐξαποστεῖλαι πρὸς ἡμᾶς εἰς παραφυλακὴν
τῆς πόλεως στρατιώτας καὶ ἐπ' αὐτῶν ἡγεμόνας Ποιμανηῶν (οἱ ;)
ὄντες ἡμῶν φίλοι καὶ εὐνόως διακείμενοι πρὸς τὸν δῆμον ἡμῶν
ἐξαπέστειλαν τούς τε στρατιώτας καὶ ἐπ' αὐτῶν ἡγεμόνα Νίκ(αν-)⁻
δρον Μηνοφίλου (υἱ)ός καὶ παραγενόμενος εἰς τὴν πόλιν ἡμῶν (τὴν)
τε ἐνδημίαν ποιεῖται καλὴν καὶ εὐσχήμονα καὶ ἀξί(ως τοῦ τε ἡμετέ-)
ρου δήμου καὶ τῆς ἑαυτοῦ πατρίδος, τήν τε τῶν (ὑφ' ;)
ἑαυτῷ νεανίσκων ἐνδημίαν εὐτ(ακτ)ον π(αρέχεται καὶ ἑαυ-)
τον καθάπερ ἐπιβάλλει ἀνδρ(ὶ . . . . . . καὶ τὴν ἐξουσίαν τὴν ἐγκε-)
χειρισμένην ἑατῷ πι(στῶς καὶ . . . .
τὴν ὑπὲρ τῆς φυλακ(ῆς . . . .
εἰσφέρεται σπουδ(ὴν
ἐκ καινῶν οὐδει
μον καὶ

CHAPTER XXII.

Interruptions through festivals — Opening of the tumulus of Batiea
— Pottery like that of the Trojan stratum at Hissarlik, and nothing
else — No trace of burial — Its age — Further discoveries of burnt
Trojan houses — Proof of their successive ages — Their construction
— Discovery of a double gateway, with the copper bolts of the
gates — The " SCÆAN GATE " of Homer — Tests of the extent of
ancient Troy — The place where Priam sat to view the Greek
forces — Homer's knowledge of the heroic Troy only traditional —
Description of the gates, the walls, and the " PALACE OF PRIAM." —
Vases, &c., found in Priam's house — Copper, ivory, and other
implements — The δέπα ἀμφικύπελλα — Houses discovered on the
north platform — Further excavations of the city walls — Statuettes
and vessels of the Greek period — Top of the Tower of Ilium
uncovered, and its height determined — A curious trench in it,
probably for the archers — Further excavations at Bunarbashi : only
a few fragments of Greek pottery — The site of Ilium uninhabited
since the end of the fourth century — The place confused with
Alexandria Troas — No Byzantine remains at Hissarlik — Freshness of the Greek sculptures.

Pergamus of Troy, May 10th, 1873.

SINCE my report of the 16th of last month I have had
many interruptions, for the Greek Easter festival lasts six
days, then the feast of Saint George and its after celebra-
tions again took away several days, so that during all this
time I have had only four days of actual work ; however,
on these days, with on an average 150 men, I have continued the works with great energy.

As we have had continual fine weather since the
beginning of April, my men no longer go to the neighbouring villages for the night as they have hitherto done ;
but they sleep in the open air and even in the excavations,
which is very convenient for me, as I now have them

always at hand. Besides this, the long days are of great
advantage to me, for I can continue work from a quarter
to five till a quarter past seven in the evening.

On the top of the tumulus, which is half an hour
distant from the Pergamus, and which, according to the
Iliad (II. 811–815), was called by men the tomb of
Batiea, and by the gods the tomb of Myrina, I have had
a shaft sunk, 10¾ feet broad and 17½ feet long; and I find
that the layer of soil there is scarcely more than ¾ of an
inch thick, and then follows brown earth as hard as stone,
which alternates with strata of calcareous earth. In the
brown earth I found a mass of fragments of brilliant black,
green, and brown vases, of the same description as those
which I find here in the Pergamus at a depth of from
8 to 10 meters (26 to 33 feet); also many fragments of
jars (πίθοι).   Beyond these I discovered nothing at all,
and at a depth of 4½ meters (13¾ feet) I came upon the
white limestone rock. What is most surprising to me is
that I did not even find any charcoal, much less the bones
of the burnt corpse. That I should have missed the traces
of the funeral pile, if such really existed, is inconceivable
to me, when I consider the size of my cutting and of its
perpendicular walls.

Now, although I have failed in the actual object of this
excavation, still it has this important result for archæology,
that, by means of all the fragments of pottery discovered
there, it enables us to determine with some degree of certainty the date of the erection of this mound; for it evidently belongs to a time when the surface of the Pergamus
was from 26 to 33 feet lower than it is now. It is therefore
of the same date as the Tower-road already described, which
is paved with large flags of stone, and above which I have
carried on the excavations with the greatest industry.   I
finished these excavations to-day. They have brought to
light two large buildings of different ages, the more recent
of which is erected upon the ruins of the more ancient one.

Both have been destroyed by terrible fires, of which the walls bear distinct traces; moreover all the rooms of both houses are filled with black, red, and yellow wood-ashes and with charred remains. The more recent house was erected when the ruins of the more ancient house were perfectly covered with ashes and with burnt *débris*, as is obvious from the fact that the more recent walls run in all directions above the more ancient ones, never standing directly upon them, and are frequently separated from them by a layer of calcined *débris*, from 6½ to 10 feet high. The lower, as well as the upper house, is built of stones joined with earth, but the walls of the lower house are much thicker and much more solidly built than those of the upper one. The Tower-road can only have been used when the more ancient house was still inhabited, for it leads directly into it, and the more recent house was not built till the street was covered to a height of 10 feet by the ruins of the more ancient house.

I was firmly convinced that this splendid street, paved with large flags of stone, must proceed from the principal building of the Pergamus, and I therefore confidently carried on the excavation in order to bring that edifice to light. To accomplish this, I was most unfortunately compelled to break down three of the large walls of the more recent house. The result has, however, far surpassed my expectations, for I not only found two large gates, standing 20 feet apart, but also the two large copper bolts belonging to them, of which

No. 218.   Copper Bolts, found exactly in the middle (*a*) of the first (*b*) of the second Scæan Gates.

PLATE XII.

Tower of Ilium.

Wall
of
Débria.

Scæan
Gate
and
Paved
Road.

οἱ Σκαιαι Πυλαι

Ruins
of the
Palace
of
Priam.

Wall of Troy.

THE DOUBLE SCÆAN GATE, PALACE OF PRIAM, AND TOWER OF ILIUM.
From the North-West.

I give drawings. The first gate is 12¼ feet broad, and is formed by two projections of the wall, one of which stands out 2½ feet, the other 2¾ feet; both are 3¼ feet high, and 3¾ feet broad. The street paved with the large flags of stone ends at the first gate, and the road from this to the second gate, which is situated a little more than 20 feet further to the north-east, is very roughly paved with large unhewn stones. The pavement has probably become uneven through the walls of the more ancient house having fallen upon it. (*See Plan II., and Plates XII. and XIII.*)

The second gate is likewise formed by two projections in the wall, which are 2 feet high, above 3 feet broad, and project about 2½ feet.

I have cleared the street as far as 5 feet to the north-east of the second gate, but I have not ventured to proceed further, as this could not be done without breaking down more of the walls of the second house, the preservation of which is of the greatest interest to archæology. For, although it must be of a much more recent date than the lower one upon the ruins of which it stands, yet, as is proved by the terra-cottas and the idols with owls' heads, as well as by its position at a depth of from 6 to 7 meters (20 to 23 feet) below the surface, it was built centuries before the time of the Greek settlement, the ruins of which extend only to a depth of 6½ feet. This upper and later house is therefore certainly older than the Homeric poems.

In my last report I expressed the firm conviction that the Tower-road, which inclines abruptly towards the Plain to the south-west, must lead to the Scæan Gate, which I thought could at most be 492 feet distant. I now venture positively to assert that the great double gate which I have brought to light must necessarily be the SCÆAN GATE. For in the mound, which runs out far to the south-west from the foot of the Pergamus and in a straight line with the Tower-road— which mound I had supposed to contain the great city wall of Ilium and the Scæan Gate,—

in this mound, close to the main hill, I have sunk a shaft, nearly 6 feet broad and 11 feet long. Here I found exclusively Greek fragments of pottery, and I came upon the rock at the small depth of 7½ feet; thus I convinced myself that ancient Troy can never have extended so far towards the Plain. A second excavation, 11¼ feet long and 6½ feet broad, which I made exactly 443 feet further to the east up the plateau, had a similar result, for I came upon the rock at a depth of 16½ feet, and here also I found exclusively fragments of Hellenic pottery (which in the Pergamus I meet with only at a depth of 6½ feet), and no trace of Trojan pottery.

This sufficiently proves that the ancient city cannot even have extended as far as this point, and its area must have been connected with the Pergamus still further eastwards.* I am at present occupied in making fifteen other shafts in this direction, and I hope, in spite of the great depth I have to sink them, that I shall succeed, at least to some extent, in determining the topography of Troy. I shall leave all the shafts open, so that every visitor may convince himself about the truth of my statements.

Meanwhile the two shafts described above have gained this much for archæology, that the street which runs down abruptly at an angle of 65 degrees towards the Plain, in a south-western direction from the double gate and the Great Tower, cannot possibly have led to a second gate, so that the double gate which I have laid bare must necessarily have been the Scæan Gate; it is in an excellent state of preservation, not a stone of it is wanting.

Here, therefore, by the side of the double gate, upon Ilium's Great Tower, at the edge of the very abrupt western declivity of the Pergamus, sat Priam, the seven elders of the city, and Helen; and this is the scene of the most

---

* It will be seen presently that Dr. Schliemann ultimately limited the ancient city of Troy to the " Pergamus " itself.—[Ed.]

splendid passage in the Iliad.*   From this spot the company surveyed the whole Plain, and saw at the foot of the Pergamus the Trojan and the Achæan armies face to face about to settle their agreement to let the war be decided by a single combat between Paris and Menelaus.

When Homer † makes Hector descend from the Pergamus and rush through the city in order to arrive at the Scæan Gate, this can only have arisen from the fact that, after the destruction of Troy, the gate, as well as the street which led down from it to the Plain, were covered with a layer of *débris* 10 feet thick, so that the names only were known from tradition, and their actual site was unknown.

In order not to weary the reader with a detailed description of the Scæan Gate, I give an exact plan of it, where all the details may be seen.   (Plan III., p. 306.)   This gate, as well as the large ancient building, stands upon the wall or buttress already mentioned as leaning on the north side of the Tower.   At this place the buttress appears to be about 79 feet thick, and to be made of the *débris* which was broken off the primary soil when the Tower was erected.   The site of this building, upon an artificial elevation directly above the gate, together with its solid structure, leave no doubt that

---

* *Iliad*, III. 146–244 :—

> " Attending there on aged Priam, sat
> The Elders of the city ; . . . . .
> All these were gathered at the Scæan Gates.
> . . . . .   so on Ilion's Tower
> Sat the sage chiefs and councillors of Troy.
> Helen they saw, as to the Tower she came."

† *Iliad*, VI. 390–393 :—

> Ἦ ῥα γυνὴ ταμίη · ὁ δ' ἀπέσσυτο δώματος Ἕκτωρ
> Τὴν αὐτὴν ὁδὸν αὖτις ἐϋκτιμένας κατ' ἀγυιὰς.
> Εὖτε πύλας ἵκανε διερχόμενος μέγα ἄστυ
> Σκαιάς τῇ γὰρ ἔμελλε διεξίμεναι πεδίονδε——

> " So spoke the ancient dame ; and Hector straight
> Through the wide streets his rapid steps retraced.
> But when at last the mighty city's length
> Was traversed, and the Scæan Gates were reached,
> Whence was the outlet to the plain——"

it was the grandest building in Troy; nay, that it must have been the PALACE OF PRIAM.* I am having an accurate plan made, so far as I can, of the portion that has been laid bare; I cannot, however, bring to light the whole of it, for in order to do this I should have to pull down both my stone and my wooden house, beneath which it extends; and even if I did pull down my own houses, I should still be unable to make a complete plan of the house till I had

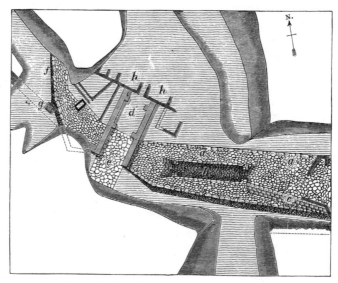

PLAN III.—THE TOWER AND THE SCÆAN GATE.

a a. The Great Tower of Ilium. *b.* Depression to shelter archers. *c.* Steps. *d.* The Double Scæan Gate. *e.* Steep paved road leading to the Plain. *f.* The City Wall. *g.* Place where the Treasure was found. *h h.* The Palace of Priam.

removed the building which stands upon it, and this I cannot at once make up my mind to do.

Anyone may convince himself that the elevation, upon which stands the Palace of King Priam above the Scæan

---

* This edifice, now first laid open from beneath the ashes which covered it in the burning of the city, was found by Dr. Schliemann in the very state to which, in Homer, Agamemnon threatens to reduce it: " The house of Priam *blackened with fire*" (Iliad, II. 414, 415) :

Πρίν με κατα πρηνὲς βαλέειν Πριάμοιο μέλαθρον
Αἰθαλόεν, πρῆσαι δὲ πυρὸς δηΐοιο θύρετρα.

Gate, is in reality an artificial one, by examining my last year's great cutting, which pierces through a portion of this elevation. The walls of that cutting, from the shaft as far as the gate, show that the mound consists of the native earth which has been thrown up, mixed with fragments of rare pottery and shells.

Now, with regard to the objects found in these houses, I must first of all mention having discovered, at a depth of 26 feet, in the palace of Priam, a splendid and brilliant brown vase, 24¼ inches high, with a figure of the tutelar goddess of Troy, that is, with her owl's head, two breasts,

No. 219.   Wonderful Vase of Terra-cotta from the Palace of Priam (8 M.).*

---

* In the letter-press to the Atlas of Photographs this object is described as "a brilliant dark-red Vase, 62 centimeters (above 2 feet) high, with the owl-face of Troy's tutelar goddess, her two breasts, a necklace, and a royal scarf round the whole body. It is remarkable that this vase has not the two uplifted arms of the goddess, which are wanting in no other case, and that it has only two handles."

a splendid necklace, indicated by an engraved pattern, a very broad and beautifully engraved girdle, and other very artistic decorations; there are no arms, nor are there any indications of them. Unfortunately this exquisite vase has suffered from the weight of stones which lay upon it, and although I myself cut it with a knife from among the stones and the stone-hard *débris* with the greatest care, I did not succeed in getting it out without breaking it to pieces. I have, however, carefully collected all the fragments and sent them to Athens to be put together, that I may give a drawing of it. (This is No. 219.)

Among the very remarkable vases discovered in this palace, I must also mention one nearly a foot high, with two handles, and an encircling row of cuneiform engravings,

No. 220.   Terra-cotta Vase from the House of Priam, with remarkable Decorations (9 M.).

above which, on both sides, there is a very prominent decoration, in the form of spectacles, which is connected with a kind of necklace by an engraved tree. I must further draw special attention to an exceedingly remarkable vase, which was found in the same house, and upon which there are actual letters in a circle round it. One piece of the vase is wanting, and with it a portion of the inscription; but, in order to lay before the reader all that has been preserved of it, I give the inscription separately, for it would be impossible to give it accurately on the drawing of the vase. (See No. 3, p. 23.) It would please me immensely if anyone could decipher the Trojan writing,

and thus throw some light upon the great people to whom it belonged, and upon the epoch at which it was written.* I must also draw attention to a vase, upon which at first sight it seems as if there were a row of letters; at a closer examination, however, it appears not to be writing, but symbolical signs, as the cross is conspicuous in almost every figure.†

No. 221. A Terra-cotta Vase with two little Ears, and two large perforated Handles, marked with eleven strange characters (5¼ M.).

The *depth* must refer to the *upper house* above the Palace. It is given as 8¼ M. in the Photograph, but corrected in the descriptive letter-press to 5¼ M.; and a like correction seems to have been neglected in the Book.—[ED.]

In the same house I found three brilliant red vases, with two handles, a prominent decoration on either side in the form of spectacles, and two mighty wings, standing erect by the side of the neck;—half-a-dozen vases of various sizes, with uncommonly long tubes at the sides and with holes in the mouth for suspending them by strings;— a very large and brilliant black vase, with two handles and two ornaments in the form of large ears;—likewise a smaller vase, with large perforated ears for the string by which it was hung up;—a vase with three feet, rings for hanging it up, and beautiful engraved

---

* The Inscription on this Vase has been discussed by Professor Gomperz, who also pronounces the characters on it as well as on the other vase (No. 221) to be Cyprian writing. (See Appendix.)

† Compare the Introduction, p. 50.

decorations, namely, two encircling stripes with zigzag lines, and five lines round the neck. (No. 222.) Further, I found a vase rounded at the bottom, with perforated handles, and completely covered with dots (No. 223) ;— also two covers with pretty owls' heads, one of which has remarkably large eyes ;—also a fragment of the fore part of a vase with a sheep's head ;—a curious small but very broad vase, with three feet and long tubes for hanging

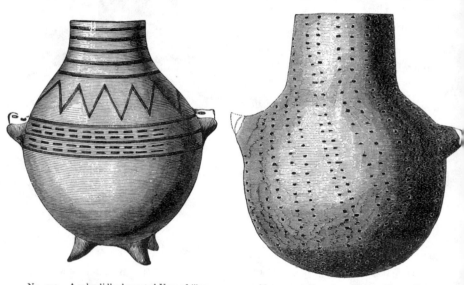

No. 222. A splendidly-decorated Vase of Terra-cotta, with three Feet and two Ears. From the Palace (7¼ M.).

No. 223. A Terra-cotta Vase, with two Ears and covered with dots. From the Palace (7 M.).

it up by strings ;—a peculiar terra-cotta lamp, with a per-forated handle in the form of a crescent, and two other projecting handles, with tubes for suspension ;—a red jug with a handle, a neck completely bent back, a beak-shaped mouth, and two eyes ;*—a small vase, covered with dots and possessing two handles and two immense erect ears ;— a jug, with two female breasts ;—a vase, with the owl's face and the body of the Ilian Athena, and two upraised arms ;— also the upper portion of another vase, upon which may be

* See Cut, No. 54, p. 87.

seen a mouth below the beak of the Trojan tutelary goddess ; and a vase, with a large hollow foot, very long tubes at the sides for hanging it up, and two prominent decorations in the form of spectacles.

No. 224. Fine decorated Vase of Terra-Cotta, with two Handles and two great upright Wings. From the Palace (7¼ M.).

Among the smaller terra-cottas found in the palace of Priam, I have particularly to mention a vessel 2¾ inches long, in a human form, with the owl's head of the Ilian Athena and unusually large eyes : two lines on the temples appear to indicate the helmet, three horizontal lines on the neck her armour.* The body is covered with an arched shield 1½ inch long, upon which there are ten rows of dots, which are probably intended to represent the heads of the small nails with which the layers (πτύχες) were fastened together; the shield of Ajax, for instance, consisted of seven layers of hides and an outer case of copper.† The Trojan goddess carries on both sides a large wing, in the form of a bottle, which is decorated with horizontal lines. The long hair at the back of the goddess's head is very distinct; it is gathered into a plait, and falls down almost as far as her ankles, and is wrought with great care, reminding one extremely of the very similar plaits of the Caryatides in the Erechtheum of the Acropolis of Athens. Not only is the idol hollow, but so also are the wings; the latter must positively have some symbolical significance.

In the palace of Priam I further met with four marble and three bone idols, with the owl's head of the tutelar goddess of Troy: one of the bone idols is painted with a

---

* This most curious vase is engraved in the Introduction, No. 31, p. 37.

† See the passage quoted below to illustrate the shield found among the Treasure (Chapter XXIII., p. 324).

white colour.   I likewise discovered there ten marble idols, without the owl's head; also the fragment of a sword, as well as of a lance, a knife, and some copper implements; further, a dozen long, thin copper nails, which must have served as hair or dress pins; besides these, a packet of five dress pins, which have been molten together in the heat of the conflagration: one of the pins has two heads, one above

No. 225.   Five Copper Dress Pins, molten together by the conflagration.   From the Palace (8 M.).

the other, the lower head being perfectly round.   I also discovered here a perforated cylinder, 1¾ inch long, made of blue felspar, and ornamented all round with extremely remarkable engraved symbols.   I there also discovered an extremely curious ivory article, which must be part of a musical instrument;* six sling bullets of loadstone and an arrow-head.

No. 226.   Engraved Cylinder of blue Felspar.   No. 227.   Terra-cotta, engraved with ten rude
From the Palace (9 M.).†   Owls' Faces.   From the Palace (8 M.).

Of 210 whorls found in the Palace adorned with Aryan religious symbols, there are 60 with engravings that I have not hitherto met with, and three terra-cotta balls with

---

* See the illustration, No. 7, p. 25.

† This looks very much like the signet-cylinders of the Assyrian and Babylonian kings.---[ED.]

symbolical signs.   One of these is especially remarkable *: it
has ten roughly-engraved owls' faces, so coarsely drawn
that I should not even know them to be owls' faces, were
it not that I have occasionally found just as rude representations of the owl's head upon idols.   I also discovered
in the same house six beautifully-polished axes of diorite ;
also one of those round twice-perforated terra-cottas,
arched on both sides and flattened on the edge of one side,
the whole of this flat side being filled with a stamp bearing the impression of an eagle and a stag or an antelope ;
further, four of those frequently-described large red goblets,
round below and with two large handles, which can only
stand on the mouth.   These four goblets are, unfortunately, all broken, and I shall not be able to have them
repaired till I return to Athens.

I now venture positively to maintain that these goblets,
which, from my former reports and drawings are known to
be from 5 to nearly 16 inches high, must necessarily be the
Homeric " δέπα ἀμφικύπελλα," and that the usual interpretation of these words by " *double cups, with a common
bottom in the centre*," is entirely erroneous.   It really appears
as if this wrong translation arose solely through Aristotle ;
for, as is clear from his *Hist. Anim.* (9, 40), there were
in his time double cups with a common bottom in the
centre ; and, in fact, many years ago it is said that such a
cup was discovered in Attica, and bought by the Museum
in Copenhagen.   But in the Homeric Troy there were
no such cups, otherwise I should have found them.   As
already remarked in one of my previous reports (p. 129), l
found on the primary soil, at a depth of from 46 to 52½ feet,
several fragments of brilliant black goblets, which I then
considered to be fragments of double cups, because there

---

* This is drawn as a *whorl*, and is so called by Dr. Schliemann in a
letter, informing us that it is found to bear an Inscription.   It is not
described in the letter-press to the Photographs.—[Ed.]

was a hollow upon both sides of the bottom ; but the one hollow was in all cases quite small in comparison with the other, and must, therefore, have been in the foot of the cup. If δέπας ἀμφικύπελλον means *double cup*, then ἀμφιφορεύς must mean *double urn*, which is not possible either in the Iliad (XIII. 92), the Odyssey (XXIV. 74), or elsewhere in Homer ; moreover, it has never occurred to anyone to translate it otherwise than " urn with two handles ;" consequently, δέπας ἀμφικύπελλον cannot be translated otherwise than by " cup with two handles." As an actual double cup can, of course, only be filled on one side at a time, Homer would certainly never have constantly described the filled cup as a double cup, for there would have been no sense in the name. By the term ἀμφικύπελλον, however, he wished to signify that the filled cup was presented by one handle and accepted by the other handle. Interpreted in this manner, there is a great deal of meaning in the name.*

The palace of King Priam furnished me also with two large fragments of a large brilliant yellow urn, adorned in the most beautiful manner with engraved decorations. Among others, it has several rows of circles running round it, in each of which there is a triple cross. The elegance of the vessel is enhanced by the broad handles, which also have circles with triple crosses. In the king's palace I also discovered the handle of a vessel, broken off ; it is 4¼ inches long, and in the form of a serpent.

In the upper and more recent house, above the Scæan Gate, I found the vase here represented, which is pointed below, has two handles and decorations in the form of spectacles (No. 228) ; also the beautiful vase, with four handles and a lid (No. 229) ; the large jug, with one large and two small handles (No. 230) ; and a number of other vases and

---

* Thus Hephæstus places a δέπας ἀμφικύπελλον in the hand of his mother, Hera, and she takes it from his hand (Homer's *Iliad*, I. 584–5, 596). —[Ed.]

jugs which I shall not describe, as they have already been frequently met with. Of idols with owls' faces I have found only one. There also I discovered many fragments of those large red goblets with two handles, which I now recognise to be the Homeric δέπας ἀμφικύπελλον.

No. 228.　Terra-cotta Vase, with a curious Decoration. From the upper and later House above the Scæan Gate (6 M.).

As the excavation above the Scæan Gate is finished, I am now again vigorously at work on the great platform on the north side, which I have lately had worked whenever I had workmen

No. 229.　Terra-cotta Vase, with four Handles and a Lid. From the upper House above the Scæan Gate (6 M.).

No. 230.　A great Jug, with Handle and two Ears. From the upper House above the Scæan Gate (6 M.).

to spare. We now come upon several houses there at a depth of from 33 to 20 feet; also, as it seems, upon a great wall of fortification in the lower strata.

As it is extremely important to know what were the fortifications on the west and north-west of the Pergamus at the time of the Trojan war, and as I see another wall, 11½ feet thick, running in a north-western direction from the Scæan Gate, which however it is impossible to follow from this side,—during the last eight days I have been making a cutting, 33 feet broad and 141 long, on the north-west side of the hill, at the point where, in April 1870, I made the first cutting, which therefore my men call ἡ μάμμη τῶν ἀνασκαφῶν ("the grandmother of the excavations"). I am having the *débris* removed simultaneously by a small platform, made at a depth of 34¼ feet on the declivity of the hill, and by three galleries. The distance is not great, and the wheel-barrows proceed across level ground, and moreover the *débris* here is very light, and only requires to be thrown down the declivity; so the work advances very rapidly. Upon the lower platform I came upon the surrounding wall built by Lysimachus, which is 13 feet high and 10 feet thick, and is composed of large hewn blocks of limestone laid upon one another without any kind of cement. I have just finished breaking through this wall. Directly behind it I came upon an older wall, 8¾ feet high and 6 feet thick, which is composed of large hewn stones joined with earth, and which of course I am also having broken through. This second wall is immediately followed by that wall of large hewn stones which I laid bare three years ago, and which I have hitherto regarded as a bastion; it is, however, probable that it will prove to be something else, and I shall describe it in detail in my next report.

This part of the Pergamus was evidently much lower in ancient times; as seems to be proved not only by the surrounding wall, which must at one time have risen to a considerable height above the surface of the hill, whereas it is now covered with 16½ feet of *débris*, but also by the remains of the Hellenic period, which here extend down to a great depth. It appears, in fact, as if the rubbish and refuse of habitations had been thrown down here for centuries, in order to increase the height of the place. This also explains how it is that I find here a quantity of small but interesting objects from the Greek period. Among others are 24 heads of terra-cotta figures, 17 of which are of great beauty; also a great number of other fragments of statuettes of the same description, which display skilful workmanship; a terra-cotta slab 5½ inches in length, upon which is a representation of a woman; also eight small terra-cotta slabs, nearly 2 inches in length, upon which I find very curious and to me utterly unknown objects in high relief.* I also found here the fragments of some vessels of exquisite workmanship; two beautifully decorated lamps; and a leaden plate, 2¾ inches long and broad, with a pig's head in bas-relief, which, as I conjecture, may have been a coin. We also discovered here a vessel 28¾ inches long, of an extremely fanciful shape, with a long and very thin foot, a long thin neck, and two enormous handles.

Upon the great platform, at a depth of 4 meters (13 feet), we found a very remarkable cup, which has a handle, and in its hollow foot four oval holes, pierced opposite to one another. Last year I repeatedly found the feet of cups of this sort at a depth of from 46 to 52½ feet, but hitherto I have never met with an entire goblet of this form.

No. 231. A remarkable Terra-cotta Cup
(4 M.).

---

* See the Cuts placed as headings to the "Table of Contents," and "List of Illustrations."

As I no longer require the surface of the Tower for removing the *débris*, I have had it quite cleared, and I find in the centre of it a depression, $45\frac{1}{4}$ feet long, from $8\frac{1}{4}$ to $14\frac{3}{4}$ feet broad, and barely 3 feet deep, which may have been used for the archers.* It has now become evident to me that what I last year considered to be the ruins of a second storey of the Great Tower are only benches made of stones joined with earth, three of which may be seen rising behind one another like steps.† From this, as well as from the walls of the Tower and those of the Scæan Gate, I perceive that the Tower never can have been higher than it now is.

The excavations of the north side of the field belonging to Mr. Calvert, which I opened to discover other sculptures, have been stopped for some time, as I can no longer come to terms with him. At present, I have only two foremen, for I was obliged to dismiss Georgios Photidas, three weeks ago, for urgent reasons.

In conclusion, I have to mention that, during the Greek Easter festival, accompanied by my esteemed friend, Judge Schells of Ratisbon, and my wife, I visited Bunarbashi and the neighbouring heights. In their presence, I made some small excavations, and I have proved that even in the village the accumulation of *débris* amounts only to $1\frac{3}{4}$ foot in the court-yards of the buildings, and that upon and beside the street there is nothing but the virgin earth; further, that upon the small site of Gergis, at the end of the heights, which was formerly regarded as identical with Troy, the naked rock projects everywhere; and besides, in the accumulation of *débris*, which nowhere amounts to $1\frac{3}{4}$ foot in the town itself, and to only a little more in the Acropolis, I found nothing but fragments of pottery from the Hellenic period, that is, from the third and fifth centuries B.C.

---

* See Plan II., and Plan III. on p. 306, at the mark *b*.
† See Plan II., and *c* on Plan III., p. 306. Compare p. 213.

I must also add that I now positively retract my former opinion, that Ilium was inhabited up to the ninth century after Christ, and I must distinctly maintain that its site has been desolate and uninhabited since the end of the fourth century.   I had allowed myself to be deceived by the statements of my esteemed friend, Mr. Frank Calvert, of the Dardanelles, who maintained that there were documents to prove that the place had been inhabited up to the thirteenth and fourteenth centuries after Christ.   Such documents, if they really do exist, must necessarily refer to Alexandria Troas, which is always, as for instance in the New Testament, simply called Troas; for on its site quantities of Byzantine antiquities are found even on the surface, which seem to prove that the city was inhabited up to the fourteenth century, or still longer.   Here in Ilium, on the other hand, there is no trace of Byzantine architecture, of Byzantine sculpture, of Byzantine pottery, or of Byzantine coins. Altogether I found only two copper medals of Byzantine monasteries, which may have been lost by shepherds.   I found hundreds of coins belonging to the time of Constantine the Great, Constans II., but no medals whatever of the later emperors.

As hitherto it was in the Pergamus alone that I found no trace of the Byzantine period, I thought that it was only the fortress that was uninhabited during that period, but that the region of the city had been occupied. But my fifteen shafts, which I am having made on the most various points of the site of Ilium, as well as the two shafts made upon the primary soil, prove, as anyone may convince himself, that below the surface there is no trace of the Byzantine period, nay that, beyond a very thin layer of earth, which however only exists in some parts, the ruins of the Greek period extend up to the very surface, and that in several of the shafts I came upon the walls of Greek houses even on the surface.

It is impossible that a Byzantine town or a Byzantine village, nay, that even a single Byzantine house, can have stood upon this hilly and stone-hard ground, which covers the ruins of a primeval city, without leaving the most distinct traces of its existence, for here, where for nine or ten months of the year it never rains, except during rare thunderstorms, the productions of human industry do not become weather-beaten and destroyed, as in other countries where there is frequent rain. The very fragments of sculptures and inscriptions, which I find here in the Pergamus and in the other districts of the city, upon the surface, and which have lain exposed to the open air for at least 1500 years, are still almost as fresh as if they had been made yesterday.

Trusting to the statements of Mr. Frank Calvert, and under the impression that Ilium had been inhabited for a long time under the Byzantine dominion, I described the wall, composed of Corinthian pillars and cement, 10 feet thick, and which gave me so much trouble to break through at the south-east corner of the Pergamus, as of Byzantine architecture. (Pp. 230, 250.) I am now, however, forced to believe that the Temple of Athena, to which these pillars belong, was destroyed by the religious zeal of the first Christians as early as the reign of Constantine the Great, or at latest during that of Constantine II., and that this wall was built of its ruins about the same time.

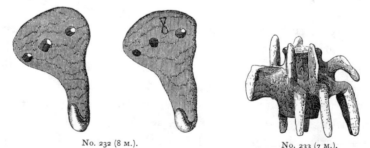

No. 232 (8 M.).   No. 233 (7 M.).

Curious Terra-cottas from the Trojan Stratum. Dr. Schliemann takes No. 232 for a pair of pegs for hanging up clothes. No. 233 is a strange animal figure, solid, except for a tube passing through the body and open at both ends, so that it cannot have been a vessel. Dr. Schliemann thinks it may represent the *chimæra* (*Iliad*, VI. 179, foll., "In front a lion, behind a serpent, and in the middle a chimæra"). In one sense, certainly, the name seems appropriate.

PLATE XIII.

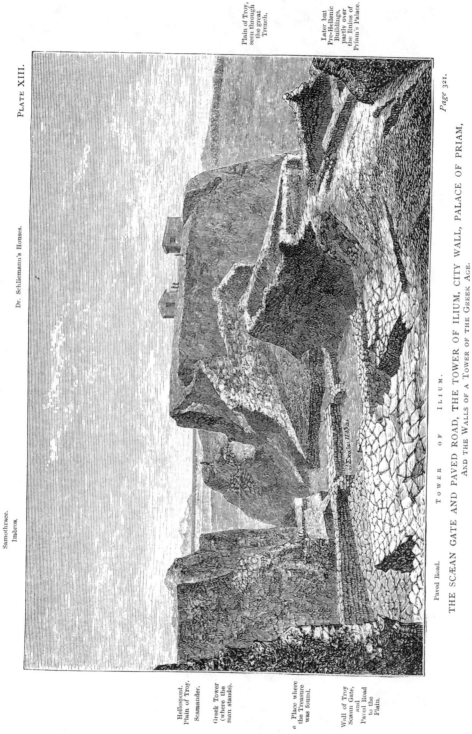

Samothrace.
Imbros.

Dr. Schliemann's Houses.

Plain of Troy,
seen through
the great
Trench.

Later but
Pre-Hellenic
Buildings,
partly over
the Ruins of
Priam's Palace.

Hellespont.
Plain of Troy.
Scamander.

Greek Tower
(where the
man stands).

αἱ Σκαιαὶ Πύλαι

a Place where
the Treasure
was found.

Wall of Troy
Scæan Gate,
and Paved Road
to the
Plain.

Paved Road.   T O W E R   O F   I L I U M.

THE SCÆAN GATE AND PAVED ROAD, THE TOWER OF ILIUM, CITY WALL, PALACE OF PRIAM,
AND THE WALLS OF A TOWER OF THE GREEK AGE.

From the South-East.

Page 321.

CHAPTER XXIII.

Further discoveries of fortifications — The *great discovery of the* TREASURE *on the city wall* — Expedient for its preservation — The articles of the Treasure described — The Shield — The Caldron — Bottle and Vases of Gold — The golden δέπας ἀμφικύπελλον — Modes of working the gold — A cup of electrum — Silver plates, probably the *talents* of Homer — Vessels of Silver — Copper lance-heads : their peculiar form — Copper battle-axes — Copper daggers — Metal articles fused together by the conflagration — A knife and a piece of a sword — Signs of the Treasure having been packed in a wooden chest — The Key found — The Treasure probably left behind in an effort to escape — Other articles found near the Treasure — The thousands of gold jewels found in a silver vase — The two golden Diadems — The ear-rings, bracelets, and finger-rings — The smaller jewels of gold — Analysis of the copper articles by M. Landerer — Discovery of another room in the Palace containing an inscribed stone, and curious terra-cottas — Silver dishes — Greek terra-cotta figures — Great abundance of the owl-faced vases.

Limited extent of Troy — Its walls traced — Poetic exaggerations of Homer — *The one great point of* TROY'S *reality established* — It was as large as the primitive Athens and Mycenæ — The wealth and power of Troy — Great height of its houses — Probable population — Troy known to Homer only by tradition — Question of a Temple in Homer's time — Characteristics of the Trojan stratum of remains, and their difference from those of the lowest stratum — The former opinion on this point recalled — Layer of metallic *scoriæ* through the whole hill — Error of Strabo about the utter destruction of Troy — Part of the real Troy unfortunately destroyed in the earlier excavations ; but many Trojan houses brought to light since — The stones of Troy not used in building other cities — The Trojan houses of sun-dried bricks, except the most important buildings, which are of stones and earth — Extent and results of the excavations — Advice to future explorers.

Further excavations on the North side — Very curious terra-cotta vessels — Perforated vases — A terra-cotta with hieroglyphics — Heads of oxen and horses ; their probable significance — Idols of the Ilian Athena — Greek and Roman medals — Greek inscriptions — Final close of the excavations : thanksgiving for freedom from serious accidents — Commendations of Nicolaus Saphyros Jannakis, and other assistants, and of the artist Polychronios Tempesis and the engineer Adolphe Laurent.

Troy, June 17th, 1873.

SINCE my report of the 10th of last month I have been
especially anxious to hasten the great excavation on the
north-west side of the hill, and for this purpose I have made
a deep cutting on the west side also, in which, unfortunately,
I came obliquely upon the enclosing wall of Lysimachus,
which is 13 feet high and 10 feet thick. I was therefore
compelled to break out from this wall a double quantity of
stones in order to gain an entrance; but I again came upon
the ruins of colossal buildings of the Hellenic and pre-
Hellenic periods, so that this excavation can only proceed
slowly. Here, at a distance of 69 feet from the declivity
of the hill, at a depth of 20 feet, I met with an ancient
enclosure 5 feet high, and with a projecting battlement. It
is not connected with the wall which runs out from the
Scæan Gate in a north-westerly direction, and, on account of
its very different structure and small height, it must belong
to a post-Trojan period. In any case, however, it is much
older than the Greek colony, because it is built of stones
and earth, and because I found by the side of it several
marble idols of the tutelar goddess of Ilium. I am, unfortunately, obliged to break down a portion of this wall to
a length of 17½ feet, in order to proceed further, but I have
left standing nearly 8 feet of the part I have excavated,
so that the wall may be examined. Behind it I found a
level place paved partly with large flags of stone, partly
with stones more or less hewn, and after this a wall of
fortification 20 feet high and 5 feet thick, built of large
stones and earth; it runs below my wooden house, but
6½ feet above the Trojan city wall which proceeds from
the Scæan Gate.

In the new large excavation on the north-west side,
which is connected with the one I have just been describing,
I have convinced myself that the splendid wall of large
hewn stones, which I uncovered in April 1870, belongs to

a tower, the lower projecting part of which must have been built during the first period of the Greek colony, whereas its upper portion seems to belong to the time of Lysimachus. (See Plate XIII.) To this tower also belongs the wall that I mentioned in my last report as 9 feet high and 6 feet broad, and as continuous with the surrounding wall of Lysimachus; and so does the wall of the same dimensions, situated 49 feet from it, which I have likewise broken through. Behind the latter, at a depth of from 26 to 30 feet, I uncovered the Trojan city wall which runs out from the Scæan Gate.

In excavating this wall further and directly by the side of the palace of King Priam,* I came upon a large copper article of the most remarkable form, which attracted my attention all the more as I thought I saw gold behind it. On the top of this copper article lay a stratum of red and calcined ruins, from $4\frac{3}{4}$ to $5\frac{1}{4}$ feet thick, as hard as stone, and above this again lay the above-mentioned wall of forti-fication (6 feet broad and 20 feet high) which was built of large stones and earth, and must have belonged to an early date after the destruction of Troy. In order to withdraw the Treasure from the greed of my workmen, and to save it for archæology, I had to be most expeditious, and although it was not yet time for breakfast, I immediately had "païdos" called. This is a word of uncertain derivation, which has passed over into Turkish, and is here employed in place of ἀνάπαυσις, or time for rest. While the men were eating and resting, I cut out the Treasure with a large knife, which it was impossible to do without the very greatest exertion and the most fearful risk of my life, for the great fortification-wall, beneath which I had to dig, threatened every moment to fall down upon me. But the sight of so many objects, every one of which is of inesti-mable value to archæology, made me foolhardy, and I never thought of any danger. It would, however, have been im-

---

* See the spot marked on Plan II. No. 42, and Plate XIII. a.

possible for me to have removed the Treasure without the
help of my dear wife, who stood by me ready to pack the
things which I cut out in her shawl and to carry them away.*

The first thing I found was a large copper shield (the
ἀσπὶς ὀμφαλόεσσα of Homer) in the form of an oval salver,
in the middle of which is a knob or boss encircled by a
small furrow (αὖλαξ). This shield is a little less than 20
inches in length; it is quite flat, and surrounded by a rim
(ἄντυξ) $1\frac{1}{2}$ inch high; the boss (ὀμφαλός) is $2\frac{1}{3}$ inches high
and $4\frac{1}{3}$ inches in diameter; the furrow encircling it is 7
inches in diameter and $\frac{2}{5}$ of an inch deep.†

---

* The articles belonging to the Treasure are partly engraved on seven
separate Plates (XIV.—XX.), and partly marked with Tr. in the cuts.
They were found at a depth of $8\frac{1}{2}$ meters, nearly 28 feet. The *General
View of the Treasure* (Plate III., opposite p. 22) shows a few objects
which are either so like others, or so insignificant, as not to need a
separate delineation.

† See Plate XIV., No. 234. This round shield of copper (or bronze?),
with its central boss, and the furrow and rim so suitable for holding
together a covering of ox-hides, reminds us irresistibly of the seven-fold
shield of Ajax :—*Iliad*, VII. 219–223 (cf. 245–247) :—

> Αἴας δ' ἐγγύθεν ἦλθε φέρων σάκος ἠΰτε πύργον,
> Χάλκεον ἑπταβόειον, ὅ οἱ Τυχίος κάμε τεύχων,
> Σκυτοτόμων ὄχ' ἄριστος, Ὕλῃ ἔνι οἰκία ναίων,
> Ὅς οἱ ἐποίησεν σάκος αἰόλον ἑπταβόειον,
> Ταύρων ζατρεφέων, ἐπὶ δ' ὄγδοον ἤλασε χαλκόν.

> " Ajax approached ; before him, as a tower,
>   His mighty shield he bore, seven-fold, brass-bound,
>   The work of Tychius, best artificer
>   That wrought in leather ; he in Hyla dwelt.
>   Of seven-fold hides the ponderous shield was wrought
>   Of lusty bulls : the eighth was glittering brass."

It is equally striking to compare the shield of the Treasure with the
description of Sarpedon's shield, with its round plate of hammered
copper (or bronze), and its covering of ox-hides, fastened to the inner
edge of the rim by gold wires or rivets (*Iliad*, XII. 294–297) :—

> Αὐτίκα δ' ἀσπίδα μὲν πρόσθ' ἔσχετο πάντοσ' ἐΐσην
> Καλὴν χαλκείην ἐξήλατον, ἣν ἄρα χαλκεὺς
> Ἤλασεν, ἔντοσθεν δὲ βοείας ῥάψε θαμειὰς
> Χρυσείῃς ῥάβδοισι διηνεκέσιν περὶ κύκλον.

[" His

PLATE XIV.

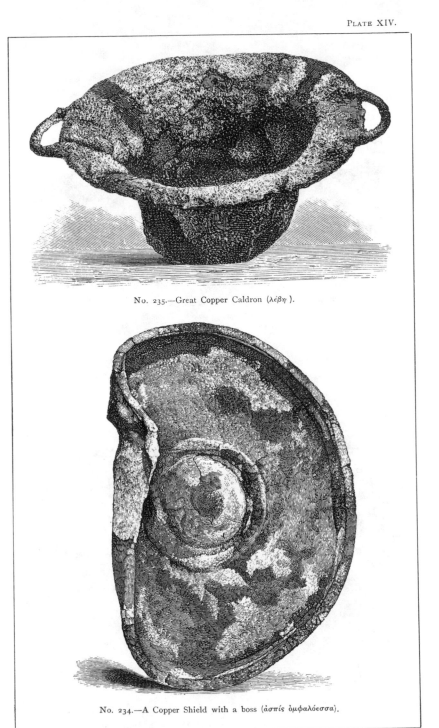

No. 235.—Great Copper Caldron (λέβη).

No. 234.—A Copper Shield with a boss (ἀσπίς ὀμφαλόεσσα).

THE TREASURE OF PRIAM.   *Page 324.*

PLATE XV.

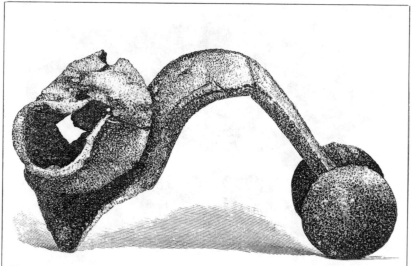

No. 236.—Curious Plate of Copper (perhaps a Hasp of the Chest), with Discs fixed on one end, and a Silver Vase welded to the other by the conflagration.

No. 237.—Bottle of pure Gold, weighing about 1 lb. Troy.

No. 238.—Cup of pure Gold, panelled, weighing 7¼ oz. Troy.

THE TREASURE OF PRIAM.

The second object which I got out was a copper cal-dron with two horizontal handles, which certainly gives us an idea of the Homeric λέβης; it is 16½ inches in diameter and 5½ inches high; the bottom is flat, and is nearly 8 inches in diameter.*

The third object was a copper plate $\frac{2}{5}$ of an inch thick, 6⅓ inches broad, and 17⅓ inches long; it has a rim about $\frac{1}{12}$ of an inch high; at one end of it there are two im-movable wheels with an axle-tree. This plate is very much bent in two places, but I believe that these curvatures have been produced by the heat to which the article was exposed in the conflagration; a silver vase 4¾ inches high and broad has been fused to it; I suppose, however, that this also happened by accident in the heat of the fire.†
The fourth article I brought out was a copper vase 5½ inches high and 4⅓ inches in diameter. Thereupon followed a globular bottle of the purest gold, weighing 403 grammes (6220 grains, or above 1 lb. troy); it is nearly 6 inches high and 5½ inches in diameter, and has the com-mencement of a zigzag decoration on the neck, which, however, is not continued all round. Then came a cup, likewise of the purest gold, weighing 226 grammes (7¼ oz. troy); it is 3½ inches high and 3 inches broad.‡

" His shield's broad *orb* before his breast he bore,
Well wrought, *of beaten brass*, which the armourer's hand
Had beaten out, and lined with stout bull's hide
With golden rods, continuous, all around."—[ED.]

* See Plate XIV., No. 235. In the Iliad the λέβης is used almost always as a caldron, and is often given as a prize at games; in the Odyssey it is always used for washing the hands or feet. This one shows the marks of a fearful conflagration, and near the left handle are seen two fragments of copper weapons (a lance and a battle-axe) firmly molten on. (Description to the Atlas of Photographs.)
† See Plate XV., No. 236. This remarkable object lay at the top of the whole mass, and Dr. Schliemann supposes it to have formed a hasp to the lid of the wooden chest in which the Treasure was packed. (Description in Atlas.)
‡ These vessels of gold are shown on Plate XV., Nos. 237, 238.

Next came another cup of the purest gold, weighing exactly 600 grammes (about 1 lb. 6 oz. troy) ;* it is $3\frac{1}{2}$ inches high, $7\frac{1}{4}$ inches long, and $7\frac{1}{5}$ inches broad ; it is in the form of a ship with two large handles ; on one side there is a mouth, $1\frac{1}{5}$ inch broad, for drinking out of, and another at the other side, which is $2\frac{3}{4}$ inches broad, and, as my esteemed friend Professor Stephanos Kumanudes, of Athens, remarks, the person who presented the filled cup may have first drunk from the small mouth, as a mark of respect, to let the guest drink from the larger mouth.† This vessel has a foot which projects about $\frac{1}{12}$ of an inch, and is $1\frac{1}{3}$ inch long, and $\frac{4}{5}$ of an inch broad. It is assuredly the Homeric δέπας ἀμφι-κύπελλον. But I adhere to my supposition that all of those tall and brilliant red goblets of terra-cotta, in the form of champagne-glasses with two enormous handles, are also δέπα ἀμφικύπελλα, and that this form probably existed in gold also. I must further make an observation which is very important for the history of art, that the above-mentioned gold δέπας ἀμφικύπελλον is of *cast gold*, and

---

* Plate XVI., Nos. 239, 240.

† Or, as suggested in the 'Quarterly Review' for April 1874, a person, holding the cup before him by the two handles, may have poured a libation from the further spout and then have drunk out of the nearer. Thus Achilles used a choice goblet (δέπας) for drinking wine and pouring libations to the gods. (*Iliad*, XVI., 225–228.)

We are indebted to Mr. J. W. Lockhart for the following account of a double-spouted boat-shaped bronze vessel, used in a similar manner in the Chinese temples :—"In China there is a vessel of very nearly the same shape, but with ears prolonged till they rise an inch above the cup : the cup stands on three legs and is, in fact, a tripod. Such cups are used in the temples, especially in the ancestral temples of the real religion of China, when offerings are made to the *manes* of ancestors. The cups are filled with wine, when placed on the altar before the idol shrine, or before the ancestral tablet ; and the wine is afterwards partly drunk and partly poured out as a libation." Such vessels are used in pairs, and our drawing is made from one of a pair in Mr. Lockhart's possession. It is of *bronze*, 6 inches long, and $6\frac{1}{2}$ inches high, including the legs. The width is 2 inches between the upright ears, and $2\frac{3}{8}$ inches at the broadest part. There is only *one* handle. Mr. Lockhart calls

PLATE XVI.

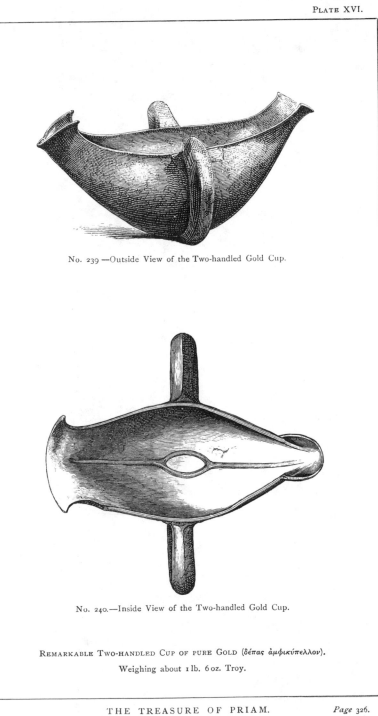

No. 239 —Outside View of the Two-handled Gold Cup.

No. 240.—Inside View of the Two-handled Gold Cup.

REMARKABLE TWO-HANDLED CUP OF PURE GOLD (δέπας ἀμφικύπελλον).

Weighing about 1 lb. 6 oz. Troy.

THE TREASURE OF PRIAM. *Page* 326.

that the large handles, which are not solid, have been fused on to it.   On the other hand the gold bottle and the gold cup mentioned above have been *wrought with the hammer*.

No. 241.   Bronze Cup used in China for Libations and Drinking.

The Treasure further contained a small cup of gold alloyed with 20 per cent. of silver, that is. the mixed metal called *electrum*.*   It weighs 70 grammes (2¼ oz. troy), and is above 3 inches high, and above 2½ inches broad.   Its foot is only ⅘ of an inch high and nearly an inch broad, and is

---

attention to the " key" ornament round the cup, which is so well known in the purest Greek art, as a sign of Chinese influence on the art of Western Asia and Europe.   Mr. Lockhart also reads Chinese characters on some of the Trojan whorls.   We are under a deep obligation to Mr. Lockhart for his spontaneous offer of this very interesting illustration of one of the most striking and (as we before supposed) *unique* objects discovered by Dr. Schliemann.—[ED.]

* Plate XVIII., No. 248.

moreover not quite straight, so that the cup appears to be meant only to stand upon its mouth.

I also found in the Treasure six pieces of the purest silver in the form of large knife-blades, having one end rounded, and the other cut into the form of a crescent; they have all been wrought with the hammer.* The two larger blades are nearly 8½ inches long and 2 inches broad, and weigh respectively 190 and 183 grammes. The next two pieces are about 7¼ inches long and 1½ broad, and weigh respectively 174 and 173 grammes. The two other pieces are nearly 7 inches long and 1⅕ inch broad, and weigh respectively 173 and 171 grammes.† It is extremely probable that these are the Homeric *talents* (τάλαντα), which could only have been small, as, for instance, when Achilles offers for the first prize a woman, for the second a horse, for the third a caldron, and for the fourth two gold talents.‡

---

* See Plate XVII., No. 242.

† The two largest weigh, respectively, a little over and a little under 6 oz., and the other four are all a little over 5½ oz., troy. The *gramme* is 15·43235 grains, that is, a little less than 15½ grains.

‡ *Iliad*, XXIII. 262–270 (cf. vv. 612–616). The passage furnishes other striking parallels to Dr. Schliemann's discoveries. The *tripod with ears containing 22 measures*, which is added to the woman for the first prize (καὶ τρίποδ' ὠτώεντα δυωκαιεικοσίμετρον) calls to mind the vessel from the Trojan stratum, No. 199, p. 285. The *fifth* prize is a *double-handled flat cup (or dish) untouched by fire*, i. e. wrought with the hammer (ἀμφίθετον φιάλην ἀπύρωτον ἔθηκεν). The *metal* is not specified, but its coming next to the two *gold talents* suggests *silver*, and Dr. Schliemann found silver φίαλαι with side-rings in the Treasure and the Palace. The passage seems to confirm Schliemann's interpretation of δέπας ἀμφικύπελλον, for what sort of a vessel can we conceive of as a double dish joined bottom to bottom? We know side-dishes with their covers can be used as two dishes, but what would be the use of joining them? Aristarchus, indeed, explained ἀμφίθετος as *double*, i.e. *standing on both ends*, after the supposed analogy of ἀμφικύπελλον, but Eustathius interpreted it as *with handles on both sides*, after the sounder analogy of ἀμφιφορεύς. These cumulative analogies between Hissarlik and Homer, gathered incidentally to a climax at the end of each work, are very striking.—[Ed.]

Plate XVII.

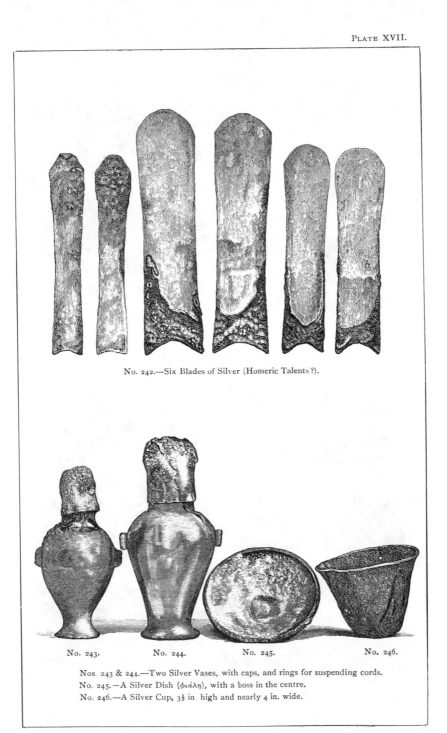

No. 242.—Six Blades of Silver (Homeric Talents ?).

No. 243.   No. 244.   No. 245.   No. 246.

Nos. 243 & 244.—Two Silver Vases, with caps, and rings for suspending cords.
No. 245.—A Silver Dish (φιάλη), with a boss in the centre.
No. 246.—A Silver Cup, 3⅜ in. high and nearly 4 in. wide.

THE TREASURE OF PRIAM.   *Page* 328.

PLATE XVIII.

No. 247.—A small Silver Cover.

No. 248.—A small Cup of Electrum, (*i.e.* 4 parts of Gold to 1 of Silver).

No. 249.—Large Silver Jug, with handle, in which the small Ornaments were found.

No. 251.

No. 250.

No. 250.—Has part of another Silver Vase welded to it by the fire.

No. 251.—Silver Vàse with a quantity of copper fixed to its bottom by the fire.

VESSELS OF SILVER AND ELECTRUM.

THE TREASURE OF PRIAM.

I also found in the Treasure three great silver vases, the largest of which is above 8¼ inches high and nearly 8 inches in diameter, and has a handle 5½ inches in length and 3½ in breadth.* The second vase is 6·9 inches high and nearly 6 inches in diameter; another silver vase is welded to the upper part of it, of which, however, only portions have been preserved.† The third vase is above 7 inches high and above 6 inches in diameter; the foot of the vase has a great deal of copper fused onto it, which must have dripped from the copper objects contained in the Treasure during the conflagration.‡ All of the three vases are perfectly round below, and therefore cannot stand upright without resting against something.

I found, further, a silver goblet above 3⅓ inches high, the mouth of which is nearly 4 inches in diameter; also a silver flat cup or dish (φιάλη) 5½ inches in diameter, and two beautiful small silver vases of most exquisite workmanship. The larger one, which has two rings on either side for hanging it up by strings, is nearly 8 inches high with its hat-shaped lid, and 3½ inches in diameter across the bulge. The smaller silver vase, with a ring on either side for suspension by a string, is about 6¾ inches high, with its lid, and above 3 inches broad. §

Upon and beside the gold and silver articles, I found thirteen copper lances, from nearly 7 to above 12½ inches in length, and from above 1½ to 2⅓ inches broad at the broadest point; at the lower end of each is a hole, in which, in most cases, the nail or peg which fastened the lance to the wooden handle is still sticking. The pin-hole is clearly visible in a lance-head which the conflagration

---

* See Plate XVIII., No. 249.

† Ibid., No. 250.

‡ Ibid., No. 251.

§ For these four vessels see Plate XVII., Nos. 243–246. The silver bottles, with the caps and the side-rings to both, remind us of modern travelling flasks.—[ED.]

No. 252.   No. 253.   No. 254.   No. 255.   No. 256.

Trojan Lance-Heads of Copper.—TR.

No. 256.   Copper Lance and Battle-Axe welded together by the Conflagration.   The Pin-hole
of the Lance is visible.—TR.

No. 257.   No. 258.   No. 259.   No. 26c.

Trojan Battle-Axes of Copper.—TR.

Nos. 258 and 260 have pieces of other weapons welded onto them by the fire.

has welded to a battle-axe. The Trojan lances were therefore quite different from those of the Greeks and Romans, for the latter stuck the shaft into the lance-head, the former fastened the head into the shaft.

I also found fourteen of those copper weapons, which are frequently met with here, but which have never been discovered elsewhere; at one end they are pointed but blunt, and at the other they end in a broad edge. I formerly considered them to be a species of lance, but now after mature considera-tion I am convinced that they could have been used only as battle-axes. They are from above 6 to above 12 inches in length, from nearly ½ to above ¾ of an inch thick, and from above 1 to nearly 3 inches broad; the largest of them weighs 1365 grammes (about 3 lbs. avoirdu-pois). The following cut shows an axe more like those of later ages.

No. 261.
Trojan Battle-axe.
—Tr.

There were also seven large double-edged copper daggers, with a handle from about 2 to 2¾ inches long, the end of which is bent round at a right angle. These handles must at one time have been encased in wood, for if the cases had been made of bone they would still have been wholly or partially preserved. The pointed handle was inserted into a piece of wood, so that the end projected about half an inch beyond it, and this end was simply bent round. (See page 332.) The largest of these daggers is 10⅔ inches in length and above 2 inches broad at the broadest part; a second dagger, which is above 1¾ inch broad, has the point broken off, and is now less than 9 inches long, but appears to have been 11 inches; a third dagger is 8⅔ inches long, and measures above 1¼ inch at the broadest point; a fourth has become com-pletely curled up in the conflagration, but appears to have been above 11 inches long. Of the fifth, sixth, and seventh daggers I only discovered the fragments; these are from nearly 4 to 5⅓ inches in length. But in a packet of four

lances and battle-axes, which have been welded together in
the heat of the fire, I believe I can recognise another dagger.

Of common one-edged knives I only found one in the
Treasure; it is above 6 inches in length. I also found a
piece of a sword which is $8\frac{2}{3}$ inches long and nearly 2 inches

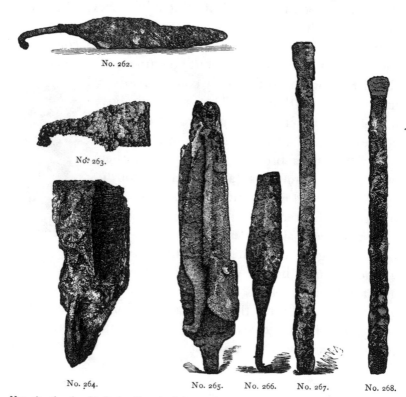

No. 262.

No. 263.

No. 264.   No. 265.   No. 266.   No. 267.   No. 268.

Nos. 262, 263, 264, 266, Trojan Two-edged Copper Daggers, with hooked Stems that have been
fastened into Wooden Handles; No. 264 is doubled up by the Conflagration. No. 265, Weapons
molten together. No. 267, a Copper Sword-Blade, with a sharp edge at the end. No. 268, a
Four-sided Copper Bar, ending in a sharp edge.—Tr.

broad: also a four-cornered copper bar ending in an edge;
it is nearly 15 inches long, and also appears to have served
as a weapon.

As I found all these articles together, forming a rect-
angular mass, or packed into one another, it seems to
be certain that they were placed on the city wall in a
wooden chest (φωριαμός), such as those mentioned by

Homer as being in the palace of King Priam.* This appears to be the more certain, as close by the side of these articles I found a copper key above 4 inches long, the head of which (about 2 inches long and broad) greatly resembles a large safe-key of a bank. Curiously enough this key has had a wooden handle; there can be no doubt of this from the fact that the

No. 269. Copper Key, supposed to have belonged to the Trea-sure-chest.—TR.

end of the stalk of the key is bent round at a right angle, as in the case of the daggers.

It is probable that some member of the family of King Priam hurriedly packed the Treasure into the chest and carried it off without having time to pull out the key; that when he reached the wall, however, the hand of an enemy or the fire overtook him, and he was obliged to abandon the chest, which was immediately covered to a height of from 5 to 6 feet with the red ashes and the stones of the adjoining royal palace.

Perhaps the articles found a few days previously in a room of the royal palace, close to the place where the Treasure was discovered, belonged to this unfortunate person. These articles were a helmet, and a silver vase

---

* _Iliad_, XXIV. 228:—ʼΗ, καὶ φωριαμῶν ἐπιθήματα κάλ᾽ ἀνέῳγεν, where the " beautiful lids" remind us of the terra-cotta pattern which Dr. Schliemann takes for the inlaying of a chest. (No. 77, p. 129). In the _Iliad_, XVI., 221, Achilles opens the lid of the beautiful deco-rated chest (χηλοῦ δ᾽ ἀπὸ πῶμ᾽ ἀνέῳγεν καλῆς δαιδαλέης), to take out the goblet for pouring his libation. The contents of Priam's chests may also be well compared with the articles of the Treasure :—

> " He chose twelve gorgeous shawls, twelve single cloaks,
> As many rugs, as many splendid robes,
> As many tunics ; then of gold he took
> Ten _talents_ full ; two tripods, burnished bright,
> Four _caldrons_ ; then a _cup of beauty rare_,
> A rich possession, which the men of Thrace
> Had given, when there he went ambassador ;
> E'en this he spared not, such his keen desire
> His son to ransom."—[ED.]

7 inches high and 5½ inches broad, containing an elegant cup of electrum 4⅓ inches high and 3½ inches broad. The helmet was broken in being taken out, but I can have it mended, as I have all the pieces of it. The two upper

No. 270.   No. 271.
Cups of Electrum and Silver. Found in the Palace, near the Treasure, 270 inside 271.

Nos. 272–275.   Pieces of Helmet-crests found in a Room of the Palace.

portions, composing the crest (φάλος), are uninjured. Beside the helmet, as before, I found a curved copper pin, nearly 6 inches in length, which must have been in some way attached to it, and have served some purpose. (Compare No. 192, p. 281.)

At 5 or 6 feet above the Treasure, the successors of the Trojans erected a fortification wall 20 feet high and 6 feet broad, composed of large hewn and unhewn stones and earth; this wall extends to within 3¼ feet of the surface of the hill.

That the Treasure was packed together at terrible risk of life, and in the greatest anxiety, is proved among other things also by the contents of the largest silver vase,

PLATE XIX.

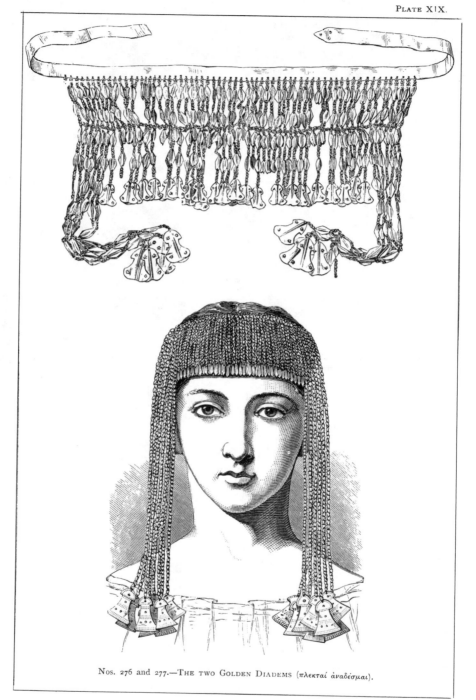

Nos. 276 and 277.—THE TWO GOLDEN DIADEMS (πλεκταί ἀναδέσμαι).

THE TREASURE OF PRIAM.

at the bottom of which I found two splendid gold diadems (κρήδεμνα)* ; a fillet, and four beautiful gold ear-rings of most exquisite workmanship : upon these lay 56 gold ear-rings of exceedingly curious form and 8750 small gold rings, perforated prisms and dice, gold buttons, and similar jewels, which obviously belonged to other ornaments ; then followed six gold bracelets, and on the top of all the two small gold goblets.†

The one diadem consists of a gold fillet, $21\frac{2}{3}$ inches long and nearly $\frac{1}{2}$ an inch broad, from which there hang on either side seven little chains to cover the temples, each of which has eleven square leaves with a groove ; these chains are joined to one another by four little cross chains, at the end of which hangs a glittering golden idol of the tutelar goddess of Troy, nearly an inch long. The entire length of each of these chains, with the idols, amounts to $10\frac{1}{4}$ inches. Almost all these idols have something of the human form, but the owl's head with the two large eyes cannot be mistaken ; their breadth at the lower end is about $\frac{9}{10}$ of an inch. Between these ornaments for the temples there are 47 little

---

* The diadem discovered by Dr. Schliemann can scarcely have been the κρήδεμνον of Homer, which was a large veil or mantilla, such, for instance, as the sea-goddess Ino gives to Ulysses, to buoy him up on the water (*Od.* v. 346). This diadem would rather seem to be, as Mr. Gladstone has suggested, the πλεκτὴ ἀναδέσμη, which Andromache casts from her head in her mourning for Hector, where the order of the words implies that it was worn over the κρήδεμνον. *Il.* XXII. 469–471 :—

Τῆλε δ' ἀπὸ κρατὸς βάλε δέσματα σιγαλόεντα,
Ἄμπυκα κεκρύφαλόν τε ἰδὲ πλεκτὴν ἀναδέσμην
Κρήδεμνόν θ', ὅ ῥά οἱ δῶκε χρυσέη Ἀφροδίτη.

" Far off were flung the adornments of her head,
    The net, the *fillet*, and the *woven band*,
    The nuptial-veil by golden Venus given."—[ED.]

Our illustration (Plate XIX., Nos. 276, 277) represents one diadem as set up by Dr. Schliemann, and the other as it might have been worn on the head of a Trojan lady.—[ED.]

† These objects are more fully described, and figured, in the following pages.

pendant chains adorned with square leaves; at the end of each little chain is an idol of the tutelary goddess of Ilium, about ¾ of an inch long; the length of these little chains with the idols is not quite 4 inches.

The other diadem is 20 inches long, and consists of a gold chain, from which are suspended on each side eight chains completely covered with small gold leaves, to hang down over the temples, and at the end of every one of the sixteen chains there hangs a golden idol 1¼ inch long, with the owl's head of the Ilian tutelary goddess. Between these ornaments for the temples there are likewise 74 little chains, about 4 inches long, covered with gold leaves, to hang down over the forehead; at the end of these chains there hangs a double leaf about ¾ of an inch long.

The fillet ἄμπυξ is above 18 inches long and ⅖ of an inch broad, and has three perforations at each end. Eight quadruple rows of dots divide it into nine compartments, in each of which there are two large dots; and an uninterrupted row of dots adorns the whole edge. Of the four ear-rings only two are exactly alike. From the upper part, which is almost in the shape of a basket, and is ornamented with two rows of decorations in the form of beads, there hang six small chains on which are three little cylinders; attached to the end of the chains are small idols of the tutelar goddess of Troy. The length of each ear-ring is 3½ inches. The upper part of the other two ear-rings is larger and thicker, but likewise almost in the shape of a basket, from it are suspended five little chains entirely covered with small round leaves, on which are likewise fastened small but more imposing idols of the Ilian tutelar divinity; the length of one of these pendants is 3½ inches, that of the other a little over 3 inches.*

---

* See Plate XX., Nos. 279, 280, for a representation of the fillet and ear-rings. The four " ear-rings " remind us, both by their *form* and *material*, of the " *beautifully twined tassels of solid gold* " which fringed the *Ægis* of Athena : *Iliad*, II. 448, 449 :—

PLATE XX.

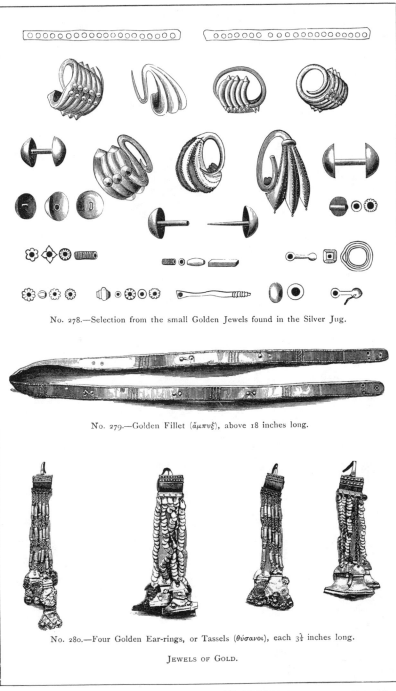

No. 278.—Selection from the small Golden Jewels found in the Silver Jug.

No. 279.—Golden Fillet (ἄμπυξ), above 18 inches long.

No. 280.—Four Golden Ear-rings, or Tassels (θύσανοι), each 3½ inches long.

JEWELS OF GOLD.

Of the six gold bracelets, two are quite simple and closed, and are about $\frac{1}{5}$ of an inch thick; a third is likewise closed, but consists of an ornamented band $\frac{1}{25}$ of an inch thick, and $\frac{1}{4}$ of an inch broad. The other three are double, and the ends are turned round and furnished with a head. The princesses who wore these bracelets must have had unusually small hands, for they are so small that a girl of ten would have difficulty in putting them on.

No. 281.
Six golden Bracelets welded together by the conflagration.
—[Tr.]

The 56 other gold ear-rings are of various sizes, and three of them appear to have also been used by the princesses of the royal family as finger-rings.* Not one of the ear-rings has any resemblance in form to the Hellenic, Roman, Egyptian, or Assyrian ear-rings; 20 of them end in four leaves, ten in three leaves, lying beside one another and soldered together, and they are thus extremely like those ear-rings of gold and electrum which I found last year at a depth of 9 and 13 meters (29½ and 42½ feet). Eighteen other ear-rings end in six leaves; at the commencement of these there are two small studs,

---

Τῆς ἑκατὸν θύσανοι παγχρύσεοι ἠερέθονται,
Πάντες ἐϋπλεκέες, ἑκατόμβοιος δὲ ἕκαστος.

"all around
A hundred tassels hung, rare works of art,
All gold, each one a hundred oxen's price."

Again, when Hera adorns herself to captivate Jove, her zone is fringed with a hundred tassels, and her *ear-rings* are described in terms corresponding exactly to the *triple leaves* seen on some of Schliemann's (*Iliad*, XIV. 181–3) :—

Ζώσατο δὲ ζώνην ἑκατὸν θυσάνοις ἀραρυῖαν,
Ἐν δ' ἄρα ἕρματα ἧκεν ἐϋτρήτοισι λοβοῖσιν
Τρίγληνα μορόεντα· χάρις δ' ἀπελάμπετο πολλή.

"Her zone, from which a hundred tassels hung,
She girt about her; and, *in three bright drops*,
Her glittering gems suspended from her ears;
And all around her grace and beauty shone."—[Ed.]

* Some of these are shown on Plate XX., No. 278.

in the centre two rows of five small studs each, and at the end three small studs. Two of the largest rings, which, owing to the thickness of the one end, certainly cannot have been used as ear-rings, and appear to have been finger-rings only, terminate in four leaves, and at the commencement of these there are two, in the middle three, and at the end again two small studs. Of the remaining ear-rings two have the form of three, and four the form of two, beautifully ornamented serpents lying beside one another.

Besides the ear-rings, a great number of other ornaments strung on threads, or fastened on leather, had been put into the same large silver vase; for above and below them, as already said, I found 8750 small objects;* such as gold rings, only $\frac{1}{8}$ of an inch in diameter; perforated dice, either smooth or in the form of little indented stars, about $\frac{1}{6}$ of an inch in diameter; gold perforated prisms $\frac{1}{10}$ of an inch high and $\frac{1}{8}$ of an inch broad, decorated longitudinally with eight or sixteen incisions; small leaves about $\frac{1}{5}$ of an inch long, and $\frac{1}{6}$ of an inch broad, and pierced longitudinally with a hole for threading them; small gold pegs $\frac{1}{3}$ of an inch long, with a button on one side, and a perforated hole on the other; perforated prisms about $\frac{1}{5}$ of an inch long and $\frac{1}{10}$ of an inch broad; double or triple gold rings soldered together and only $\frac{1}{4}$ of an inch in diameter, with holes on both sides for threading them; gold buttons or studs $\frac{1}{5}$ of an inch high, in the cavity of which is a ring above $\frac{1}{10}$ of an inch broad for sewing them on; gold double buttons, exactly like our shirt studs, $\frac{3}{10}$ of an inch long, which, however, are not soldered, but simply stuck together, for from the cavity of the one button there projects a tube

---

* Dr. Schliemann has strung these in two sets, one of which, consisting of 4610 pieces, is represented as Cut No. 282. The other set, of 4090 pieces, is precisely similar. The small jewels described are shown in detail on Plate XX., No. 278.

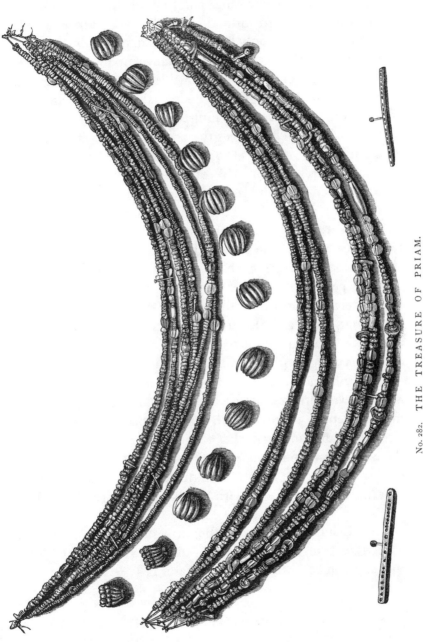

No. 282. THE TREASURE OF PRIAM.

4610 SMALL JEWELS OF GOLD.

(αὐλίσκος) nearly $\frac{1}{4}$ of an inch long, and from the other a pin (ἔμβολον) of the same length, and the pin is merely stuck into the tube to form the double stud. These double buttons or studs can only have been used, probably, as ornament upon leather articles, for instance upon the handle-straps (τελαμῶνες) of swords, shields, or knives. I found in the vase also two gold cylinders above $\frac{1}{10}$ of an inch thick and $\frac{3}{4}$ of an inch long; also a small gold peg above $\frac{4}{5}$ of an inch in length, and from $\frac{6}{100}$ to $\frac{8}{100}$ of an inch thick; it has at one end a perforated hole for hanging it up, and on the other side six encircling incisions, which give the article the appearance of a screw; it is only by means of a magnifying glass that it is found not to be really a screw. I also found in the same vase two pieces of gold, one of which is $\frac{1}{7}$ of an inch, the other above 2 inches, long; each of them has 21 perforations.*

The person who endeavoured to save the Treasure had fortunately the presence of mind to stand the silver vase, containing the valuable articles described above, upright in the chest, so that not so much as a bead could fall out, and everything has been preserved uninjured.

My esteemed friend M. Landerer, of Athens, a chemist well known through his discoveries and writings, who has most carefully examined all the copper articles of the Treasure, and analysed the fragments, finds that all of them consist of pure copper without any admixture of tin or zinc,† and that, in order to make them more durable, they have been wrought with the hammer (σφυρήλατον).

As I hoped to find other treasures here, and also wished to bring to light the wall that surrounded Troy, the erection of which Homer ‡ ascribes to Poseidon and

---

* See Plate XX., at top.

† The subsequent analysis by M. Damour, of Lyon, has, however, shown the presence of tin in some of the articles of the Treasure, see Note C, p. 361.—[ED.]   ‡ *Iliad*, VII. 452–453.

Apollo, as far as the Scæan Gate, I have entirely cut away the upper wall, which rested partly upon the gate, to an extent of 56 feet. Visitors to the Troad can, however, still see part of it in the north-western earth-wall opposite the Scæan Gate. I have also broken down the enormous block of earth which separated my western and north-western cutting from the Great Tower; but in order to do this, I had to pull down the larger one of my wooden houses, and I had also to bridge over the Scæan Gate, so as to facilitate the removal of the *débris*. The result of this new excavation is very important to archæology; for I have been able to uncover several walls, and also a room of the Royal Palace, 20 feet in length and breadth, upon which no buildings of a later period rest.

No. 283.   Terra-cotta Vessel in the shape of a Cask.   From the Palace (8 M.).

Of the objects discovered there I have only to mention an excellently engraved inscription found upon a square piece of red slate, which has two holes not bored through it and an encircling incision, but neither can my learned friend Émile Burnouf nor can I tell in what language the inscription is written.* Further, there were some interesting terra-cottas, among which is a vessel, quite the form of a modern cask, and with a tube in the centre for pouring

---

* No. 5, on p. 24.   (See Appendix.)

in and drawing off the liquid. There were also found upon the wall of Troy, 1¾ feet below the place where the Treasure was discovered, three silver dishes (φιάλαι), two of which were broken to pieces in digging down the

No. 284.   Large Silver Vase found in the House of Priam (8 m.).

débris; they can, however, be repaired, as I have all the pieces.*   These dishes seem to have belonged to the Treasure, and the fact of the latter having otherwise escaped our pickaxes is due to the above-mentioned large copper vessels which projected, so that I could cut everything out of the hard *débris* by means of a knife.

---

* These silver φιάλαι, as shown in the photographs, are too much battered to be worth engraving; but we give a very fine large silver vase, which was found in a room of the Palace.—[ED.]

I now perceive that the cutting which I made in April 1870 was exactly at the proper point, and that if I had only continued it, I should in a few weeks have uncovered the most remarkable buildings in Troy, namely, the Palace of King Priam, the Scæan Gate, the Great Surrounding Wall, and the Great Tower of Ilium; whereas, in consequence of abandoning this cutting, I had to make colossal excavations from east to west and from north to south through the entire hill in order to find those most interesting buildings.

In the upper strata of the north-western and western excavations we came upon another great quantity of heads of beautiful terra-cotta figures of the best Hellenic period, and at a depth of 23 feet upon some idols, as well as the upper portion of a vase with the owl's face and a lid in the form of a helmet. Lids of this kind, upon the edge of which female hair is indicated by incisions, are frequently found in all the strata between 4 and 10 meters (13 and 33 feet) deep, and as they belong to vases with owls' faces, the number of lids gives us an idea of the number of the vases with the figure of the owl-headed Athena, which existed here in Troy.

But Troy was not large. I have altogether made twenty borings down to the rock, on the west, south-west, south, south-east and east of the Pergamus, directly at its foot or at some distance from it, on the plateau of the Ilium of the Greek colony. As I find in these borings no trace either of fragments of Trojan pottery or of Trojan house-walls, and nothing but fragments of Hellenic pottery and Hellenic house-walls, and as, moreover, the hill of the Pergamus has a very steep slope towards the north, the north-east, and the north-west, facing the Hellespont, and is also very steep towards the Plain, the city could not possibly have extended in any one of these directions. I now most emphatically declare that the city of Priam cannot have extended on any one side

beyond the primeval plateau of this fortress, the circumference of which is indicated to the south and south-west
by the Great Tower and the Scæan Gate, and to the
north-west, north-east and east by the surrounding wall
of Troy. The city was so strongly fortified by nature
on the north side, that the wall there consisted only of
those large blocks of stone, loosely piled one upon another
in the form of a wall, which last year gave me such
immense trouble to remove. This wall can be recognized at once, immediately to the right in the northern
entrance of my large cutting, which runs through the
entire hill.

I am extremely disappointed at being obliged to give
so small a plan of Troy; nay, I had wished to be able to
make it a thousand times larger, but I value truth above
everything, and I rejoice that my three years' excavations
have laid open the Homeric Troy, even though on a
diminished scale, and that I have proved the Iliad to be
based upon real facts.

Homer is an epic poet, and not an historian: so it is
quite natural that he should have exaggerated everything
with poetic licence. Moreover, the events which he describes
are so marvellous, that many scholars have long doubted the
very existence of Troy, and have considered the city to be a
mere invention of the poet's fancy. I venture to hope that
the civilized world will not only not be disappointed that
the city of Priam has shown itself to be scarcely a twen-
tieth part as large as was to be expected from the statements
of the Iliad, but that, on the contrary, it will accept with
delight and enthusiasm the certainty that Ilium did really
exist, that a large portion of it has now been brought to
light, and that Homer, even although he exaggerates, nevertheless sings of events that actually happened. Besides, it
ought to be remembered that the area of Troy, now reduced
to this small hill, is still as large as, or even larger than, the
royal city of Athens, which was confined to the Acropolis,

and did not extend beyond it, till the time when Theseus added the twelve villages, and the city was consequently named in the plural Ἀθῆναι. It is very likely that the same happened to the town of Mycenæ (Μυκῆναι), which Homer describes as being rich in gold, and which is also spoken of in the singular, εὐρυάγυια Μυκήνη.*

But this little Troy was immensely rich for the circumstances of those times, since I find here a treasure of gold and silver articles, such as is now scarcely to be found in an emperor's palace; and as the town was wealthy, so was it also powerful, and ruled over a large territory.

The houses of Troy were all very high and had several storeys, as is obvious from the thickness of the walls and the colossal heaps of *débris*. But even if we assume the houses to have been of three storeys, and standing close by the side of one another, the town can nevertheless not have contained more than 5000 inhabitants, and cannot have mustered more than 500 soldiers; but it could always raise a considerable army from among its subjects, and as it was rich and powerful, it could obtain mercenaries from all quarters.

As I do not find in my shafts (that is, beyond the hill itself) a trace of earthenware belonging to the successors of the Trojans up to the time of the Greek colony, it may with certainty be assumed that Troy had increased in size at Homer's time only to the small amount of what was added through the heaps of rubbish caused by the destruction of the city. Homer can *never* have seen Ilium's Great Tower, the surrounding wall of Poseidon and Apollo, the Scæan Gate or the Palace of King Priam, for all these monuments lay buried deep in heaps of rubbish, and he made no excavations to bring them to light. He knew of these monuments of immortal fame only from hearsay, for the tragic fate of ancient Troy was

---

* *Iliad*, IV. 52.

then still in fresh remembrance, and had already been for centuries in the mouth of all minstrels.*

Homer rarely mentions temples, and, although he speaks of the temple of Athena, yet, considering the smallness of the city, it is very doubtful whether it actually existed. It is probable that the tutelar goddess at that time possessed only the sacrificial altar which I discovered, and the crescent form of which greatly resembles the upper portion of the ivory idol found in the lowest strata,† as well as the one end of the six talents contained among the Treasure.

The position, size, and depth of all my shafts will be found most accurately specified on my plan of the Ilium of the Greek colony;‡ I therefore refrain from repeating these statements here, so as not to weary the reader. I also add an accurate plan of my excavations,§ a plan of the Scæan Gate and of the Great Tower of Ilium,‖ and lastly, a plan of the city of Troy at the time of the great destruction (Plan IV.).

The Scæan Gate gives us the age of the royal edifice in front of which it stands, and of the vessels of pottery which are found in that house. This earthenware is indeed better than what is generally found here at a depth of from 7 to 10 meters (23 to 33 feet), but it is exactly similar; and consequently all the strata of *débris* from these depths

---

* Nothing can be clearer than Homer's own testimony on this point, when he invokes the Muses to inspire him with the knowledge of what he had only heard by report (*Iliad*, II. 484–487) :—

Ἔσπετε νῦν μοι, Μοῦσαι Ὀλύμπια δώματ' ἔχουσαι,—
Ὑμεῖς γὰρ θεαί ἐστε, πάρεστέ τε, ἴστε τε πάντα,
Ἡμεῖς δὲ κλέος οἶον ἀκούομεν, οὐδέ τι ἴδμεν—
Οἵ τινες ἡγεμόνες Δαναῶν καὶ κοίρανοι ἦσαν.

" Say now, ye Nine, who on Olympus dwell,
    Muses—for ye are Goddesses, and ye
    Were present, and know all things : *we ourselves*
    But hear from Rumour's voice, and nothing know—
    Who were the chiefs and mighty lords of Greece."—[ED.]

† See No. 14 on the Plate of Idols, p. 36.
‡ Plan I.   § Plan II.   ‖ Plan III. (see p. 306).

belong to the Trojan people. These strata are composed
of red, yellow, and occasionally black wood-ashes, and
every stone found there bears the marks of the fearful heat
to which it has been exposed. In these strata we never
meet with those brilliant black plates and dishes, with a
long horizontal ring on either side, found at the depth of
from 13 to 16 meters (42½ to 52½ feet), nor do we meet
with the vases with two long tubes on either side. Besides

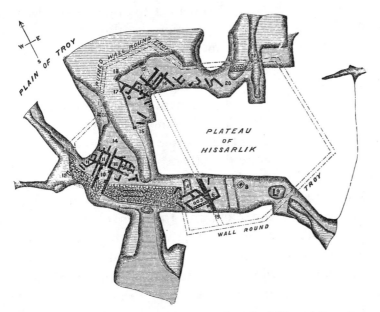

Plan IV.—Plan of Troy at the Epoch of Priam, according to Dr. Schliemann's Excavations.

the vessels in the lowest strata are entirely different in
quality and in form from those found at a depth of from
23 to 33 feet, so that they certainly cannot have belonged to
the same people. But they belong, at all events, to a kindred
Aryan nation, as these too possessed in common with the
Trojans the whorls ornamented with Aryan religious
symbols, and also idols of the Ilian Athena. I formerly
believed that the most ancient people who inhabited this
site were the Trojans, because I fancied that among their
ruins I had found the δέπας ἀμφικύπελλον, but I now

perceive that Priam's people were the succeeding nation, because in their ruins I have discovered the actual δέπας ἀμφικύπελλον, made of gold and also of terra-cotta, and likewise the Scæan Gate.

Several geologists, who have visited me here, maintain that the stratum of scoriæ, which runs through the greater part of the hill, at an average depth of 9 meters (29½ feet), has been formed by melted lead and copper ore, quantities of which must have existed here at the time of the destruction of Troy; and this opinion is also shared by the engineer, Adolphe Laurent, who has returned to help me with my last works, and to make some new plans.

Strabo says,* "No trace of the ancient city (Troy) has been preserved. This is very natural; for, as all the towns round about were desolated, yet not completely destroyed, while Troy was razed to the ground, so all the stones were carried off to renovate the others. Thus, at least, Archæanax of Mitylene is said to have built a wall round Sigeum with the stones." These statements of Strabo are, however, completely erroneous, and the tradition of antiquity, that Troy was razed to the ground, can only be explained by its having been buried deep beneath colossal masses of woodashes and stone, which were built over by a new town; the latter being again destroyed, and again surmounted by buildings which had a similar fate; till at last the mass of *débris* lying upon Troy reached a height of from 6 to 8 meters (20 to 26 feet), and upon this was established the Acropolis of the Ilium of the Greek colony.

In consequence of my former mistaken idea, that Troy was to be found on the primary soil or close above it, I unfortunately, in 1871 and 1872, destroyed a large portion of the city, for I at that time broke down all the housewalls in the higher strata which obstructed my way. This year, however, as soon as I had come by clear proofs to the

---

* XIII. p. 599, ed. Forbiger.

firm conviction that Troy was not to be found upon the primary soil, but at a depth of from 23 to 33 feet, I ceased to break down any house-wall in these strata, so that in my excavations of this year a number of Trojan houses have been brought to light. They will still stand for centuries, and visitors to the Troad may convince themselves that the stones of the Trojan buildings can *never* have been used for building other towns, for the greater part of them are still *in situ*. Moreover, they are small, and millions of such stones are to be found upon all the fields of this district.

Valuable stones, such as those large flags which cover the road leading from the Scæan Gate to the Plain, as well as the stones of the enclosing wall and of the Great Tower, have been left untouched, and not a single stone of the Scæan Gate is wanting. Nay, with the exception of the houses which I myself destroyed, it would be quite possible to uncover the "carcasses" of all the houses, as in the case of Pompeii. The houses, as I have already said, must have been very high, and a great deal of wood must have been used in their construction, for otherwise the conflagration could not have produced such an enormous quantity of ashes and rubbish.

In my excavations of 1871 and 1872, at a depth of from 7 to 10 meters (23 to 33 feet), I found only house-walls composed of sun-dried bricks; and, as anyone may convince himself by examining the houses which I have uncovered, this style of building was almost exclusively met with during that year. It is only the buildings by the side of the Scæan Gate, and a few houses in the depths of the Temple of Athena, that are made of stones and earth.

As may be seen from my plan of the site of Troy, I have excavated two-thirds of the entire city; and, as I have brought to light the Great Tower, the Scæan Gate, the city wall of Troy, the royal palace, the sacrificial altar of the Ilian Athena, and so forth, I have uncovered

the grandest buildings, and, in fact, the best part of the
city. I have also made an exceedingly copious collection of
all the articles of the domestic life and the religion of the
Trojans; and therefore it is not to be expected that science
would gain anything more by further excavations. If,
however, my excavations should at any time be continued,
I urgently entreat those who do so to throw the *débris*

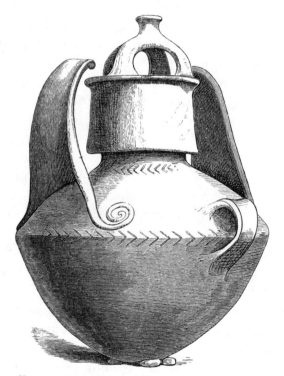

No. 285.   Splendid Terra-cotta Vase from the Palace of Priam.

This is the largest vase of the type frequent in the ruins, with two small handles and two great
upright wings.   The *cover* was found near it.

of their diggings from the declivity of the hill, and *not* to
fill up the colossal cuttings which I have made with such
infinite trouble and at such great expense, for they are of
great value to archæology, inasmuch as in these cuttings
all the strata of *débris*, from the primary soil up to the
surface of the hill, can be examined with little trouble.

On the north side of the hill, I have now also uncovered several house-walls at a depth of 13 meters (42½ feet), and also the beginning of that remarkable wall of fortification already mentioned, the continuation of which may be seen in the labyrinth of house-walls in the depths of the Temple of Athena. On the north side, above the primary soil, I have also brought to light a portion of the pavement already mentioned, composed of small, round white sea-

pebbles, below which are the calcined ruins of a building which formerly stood there.

Among some very remarkable terra-cottas discovered since my last report, I must mention two jugs found on the

No. 286.   Curious double-necked Jug (8 M.).

No. 287.   Terra-cotta Vessel consisting of three Goblets rising out of a tube on three feet (4 M.).—[6 M. in Atlas.]

north side, at a depth of from 23 to 26 feet, each of which has two upright necks standing side by side, but their handles are united. One of them has also beside the mouths two small elevations, which may probably indicate eyes. Of a third jug of this kind, I only found the upper portion. I must also mention an exceedingly curious cup, discovered at a depth of 4 meters (13 feet), which consists of a tube resting upon three feet and ending in one large and two small goblets; the larger goblet is connected with the opposite side of the tube by a handle. At the same depth I met with a large vase, from which projects a separate small vase; it is ornamented with incisions, and has three feet and two very pretty handles and rings for hanging it up. I found likewise, at the depth of 13 feet, a vase with two female breasts, two large handles and engravings resembling letters. Among other extremely curious terra-cottas, I must also mention three pots with three rows of perforations; they have the usual handle on one side and three feet on the other; also three large vases with

No. 288. Terra-cotta Vessel in the form of a Pig, with   No. 289. A round Terra-cotta, stamped
         legs too short to stand it on (7 M.).   with Hieroglyphics (1¼ M.).

perforations right round, on all sides from the bottom to the top; their use is a riddle to me; can they have served as bee-hives?* Also a vessel in the form of a pig with four feet, which are, however, shorter than the belly, so that the vessel cannot stand upon them; the neck of the vessel, which is attached to the back of the pig, is connected with the hinder part by a handle. I further found a pot in the form of a basket with a handle crossing the mouth, and with a tube in the bulge for drawing off the liquid. Also two terra-cotta funnels, at a depth of 10 feet, with a letter, which I have repeatedly met with on some of the terra-cottas of which I have given drawings,

---

* Certainly not; but they may have served for burning charcoal or incense.—[ED.]

and which therefore will probably be deciphered. At a depth of 5 feet I found one of those round twice-perforated terra-cottas with a stamp, in which there are Egyptian hieroglyphics; also a dozen of the same articles in the stamps of which are a crowned head, a bird, a dog's head, a flying man or an eagle and a stag. At a depth of 16½ feet, I found the handle of a cup with the beautifully modelled head of a bull, which probably represents the βοῶπις πότνια Ἥρη:* however, this cannot be proved, for up to that time I had never found an idol with the head of an ox. Neither can I prove that the terra-cottas here frequently met with, in the form of horses' heads, represent the mother of Hera, Cybele or Rhea; but it is very likely,

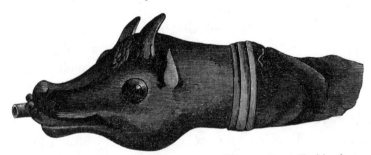

No. 290. Fragment of a Terra-cotta Vessel, in the shape of a Horse's Head (4 M.).

for, as is well known, in Phrygia she was represented with a horse's head. Terra-cotta idols of the Ilian Athena are rarely met with; but we daily find marble idols of this goddess, most of which have almost a human form. We also frequently come upon oblong flat pieces of rough marble, upon which the owl's face of the goddess is more or less deeply engraved. It is often so finely scratched that the aid of a magnifying glass is required to convince one that it actually exists; we found several such pieces of marble where the owl's head was painted in a black colour. Since I have come to the conclusion that they are idols of the tutelary divinity of Troy, I have carefully collected

---

* See the similar example, No. 208, p. 294.

them; but in 1871 and 1872 seven-eighths of all the marble
idols must have escaped my notice, for at that time I had
no idea of their significance.

In excavating the ground upon which my wooden
house had stood, we found, at a depth of from 9 to
19 inches, eighteen copper and two silver medals; one of
the latter is of Marcus Aurelius. The other is a tetra-
drachm of the island of Tenedos; on the obverse, to the
right, is the head of Jupiter, to the left that of Juno, both
having one neck in common, like the heads of Janus. The
head of Jupiter is crowned with laurels, that of Juno has a
wreath or crown. Upon the reverse of the coin there is
a laurel wreath round the edge, and in the centre a large
double axe, above which stands the word ΤΕΝΕΔΙΩΝ:
below and to the right of the handle of the double axe
there is a winged Eros, who is holding up an object which
it is difficult to distinguish; to the left is a bunch of grapes
and a monogram, which looks like the letter A.

Of the copper coins, five are of Alexandria Troas, two
of Ophrynium, one of Tenedos, two of Abydos, and one of
Dardania. Two have on one side the bust of Julia Domna,
with the inscription ΙΟΥΛΙΑ ΣΕΒΑΣΤΗ; one of these has
on the reverse the full-length figure of this empress with
the inscription ΙΛΙΕΩΝ, and the other has the figure of
Hector with the inscription ΙΛΙΕΩΝ ƎΚΤΩΡ. The other
medals belong to an earlier period of Ilium, and have on
the one side the bust of Athena, and on the other the
inscription ΙΛΙΕΩΝ.

In April of this year, when I uncovered the road paved
with large flags of stone, which leads from the Scæan Gate
to the Plain, the stones looked as new as if they had just
been hewn. But since then, under the influence of the
burning sun, the flags of the upper portion of the road,
which have specially suffered from the conflagration that
destroyed the city, are rapidly crumbling away, and will
probably have quite disappeared in a few years. However,

the flags of stone on the north-western half of the road which have been less exposed to the heat, may still last many centuries.

The following inscriptions were found at a depth of from 19 inches to 3½ feet below my wooden house.

```
. . . . . . . . . . . . . . . ⸱ . . . . . . . . . . . . . . .
. . . . . . . . . . . . . ⸱ . . . . . . . . . . . . . . . . .
. . . . . . ΣΑ . . . . . . . . . . . . . . . . . . . . .
, . . ΕΣΑΙ . . . . . . . . . ⸱ . . . . ΝΟΥ . . . . . . . . . . .
5 . . . . . . ΑΒΟΥΚΟΛ . . . . . . ΕΤΡΑΝΦ . . . . . . . . . ⸱ ⸱
. . . . ΣΚΑΤΑΠΛΗΘΟΣΕΙΣΟΙΝΙΣΤΡΑ . . . . .
. . ΤΩΝΕΨΗΦΙΣΘΑΙΣΚΑΔΡΕΙΣΟ . . . . .
. . ΣΑΝΔΡΑΣΤΟΥΣΣΥΝΘΗΣΟΜΕΝ . . . . .
. . . . ΕΡΟΝΥΠΗΡΧΕΝΚΑΙΣΤΗΛΩ . . . . .
10 . . . . ΙΕΝΤΩΤΩΝΣΑΜΟΘΡΑΚ . . . . . . . . .
. . . . ΙΣΑΠΟΚΑΘΙΣΤΑΜΕΝΟ . . . . . . . . . .
. . . . ΕΝΟΥΣΤΗΝΣΥΝΘΕΣΙΝ . . . . . . . . . .
. . . . . . ΜΟΛΟΓΙΑΣΤΟΑΝΤΙΓΡΑ . . . . . . . . . . .
. . . . . . ΟΙΚΗΣΟΝΤΕΣΗΡΕΘΗΣ . . . . . . . . . . . ⸱ ⸱
15 . . . . . . ΟΠΕΙΘΟΥΜΙΛΗΣΙΟΣ . . . . . . . . . . . . . .
. . . . . . ΘΟΥΔΙΟΠΕΙΔΗΣΒ . . . . . . . . . . . . . .
. . . . . ΤΙΦΑΝΗΣΑΠ . . . . . . . . . . . . . . . . . . .
. . . . . . . . . . . . . . . . . . . . . . . . .
. . . . . . σα . . . . . . . . . . . . . . . . . . . .
. . . . εσαι . . . . . . . . . . . . . . . νου(ς . . .
5 . . . . . . . . αβουκολ . . . . . . ετραν φ . . .
. . . . ς κατὰ πλῆθος εἰς οἴνιστρα . . . . .
. . των ἐψηφίσθαι Σκαδρεῖς ο . . . . . . .
. . ς ἀνδρὰς τοὺς συνθησομέν(ους . . . .
. . . . ερον ὑπῆρχεν καὶ στηλω . . . . . .
10 . . . . ι ἐν τῷ τῶν Σαμοθράκ(ων . . . . . .
. . . . ις ἀποκαθισταμέν(ο . . . . . . . . .
. . . . ενους τὴν σύνθεσιν . . . . . . . . . .
. . . . . . ὁ)μολογίας τὸ ἀντίγρα(φον . . .
. . . . . . οἰκήσοντες ἡρέθησ(αν . . . . . .
15 . . . . . . Δι)οπείθου Μιλήσιος . . . . . . .
. . . . . . θου Διοπείδης Β . . . . . . . . . . .
. . . . . . Αν)τιφάνης Ἀπ . . . . . . . . . . .
```

This inscription contains a contract for a settlement and gives the names of the men selected for founding it; Σκαδρεῖς is an unknown word, which has never before been met with.

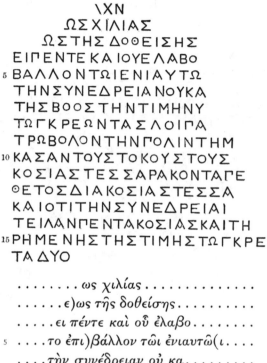

```
              \ΧΝ
            ΩΣ ΧΙΛΙΑΣ
          ΩΣ ΤΗΣ ΔΟΘΕΙΣΗΣ
        ΕΙΠΕΝΤΕ ΚΑΙΟΥΕΛΑΒΟ
      5 ΒΑΛΛΟΝΤΩΙΕΝΙΑΥΤΩ
        ΤΗΝΣΥΝΕΔΡΕΙΑΝΟΥΚΑ
        ΤΗΣ ΒΟΟΣ ΤΗΝΤΙΜΗΝΥ
        ΤΩΓΚΡΕΩΝΤΑΣΛΟΙΓΑ
        ΤΡΩΒΟΛΟΝΤΗΝΓΟΛΙΝΤΗΜ
     10 ΚΑΣΑΝΤΟΥΣΤΟΚΟΥΣΤΟΥΣ
        ΚΟΣΙΑΣΤΕΣΣΑΡΑΚΟΝΤΑΓΕ
        ΘΕΤΟΣΔΙΑΚΟΣΙΑΣΤΕΣΣΑ
        ΚΑΙΟΤΙΤΗΝΣΥΝΕΔΡΕΙΑΙ
        ΤΕΙΛΑΝΠΕΝΤΑΚΟΣΙΑΣΚΑΙΤΗ
     15 ΡΗΜΕΝΗΣΤΗΣΤΙΜΗΣΤΩΓΚΡΕ
        ΤΑ ΔΥΟ
```

.... ως χιλίας ....

...... ε)ως τῆς δοθείσης..........

..... ει πέντε καὶ οὗ ἔλαβο........

5 .... το ἐπι)βάλλον τῶι ἐνιαυτῶ(ι....

.... τὴν συνέδρειαν οὐ κα.........

.... τῆς βοὸς τὴν τιμὴν ὑ.........

.... τῶγ κρεῶν τὰς λοιπὰ(ς ....

.... τε) τρώβολον τὴν πόλιν τημ...

10 .... ἠνάγ;)κασαν τοὺς τόκους τοὺς..

.... α)κοσίας τεσσαράκοντα πέ(ντε.

.... θετος διακοσίας τεσσα(ρα.....

...καὶ ὅτι τὴν συνέδρεια(ν........

... ἀπέσ)τειλαν πεντακοσίας καὶ τη.

15 ...ρημένης τῆς τιμῆς τῶγ κρε(ῶν...

...τάλαν;)τα δύο..............

In this day closing the excavations at Ilium for ever, I cannot but fervently thank God for His great mercy, in that, notwithstanding the terrible danger to which we have been exposed owing to the continual hurricanes, during the last three years' gigantic excavations, no misfortune has happened, no one has been killed, and no one has even been seriously hurt.

In conclusion, I cannot refrain from most strongly recommending Nikolaos Saphyros Jannakis, of the neighbouring village of Renkoï, to all those who, sooner or later, may wish to make excavations in the Plain of Troy or in the neighbourhood. During all my excavations here, since April 1870, he has been my attendant, cook, and cashier. It is in the latter capacity especially that I find him incomparably useful on account of his honesty, which has been well tested, and also on account of his knowing the names and capabilities of every workman in the Troad. In addition to this, his size and herculean strength, his cleverness, and his thorough knowledge of the Turkish language, are excellently adapted for settling the difficulties which continually arise in reference to the excavations with the Turkish officials. I must also specially recommend my foreman Spiridion Demetrios of Athens, and Captain Georgios Tsirogiannis of Limme in Eubœa, for they have here learnt by long experience the easiest way of removing colossal masses of *débris*, and they have in addition the gift of command. I can also most strongly recommend my accomplished draughtsman, Polychronios Lempessis, of Salamis, who has here made all the drawings of my work from Plate 119 to 190.* Lastly, I can speak with the utmost satisfaction of my engineer Adolphe Laurent, who has made the ground plans for me from first to last.

---

* This refers, of course, to Dr. Schliemann's Atlas of photographic illustrations, of which all the most valuable are reproduced in the present translation in a greatly improved style of execution.—[ED.]

NOTE A.

THE RIVER SIMOÏS.

As the present name of the Simoïs, *Dumbrek*, is not a Turkish word, some take it for a corruption of the name Thymbrius, and use it to prove that the river—which, flowing past the foot of the ruins of Ophrynium, runs through the north-eastern valley of the Plain of Troy, and falls into the Kalifatli Asmak, the very ancient bed of the Scamander, in front of Ilium—is the Thymbrius, and cannot possibly be the Simoïs.

To this I reply : that there is no example of a Greek word ending in *os* being rendered in Turkish by a word ending in a *k*; further that Dumbrek must certainly be a corruption of the two Turkish words طوك برق *Don barek*. *Don* signifies 'ice,' and *barek* the 'possession' or the 'habitation'; the two words therefore mean much the same thing as containing ice, and the name might be explained by the fact that the inundations caused by the Simoïs are frequently frozen over in winter, when the whole north-eastern plain forms a sheet of ice. Throughout antiquity, however, the river was called the Simoïs, for according to Strabo (XIII. I. p. 103), the grove dedicated to Hector was situated on a hill near Ophrynium ; according to Lycophron (*Cassandra*), the hero was buried in Ophrynium ; and according to Virgil,* who is the most conscientious preserver of ancient traditions, Hector's tomb was situated in a little grove on the shores of the Simoïs.

---

* *Æneid*, III. 302–305 :—

> " Ante urbem in luco, falsi Simoëntis ad undam,
> Libabat cineri Andromache manesque vocabat
> Hectoreum ad tumulum, viridi quem cæspite inanem,
> Et geminas, causam lacrimis, sacraverat aras."

NOTE B.

I.—List of the specific weight in Grammes, of the terra-cottas in the form of cylinders, balls, pyramids, &c., found in the various depths of the Pergamus of Troy, and which appear to have been used as weights.* (The depths are given in meters.)

1	2	3	4	5	6	7	8	9	10	11	12	13	14	15
67	98	73	58	107	177	·95	70	38	26		210			
125	149	202	298	110	221	198	74	75	42					
134	162	205		120	259	215	90	83	144					
430	197	328			400	334	91	154	148					
545	220				400		109	73	167					
1005	228				442		112		176					
	306				443		133		224					
	495				448		141		248					
	509				455		177		279					
					456		403		300					
					458		458		308					
					458		472		315					
					464		748		320					
					465				322					
					470				336					
					475				338					
					475				350					
					555				355					
									365					
									366					
									368					
									374					
									384					
									430					
									435					
									450					
									458					
									500					
									520					
									575					

* The *gramme* = 15·43235 *grains*; or, approximately, 15¼ *grains*. The *ounce* (avoirdupois) = 437½ *grains*; and the *pound*, 16 oz., = 7000 grs.

NOTE B—(continued).

II. List of the specific weight in Grammes of the round stones found in the various depths of the Pergamus of Troy, and which have apparently served as weights. (The depths are in meters.)

1	2	3	4	5	6	7	8	9	10	11	12	13	14	15
418	183	79	69	100	100	169	102	223	145	555	485	190	135	332
576	275	109	71	112	185	186	150	224	146		1710	468	413	363
757	442	135	100	140	300	186	207	227	182			1475	450	447
	472	414	136	215	330	189	244	372	190				485	475
		448	195	230	412	219	254	390	214				505	557
		584	388	262	420	229	257	420	225				1250	585
		726	400	268	427	245	288	500	280				1852	680
			513	293	446	266	295	852	310					3148
			583	318	460	290	381		334					
			608	335	462	291	385		341					
			624	335	515	346	402		372					
			635	368	528	369	408		450					
			662	478	546	380	429		545					
			688	490	572	384	440		605					
			893	498	602	400	472		627					
				537	628	435	536		755					
				637	640	437	551							
				688	670	468	568							
				728	738	483	620							
				757	770	491	638							
				790	1288	515	658							
				4260	3000	534	660							
						560	712							
						569	764							
						606	825							
						632	1145							
						825	1160							
						895	1232							
						904	1710							
						1005	1950							
						1082								
						1193								
						1877								

Note C.

Monsieur Ernest Chantre, Assistant Director of the Museum in Lyon, has just sent me the result of the analysis of the Trojan weapons made by the celebrated chemist, M. Damour, of Lyon. I had drilled three weapons, and sent him the drillings.

No. 1.—Drillings from one of the battle-axes of the treasure.

Analysis.

	Grammes.
	0·3020
Deducting the sand contained in it	0·0160
Analysed metal	0·2860

In 10·000 parts.

	Grammes.	
This consists of copper . .	0·2740	= 0·9580
„ „ tin . . .	0·0110	= 0·0384
	0·2850	= 0·9964

No. 2.—Drillings of another battle-axe of the treasure.

Analysis.

	Grammes.
	0·2970
Deducting the sand contained in it	0·0020
Analysed metal	0·2950

In 10·000 parts.

	Grammes.	
This consists of copper . .	0·2675	= 0·9067
„ „ tin . .	0·0255	= 0·0864
	0·2930	= 0·9931

No. 3.—Drillings from a common two-edged axe, found at a depth of $3\frac{1}{4}$ feet, and therefore in the remains of the Greek colony.

Analysis.

	Grammes.
	0·5280
Deducting the sand contained in it	0·0070
Analysed metal	0·5210

In 10·000 parts.

	Grammes.	
This consists of copper . .	0·4810	= 0·9232
„ „ tin . . .	0·0385	= 0·0739
	0·5195	= 0·9971

No. 4.—Drillings of one of the Trojan sling-bullets, externally covered with verdigris, and internally the colour of iron.

Analysis.

	Grammes.
Quantity of analysed metal	0·2410

In 10·000 parts.

	Grammes.	
Consisting of sulphur . .	0·0470	= 0·1950
„ „ copper . . .	0·1920	= 0·7966
„ „ iron . . .	0·0002	= 0·0008
„ „ quartzose . .	0·0005	= 0·0020
	0·2397	= 0·9944

DR. H. SCHLIEMANN.

Athens, January 1, 1874.

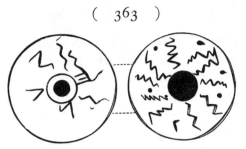

No. 291. An Inscribed Trojan Whorl (8 M.).

APPENDIX.

ON THE INSCRIPTIONS FOUND AT HISSARLIK.

By The Editor.

As soon as Dr. Schliemann's wonderful discoveries at Hissarlik were made known, one of the most important questions that arose in the mind of all scholars was :— Has he found any *Inscriptions*, to throw the certain light of written testimony on the language and ethnic affinities, the history and social condition, the religion, science, and literature, of the old inhabitants of the hill, whose records form as yet no part of ancient history?

Dr. Schliemann's private communications during the progress of his work had called forth the efforts of eminent Orientalists — such as Martin Haug, Émile Burnouf, and Max Müller—to attempt the discovery of true writing among the vast variety of strange and novel patterns impressed upon the terra-cotta whorls, balls, seals, vases, and other objects in his collection; for some of these bore a likeness to written characters which could hardly be deceptive.* It mattered not for this enquiry, by what name the habitations, whose successive strata were

---

* Dr. Schliemann's work records several interesting examples of his first impressions on this point, and he appears more often to have mistaken written characters for mere symbols or ornaments than the other way.

revealed, had been called of old. No one whose opinion
was worth regarding disputed their very high antiquity,
which implied the great age of the objects found. Apart
even from its traditional claim to be the Ilium of Homer,
the site lay in the track of the primitive migrations of
the Indo-European race from their cradle in the East to
their settlements in the West; and not of one migration
only, but of their passage to and fro between the shores of
Asia and of Europe; as well as upon the path of their commerce and military expeditions, after they were settled in their
homes. For, lest we be misled by the arbitrary distinction
between the continents, which is stereotyped in the names
of Asia and Europe—that is, East and West—it must be
borne in mind that the Hellespont and Bosporus (as the
latter name expresses) were *ferries* rather than sundering
seas, and the islands of the Ægean were stepping-stones.
The close affinities of the early settlers on both shores had
long since been proved; and, in particular, the presence of
the great Pelasgo-Hellenic or Græco-Italic family had been
traced on both. The very ancient habitation of the north-
western parts of Asia Minor by the *Ionians*—the oriental
name of the whole Hellenic race—long before their traditional colonization from the peninsula of Hellas—had been
maintained by Ernst Curtius twenty years ago,* and more
fully established by recent Egyptologers †—thus confirming
the most ancient ethnic record, that the *Isles of the Gentiles*
were divided among the families of the *Sons of Javan.*‡

---

* Curtius, *Die Ionier vor der Wanderung*, Berlin, 1855.

† Chabas, *Études sur l'Antiquité historique*, Paris, 1872, p. 190.

‡ Genesis x. 4, 5.   The essential letters of the Hebrew name יון
are identical with the Greek ΙΩΝ (Ion), and both are equivalent to the
Yavanas, the "younger race" of the old Aryan traditions, who migrated
to the West, while the elder branch remained in the East. On the
whole subject the Editor may be permitted to refer to the *Student's
Ancient History of the East*, especially to Chapter XX., on the Nations
of Asia Minor, which contains a discussion of the Hellenic affinities of
the Phrygians and Trojans in particular.

Thus, before the first trench was dug at Hissarlik, a clue was already supplied to the race of the primitive inhabitants, if any such had dwelt there, and to the nature of their language, if they had left any written records.

Among the patterns engraved upon the whorls and other terra-cottas, many were soon found, as Dr. Schliemann has fully shown, to be the most ancient sacred emblems of the Aryan race; and the discovery of these at all depths, below the ruins of Greek Ilium, attested the common Aryan descent of all the nations that had dwelt successively on the hill before the historic Grecian colony. The absence of any trace of Egyptian influence, and almost equally of Assyrian, seemed to attest an independent and very ancient Aryan civilization; while the general character of the works in terra-cotta, resembling those found in Cyprus and some of the islands of the Ægean, appeared to belong to the style which Professor Conze, of Vienna, had defined as the earliest Greek or European Indo-Germanic. The characters, which looked so exactly like writing, were certainly not hieroglyphs in any of their varieties; nor—though there were some cuneiform marks—was there any true cuneiform writing; while the few semblances of Phœnician characters were soon found to be deceptive. This last fact, again, helped to carry back the time of the settlement of Hissarlik beyond the age when Greeks and Phœnicians had entered into close relations of civilization on the shores of the Ægean, that is, before the date of the Homeric poems, which are full of allusions to Phœnician influence.

It has often been observed how remarkably new discoveries coincide in point of time, just when they are needed to throw light upon one another. At the very moment when Dr. Schliemann was bringing to light the remains buried in the Hill of Hissarlik, Orientalists were engaged in deciphering the inscriptions found among the antiquities of Cyprus, and upon the rock tablets in the island, by the aid of the still recent results of cuneiform interpretation. The Cyprian characters were proved to belong to a syllabic alphabet, which is a varied form of the cuneiform writing of Babylonia and Assyria, and of an origin older than the Phœnician. The leaders in this work were Mr. George Smith and Dr. Samuel Birch, who assigned a phonetic value to 33 characters of the Cypriote syllabary; and it was followed up with especial zeal by the lamented young scholar, Dr. Johannes Brandis, who determined (as was thought) the remainder of the 60 signs. His unfinished posthumous *Essay on the Decipherment of the Cyprian Inscriptions* forms the landmark of the state of enquiry in the year in which Dr. Schliemann finished his excavations.*

To Dr. MARTIN HAUG belongs the honour of first applying this key to the decipherment of the Hissarlik inscriptions. He traced such striking resemblances in some of the characters to those of the Cyprian alphabet, as to make out a good *primâ facie* case for their identity, and he seemed to have succeeded in deciphering three words. Two of these were formed by the six characters on a whorl from the Trojan stratum, which were afterwards seen to be identical with those on another from the same depth (7 meters), a repetition which seems to show the importance of the inscription. Both had been specially noticed and discussed by Dr. Schliemann on their discovery; † and they will be always memorable in the history of this investigation. Haug read these characters *ta. i. o. si. i. go.*, which he interpreted as a dedication, θείῳ Σιγῷ, "to the divine Sigo," a deity whose name was found in Sigeum, the Scamander, and even Sicyon; and he thought he traced the same name on two of Schliemann's small funnels (Nos. 145, 146, p. 191).‡ But the deity was otherwise as

---

* Brandis, *Versuch zur Entzifferung der Kyprioten Schrift*, Berlin, 1873. See also the Life of Brandis by Curtius: *Johannes Brandis, ein Lebensbild*, von Ernst Curtius, 1873.   † See pp. 83, 137, 161.

‡ 'The Augsburg Gazette' (*Augsburger Allgemeine Zeitung*), 1874, p. 32.

unknown as the transmutation of *ta. i. o.* into θείῳ was forced; and, while Haug was doubtless right in his *method,* his results must be pronounced at best :—

"Fragments of broken words and thoughts,
Yet glimpses of the true."

Nos. 292, 293.   Two Trojan Whorls from the same depth (7 M.) with an identical inscription.*

It was with such a conviction that the enquiry was taken up by Professor Theodore Gomperz, of Vienna,† whose words are well worth quoting as a lesson in the method of investigation: "One circumstance alone appeared to me consoling, namely, that I did not find myself obliged to add a new hypothesis to the numerous ones already existing, and that I felt it still possible to abide by Haug's discovery, were it only as a starting-point for further efforts. *For the beginning of continuity in enquiry is always the surest harbinger of approaching success.*" After making one correction in Haug's reading of the above inscription, he still found it quite unintelligible, till the thought struck him of reading it from right to left round

---

* The whorl on the left hand (the one discussed by Haug and Gomperz) is engraved from M. Burnouf's more accurate drawing in our lithographed Plate LI., No. 496; the other is given at page 161; but they are repeated here (from Schliemann's Atlas, Pl. 13, No. 432, Pl. 6, No. 208) in order to exhibit their identity. It is remarkable that these whorls, belonging to an age when writing was already known, are very coarse, both in material and work.

† Professor Gomperz gave an interesting and eloquent account of his labours and their results in two papers in the 'Vienna Evening Post' (*Wiener Abendpost*) for May 6th, and June 26th, 1874.

the whorl, instead of from left to right, and the confused syllables flashed, as by a sudden crystallization, into the pure Greek *ta. go. i. di. o. i.,* that is Ταγῶ δίῳ. "To the

No. 294. *ta.   go.   i.   di.   o.   i.*

No. 294. The above Inscription developed (7 M.).

divine General or Prince," an interpretation which Professor Max Müller pronounced to be "almost beyond reasonable doubt."* We deem this solution worthy of special record, both as a landmark in the history of the investigation, and still more as a striking example of the power of mere coincidence to produce combinations that seem to bear the stamp of truth.

The other inscriptions, of which Professor Gomperz proposed solutions, were the following: First, three letters on the terra-cotta seal, also from the Trojan stratum, mentioned in the 'Introduction' (No. 4, p. 24; Pl. 19, No. 555 in Schliemann's Atlas), which Professor Max Müller

No. 295.   Inscription on a Trojan Seal (7 M.)

was at one time tempted to read as the very name of *Ilion* (See the 'Academy' for May 16, 1874, p. 546). The

No. 296.   Inscription on a Trojan Whetstone (7 M.).

second was the "splendidly engraved inscription" round the base of the whetstone of red slate (No. 5, p. 24, Pl. 190,

---

* The '*Academy*' for June 6th, 1874.

No. 3474, Atlas). The third is round the shoulder of a vase from the Palace of Priam (No. 3, p. 23; Pl. 168, Nos. 3273 and 3278, Atlas), where, however, about one-

(gap)  (gap)

No. 297. Inscription on a Trojan Vase from the Palace (8 M.).

third of the inscription is wanting. The fourth is on a whorl from *the lower limit* of the Trojan stratum.

No. 298. Trojan Whorl, with   No. 299. The Inscription developed (10 M.).
an Inscription (10 M.).
        Comp. Pl. XXVII., No. 369. This also is of very coarse work.

The above record of the process of the investigation will still possess great historical interest, long after the results shall have emerged (as we trust) from the cloud which, for the moment, has come over our hopes; and we believe that its interest will be increased by stating the present position of the case in the words of Professor Gomperz himself * :—

" There is not, and there cannot be, the slightest doubt that Professor Haug at Munich was perfectly right, when he first identified the symbols found on several of the Hissarlik vases, &c., with Cypriote characters. I was right too in following up the track, and I think still that I have scarcely once been wrong in identifying those symbols with these characters. Furthermore, my general inferences drawn from the fact, that the Cypriote syllabic writing occurs out of Cyprus, and associated with what I rightly have called *pre-Homeric* objects of art, I still think unassailable. But—I cannot go further than this! My attempt at *deciphering* those inscriptions I now look upon as abortive! I hasten to add, that I do not think I deserve any reproach in the matter. I utilized to the best of my abilities the progress which till then had been made in the decipherment of the Cypriote inscriptions found in Cyprus.

---

* From a letter to the Editor, dated Vienna, Dec. 9th, 1874, written in English, as here quoted.

I used as a key for my decipherment of the Hissarlik inscriptions the phonetic values which Mr. George Smith and Dr. Johannes Brandis had ascertained for those characters. But both these investigators had been only partially right! Wonderful indeed it is, that, applying as I did a key partially right and partially wrong, good and intelligible Greek words emerged. It was a most marvellous coincidence—but nothing else, a mere fortuitous coincidence.

"The labour of ascertaining the phonetic value of the Cypriote characters has since been taken up by several German scholars, Dr. Moritz Schmidt, Professor at Jena, and Messrs. Deecke and Siegismund at Strasburg, and to a candid critic there cannot remain a doubt that *they are right*, and that I (together with Smith and Brandis) *was wrong*." *

Such a frank, truth-loving spirit in the enquirer is as sure a guarantee of ultimate success as that "continuity in the enquiry," which Gomperz still holds to be established. In a word, the right track is known, but the sign-posts have to be rectified; the key is found, but its wards need some fresh adjustment; and we may soon hope for results far more fruitful than those of which, for a moment only, we have been disappointed.

Meanwhile it is well to put on record Professor Gomperz's reply to the objections that may be brought forward against the probable conclusion that, even before the

---

* Professor Gomperz adds that his change of opinion was at once communicated to Moritz Schmidt, and published by him in a postscript to his work, 'Die Inschrift von Idalion und das Kyprische Syllabar.' It has also been published by Gomperz's colleague, Professor Conze, in an article on Schliemann's discoveries in the 'Preussische Jahrbücher.'

The *Academy* of November 28th, 1874 (p. 591), quotes from the *Nation* the following summary of the proceedings at the meeting of the *Oriental Society*, held in New York at the end of October :—

"One of the most elaborate and interesting of the papers presented was a review and criticism of the *Progress of Decipherment of the Cypriote Inscriptions, with original additions*, by Mr. J. H. HALL. The latest and best German investigator in this field, MORITZ SCHMIDT, laments that he has not, in trustworthy form, the material from the *Di Cesnola collections ;* this Mr. Hall has undertaken to furnish him."

We have now a fresh reason to lament the misfortune by which the Di Cesnola collection was lost to our Museum.

Homeric times, there existed Greeks acquainted with a written language.

" For this supposition is not only opposed by ancient, though possibly unhistoric traditions, such as the denial of the settlement of Asia Minor by European Greeks, but by really historical facts—for instance, the total absence of any mention of the art of writing in these very Homeric poems.

" However this objection—let it count for as much or as little as it may—affects not only our decipherings, but also a firmly established and quite undeniable fact, the existence of a Cyprian syllabic writing. For that a nation which knew of a written language, simple and handy as the Phœnician with its facility of supplying the vowels, should prefer one like the Cyprian, full of the most troublesome characters and yet subject to the worst ambiguity, is surely as unlikely as that a nation in possession of the needle-gun should return to the use of the battle-axe. However, in the ninth and at latest in the eighth century (and very probably much earlier) the Greeks *must* already have been acquainted with the so-called Phœnician writing, which at that time was employed with equal readiness both in Moab and in Nineveh. Hence the Cyprian writing must have found its way among the Greeks before this epoch (and we may almost safely say a considerable time before this epoch, for otherwise how could it have taken firm root in Cyprus only?) My opinion is that we shall soon find the definite outlines of an epoch of Greek culture, or semi-culture, which I should be inclined to name the *pre-Cadmean*, the decline of which may probably be dated from the mighty impulse which the conquest of Canaan by the Israelites (about 1300) gave to the migration and the colonization of the Phœnicians." *

We are enabled, by a communication from Dr. Schliemann, to present a list of all the objects in his collection, which Professor Gomperz has recognised as bearing Inscriptions, all of which are figured in our work. We also append the *depth* at which each object was found, inasmuch as this determines to which of the nations, that dwelt successively on the site of Ilium, each inscription is to be referred; and this is by no means the least interesting point in the investigation.

It will be understood, of course, that this is, in the strongest sense, a "first provisional list" of the results of

---

* See B. Schröder, *Die phonicische Sprache ;* Halle, 1869, p. 2, fol.

an enquiry only just begun. We believe that we could make no inconsiderable additions to it; but we await the verdict of the more competent enquirers who are now engaged in the research. Their labours may show that the *lowest stratum* of remains is not destitute of traces of a written language, as would appear at first sight from the List. Meanwhile the great preponderance of known inscriptions from the "Trojan stratum" (7–10 M.) of Dr. Schliemann is very striking: 11 out of the 18 belong to it. But the ethnic affinity between the Trojans and their successors, already attested by many proofs, is now confirmed by five inscriptions in the Cyprian character from the depths of 4, 5, and 6 meters (Nos. 5, 6, 7, 12 and 16 in the List). The two funnels (Nos. 17, 18) are furnished by the uppermost stratum: each bears only a single letter, which appears also to be Cyprian; but there would seem to be still some doubt whether it may not be Phœnician.

No. 300.   Terra-cotta Ball (4 M.).
a. Side View.   *b*. Upper Hemisphere.   *c*. Lower Hemisphere, with the Inscription.

LIST OF INSCRIPTIONS

RECOGNIZED TO THE PRESENT TIME ON OBJECTS IN DR. SCHLIEMANN'S COLLECTION.*

I.—INSCRIPTIONS ON WHORLS.

	In Translation.	In Atlas.	Depth.	References.
1.	Pl. XXIV. No. 353.	Pl. 5, No. 166.	·9 M.	
2.	Pl. XXVII. No. 369.	Pl. 11, No. 356.	10 M.	Pp. 137, 369.
3.	Pl. LI. No. 496.	Pl. 13, No. 432.	7 M.	Identical inscription: pp. 83, 137, 161, 365–368.
4.	No. 115, p. 161.	Pl. 6. No. 208.	7 M.	
5.	Pl. XXXIX. No. 435.	Pl. 122, No. 2442.	5 M.	
6.	Pl. XLVI. No. 472.	Pl. 162, No. 3134.	6 M.	
7.	Pl. XXV. No. 360.	Pl. 173, No. 3364.	4 M.	
8.	Pl. LI. No. 494.	Pl. 187, No. 3415.	7 M.	
9.	No. 227, p. 312.	Pl. 164, No. 3193.	8 M.	Page 312.
10.	No. 291, p. 363.	Pl. 166, No. 3233.	8 M.	

II.—INSCRIPTIONS ON TERRA-COTTA BALLS.

11.	Pl. LII. No. 497.	Pl. 166, No. 3229.	8 M.	
12.	No. 300, p. 372.	Pl. 135, No. 2699.	4 M.	

III.—ON OTHER OBJECTS.

13.	*Seal*, No. 4, p. 24.	Pl. 19, No. 555.	7 M.	Pp. 24, 368.
14.	*Whetstone*, No. 5, p. 24.	Pl. 190, No. 3474.	7 M.	Pp. 24, 368.
15.	*Vase*, No. 3, p. 23.	Pl. 168, No. 3273, 3278.	8 M.	Pp. 307, 369.
16.	*Vase*, Nos. 31, 32, p. 50.	Pl. 161, No. 3092.	5½ M.	Pp. 50, 309.
17.	Pair of Funnels, Nos.	Pl. 171, No. 3292.	3. M.	Pp. 191, 366.
18.	145, 146, p. 191.	Pl. 171, No. 3295.		

* Besides the numbers of our own engravings, those of Schliemann's Atlas are given, as they have been hitherto used for reference in the discussion by Haug, Gomperz, Max Müller, and other scholars.

INDEX.

ERRATUM.

Page 345.—After the third paragraph, ending "from all quarters," insert the following :—

"Troy had therefore no separate Acropolis ; but as one was necessary for the great deeds of the Iliad, it was added by the poetical invention of Homer, and called by him *Pergamus,* a word of quite unknown derivation."

COMPARATIVE TABLE OF THE ILLUSTRATIONS IN Dr. SCHLIEMANN'S ATLAS AND THE TRANSLATION.

Atlas.		Translation.		Atlas.		Translation.	
Pl.	No.	No.	Pl.	Pl.	No.	No.	Pl.
1,	1	317,	XXII.	4,	133	330,	XXII.
	4	318,	XXII.	5,	134	430,	XXXVIII.
	10	475,	XLVI.		136	398,	XXXIII.
	12	319,	XXII.		140	460,	XLIII.
	20	320,	XXII.		142	489,	XLIX.
2,	34	381,	XXX.		143?	354,	XXIV.
	35	380,	XXIX.		145	476,	XLVI.
	36	382,	XXX.		156	408,	XXXIV.
	37	321,	XXII.		160	419,	XXXVI.
	42	410,	XXXV.		161	332,	XXII.
	51	322,	XXII.		166	334,	XXIV.
	53	329,	XXII.		168	423,	XXXVII.
	57	42,	p. 80.	6,	174	44,	p. 80.
	58	324,	XXII.		175	478,	XLVII.
	60	325,	XXII.		176	389,	XXXI.
	61	482,	XLVIII.		193	335,	XXIII.
	64	323,	XXII.		208	115,	pp. 161, 367
	65	413,	XXXV.	7,	224	337,	XXIII.
	66	327,	XXII.		231	336,	XXIII.
3,	70	328,	XXII.	8,	237	352,	XXIV.
	93	471,	XLV.		242	490,	XLIX.
4,	105	437,	XXXIX.		245	384,	XXX.
	124	480,	XLVIII.		252	403,	XXXIV.
	125	81,	p. 138.		253	400,	XXXIII.
	132	333,	XXIII.		259	483,	XLVIII.

NOTE.—In the columns headed "Translation" the *Roman numerals* refer to the *Plates*.

A (?) against Schliemann's Numbers signifies that we have not been able to identify the objects *certainly* with those engraved by us from M. Burnouf's drawings.

Atlas.		Translation.		Atlas.		Translation.
Pl.	No.	No. Pl.		Pl.	No.	No. Pl.
8,	260	402, XXIII.		13,	422	342, XXIII.
	261	331, XXII.			424	346, XXIII.
	263	43, p. 80.			426	444, XL.
	264?	396, XXXII.			427	343, XXIII.
	266	80, p. 137.			428	347, XXIII.
	270	361, XXVI.			430 ?	466, XLV.
9,	272	416, XXXVI.			431	465, XLIV.
	273	414, XXXV.			432	496, LI. & p. 367.
	274	365, XXVII.			433	345, XXIII.
	276	424, XXXVII.			434	348, XXIII.
	279	338, XXIII.			436	301, XXI.
	282	356, XXV.			438	302, XXI.
	285	359, XXV.			442	303, XXI.
	288	377, XXVIII.			443	304, XXI.
	289?	372,* XXVIII.			445	305, XXI.
	289?	411,* XXXV.			446	306, XXI.
	294	370, XXVII.			448	307, XXI.
	295	362, XXVI.			449	308, XXI.
	296	380, XXIX.		14,	450	493, LI.
	297	447, XLI.			452	491, L.
	298	381, XXX.		15,	460	498, LII.
	299	379, XXIX.			471	486, XLIX.
10,	307	339, XXIII.		16,	472	484, XLVIII.
	326	340, XXIII.			473	149, p. 199.
	327	341, XXIII.			474	62, p. 95.
	337	458, XLIII.			485	309, XXI.
11,	344	387, XXXI.			486	310, XXI.
	346	392, XXXII.			487	311, XXI.
	356	369, XXVII.			488	312, XXI.
	356	298–9, p. 369.			489	313, XXI.
12,	384	428, XXXVIII.			491	314, XXI.
	410	391, XXXII.			494	315, XXI.
13,	418	344, XXIII.			497	316, XXI.

* Identical design, but different material.

Atlas.	Translation.	Atlas.	Translation.
Pl. No.	No. Page.	Pl. No.	No. Page.
17, 503–4	2, 21	24, 646	50, 83
512	142, 173	656	67, 101
513	37, 65	657	68, 101
518	38, 65	660	122, 165
519	39, 65	661	123, 165
18, 529	40, 65	662	124, 165
537	162, 232	25, 665	14, 36
540	290, 353	666	92, 150
19, 541	143, 188	669	93, 150
546	116, 162	670	94, 150
553	147, 192	671	95, 150
554	148, 192	672	96, 150
555	4, 24, 368	674	97, 150
556	78, 130	675	98, 150
20, 562	109, 155	678	99, 150
564	24, 36	681	100, 150
565	18, 36	682	101, 150
566	15, 36	683	58, 94
567	12, 164	685	61, 94
568	16, 36	687	59, 94
570	20, 36	689	60, 94
572	141, 172	26, 700	83, 150
577	23, 36	701	84, 150
578a	77, 129	702	85, 150
578b	76, 129	703	86, 150
21, 583	26, 36	705	87, 150
586	28, 36	713	90, 150
587	144, 190	718	88, 150
22, 592	71, 110	719	89, 150
601	56, 94	720	91, 150
610	57, 94	721	79, 135
24, 639	66, 101	27, 722	1, 15
643	47, 83	732	110, 157
644	48, 83	734	19, 36
645	49, 83	PLATE 30	PLATE III.

Atlas.		Translation.		Atlas.		Translation.	
Pl.	No.	No.	Page.	Pl.	No.	No.	Page.
32,	774	131,	170	69,	1541	45g,	82
	775	10,	34		1553	46,	82
	776	11,	34	72,	1582	6,	25
	779	64,	97	75,	1623	74,	115
	782	136,	171		1628	155,	214
	786	137,	171		1630	113,	159
	787	134,	171		1632	51,	86
	788	135,	171	84,	1762	53,	87
34,	867	138,	172		1768	111,	158
	868	139,	172		1770	112,	158
35,	872a	129,	169	90,	1864	117,	163
	874	132,	171		1880	118,	163
	882	133,	171		1886	119,	163
41,	994	125,	166	91,	1893	151,	208
	996	130,	170	97,	2022	153,	209
	1003	70,	106		2025	104,	151
48,	1152	127,	167	98,	2044	8,	25
52,	1158	128,	167	101,	2272a–d	108,	155
	1257	126,	166		2272g	120,	163
54,	1275	13,	35		2272l	154,	211
55,	1287	41,	74	102,	2290–1	73,	114
61,	1374	233,	320		2292	102,	151
64,	1433–5	157,	215		2293	103,	151
65,	1440	150,	208	103,	2294	107,	153
	1441	55,	87		2296	106,	152
	1446	12,	34	104,	2298	105,	152
67,	1497–8	232,	320		2299	152,	209
	1505	184,	268	PLATE 110		PLATE VIII.	
68,	1520	158,	219	114,	2317	156,	214
69,	1535	45a,	82		2325	72,	110
	1536	45b,	82	PLATE 118		MAP.	
	1537	45c,	82	119,	2330	159,	228
	1538	45d,	82		2331	65,	97
	1539	45e,	82	120,	2352	160,	229
	1540	45f,	82		2362	161,	229

Atlas.		Translation.		Atlas.		Translation.	
Pl.	No.	No.	Page.	Pl.	No.	No.	Page.
120,	2363	170,	237	138,	2746	63,	95
121,	2389	454,	XLII.	139,	2755	178,	262
	2390–1?	477,	XLVII.	140,	2768	52,	86
	2392	451,	XLII.		2769	196,	283
	2393	367,	XXVII.	141,	2778	36,	63
122,	2423	384	XXX.		2780	197,	284
	2432	171.	238		2782	194,	282
	2435	9,	27		2784	199,	285
	2438	165,	235	142,	2791	191,	280
	2442	435,	XXXIX.		2803	198,	285
	2444	167,	236		2806	200,	286
123,	2467	166,	236		2815	422,	XXVII.
125,	2515	489,	XLIX.	143,	2827	201,	p. 286
126,	2554	455,	XLIII.		2840	395,	XXXII.
	2555	164,	235	145,	2838 *bis*	215,	296
	2560	163,	234		2839 *bis*	204,	292
PLATE 127		PLATE IV.		146,	2850	190,	280
130,	2561	176,	261	147,	2862	209,	294
	2577	177,	261		2865	210,	295
132,	2613	172,	255		2889	29,	36
	2615	473,	XLVII.		2892	371,	XXVII.
133,	2633	179,	264	148,	2898	439,	XL.
	2638	180,	264		2899	29,	p. 36.
	2639	174,	260		2912	206,	293
	2662	202,	286		2921	216,	296
134,	2664	193,	282		2924	217,	297
	2674	195,	283	149,	2951	213,	296
	2683	192,	281		2952	209,	296
135,	2694	404,	XXXIV.		2964	378,	XXVIII.
	2699	300,	372	150,	2975	211,	295
	2706	187,	268		2977	203,	291
	2707	186,	268		2981	205,	292
	2708	181,	265		2984	487,	XLIX.
	2721	189,	279		2988	212,	p. 295
138,	2741	82,	139		2998	214,	296

Atlas.	Translation.	Atlas.	Translation.
Pl.　No.	No.　Page.	Pl.　No.	No.　Page.
PLATE 153	PLATE V.	166, 3252	388,　XXXI.
154, 3050	168, 237	3258	7,　25
3051	169, 237	168, 3273	3a, 23
PLATE 156	PLATE XI. B.	3278	3b, 23, 369
PLATE 157	PLATE IX.	PLATE 169	PLATE X.
158, 3063	231, 317	PLATE 170	PLATE XI. A.
3065	220, 308	171, 3290	349, XXIV.
PLATE 159	188, 278	3292	145, 191
160, 3084	229, 315	3295	146, 191
161, 3087	228, 315	3296	289, 352
3088	230, 315	172, 3323	386, XXXI.
3089	54,　87	3341	405, XXXIV.
3092	221, 309	173, 3364	360, XXV.
3092*	33-4,　50	174, 3380	288, 352
3094	224, 311	175, 3384	287, 351
3095	222, 310	3390	286, 351
3096	223, 310	176, 3401	284, 342
162, 3111	363, XXVI.	PLATE 177	PLATE VII. A.
3117	464, XLIV.	PLATE 178	PLATE VII. B.
3124	448, XLI.	PLATE 180	PLATE I.
3131	226, 312	PLATE 186	PLATE VI.
3134	472, XLVI.	187, 3407	182, 265
163, 3143	385, XXXI.	3415	494, LI.
3158	421, XXXVI.	188, 3439	207, 294
3166	225, 312	3450	114, 160
164, 3171-3	HEADING TO CONTENTS.	189, 3455	173, 258
3174-7	LIST OF ILLUSTRATIONS.	3462	283, 341
3187	366, XXVII.	190, 3464	374, XXVIII.
3189	431, XXXVIII.	3474	5,　24, 368
3193	227, 312	191, 3483	219, 307
165, 3224	453, XLII.	192, 3484	262, 332
166, 3229	497, LII.	3485	264, 332
3233	291, 363	3486	247, XVIII.
3248	21,　36	3489	256, 330
3249	31,　37	3490	269, 333

Atlas.		Translation.		Atlas.		Translation.	
Pl.	No.	No.	Page.	Pl.	No.	No.	Page.
192,	3490a	243,	XVII.	199,	3588	235,	XIV
	3490b	244,	XVII.	200,	3489-94	242,	XVII
	3490c	245,	XVII.		3595	250,	XVIII
	3490d	246,	XVII.		3596	251,	XVIII
193,	3492	257,	330	201,	3600	265,	332
	3493	258,	330		3600a	266,	332
	3495d	259,	330		3600b	268,	332
	3495e	260,	330		3600c	249,	XVIII
	3495	218,	302	202,	3601	281,	337
	3495a	218,	302		3602	238,	XV.
	3495g	267,	332		3603	248,	XVIII.
194,	3496	273,	334		3603a	237,	XV.
	3497a	274,	334		3603b	240,	XVI.
	3497b	275,	334	203a		239,	XVI.
	3499	263,	332	204		PLATE II.	
	3502	252,	330	205		276,	XIX.
	3503	253,	330	206		277,	XIX.
	3504a	261,	331	208		282,	339
	3504f	254,	330	209		279–80, XX.	
	3504g	255,	330	211		PLATE XII.	
	3504i	272,	334	212		PLATE XIII.	
195,	3511	285,	350	213		PLAN I.	
196,	Selection.	278,	XX	214		PLAN II.	
197,	3585	270,	334	215		PLAN IV. 347	
	3586	271,	334	216		PLAN III. 306	
	3586a	236,	XV	217 and last.		32, 48.	
198,	3587	234,	XIV				

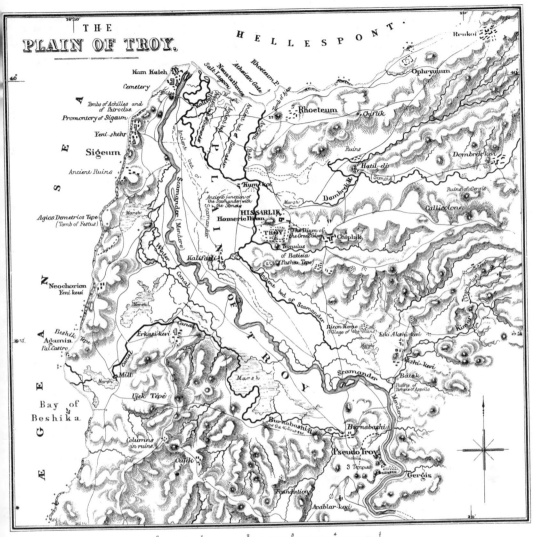

THE
PLAIN OF TROY.

HELLESPONT.

Renkoi

Ophrynium

Kum Kaleh
Cemetery
Tombs of Achilles and of Patroclus.
Promontory of Sigeum
Yeni-shehr

SEA

Sigeum

Ancient Ruins

Agios Demetrios Tepe
(Tomb of Festus)

Rhoeteum P.
Achaian Gate
Neustathmos
Rhoeteum
Chiflik

Ruins
Hotil-elin
Dombrek-kevi

Ruins of Gergis
Callicolone

Kum Kioi
Ancient junction of the Scamander with the Simois
HISSARLIK
Homeric Ilium
TROY
The Ilium of the Greek Colony
Tumulus of Batiæa
Pasha Tepe
Chiplak

Dombrek

AEGEAN SEA

Neochorion
Yeni-keui

Beshik
Agamia
Pal Castro

Marsh
Kalifatli

Canal

PLAIN OF TROY

Ancient bed of Scamander

Rizen-Korne
(Village of the Titans)
Eski Alashi-kevi

Kirgos

Marsh

Bay of Beshika

Erkassi-kevi
Canal
Canal
Mill
Marsh

Ujek Tepe

Marsh

Akshi-kevi
Batak
Ruins of Temple of Apollo

Scamander

Columns in ruins

Oujek

Bunabashi R.
near the 40 sources.

Foundation

Bunabashi

Pseudo Troy
3 Temples
Gergis

Anablar-keui

Scale of English Miles.
0   1   2   3   4   5

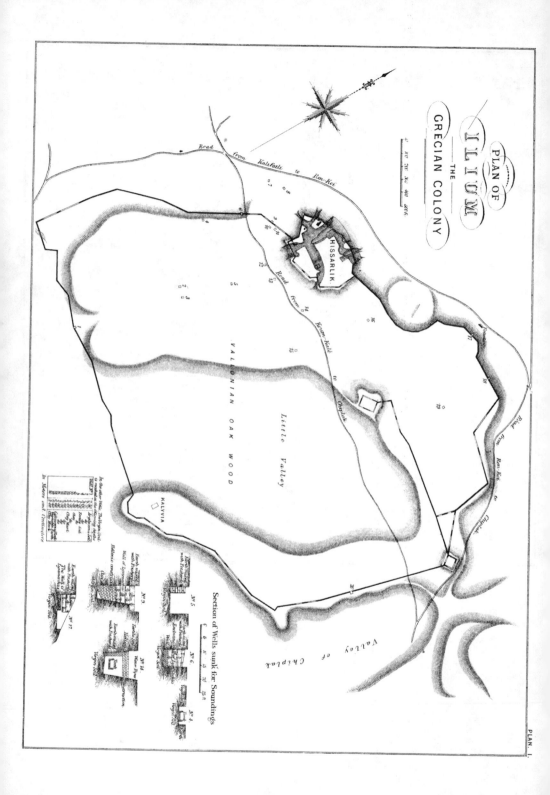

PLAN OF
ILIUM
THE
GRECIAN COLONY

HISSARLIK

Road from Kalifatti to Ren-Kei

Road from Koum-Kale to Chiplak

VALLONIAN OAK WOOD

Little Valley

KALIVVIA

Valley of Chiplak

River from Ren-Kei to Church

Section of Wells sunk for Soundings

PLAN. I.

RUINS OF TROY.

GENERAL PLAN
of researches made by
M. SCHLIEMANN.
IN
1870, 1871, 1872 & 1873.

RUINS OF TROY.

GENERAL PLAN OF RESEARCHES MADE BY M. SCHLIEMANN
IN 1870, 1871, 1872 AND 1873.

- - - - - - Outer Wall of Lysimachus.
——— Outer Wall of Troy.

1. Greek Wall.
2. Great Hellenic Construction.
3. Interior Bastion of Lysimachus.
4. Great Tower of Ilium.
5. Trenches for the protection of Archers.
6. Courses of stone in form of seats.
7. Ruins of Palace of Priam and later superincumbent constructions.
8. Trojan constructions erected upon old Trojan houses in the depths of the Temple of Minerva.
9. Large jars of earthenware enclosed in the wall.
10. Wall of the Temple of Minerva under Lysimachus.
11. Remains of the same Temple of Minerva.
12. House of two storeys in the basement of the Temple anterior to the taking of Troy.
13. Trojan houses.
14. Sacrificial Altar of the Trojan Minerva, with drain for carrying away the blood.
15. Inner Cistern of the Temple of Minerva of Lysimachus.
16. Remains of the Wall of the Temple of Minerva under Lysimachus.
17. Remains of Trojan houses.
18. Remains of the Temple of Minerva.
19. Wall constructed of fragments of the columns of the Temple of Minerva.
20. Outer Wall later than Troy.
21. Wall later than Troy.
22. Artificial Mound.
23. Wall of Troy.
24. Trojan houses and later walls built upon them.
25. Wall anterior to Troy.
26. Mosaic anterior to the Epoch of Priam.
27. Wall of Fortification anterior to the time of Troy.
28. Sustaining Wall anterior to Troy.
29. Mound of natural or virgin soil.
30. Hellenic Wall.
31. Excavations of Mr. Frank Calvert.
32. Outer Wall of Troy.
33. Encircling Wall later than Troy.
34. Tower later than Troy.
35. Encircling Wall later than Troy.
36. Hellenic Tower.
37. Scaean Gate, and paved road.
38. Dwelling-houses.
39. Magazine.
40. Lodging for Workpeople.
41. Workpeople's Canteen.
42. Place where the treasure of Priam was found.

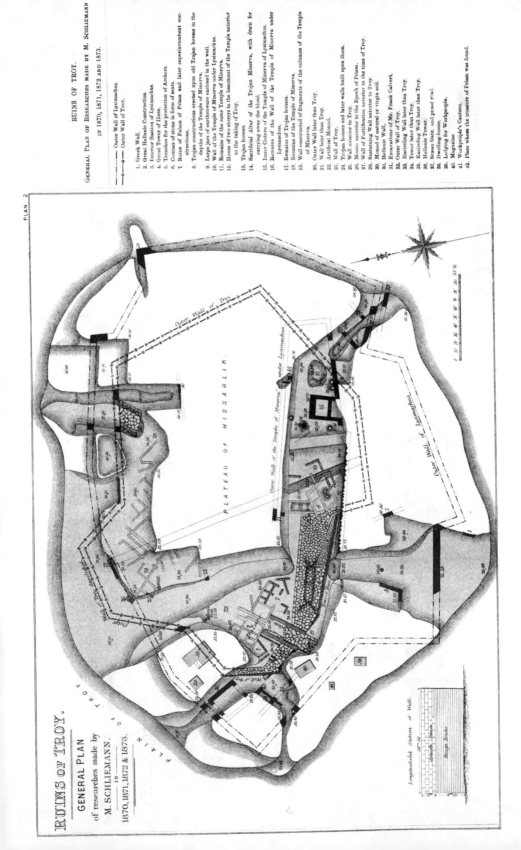

Longitudinal Section of Wall.

PLATEAU OF HISSARLIK.

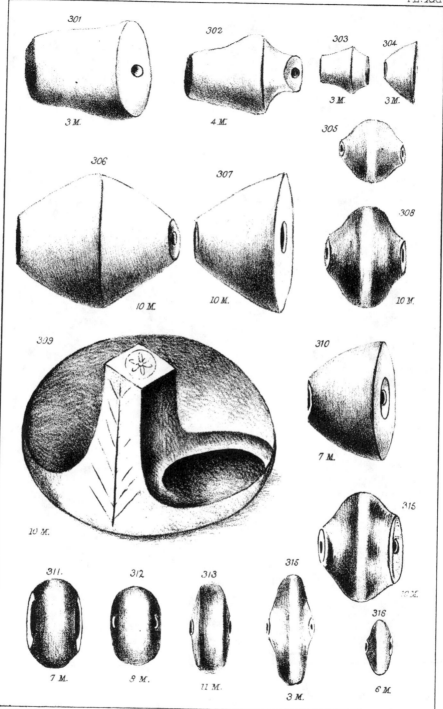

SPECIMENS OF WHORLS, &c. DUG UP AT TROY.

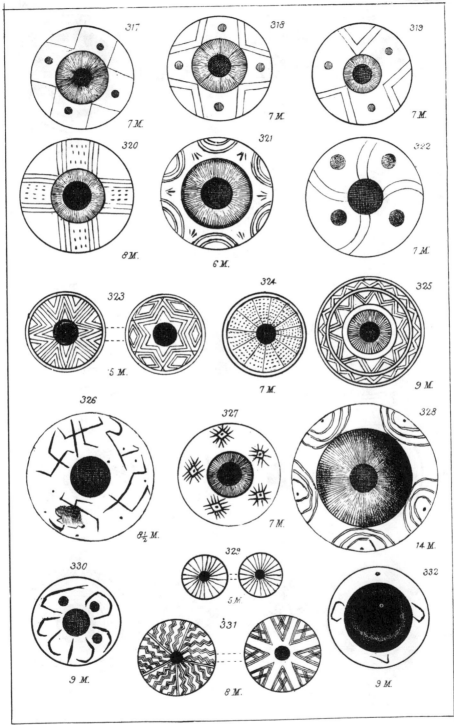

SPECIMENS OF WHORLS, &c. DUG UP AT TROY.

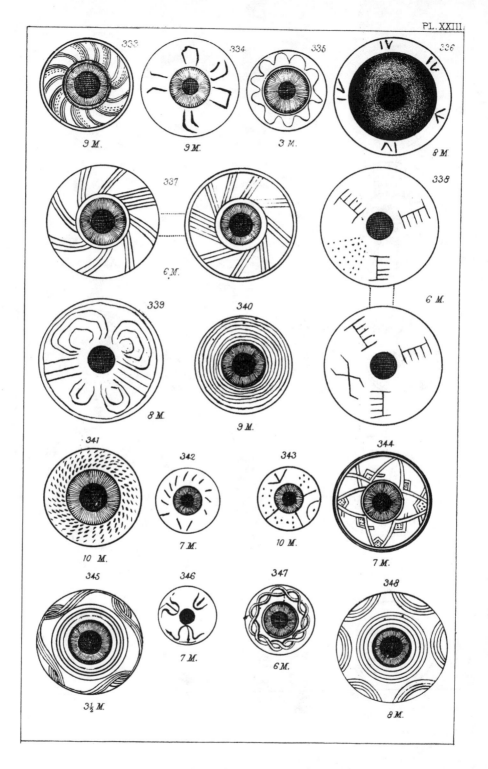

333   334   335   336
9 M.   9 M.   3 M.   8 M.

337   338
6 M.   6 M.

339   340
8 M.   9 M.

341   342   343   344
10 M.   7 M.   10 M.   7 M.

345   346   347   348
3½ M.   7 M.   6 M.   8 M.

SPECIMENS OF WHORLS, &c. DUG UP AT TROY.

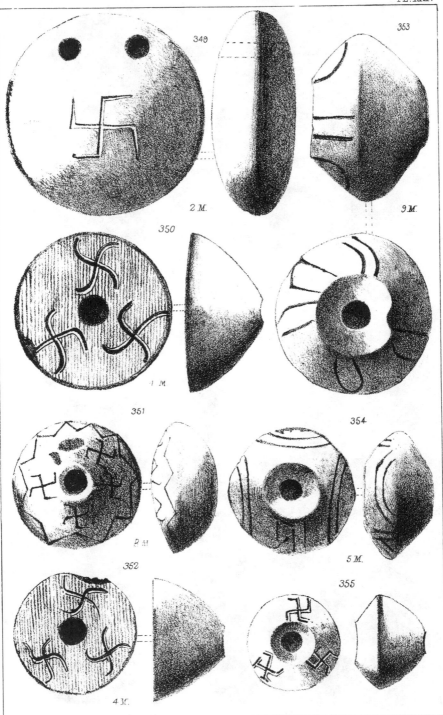

349
2 M.
353
9 M.
350
4 M.
351
3 M.
354
352
4 M.
5 M.
355

SPECIMENS OF WHORLS, &c. DUG UP AT TROY.

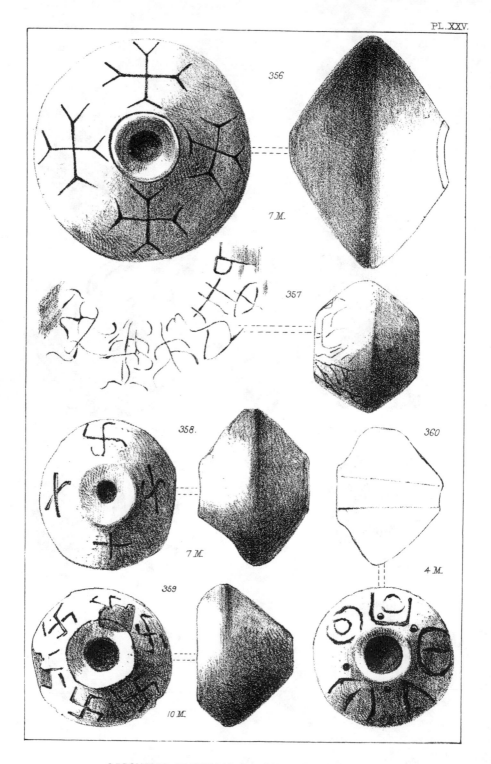

356

7 M.

357

358.

7 M.

360

4 M.

359

10 M.

SPECIMENS OF WHORLS, &c. DUG UP AT TROY.

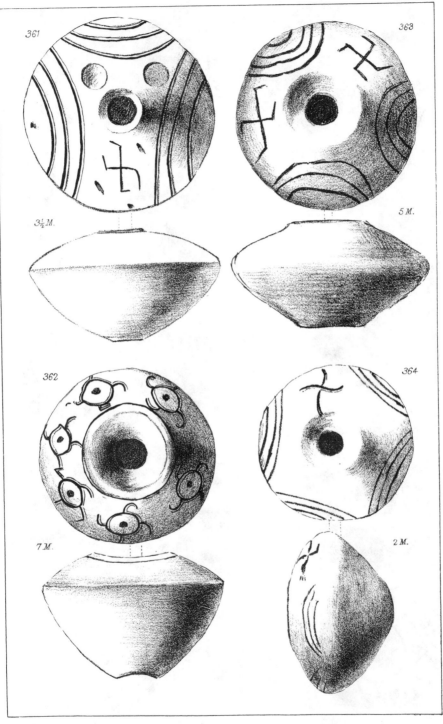

361

363

3½ M.

5 M.

362

364

7 M.

2 M.

SPECIMENS OF WHORLS, &c. DUG UP AT TROY.

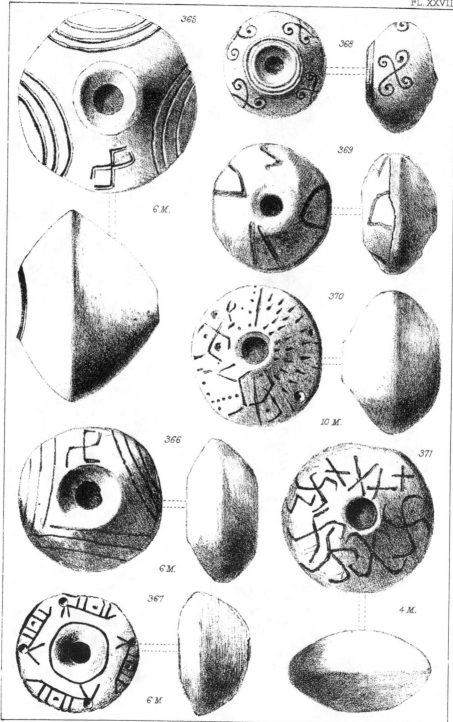

SPECIMENS OF WHORLS &c DUG UP AT TROY.

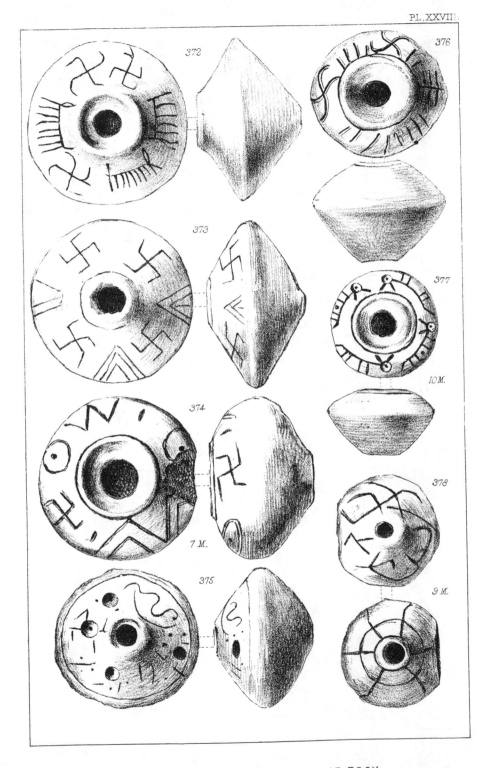

372

376

373

377

10 M.

374

378

7 M.

375

9 M.

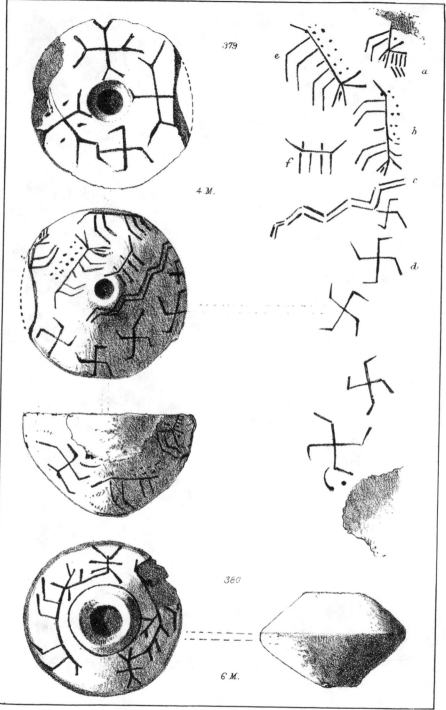

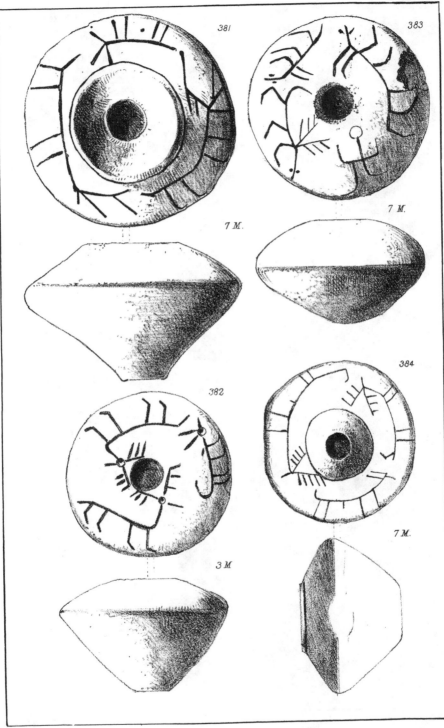

SPECIMENS OF WHORLS, &c. DUG UP AT TROY.

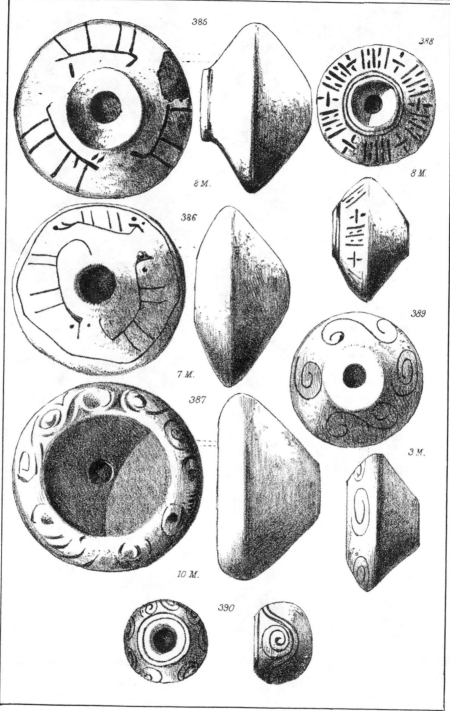

SPECIMENS OF WHORLS, &c. DUG UP AT TROY.

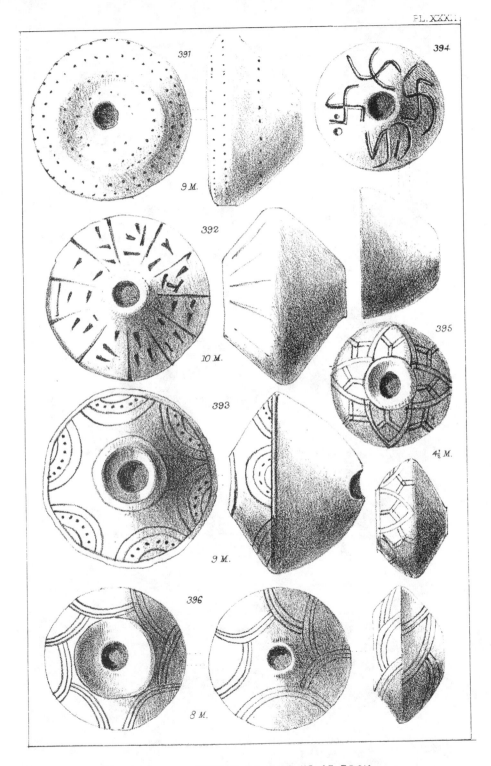

SPECIMENS OF WHORLS, &c. DUG UP AT TROY.

Pl. XXXIII.

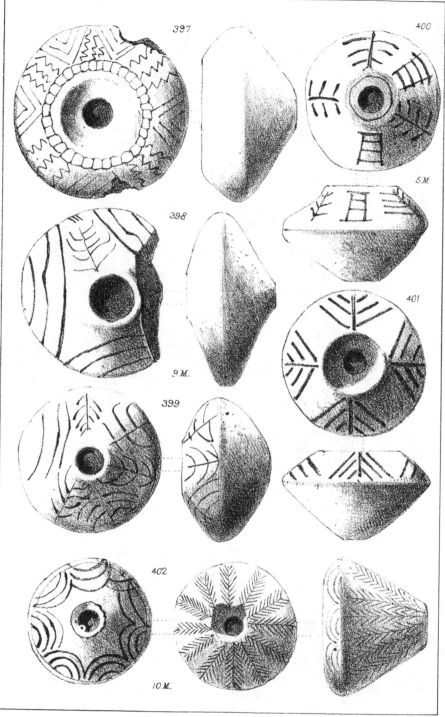

SPECIMENS OF WHORLS, &c. DUG UP AT TROY.

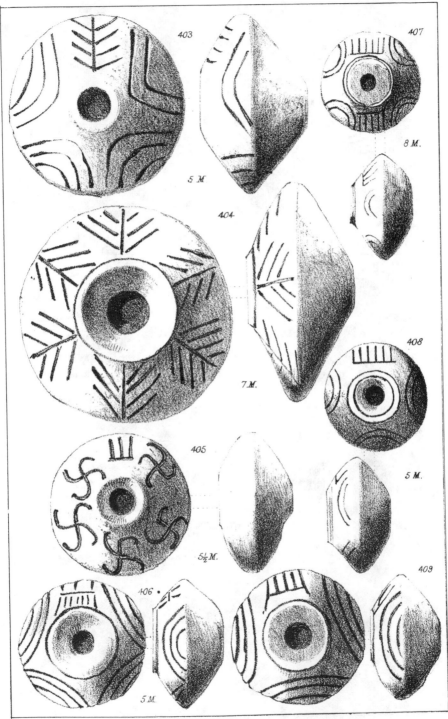

SPECIMENS OF WHORLS, &c. DUG UP AT TROY.

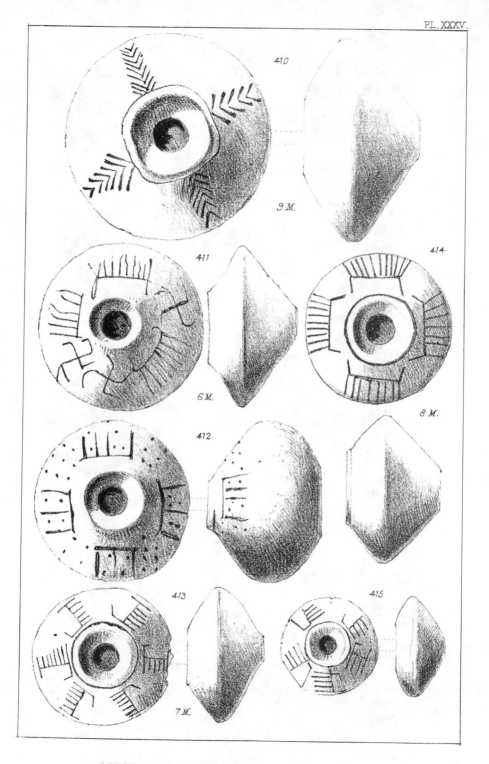

SPECIMENS OF WHORLS, &c. DUG UP AT TROY.

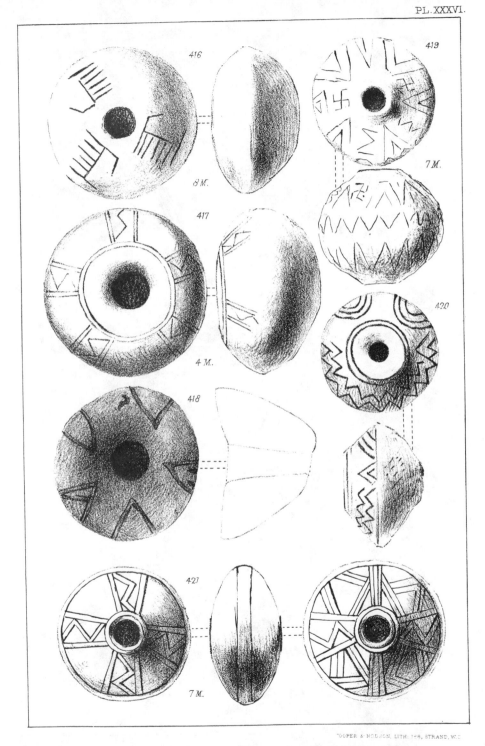

416

419

8 M.

7 M.

417

4 M.

420

418

421

7 M.

SPECIMENS OF WHORLS, &c. DUG UP AT TROY.

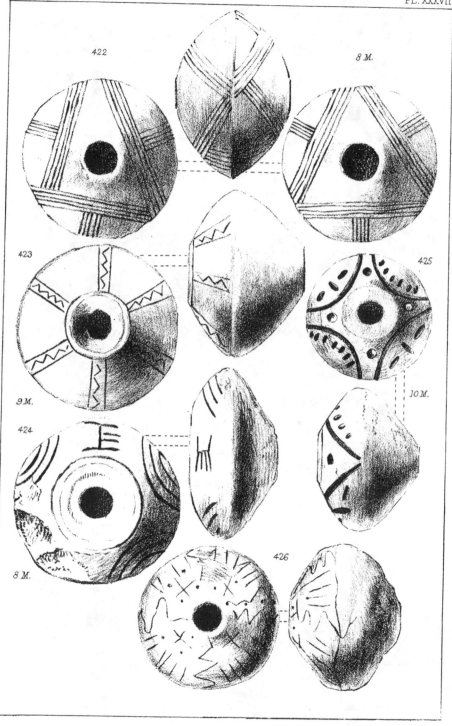

422   8 M.

423   425

9 M.   10 M.

424

8 M.   426

SPECIMENS OF WHORLS, &c. DUG UP AT TROY.

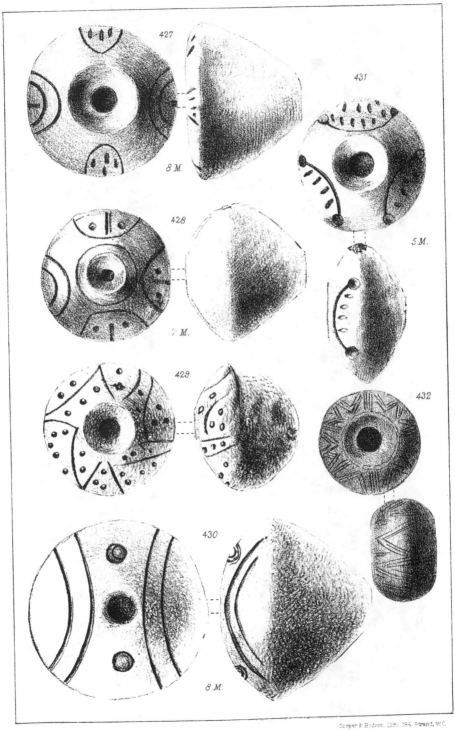

SPECIMENS OF WHORLS, &c. DUG UP AT TROY.

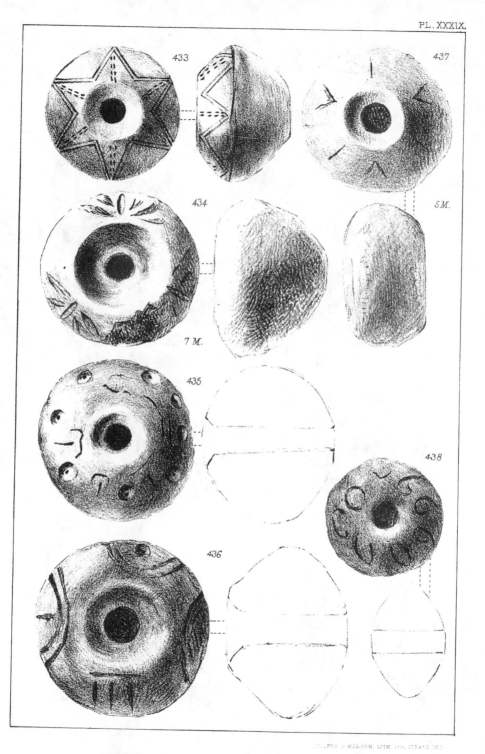

433
437
5 M.
434
7 M.
435
438
436

SPECIMENS OF WHORLS, &c. DUG UP AT TROY.

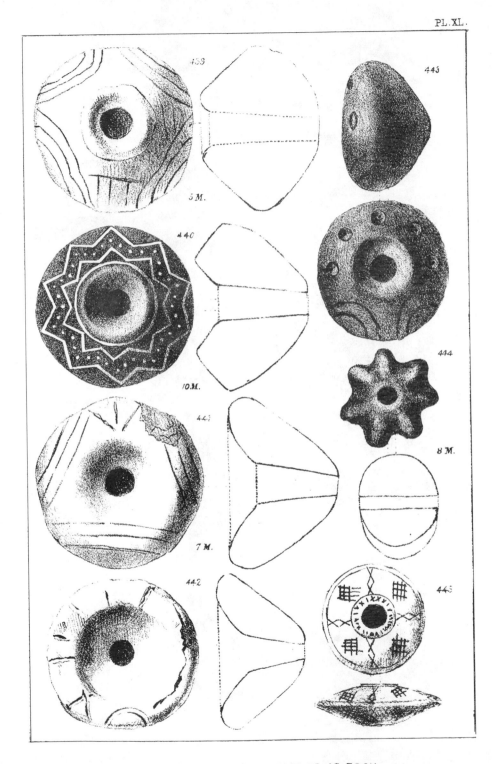

SPECIMENS OF WHORLS, &c. DUG UP AT TROY.

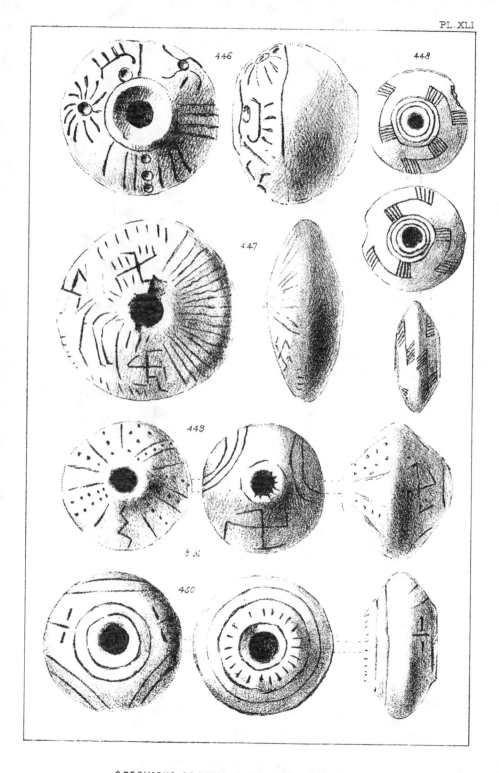

446
448
447
449
450

SPECIMENS OF WHORLS, &c. DUG UP AT TROY.

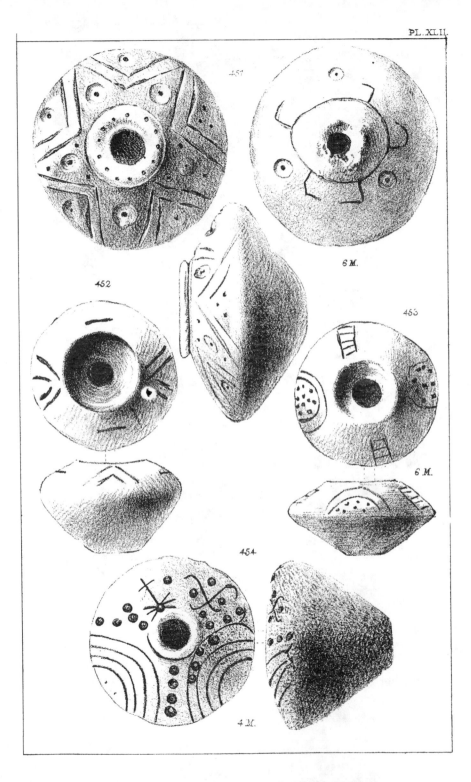

451

6 M.

452

453

6 M.

454

4 M.

SPECIMENS OF WHORLS, &c. DUG UP AT TROY.

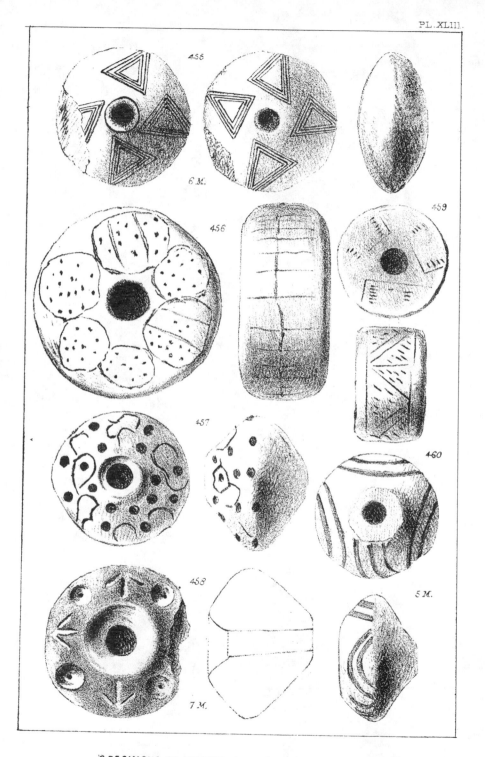

SPECIMENS OF WHORLS, &c. DUG UP AT TROY.

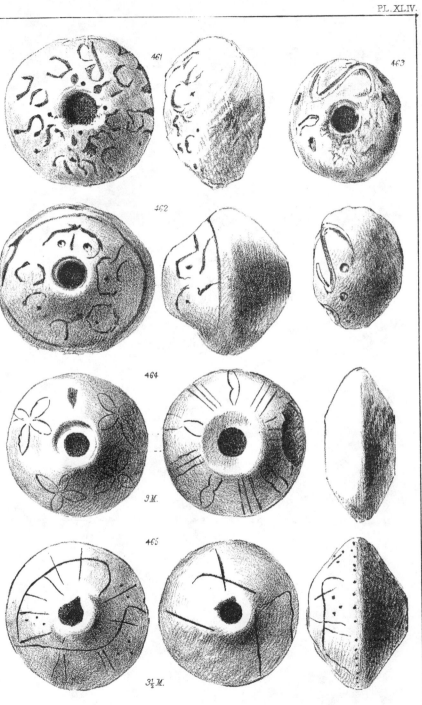

SPECIMENS OF WHORLS, &c. DUG UP AT TROY.

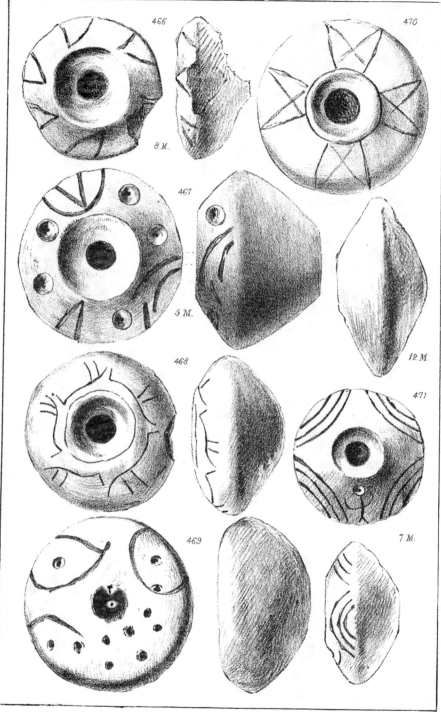

SPECIMENS OF WHORLS, &c. DUG UP AT TROY.

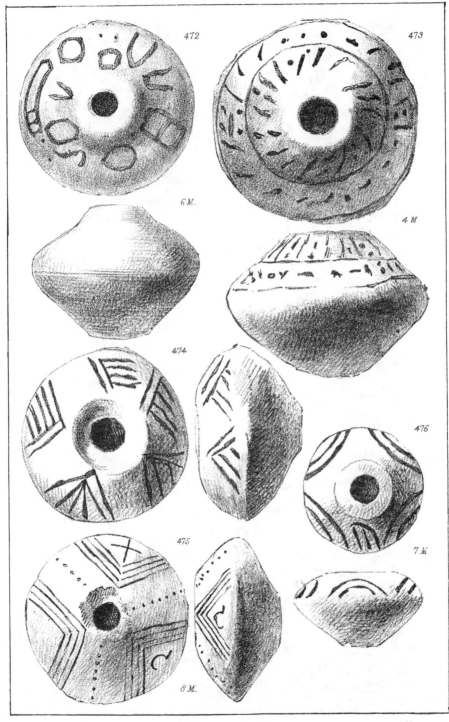

472

473

6 M.

4 M.

474

476

475

7 M.

8 M.

SPECIMENS OF WHORLS, &c. DUG UP AT TROY.

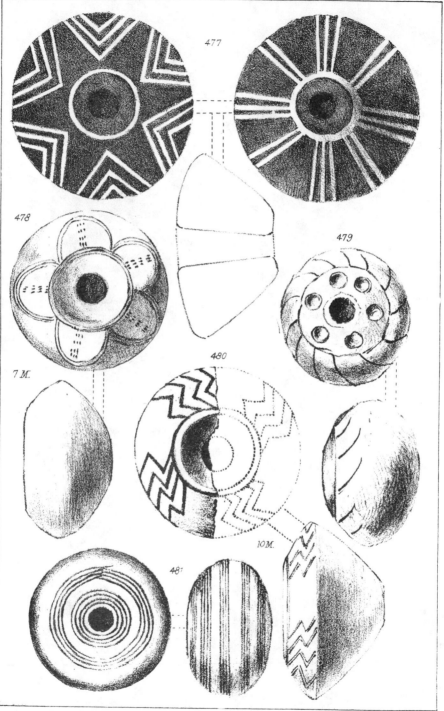

SPECIMENS OF WHORLS, &c. DUG UP AT TROY.

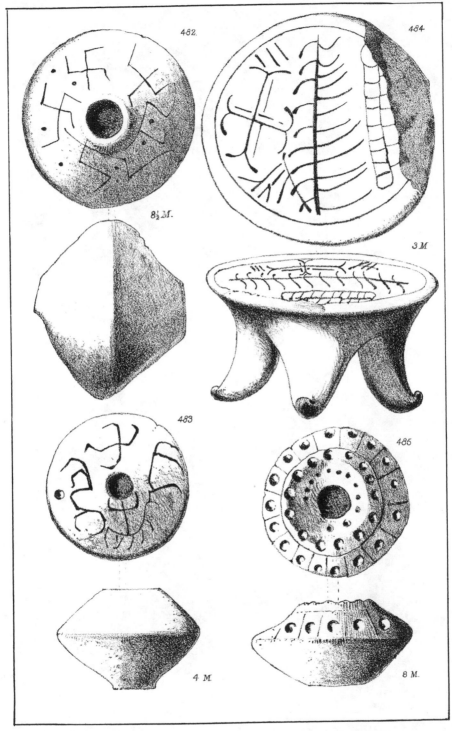

482.

8½ M.

484

3 M

483

485

4 M.

8 M.

SPECIMENS OF WHORLS, &c. DUG UP AT TROY.

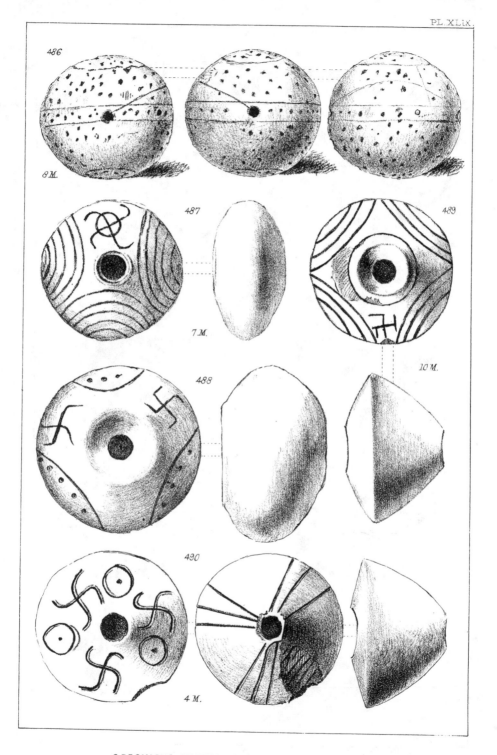

SPECIMENS OF WHORLS, &c. DUG UP AT TROY.

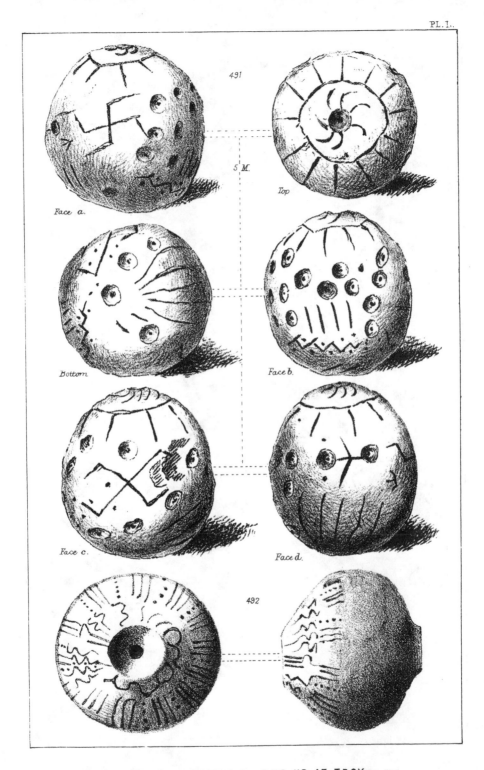

491

5 M.

Face a.

Top

Bottom

Face b.

Face c.

Face d.

492

SPECIMENS OF WHORLS, &c. DUG UP AT TROY.

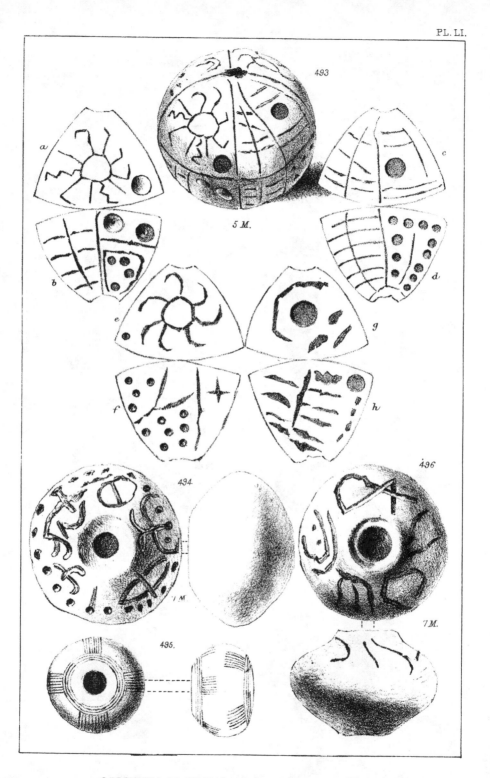

493

5 M.

a

c

b

d

e

g

f

h

494

496

7 M.

495.

7 M.

SPECIMENS OF WHORLS, &c. DUG UP AT TROY.

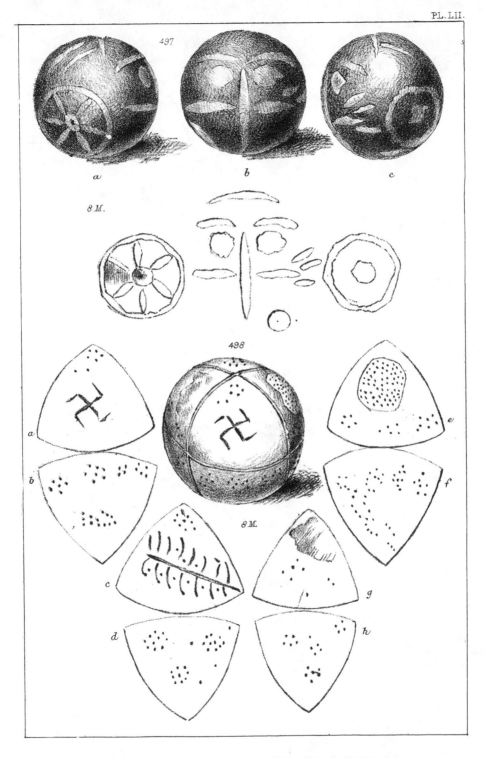

497

8 M.

498

8 M.

SPECIMENS OF WHORLS, &c. DUG UP AT TROY.